Studies in International Mediation

Also by Jacob Bercovitch

ANZUS IN CRISIS (*editor*)

CONFLICT MANAGEMENT IN THE TWENTY-FIRST CENTURY

INTERNATIONAL CONFLICT MANAGEMENT, 1945–1995

INTERNATIONAL MEDIATION

RESOLVING INTERNATIONAL CONFLICTS (*editor*)

SOCIAL CONFLICT AND THIRD PARTIES

SUPERPOWERS AND CLIENT STATES (*editor*)

Studies in International Mediation

Essays in Honor of Jeffrey Z. Rubin

Edited by

Jacob Bercovitch
Professor of International Relations
University of Canterbury
New Zealand

 Published in Association with the Program on
Negotiation, Harvard Law School

First published 2002 by
PALGRAVE MACMILLAN
Houndmills, Basingstoke, Hampshire RG21 6XS and
175 Fifth Avenue, New York, N.Y. 10010
Companies and representatives throughout the world

PALGRAVE MACMILLAN is the global academic imprint of the Palgrave
Macmillan division of St. Martin's Press, LLC and of Palgrave Macmillan Ltd.
Macmillan® is a registered trademark in the United States, United Kingdom and
other countries. Palgrave is a registered trademark in the European Union and
other countries.

ISBN 0–333–69300–0 hardback
ISBN 0–333–69301–9 paperback

This book is printed on paper suitable for recycling and made from fully
managed and sustained forest sources.

A catalogue record for this book is available from the British Library.

Library of Congress Cataloging-in-Publication Data

Studies in international mediation: essays in honor of Jeffrey Z. Rubin / edited by
Jacob Bercovitch.
   p. cm.
   Includes bibliographical references and index.
   ISBN 0–333–69300–0
   1. Mediation, International. I. Rubin, Jeffrey Z. II. Bercovitch, Jacob.

JZ6045 .S78 2002
341.5′2 – dc21   2002074842

10   9   8   7   6   5   4   3   2   1
11   10   09   08   07   06   05   04   03   02

Printed and bound in Great Britain by
Antony Rowe Ltd, Chippenham and Eastbourne

For Carol, Sally and Noah

Contents

List of Tables and Figures

Tables

Figures

Foreword

Jacob Bercovitch has gathered some of the world's foremost negotiation and mediation scholars to provide a hearty intellectual feast for readers of this book. Sadly, there is one very important person missing from the feast – the late Jeffrey Z. Rubin, a social psychologist, professor at Tufts University, expert in third-party processes in international negotiation, and leader in the intellectual life of the Program on Negotiation at Harvard Law School.

Jacob has dedicated this book to the memory of his colleague and friend; prior to Jeff's untimely death in 1995, they had planned to work together as co-editors on this project. Jeff had worked closely with nearly all of the essayists in the past; they, like all the rest of us who enjoyed the pleasure of his company, are indebted to him for his intellectual curiosity, analytic skills, enthusiasm, energy, and helpful, supportive criticism. Many of the contributors to this book were also Jeff's colleagues from the Processes of International Negotiation Project of the International Institute of Applied Systems Analysis (IIASA), a group that provided him with the intellectual challenges he was constantly seeking, and to which he was devoted.

Among the many questions considered in this book are: the nature and style of mediation itself; its effectiveness when practiced by individuals, governments, or regional organizations; the conflict management role of international organizations; mediation by international peacemakers; the influence of power in international mediation; and the mediative nature of interactive problem-solving workshops. The essayists explore answers to these questions by examining case material from both the political and business worlds, yielding generalizations that will surely add value to the growing literature on mediation theory. It is the kind of practice-to-theory-to-practice project that Jeff Rubin thrived on.

Social psychologist Kurt Lewin is frequently credited with having observed once that 'There is nothing as practical as a good theory.' That philosophy was a guiding principle in the career of Jeff Rubin, and resonates as well in the contribution this book makes to the study of mediation. The Program on Negotiation at Harvard Law School is honored to be associated with a volume that is a wonderful tribute to the memory of our late executive director and esteemed colleague, Jeffrey Z. Rubin. He would have loved this book – and I think you will too.

ROBERT H. MNOOKIN
Chair, The Steering Committee
Program on Negotiation
at Harvard Law School

Preface

I first met Jeff Rubin when he was a visiting Professor at Tel Aviv University in 1984. We soon discovered we had some common interests, and Jeff was intrigued to learn that even though I had done all my graduate work in England, the two books that influenced me the most and shaped my approach in those years were the book he wrote with Bert Brown in 1975 on the social psychology of negotiations, and the book on negotiations edited by Dan Druckman two years later.

Jeff was generous with his advice and comments on some of my early writings. We subsequently met in Amsterdam, Christchurch, Boston, San Francisco, New York and Vienna. It was a pleasure to be with Jeff at each of these places. He seemed so well briefed on any place we met, and it was a delight to witness his enthusiasm, curiosity and knowledge of all these different locations.

I was always struck, as I know many others were, by how focused and disciplined Jeff was. We could be dining at some wonderful restaurant any where in the world, and Jeff would always turn the conversation to some more productive, intellectual avenues. Neither globetrotting, nor fine cuisine ever diverted Jeff from his work, his teaching and writing.

Jeff spent two months with us as a visiting Canterbury Fellow where I got to know him really well not only as a teacher or a colleague, but as a wise, outgoing and generous friend. We spent every day together toiling in every intellectual vineyard. It was impossible not to be impressed by the alacrity of his mind and the breathtaking range of his interests. Jeff was interested in all things from astronomy to Zen Buddhism.

It was here, in Christchurch, New Zealand, that we decided to collaborate in writing a book on international mediation, one of Jeff's enduring professional interests. We were fortunate then to get some of the finest scholars to contribute to the book, and upon its publication in 1992, we were very pleased by the way the book was received – both professionally and commercially. The relative success of the book led us to consider writing another volume on mediation. We toyed with various ideas, explored different options, and finally decided that a second edition was warranted.

We had just reached some decisions regarding new contributors, new issues and all that sort of things. I rang Jeff on Thursday night 1 June 1995 to finalize a few matters. Jeff was quite excited, he was going to Europe that weekend to take over as President of the International Association of Conflict Management, and he told me with what I imagined was even more pride, he was going to climb Fort Mountain in Maine – thus climbing all 100 mountains in New England. On Saturday, 3 June 1995, Jeff Rubin died as a result of a climbing accident. He was only 54 when he died.

Jeff's death was a total shock to all who knew him. Many feel that the evolving discipline of conflict management is that much the poorer for his death. Jeff made tremendous contributions to the study of conflict management, negotiations, mediation and entrapment. His book on Kissinger in the Middle East, published in 1981, is widely considered to have set the scene for the serious and systematic study of international mediation. It was path-breaking, and it showed, for the first time, how different disciplines could bring their tools and modes of thinking to study a social phenomenon (i.e. mediation) from various perspectives and offer pieces of information which could be integrated into a whole mosaic of research. The book was and remains seminal. It inspired many people (be they psychologists, political scientists, legal scholars and anthropologists) to carry on research in this field. Jeff was undoubtedly one of the intellectual leaders who inspired many to follow in his footsteps.

Jeffrey Rubin showed us how theory and practice can interweave, how different pieces of research can be integrated, how different traditions can be brought to bear on a subject. It seems only fitting that his friends, colleagues and disciples, all of whom represent different academic traditions and approaches, should come together and produce a volume in his memory. The result is this edited book, which we dedicate to his family.

This was not an easy project to undertake. It is hard to think of a friend and a mentor in the past sense only. It is also hard to get some of the most productive scholars to prepare specially commissioned papers, and then revise them as directed. Bringing the book to the reader has taken much more time than I had ever imagined. I hope the reader holding the book now thinks the effort was worth its while.

I have accumulated quite a few debts in the course of working on this book. First and foremost I am thankful to all the contributors who remained patient to the end despite the long delays. It is not often one has the chance to work with such a remarkable team of people, and I am grateful to them all for making this project possible.

Over the years I have discussed just about every issue with most of the contributors to this book. Many are close friends; all have shaped my awareness and understanding of conflict resolution and mediation. I have also benefited from the insights, comments and ideas of such close friends as Jean Bailey, Eileen Babbit, Raymond Cohen, Mark Francis, Brian Mandell, Ray Goldstein, J. David Singer, Larry Susskind, Peter Wallensteen, and my wonderful research associates Jud Fretter and Alison Houston.

The book's gestation period was so long that our Publisher had changed both name and identity whilst we were still preparing it for publication. The fine publishing house of Macmillan metamorphosed into Palgrave Macmillan, and in the process I was guided and helped by two excellent and patient editors, Annabelle Buckley and then Alison Howson. They both deserve my sincere thanks. Thanks too to Ann Marangos for preparing the manuscript for publication with great efficiency and punctuality.

The University of Canterbury, through its Research Committee, awarded me a research grant (U6438) that enabled me to complete this project.

I owe a special thanks to my friend Bill Breslin, from the Program on Negotiation at Harvard. Bill was always there with advice, help and useful criticism. I have had the pleasure of writing a few professional papers that Bill had edited. I know just how much better they were once Bill had applied his pencil to them. I hope this book bears his marks as well.

Thanks are due to Jill Dolby who typed every word of the manuscript at least twice, and not once did she lose her temper with me. I think that is quite remarkable.

The book was completed when I was a Senior Fellow at the United States Institute of Peace in 2002. I can think of no better environment to complete such a project than the USIP. I am grateful to the Board of Directors for awarding me this fellowship, and to the many excellent people at the Institute who made it such a wonderful and memorable year for me.

My greatest debt, as ever, is to my family. To my wife, Gillian, who offered support and encouragement when I needed it most, and took care of so many things I should have, and to my two daughters; Liora, who even offered to type a few pages of the book, and sent me upstairs to my study on numerous occasions, and Daniella, who may soon enough know why her father played with the computer for so long.

Notes on the Contributors

Editor

Jacob Bercovitch is Professor of International Relations at the University of Canterbury in Christchurch, New Zealand. He is the author of eight books and numerous articles on international conflict. He has held fellowships from, and taught at, many universities including Harvard, London and Jerusalem. Currently he is on a Senior Fellowship at the United States Institute of Peace. His recent books include *Resolving International Conflicts, International Conflict, 1945–1995* and *Conflict Management in the 21st Century*.

Contributors

Pamela R. Aall is the Director of the Education Program at the US Institute for Peace. Previously, she was a consultant to the President's Committee on Arts and Humanities and held a number of position at the Rockefeller Foundation. She is co-editor of *Managing Global Chaos*, and *Herding Cats: Multiparty Mediation in a Complex World*.

Karin Aggestam is a research fellow at the Department of Political Science, Lund University, Sweden. She has authored and co-authored several articles on negotiation, conflict resolution and the Middle East peace process, including *Reframing and Resolving Conflict: Israeli–Palestinian Negotiations 1988–1998* (1999). Recent articles on peacekeeping and international mediation have been published in the *Cambridge Review of International Affairs* (2001) and *Mediterranean Politics* (2002).

Peter J. Carnevale is Professor of Psychology at New York University. He is the recipient of multiple grants and awards including grants from the social psychology program at the National Science Foundation. He is Past President of the International Association for Conflict Management and is currently Chair of the Conflict Management Division of the Academy of Management. Professor Carnevale is co-author of *Negotiation in Social Conflict*. He has published more than 70 papers in books and journals.

Chester A. Crocker is James R. Schlesinger Professor at Georgetown University and Chairman of the Board of the United States Institute of Peace, Washington, DC. From 1981 to 1989 he was Assistant Secretary of State for African Affairs and the principal mediator in Angola, and South Africa. He is the author of *High Noon in Southern Africa*, and co-editor of *Managing Globa: Chaos*, and *Herding Cats: Multiparty Mediation in a Complex World*.

Paul F. Diehl is Professor of Political Science at the University of Illinois, Urbana-Champaign. He has published widely on topics such as the causes of war, United Nations peacekeeping, international law, and arms control. His recent books include *The Dynamics of Enduring Rivalries, International Peacekeeping and Territorial Changes and International Conflict*. He is a recipient of the International Studies Association's Karl Deutsch Award.

Daniel Druckman is the Vernon and Minnie Lynch Professor of Conflict Resolution at George Mason University's Institute for Conflict Analysis and Resolution, Fairfax, Virginia. He has directed National Academy of Science committees from 1985 to 1997. He has published widely on such topics as conflict resolution and negotiation, nationalism, group processes, nonverbal communication, and modelling methodologies, including simulation. He received the 1995 Otto Klineberg intercultural and international relations award from the Society for the Psychological Study of Social Issues for his work on nationalism.

Larry A. Dunn has worked for 15 years as a mediator, trainer, consultant and educator in the field of conflict resolution. He has been associated with the Mennonite Conciliation Service since 1985, and has taught courses on Interpersonal Conflict Resolution and Mediation Theory and Practice in a variety of settings. He has written and co-authored several articles and chapters on a variety of topics, including mediation role plays and ethnic conflict in the former Yugoslavia. He completed his PhD at Syracuse University and is currently the Director of Academic Programs in the Center for Peacemaking and Conflict Studies at Fresno Pacific University.

Judith Fretter has completed her PhD on the United Nations and regional organizations in conflict at the University of Canterbury in Christchurch, New Zealand. She is currently a research associate at the Department of Political Science.

Fen Osler Hampson is Professor of International Affairs and Director of the Norman Patterson School in Canada. Among his many publications are *Nurturing Peace: Why Peace Settlemnts Succeed or Fail, Multilateral Negotiations*, and *Managing Global Chaos* (co-editor) and *Herding Cats: Multiparty Mediation in a Complex World* (co-editor). He is also the annual editor of *Canada Among Nations*.

Herbert C. Kelman was until recently the Richard Clarke Cabot Professor of Social Ethics at Harvard University, and Chair of the Middle East Seminar at the Centre for International Affairs. He has worked for almost three decades on developing his interactive problem solving workshops as a way of bringing Palestinian and Israelis together. He was a Distinguished Fellow at the US Institute for Peace. He is the author of *A Time to Speak, Crimes of Obedience*, and editor of *International Behavior*. Professor Kelman is the recipient of numerous honors and awards, including, most recently, the Grawemeyer Award for Ideas for Improving World Order.

Marieke Kleiboer holds a post-doctoral fellowship from the Royal Dutch Academy of Sciences at the Meijerts Institute for Legal Studies (Leiden University, The Netherlands). Recipient of a PhD in International Politics from that same university, her research interests include the role of third parties in conflict resolution and the prospects and problems of Alternative Dispute Resolution. Among her publications are *The Multiple Realities of International Mediation*, and articles in the *Journal of Peace Research*, *Cooperation and Conflict*, the *Journal of Conflict Resolution*, *Knowledge and Policy* and the *Journal of Contingencies and Crisis Management*.

Louis Kriesberg is Professor Emeritus of Sociology, Maxwell Professor Emeritus of Social Conflict Studies. He was the founding director of the Program on the Analysis and Resolution of Social Conflicts (PARC) at Syracuse University, and continues as an affiliate of PARC. He has authored several books, including: *Constructive Conflicts*, *International Conflict Resolution*, and *Social Conflicts*, has edited or co-edited many books including *Intractable Conflicts and Their Transformation* and *Timing the De-Escalation of International Conflicts*, and has written numerous articles and book chapters.

Dean G. Pruitt was for many years Distinguished Professor in the Department of Psychology at the State University of New York at Buffalo. At present he is at the International Centre for Conflict Analysis and Resolution at George Mason University. He is author, co-author or editor of six books and numerous scholarly papers on conflict, negotiations and mediation. A recipient of many awards including the Harold D. Lasswell Award for Distinguished Scientific Contribution to Political Psychology, and the Lifetime Achievement Award from the International Association for Conflict Management.

Jeswald W. Salacuse is Henry J. Braker Professor of Commercial Law at the Fletcher School of Law and Diplomacy, Tufts University, Medford, Massachusetts. He was Dean of the Fletcher School from 1986 to 1995, President of the Association of Professional Schools of International Affairs, and of the Third World Legal Studies Association. His recent books include *Making Global Deal – Negotiating in the International Marketplace*, *The Art of Advice*, and *International Business Planning: Law and Taxation* (with W. P. Streng).

James A. Wall is Professor of Management in the College of Business and Public Administration at the University of Missouri, Columbia. He has published widely on negotiation and mediation including a number of studies on mediation in several Asian countries. He is the author of *Negotiation: Theory and Practice* and *Bosses*.

I. William Zartman is the Jacob Blaustein Professor of International Organization and Conflict Resolution at the Paul H. Nitze School of Advanced International Studies at Johns Hopkins University in Washington, DC. He has written extensively on conflict management and negotiations and on African politics. Professor Zartman was the recipient, in 2001, of the International Association of Conflict Management's Lifetime Achievement Award. Among his numerous books are *The Practical Negotiator, Ripe for Resolution, The 50% Solution, International Relations in the New Africa* and *Governance and Conflict Management.*

List of Abbreviations

ADR	alternative dispute resolution
AFSC	American Friends Service Committee
BET	Boukou-Ennedi-Tibetsi
CHAL	Christian Health Association of Liberia
CNS	sovereign national conferences
DOP	Declaration of Principles
ECF	Economic Cooperation Foundation
FAFO	Norwegian Research Institute for Applied Social Science (what do letters stand for?)
FroLiNat	National Liberation Front of Chad
ICC	International Chamber of Commerce
ICR	Interactive conflict resolution
ICSID	International Center for Settlement of Investment
IFOR	International Fellowship of Reconciliation
IGO	Intergovernmental Organization
IIASA	International Institute of Applied Systems Analysis
INF	intermediate nuclear forces
INGO	International Non-Governmental Organization
INN	International Negotiation Network
IRC	International Red Cross
MCC	Mennonite Central Committee
MRA	Moral Re-Armament
NGO	Non-Governmental Organization
NSC	National Security Council
OAS	Organization of American States
OAU	Organization for African Unity
OSCE	Organization for Security and Cooperation in Europe
PCT	Congolese Workers' Party
PLO	Palestinian Liberation Organization
PTSD	post-traumatic stress disorder
SNT	Single Negotiating Text
TO	Transnational Organizational
UNDOF	UN Disengagement Observer Force stationed in the Syrian Golan Heights
UNEF II	UN Emergency Force supervising a cease-fire between Egyptian and Israeli forces
UNICYP	UN Peacekeeping Mission to Cyprus
UPADS	Pan-African Union for Social Democracy

Part I
Theoretical Perspectives

1
Introduction: Putting Mediation in Context

Jacob Bercovitch

Introduction

In May, 1899 delegates from 26 countries met in The Hague, in the Netherlands, to hold what became known later as the First Hague Peace Conference. The meeting was convened by Tsar Nicholas II of Russia, and had two main objectives: (1) to stop the spread of armaments in Europe, and (2) to produce some ideas for the progress settlement of disputes. While little progress was made on the disarmament issues, the Conference did produce a series of declarations about the need to settle conflicts without resorting to arms (those declarations actually resulted in the establishment of the Permanent Court of Arbitration – the prototype of today's International Court of Justice). Foremost among these declarations was the need to use judicial methods, arbitration or mediation in the settlement of international disputes. Thus, for the first time, the norm of international mediation was given its most explicit formal espousal.

Exactly one hundred years later, in May 1999, another major peace conference was held in The Hague. This time the agenda was wider; the Conference discussed such matters as assessing and removing the root causes of war, conflict prevention and peace-building, but its overall theme was 'The Peaceful Settlement of Disputes: Prospects for the 21st Century'. Among methods of peaceful settlement, mediation figured most prominently.

In a world as interconnected and interdependent as ours is, the challenge of dealing with conflicts peacefully, and learning to interact effectively with other human beings, is truly one of the most important challenges we face today. However far-fetched the claim may seem to some, there can be no doubt that mediation can resolve conflicts, reduce hostilities, and generally allow people, organizations, and nations to confront their differences peacefully, and at times even constructively.

It is from that vantage point that we believe that a better and more systematic understanding of mediation, and a heightened awareness of just how best to apply it to human conflicts, can make a major contribution to scholarship, and hopefully, the wider community as well.

The chapters in this book, all commissioned from leading practitioners or scholars, reflect this belief, and purport to offer the most up-to-date statement on the nature, features, performance and effectiveness of mediation in international relations.

The nature of mediation

Mediation has been, and remains, one of the most significant methods of managing conflicts. Provisions for some form of third party mediation were recently discovered in the Amarna letters (those refer to the reign of King Amenhotep IV around 3,500 years ago, see Cohen and Westbrook, 2000). References to acts of mediation abound in the Bible (ca. 2000 B.C.). They are found in Homer's *Iliad* (ca. 750 B.C.) and Sophocles' *Ajax* (ca. 500 B.C.). We learn too that mediation was the principal way of resolving interpersonal disputes in ancient China (Brown, 1982). It was frequently used in the many disputes between the Greek city-states (Adcock and Mosley, 1975), and it became quite indistinguishable from the evolving pattern of Renaissance diplomacy and the codification of ambassadorial functions. Few other devices of dispute settlement receive so eloquent a testimony as that given to mediation in Shakespeare's *Romeo and Juliet*. The failure of Mercutio's ill-advised mediation changes the mood and character of the play.

In the present international environment, a heterogeneous, competitive environment characterized by a fairly loose (some might say anarchic) structure, absence of generally accepted rules and norms, or a centralized authority, the unstoppable proliferation of all sorts of non-state actors, serious security concerns, and increasing ethnic cleavages, the opportunities for conflict are multiplied manifold. So, alas, has the need for effective conflict management. Mediation seems, on the face of it, to offer a good practical method of managing conflicts and helping to establish some sort of regional or international order. It can do so because its very essence is guaranteed to guard the independence, sovereignty and freedom of choice which all actors in conflict so jealously value.

For a long time the study of mediation has been characterized by a startling lack of information. Practitioners of mediation, in all its guises, were keen to sustain its perception as a mysterious practice taking place behind closed doors, and scholars of mediation did not think it was susceptible to a systematic analysis. Neither believed that patterns of behavior could be discerned, or that any generalizations about mediation should be made. It was as if all conflicts were essentially two-sided only. The third party was introduced merely as an afterthought, and as an unrelated exogenous input.

My approach to mediation is quite different. It is largely influenced by the parameters set by such scholars as Carl Stevens and Tom Schelling.

Stevens states that 'mediation, like other social phenomena, is susceptible to systematic analysis. The key to analysis is in recognising that where mediation is employed it is an integral part of the bargaining process... an analysis of mediation is not possible except in the context of general analysis of bargaining negotiations' (Stevens, 1963: 123). In a similar vein, Schelling notes that a mediator 'is probably best viewed as an element in the communication arrangements, or as a third party with a payoff structure of his own' (Schelling, 1960: 44).

These are important points and are worth emphasizing. Mediation can and should be studied systematically. It can, and should be placed within a broader context or structure, where questions concerning its performance and effectiveness can be raised, and studied systematically. Here we want to raise questions such as who is, or should be, the third party? How should a mediator behave, and what resources does it possess? Why do some mediator parties fail, while others succeed? Which set of factors may explain success or failure? And how, finally, has the third party's role been expanded to encompass different conflicts and different mandates?

Let us begin by listing the characteristics of mediation. The following may be listed as the most significant irrespective of the context:

1. Mediation is an extension and continuation of the parties' own conflict management efforts.
2. Mediation involves the intervention of an individual, group or organization into a dispute between two or more actors.
3. Mediation is a non-coercive, non-violent and ultimately non-binding form of intervention.
4. Mediation turns a dyadic relationship into a triadic interaction of some kind. By increasing the number of actors from two to three, mediation effects considerable structural changes and creates new focal points for an agreement.
5. A mediator enters a dispute in order to affect, change, resolve, modify or influence it in some way.
6. Mediators bring with them, consciously or otherwise, ideas, knowledge, resources and interests of their own, or of the group they represent. Mediators are often important actors with their own assumptions and agendas about the dispute in question. Mediators can often be both interested and concerned parties.
7. Mediation is a voluntary form of intervention. This means the parties retain their control over the outcome (if not always the process) of their dispute, as well as their freedom to accept or reject mediation or mediator's proposals.
8. Mediation operates on an *ad hoc* basis only.

Posing questions about mediation is a meaningful exercise only when we reach a consensus on how best to define it, and can emphasize its specific features. Most definitions of mediation purport to (a) capture the gist of what mediators do, or hope to achieve, (b) distinguish between mediation and other related processes of third party intervention, and (c) describe mediators' stance. It is worth considering a few definitions and evaluating their implications.

The first set of definitions focuses on what mediators hope to achieve. Oran Young defines it as 'any action taken by an actor that it not a direct party to the crisis, that is designed to reduce or remove one or more of the problems of the bargaining relationship, and therefore to facilitate the termination of the crisis itself' (Young, 1967: 34). In much the same vein Chris Mitchell defines mediation as any intermediary activity '... undertaken by a third party with the primary intention of achieving some compromise settlement of the issues at stake between the parties, or at least ending disruptive conflict behavior' (Mitchell, 1981: 287). And in a somewhat more detailed fashion we have Blake and Mouton's definition of mediation as a process involving 'the intervention of a third party who first investigates and defines the problem and then usually approaches each group separately with recommendations designed to provide a mutually acceptable solution' (Blake and Mouton, 1985: 15).

Another set of definitions purports to capture differences between mediation and related forms of peaceful conflict management. Moore defines it as 'an extension and elaboration of the negotiation process. Mediation involves the intervention of an acceptable, impartial, and neutral third party who has no authoritative decision making power to assist contending parties in voluntarily reaching their own mutually acceptable settlement' (Moore, 1986: 6). Linda Singer defines it as a 'form of third party assistance (that) involves an outsider to the dispute, who lacks the power to make decisions for the parties' (Singer, 1990: 20). Folberg and Taylor define it 'as an alternative to violence, self-help or litigation that differs from the processes of counselling, negotiation and arbitration' (Folberg and Taylor, 1984: 7).

A great number of definitions emphasize neutrality and impartiality, as opposed to bias, as the distinguishing features of mediation. Bingham defines mediation as the 'assistance of a "neutral" third party to a negotiation' (Bingham, 1985: 5). Folberg and Taylor see mediation 'as the process by which the participants, together with the assistance of a neutral person or persons, systematically isolate disputed issued in order to develop options, consider alternatives, and reach a consensual settlement that will accommodate their needs' (Folberg and Taylor, 1984: 7). Moore draws attention to the process of mediation and the neutrality of a mediator by defining it as 'the intervention into a dispute or negotiation by an acceptable, impartial and neutral third party who has no authoritative decision-making power to assist disputing parties in voluntarily reaching their own mutually acceptable settlement of issues in dispute' (Moore, 1986: 14).

And Spencer and Yang see mediation as 'the assistance of a third party not involved in the dispute, who may be of a unique status that gives him or her certain authority with the disputants; or perhaps an outsider who may be regarded by them as suitably neutral go-between' (Spencer and Yang, 1993: 1495).

These definitions, and they are but a small sample, exemplify the enormous scope of mediation. Mediation may take place between states in conflict, within states, between groups of states, between organizations, and between individuals. Mediators enter a conflict to help those involved achieve a better outcome than they would otherwise. Once in a conflict, mediators may use a wide variety of behaviors to achieve their objective. Some mediators may make suggestions for a settlement, others consciously refrain from doing so. Some mediators are interested in achieving an acceptable outcome, others may wish to improve interactions between the parties. Some mediators may possess skills to defuse tensions, others may have the resources to 'nudge' the parties one way or another.

To quibble over definitions may seem as a futile exercise in semantic sophistry. It is decidedly not so. The myriad of possible mediators and the range of mediatory roles and strategies is so wide as to defeat many attempts to understand, as we seek to do here, the 'essence' of mediation. A corollary of this is the tendency to assume that mediators adopt one role (e.g. go-between) or one strategy (e.g. offer proposals) only. This is not a very helpful conception. Assigning a singular role or an exclusive strategy to a mediation effort is neglectful of the dynamics of the process. It is also detrimental to the search for common or divergent dimensions of mediation in international and other social contexts, and the effort to draw general lessons from these experiences.

The reality of mediation is that of a complex, changing and dynamic interaction between mediators, who have some resources and an interest in the conflict or its outcome, and parties in conflict or their representatives. As with any other social interaction, mediators may change, their role may be re-defined, issues may alter, indeed even the parties involved in a conflict may, and often do, change. A comprehensive definition seems to be a primary requisite for understanding this reality. The following broad definition provides suitable criteria for inclusion (and exclusion), and may serve as a basis for identifying differences and similarities. 'Mediation is here defined as a process of conflict management, related to but distinct from the parties' own negotiations, where those in conflict seek the assistance, or accept an offer of help, from an outsider (who may be an individual, an organization, a group, or a state), to change their perceptions of behavior, and to do so without resorting to physical force or invoking the authority of the law' (Bercovitch, 1997).

This may seem like a truly broad definition, but it is also one that can be widely applicable. It forces us to recognize, as surely we must, that any mediation situation comprises (a) parties in conflict, (b) a mediator, (c) a process of mediation, and (d) the context within which mediation occurs. All these elements are important in a mediation. Their interplay determines the nature, quality and effectiveness of any act of mediation in international relations. To understand how mediation functions, why it may succeed or fail, we need to identify and understand these dimensions.

Motives for mediation

Once we have presented our definition of mediation, a number of key questions may now be addressed. Four questions in particular appear pertinent. These are:

1. Why do parties in conflict, and a mediator for that matter, decide to enter into mediation?
2. Who may mediate in international conflicts?
3. How do mediators behave in the course of mediation, and
4. What are the general conditions that make it successful?

Let us review these questions.

Mediation is almost as common as conflict itself in international relations. It is carried out, on a daily basis, by such heterogeneous actors as private individuals, government officials, religious figures, regional or international organizations, *ad hoc* groupings, or small, medium and large states. In a way all these acts of mediation help to define the evolving culture of a global civil society. Each mediator may adopt behavior that ranges from the very passive, through the facilitative, to the highly active. But what is the rationale for mediation? Why would a mediator enter a conflict, and why would parties in conflict accept outside intervention in their affairs?

Generally speaking, mediation is an appropriate method for dealing with an international conflict when:

1. a conflict is long, complex, or intractable,
2. the parties' own efforts have reached an impasse,
3. neither party is prepared to countenance further costs or loss of life, and
4. both parties are prepared to cooperate, tacitly or openly, to end a cycle of conflict.

When these conditions are present, the presence of a mediator may, *prima facie*, be conducive to a peaceful outcome. But why would a mediator wish to intervene in other people's conflicts, and why, come to that, would those parties in conflict accept an outsider or a third party meddling in their affairs?

In some international conflicts, mediation, or more accurately, peaceful, constructive intervention is carried out by an individual without a direct interest in the conflict, or the issues in dispute. The motives for initiating individual mediation may include: (a) a genuine desire to change the course of a long-standing or escalating conflict and promote peace, (b) a desire to gain access to major political leaders and open channels of communication, (c) a desire to put into practice a set of ideas on conflict management, and (d) a desire to spread one's ideas and enhance personal standing and professional status. The presence of one or more of these motives (and they may be conscious or unconscious) with an opportune situation provide a very strong rationale for initiating informal mediation by individuals.

Where mediators represent an official government, a regional or an international organization, a different set of motives may prevail. Here the motives for initiating mediation may include: (a) a clear mandate to intervene in disputes (many regional organizations are constitutionally mandated to mediate disputes in their region), (b) a desire to do something about a conflict whose continuance may adversely affect their own political interests, (c) being approached directly by one or both parties and asked to mediate, (d) the wish to preserve intact a structure of which they are a part (e.g. the frequent mediation attempts by the United States between Greece and Turkey, two valued NATO member-states), or finally, (e) viewing mediation as a way of extending and enhancing their own influence and gaining some value from the conflict. The relationship between mediator and disputants is thus, never entirely devoid of political interest. To overlook this feature is to miss an important element in the dynamics of mediation.

What then of parties in conflict? Why would they accept external intervention and cooperate with it? At the most basic level we can argue that parties having trouble with their conflict, or their efforts to settle it, will be all too pleased to accept outside help, especially if it is non-binding. Other reasons why parties may accept mediation include: (a) a belief that mediation will help reduce the risks of escalation, (b) each party may embrace mediation in the expectation that the mediator would actually nudge, influence or 'deliver' the other, (c) both parties may see mediation as a public expression of their commitment to an international norm of peaceful conflict management, (d) the parties may want an outsider to take much of the blame should their efforts fail, (e) the parties may desire mediation because a mediator can be used to monitor, verify and guarantee any eventual agreement, and (f) the parties' belief that the integrative potential inherent in their conflict may be advanced by a mediator.

Whether we study ethnic, internal, international conflict, or organizational conflict, we should appreciate that, one way or another, both parties in conflict and a given mediator have pretty compelling reasons for initiating, accepting and engaging in mediation. We should not think of mediation as motivated solely and exclusively by an overriding sense of altruism, and a genuine mutual commitment to conflict resolution. These may certainly be present, but the motives, and rationale, for mediation are much more complex than merely altruism and a commitment to peace.

Who may mediate?

Given the inevitability and omnipresence of conflict, a limited range of widely accepted procedures for dealing with it, and the unwelcome reality of the scope of its potential destructiveness, it is hardly surprising that so many actors, each adopting different strategies and using different resources, are keen to mediate and undertake low-cost conflict management activities. In an environment lacking a centralized authority, the range of mediators, and the diversity of mediation, are truly immense. To make some sense of the bewildering range of possible mediators, I suggest that we think of them as falling within one of the following three categories: (a) individuals, (b) states, and (c) institutions and organizations. Let us examine the characteristics of each.

Individuals

The traditional image of international mediation, one nurtured by the media and popular accounts, is that of a single, usually high-ranking, individual, shuttling from one place to another, trying to search for understanding, restore communication between hostile parties, or help settle their conflict. This image is only partly accurate. The individual mediator who engages in such behavior is normally an official representing his/her government in a series of formal interactions with high-level officials from the disputing countries. This cannot accurately be described as individual mediation.

By individual mediation I mean mediation that is carried on by individuals who are not government officials or political incumbents. Although individual mediation exhibits greater variety and experimentation than other forms of mediation, it is essentially of two kinds only: formal or informal. Informal mediation refers to (a) the efforts of mediators who have a long-standing experience of, and a deep commitment to, international conflict resolution (e.g. the Quakers, see Yarrow, 1978), or to (b) the efforts of knowledgeable scholars whose background, attitudes and professional experience give them the opportunity to engage in mediation with real conflict parties (e.g. the efforts of scholars such as Burton, Doob and Kelman). Such individuals approach a conflict as private citizens only, not as official representatives. Their efforts are designed to utilize competence, credibility and experience to create situations and occasions in which communication may be facilitated, a better understanding of a conflict may be gained, and conflict resolution attempted.

Informal mediation is usually activated when a mediator enters a conflict on its own initiative. The format and arrangements of such mediation are, to say the least, novel. Those present come there in their personal capacity only, not as government appointees. The mediator relies mostly on communication strategies and social facilitation, and the whole tone of the interaction is free and flexible, and can serve as a useful input to the more formal channels of policy-making. The efforts of two Israeli academics, Pundak and Hirschfeld, and the late Johan Holst of Norway, in paving the way for more formal discussions between the Government of Israel and the Palestine Liberation Organization (PLO), exemplify the potential benefits of informal mediation.

Another example of informal mediation is the assistance given to parties in conflict by bodies such as the International Negotiation Network (INN) at the Carter Center. This initiative was set up by President Carter, with other international leaders, in 1976 to fill a major mediation gap. The vast majority of serious recent conflicts have been within nations, rather than between them. As most states and international organizations are prevented from intervening in the internal affairs of another sovereign state, a clear need was felt for an informal network of prestigious individuals (including former Presidents, Secretary-General of the UN etc.) to offer additional mediation resources to the disputants. The INN's informal mediation can range from offering facilities to clarifying issues and helping to 'save face'. The INN has been actively involved in various mediation and consultation efforts in Ethiopia, Cyprus, Zaire, Burma, Cambodia and the Sudan. The INN has shown just how much can be achieved through informal mediation by individuals.

Formal mediation, on the other hand, takes place when a political incumbent, a government representative or a high-level decision-maker, acts in an individual capacity to mediate a conflict between the official representatives of other states (e.g. Denis Ross and General Zinni in the Middle East, Richard Holbrook in Bosnia). It invariably occurs within a formal structure (e.g. conference, political forum or other official arenas), and is much less flexible than informal mediation. It is also less susceptible to the impact of personality characteristics. Its loss of flexibility, however, is more than matched by its immediacy of access to influential decision-makers. Formal mediation is often quite indistinguishable from diplomatic intercourse. Its range of roles is more limited than that of informal mediation, but its impact on outcomes is more direct.

States

Individual mediation, although significant, is not all that common in international relations. Most mediation activity is carried on by states (or, to be more accurate, their representatives) and regional and international organizations.

When a state is invited to mediate a conflict, or when it offers mediation, the services of one of its top decision-makers are normally engaged.

In these cases, figures such as Dr Henry Kissinger, Presidents Carter or Clinton, Secretary of State Christopher or Powell, or Lord Carrington, or other special representatives like Chester Crocker or Philip Habeeb, fulfill a mediatory role, usually in the full glare of the international media, as salient representatives of their countries.

Mediation, at any level, and in all its guises, is essentially a voluntary process. This dimension is particularly important in the relations between states where any unwelcome intervention may be strenuously resisted. For mediation between states to be effective, even the most highly placed decision-makers must be seen to be impartial, acceptable to the disputants and inspire their trust. The absence of any one of these attributes may well lead to a failed mediation. States in conflict will submit their conflict to mediation only when they believe that the mediator can act fairly and take cognizance of their own interests. When we talk about mediation by states, we normally distinguish between small states and large states. Each claims legitimacy and authority on the basis of different attributes. Small states such as New Zealand, Algeria, Switzerland and Austria (see Slim, 1992), have been involved in a disproportionate number of mediations in international relations. Their very size, and presumed lack of clout, makes them appear non-threatening and ideally positioned to carry out mediations between adversaries. Small states usually wait for an invitation to mediate. When they do intervene, their efforts tend to be confined to regional conflicts only, and the strategies used tend to be mostly low-profile strategies of dialogue and communication. This is where small states can be at their most useful.

Large states, by contrast, often create the opportunity to mediate, and use mediation as a vehicle to protect or promote their own interests (Touval, 1992). Large states have a greater array of resources, and can utilize a wider range of strategies. Because of their global interests, large states get involved in many conflicts in various parts of the world. When large states mediate a conflict, they can use their material capabilities to apply sticks and carrots in the course of their mediation. They can generate and maintain a momentum toward a settlement by offering a neutral environment (e.g. Camp David, Dayton), pressing for concessions, offering proposals, and generally altering the disputants' payoffs and motivation.

Mediation, whether by small states or large states, is not a form of behavior that is prescribed by international law. It is not pre-ordained; it is evolutionary and ever-changing. Its precise form and characteristics are negotiated and re-negotiated with each passing phase. There is little that is pre-determined about the course of outcome or mediation by states.

Institutions and organizations

The complexity of the international environment is such that states can no longer facilitate the pursuit of all human interests, nor satisfy the demands for an ever increasing range of services. Consequently we have witnessed a phenomenal growth in the number of international and transnational organizations, all of whom may affect issues of war and peace. These organizations have become, in some cases, more important providers of services than states. They have also become, in the modern international system, very active participants in the search for mechanisms and procedures conducive to peacemaking and conflict resolution. We would expect these organizations to play their full part in the mediation of international conflicts.

Two kinds of organizations play an important role in the area of peacemaking and conflict resolution; regional and international organizations, and transnational organizations. Regional and international organizations (e.g. the OAS, the Organization for African Unity (OAU), the UN etc.) represent local or global collections of states signifying their intention to fulfill the obligations of membership as set forth in a formal treaty. Transnational organizations (e.g. Amnesty International) represent individuals from different countries who have similar knowledge, skills or interests, and who meet together on a regular basis to promote their interests.

Of the international organizations now in existence, none has been more active in resolving conflicts through negotiations and mediation than the UN. Its Charter specifically commits it to provide answers to global problems of conflict and security. In the post Cold War world, with its outbreak of low-level violence, civil wars and ethnic conflicts, the UN is often seen as the only actor capable of acting independently and resolving conflict. The 'Agenda for Peace' report, released by former Secretary General Boutrous-Ghali, recognizes the future challenges the UN is likely to meet, and lays great emphasis on preventive diplomacy and conflict resolution.

The UN is quickly becoming a center for initiating concerted efforts to deal with the deep-rooted causes of conflict, to resolve conflicts, and not merely to keep the peace. The UN will undoubtedly use its new political latitude to expand its mediation and conflict resolution activities. Recent peacemaking efforts by the UN in Somalia, Bosnia, Cambodia, Yugoslavia, Afghanistan, Angola and Rwanda show the extent to which this, once shackled and much-criticized, organization is now prepared to go to involve itself in all kinds of difficult and intractable conflicts. Once involved, the UN can offer a forum, resources, monitoring ability, and the capacity to mobilize an international consensus.

Regional organizations, like the EU, the OAS, the OAU and the Arab League, all adhere to the principles of negotiation and mediation as their preferred means of resolving conflicts. These organizations have always had a great latitude in the field of conflict resolution. This is not surprising as most conflict occurs between regional neighbors. Some, like the EU, have made conflict resolution a major objective of their structure. Regional organizations usually engage in collective mediation. Their strength is undoubtedly in the possession of common background, culture and experience. They may not have the capacity or resources that the UN possesses, but they are all involved in some current peacemaking activities: the EU in Bosnia, the OAU in Somalia, and the OAS in El Salvador.

Transnational organizations, such as Amnesty International, the Quakers, the International Committee of the Red Cross, etc. operating independently of states, embody many of the elements commonly associated with impartiality. These organizations, with a limited resource base, and ability to use fewer strategies, often find themselves involved in what may be termed humanitarian intervention (where the issues at stake are often hostages, refugees or prisoners). Where strict secrecy may be required, a high degree of impartiality desired, and when neither governments nor international organizations can gain access to a conflict, transnational organizations come into their own. New organizations, like International Alert and the International Negotiation Network exemplify the growing number of institutions and organizations committed to peacemaking, mediation and conflict resolution.

Overall, it seems clear that, many actors, from informal individuals to formal leaders of states, can play an important role in conflict resolution and mediation. The international community can no longer afford to ignore conflict, or respond to it in an *ad hoc* manner. Mediation offers a framework for developing complementary, consistent, and effective policies for continuing, managing and resolving conflicts.

Mediator's roles and behavior

Mediation has been a prevalent form of international conflict management for many years now. It is linked to the development of international negotiations and diplomacy, and it is embedded in the creation of institutions, regimes and formal organizations to help states deal with many aspects of their relationships. But what do mediators actually do? Do they change behavior merely by chairing meetings and carrying messages, or do they develop more active roles and functions? What do mediators do once mediation is under way?

Considerable attention has been given to the question of mediator roles, functions and behavior. Some scholars see this aspect as the most useful criterion by which to evaluate the success of mediation. In an exhaustive review of the literature Wall (1981) identified more than 100 specific mediation functions and behaviors. In a later paper (Wall *et al.*, 2001) all these functions and behaviors are divided into three broad categories: (a) behavior that is designed to affect each disputant (e.g. empowerment, educative), (b) behavior that is designed to affect the relations between the conflict parties (e.g. a proper agenda, secrecy), and (c) behavior designed to change the relationship between each disputant and the mediator (e.g. offer rewards). All these forms of behavior arise from the fact that the negotiators concerned cannot reach an agreement, and their stated purpose is to change, modify, settle or resolve a conflict and/or the perceptions that sustain it. Enacting these behaviors constitutes the 'heart' of mediation.

To make sense of the many forms of behavior mediators may undertake, we usually suggest a number of role-categories that encompass related forms of behavior. Mediators' roles may be characterized in a number of ways (e.g. Jabri, 1990; Princen, 1992). The late Jeffrey Rubin, for instance, offers a set of mediation roles and distinguishes between formal mediators (e.g. by UN Secretary General) and informal mediation (e.g. by academic practitioners such as John Burton and Herb Kelman), individual mediation (e.g. Lord Owen) and mediation by a representative of a state (e.g. Colin Powell), invited mediation and non-invited mediation, advisory mediation and more directive mediation, permanent mediation v. temporary mediation, and resolution-oriented mediation v. relationship-oriented mediation. Each of these mediators has different interests, different resources and capabilities, and the behavior of each may lead to different outcomes (Rubin, 1981). Stulberg, writing in a more traditional vein, lists the following as mediators' roles: (a) a catalyst, (b) an educator, (c) a translator, (d) a resource-expander, (e) bearer of bad news, (f) an agent of reality, and (g) a scapegoat (Stulberg, 1987). Susskind and Cruickshank, whose conception of mediation is that of 'assisted negotiation', introduce a dynamic element into the discussion by identifying a number of roles (e.g. representation, inventing options, monitoring) and relating these to the various stages of the conflict (Susskind and Cruickshank, 1987).

Another, and some would argue more useful, conception for focusing on, and categorizing what mediators actually do, is that of a mediation strategy. A mediation strategy is defined by Kolb as 'an overall plan, approach or method a mediator has for resolving a dispute ... it is the way the mediator intends to manage the case, the parties, and the issue' (Kolb, 1983: 24). Which are the most important mediation strategies, and do different mediators choose different strategies?

There are a number of ways of thinking about mediation strategies. Kolb herself distinguishes two kinds of strategies: deal-making strategies (affecting the substance of a conflict) and orchestration strategies (managing the interaction) (Kolb, 1983). Janice Stein, in her study of successive American mediations in the Middle East, talks about incremental strategies (segmenting a conflict into smaller issues) and comprehensive strategies (dealing with all aspects of a conflict) (Stein, 1985). Carnevale, in a classic paper, suggests that mediators may choose one of four fundamental strategies: integration (searching for common ground), pressing (reducing range of available alternatives), compensation (enhancing attractiveness of some alternatives) and inaction (which in effect means allowing the parties to go their own way; Carnevale, 1986). Kressel, in one of the most widely used typologies of mediation strategies, presents three general strategies: reflexive (discovering issues, facilitating better interactions), non-directive (producing a favorable climate for mediation), and directive (promoting specific outcomes; Kressel, 1972).

Touval and Zartman's typology of mediation strategies is the most apposite for the scholar or practitioner of international mediation. They identify three discrete categories of third party behavior, on an ascending level of involvement, that can describe the full range of mediation techniques. This typology is particularly useful because (a) it is derived deductively from a general framework of mediation relationship that includes information, decision-making and influence, (b) it can be examined empirically (through observations or post mediation questionnaires), and (c) it includes all dimensions of mediator behavior. The three broad strategies are: (a) communication–facilitation, (b) formulation, and (c) manipulation (Touval and Zartman, 1985). Many of the limitations of past research on mediation behavior can be rectified by using this typology.

Touval and Zartman's typology permits us to study and compare what mediators actually do when they get involved in a conflict. We can observe actual mediation cases, or interview experienced mediators, and code specific aspects of their behavior in terms of one of the three strategies. The choice of any form of mediation behavior or broad strategy is rarely random. It is influenced by factors peculiar to the conflict, and factors internal to the mediator. Mediators try and vary their behavior to reflect the conflict in hand. In low intensity conflicts, for instance, communication strategies may be effective; in high intensity conflicts, more active strategies may be called for. Time pressure, mediator rank, the previous relations between the parties, may all affect the choice of a strategy. All of these factors should be studied. To be effective, mediation strategies and behavior must be congruent with the nature of a conflict, and the objectives and interests of the adversaries and the mediator.

Whichever intervention strategy mediators use, their underlying objectives in any conflict are: (a) to change the physical environment of conflict management (e.g. by maintaining secrecy, or imposing time limits as President Carter did at Camp David), (b) change the perception of what is at stake (e.g. by structuring an agenda, identifying and packaging new issues), and (c) change the parties' motivation to reach a peaceful outcome (e.g. using subtle pressure). Any international conflict presents opportunities for some form of mediation. To be effective, however, mediation strategies must reflect the reality of the conflict, and the resources of a mediator. To that extent international mediation is a truly contingent and reciprocal political activity.

Evaluating international mediation

We have seen that numerous actors and organizations may undertake and initiate international mediation, but is there any way of assessing just how much these different mediators have achieved? How can mediation outcomes be assessed, and how, come to that, can the impact of a particular mediation be evaluated? If mediation is ultimately about changing or influencing a conflict, or the way parties in conflict behave, can such changes be discerned? Furthermore, if change has been effected, and a satisfactory outcome of sorts has been achieved, can this be attributed to the wisdom and experience of the mediator or the motivation of the parties? And conversely, if the parties show no change whatsoever, should this be described as mediation failure? Evaluating success and failure in mediation poses serious conceptual and methodological problems.

As international mediation is not uniform, it seems futile to draw up one set of criteria only to cover the many objectives of all mediators. Individual mediators, for instance, may emphasize communicational–facilitative strategies, be more concerned with the quality of interaction, and seek to create a better environment for conflict resolution. States, on the other hand, may well seek to change the behavior of those in conflict and achieve a formal settlement of sorts. Such different objectives cannot be easily accommodated within a single perspective. To answer the question whether or not mediation works, we need to know something about the goals of mediation. This is why I suggest the need for two broad criteria, subjective and objective, to assess the contribution and consequences of any form of international mediation.

Subjective criteria refer to the parties', or the mediator's, perception that the goals of mediation had been achieved, or that a desired change had taken place. Using this perspective, we can suggest that mediation has been successful when the parties (a) express satisfaction with the process or outcome of mediation, or when the outcome is seen as (b) fair, (c) efficient, or (d) effective (Susskind and Cruickshank, 1987).

Aspects such as fairness of mediation, satisfaction with its performance, or improvement in the overall climate of relationship, cannot be easily demonstrated, but they are undoubtedly correlates of successful mediation. They are subjective in that they are essentially in the eyes of the parties in conflict. Even if a conflict remains unresolved, mediation – of any form – can do much to change the way the disputants feel about each other, and lead, however indirectly, to a long-term improvement in relationships and a resolution of the conflict.

Objective criteria for assessing the impact and consequences of mediation offer a totally different perspective. Objective criteria rely on substantive indicators which may be demonstrated empirically. Usually such criteria involve observations of change and judgements about the extent of change as evidence of the success or failure of mediation.

We can, thus, see a particular mediation effort as successful if it contributed to a cessation or reduction of violent behavior and hostilies, and the opening of a dialogue between the parties. Or, we can see it as being successful only when a formal and binding agreement that settles many of the issues in conflict has been signed. Thus, what we mean by 'the success rate of mediation' may vary from study to study, and from context to context.

Evaluating the success or failure of international mediation in objective terms is a relatively straightforward task. Here we can assess the permanence of the agreement achieved, the speed with which it was achieved, the reduction in the level of hostilities between the disputants, the number of issues on which agreement was achieved, etc. On the face of it, at least, objective criteria seem to offer a perfectly valid way to assess the impact, consequences and effectiveness of international mediation.

We would, however, be unwise to rely solely on objective criteria. Different mediators, and indeed different conflict parties, have different goals in mind when they enter conflict management. Behavior changes could well be only one among a set of goals. Some international mediators may focus on the substance of interactions, others may focus on its climate, setting and decision-making norms. These cannot always be easily evaluated. Each mediation should, perhaps, be evaluated in terms of the criteria that are significant to its own context. The question does mediation work and how best to evaluate it, can only be answered by collecting information and making judgements in specific cases. There are just too many problems with this question, and it seems that on this issue at least our theoretical ambitions must be tempered by the constraints of a complex and an unyielding reality.

Toward more effective mediation

Given the diversity of conflicts, different circumstances and strategies, and the range of possible actors, there cannot possibly be one 'right way' to manage or mediate international conflicts. However, it is possible to draw generalizations from various studies on mediation, and to reflect on lessons learned, to suggest some factors and conditions that impede mediation or help it to become more effective.

Scholars and practitioners alike have devoted considerable attention to the question of the conditions under which mediation can be more effective. Mediation cannot be successful (whatever that means) in each and every conflict. It is not a panacea to all the social problems and conflicts in the world. Clearly, it can be effective in some situations, and not so effective in others. Can, though, the characteristics of the situations under which mediation is effective, be distinguished?

In an overview of mediation, Jeffrey Rubin notes that 'For international mediation – indeed, for any form of intervention in any conflict setting – to be effective, three things are required; disputant motivation to settle or resolve the conflict in question, mediator opportunity to get involved, and mediator skill' (Rubin, 1992: 251). The parties' motivation, and commitment, to accept and engage in mediation will undoubtedly affect the outcome of mediation. When disputants are unenthusiastic about mediation, or believe they can get what they want through unilateral action, the likelihood of a successful mediation is extremely low. Effective mediation requires consent, high motivation and active participation.

From the perspective of a would-be mediator, a number of features can be indicative of the parties' genuine motivation and serious commitment to mediation. Foremost among these are the parties' perceptions of a 'hurting stalemate', and the receipt of a joint request for mediation. The parties reach a 'hurting stalemate' when their own efforts to manage the conflict are not going anywhere, and yet the costs, both human and economic, of pursuing the conflict continue to mount. The timing of mediation is a crucial factor affecting the chances of its success. Conflicts, like all other social processes, have their own life cycle (which may be days or months). There are times when a conflict is 'ripe for mediation' (Zartman, 1985), and times when mediation can only make a conflict worse and harm the credibility of the mediators involved (Haass, 1990). Assessing when a conflict is ready for mediation may not be easy, and may clearly vary from case to case and be dependent upon many dynamic factors. What we are saying here is that the existence of a 'hurting stalemate' (e.g. a military setback, a change in power relations, or failure to impose a unilateral outcome) provides the best guideposts for initiating mediation.

Empirical research (Bercovitch, 1986) suggests that neither premature, nor belated mediations are especially likely to be effective. The most propitious phase to initiate mediation – at least of the formal kind – is about half-way through the life cycle of a conflict, and certainly after the parties' own conflict management efforts have failed. At this stage the parties' motivation to settle may be at its highest.

Another indication of the strength of commitment to mediation is the source of request. When one party only requests mediation, the chances of a successful outcome are pretty slim. Mediation offers more rewarding opportunities when it is requested by both parties in conflict rather than by one party only, of offered by a mediator. A joint request may well be a necessary pre-condition for effective international mediation (Bercovitch, 1984; Hiltrop, 1989).

International mediation is also more likely to be effective when certain conditions and circumstances are present. These include: relative power parity between the states or other actors in conflict (Young, 1967), absence of any issues of general 'principle' or ideology (Bercovitch and Langley, 1993), a clear identification of the parties in conflict (not always as straightforward as it may appear), the absence of severe internal disorganization or civil war, and a reasonably amicable history of the parties' previous relationship (Bercovitch, 1989). These and other conditions can affect the course and outcome of mediation. Being able to identify these conditions may affect mediators' decisions to initiate, or discard, mediation, as well as decisions about likely strategies and outcomes. Knowing when to use mediation, may even be more important than knowing how to use it.

Another aspect which affects mediation is that of mediator identity and skills. Mediation is a voluntary process, so only an appropriate mediator is likely to be effective. There is wide agreement among scholars and practitioners that appropriate mediators should possess intelligence, tact, drafting skills, a sense of humor, and have specific knowledge and expertise of the conflict at hand. Mediators who possess these attributes are likely to be acceptable to all sides in a conflict, and consequently enhance the parties' motivation to reach a peaceful settlement.

A related aspect of mediator identity that can help us to differentiate potentially effective from ineffective mediators is that of mediator rank. It is important to recall that some mediators, such as a President, a Prime Minister or Secretary of State, are better able to marshal resources in the course of mediation. High-ranking mediators can be more persuasive than middle-level officials. They possess leverage and can use social influence that could be crucial in persuading the parties to make concessions or more toward an agreement. This notion is borne out in a series of empirical studies (Bercovitch and Houston, 1993) which show unmistakenly the positive association between high rank and successful mediation outcomes.

Related to this is the idea that mediation roles and strategies may affect outcomes. There are some (e.g. Burton, 1969; Kelman, 2000) who advocate a particular range of strategies, usually informal, communicational strategies as the most viable strategy a third party may use. Others (e.g. Touval and Zartman, 1985) argue for more forceful mediation. Although much may depend on the nature and circumstances of a conflict, there is strong evidence (e.g. Bercovitch and Houston, 1993) to suggest that more directive strategies are more likely to be effective. Active strategies can rely on the full gamut of influence attempts and utilize reward, persuasion, legitimacy and information to effect a desired outcome.

Mediators may appear to do little more than shuttle from here to there, chair meetings and clarify issues. In most cases, however, they quickly begin to sense what is possible, and very discreetly urge the parties to work toward some agreement. To do so, and to have the desired impact on a conflict, mediators need to do more than generating and sharing information; they have to rely on some strategies that can change the ways the parties interact.

A number of conditions relating to the context of a conflict, and some relating to the identity of a mediator, form the core of a framework for more effective mediation. This framework can offer policy implications and guidelines which may be applied in concrete cases, and ultimately explain the success and failure of mediation across a wide range of conflicts. This fruitful area of research should prove invaluable in bringing scholars and practitioners together in constructing an inventory of conditions that impede mediation, and conditions that are conducive to its success.

Structure of the book

Writing about mediation and conflict management in the current political environment is not easy. States that have held together for a long time collapsed, conflicts these days involve different actors, using different strategies and techniques, and the strident demands for ethnic separatism, all create a very confusing picture for any would-be mediator. The 'rules of the game' these days are simply more complex, and what was referred to as the 'international community of states' is that much more amorphous today. One of the challenges we face is to make intellectual sense of all this complexity, study mediation (or indeed any other response to conflict) systematically, and offer broad guidelines within which policy-makers might frame their responses to conflict.

The overriding concern of the book is with mediation effectiveness, or mediation success, and how best to achieve it. Within these parameters, three major themes are highlighted. The first theme (Part I) concentrates on some determinants of mediation success. The scene is set by Carnevale's chapter which explores strategic and tactical resources available to a mediator, and how these may be expanded to improve the chances of success. Pruitt's chapter examines psychological prerequisites for success, focusing on motivation and optimism as the best indicators for initiating mediation.

The five chapters which constitute Part II of the book highlight the second theme of the book; namely, the range and diversity of mediation in the contemporary environment. Mediators may come from all kinds of background, be associated with different states or organizations, and mediate a conflict using different resources and strategies. Aggestam focuses on individual mediation, and how such mediation can achieve success by complementing more traditional forms of mediation, Zartman studies the conditions which permit regional organizations to initiate mediation, and to do so effectively, Fretter examines the resources, and behaviors, that are available to the UN in its quest for successful mediation, Kleiboer analyses the relevance of leverage in great power mediation, and Wall, Druckman and Diehl show how responses to conflict, such as peacekeeping for instance, may merge imperceptibly into effective mediation.

The third theme of the book (Part III) shows just how wide the spectrum of mediational, and other third-party responses to conflict really is. Here scholars and practitioners focus on new strategies of intervention, or new arenas of mediation. Kelman discusses the interactive problem-solving approach to conflict with which he has been associated for more than three decades, Dunn and Kriesberg examine the expanding range of conflict sources, and the emergence of single-purpose transnational organizations as effective mediators, Salacuse discusses the expansion of mediation to new arenas, such as the business arena, and Crocker, Hampson and Aall address the challenge of a new form of mediation, multiparty mediation.

The chapters below attempt to distil much of what we know about mediation, and provide us with new insights and ideas about the process. I do not pretend to offer here the last word on mediation. The book purports to contribute to theory development, to a critical dialog between scholars and practitioners, and to the creation of better mediators. As long as we test our ideas in the different context and arenas of mediation practice, we may well achieve these objectives.

Conclusion

Until ten or fifteen years ago scholarly attempts to comprehend the nature and sources of human conflict in general, and the manner of their resolution in particular, were all too few in number and rather marginal in character. This has changed very much. The study of international conflict and conflict management has become a major focus of systematic analysis. Scholarly tracts and practitioners' reflections have helped to institutionalize the field, and enhance individual and collective capacity to deal with or manage conflicts. The risks, costs and tragedies of conflict in the later part of our century have finally forced us to search for better ways of resolving conflicts. The traditional reliance on power or avoidance is as far from being an optimal way of dealing with conflict as they are outdated. Negotiations and mediation are at last beginning to emerge as the most appropriate responses to conflict in its myriad forms and to the challenge of building a more peaceful world. Negotiations and mediations do not just happen, they are social roles subject to many influences. As with other roles, they can be learned.

The shared quest for learning the principles and practices of mediation can only make sense if it is conducted systematically, and located within some kind of an intellectual framework. This book does both; it offers a systematic analysis of some significant aspects of mediation, and it suggests the broad outlines of a framework to study mediation in the overall context of conflict management, and to draw relevant lessons from such a study.

This book embodies, I believe, Jeffrey Rubin's conviction that mediation can, and should be, studied systematically, and is an aspect of the broader process of conflict management, and that irrespective of what the conflict is all about, or who the mediators are, mediation involves the intertwining of interests, resources, positions and influence attempts. This relationship is critical for analysing the dynamics of conflict, and assessing the prospects of successful mediation. I do not assume that the chapters below offer an exhaustive account of mediation, but I believe that they adequately integrate many findings that have a bearing on conflict resolution, and provide answers to such questions as who may mediate conflicts, and how, when should mediation be initiated, how does it actually work, how to evaluate its impact, and how to improve it?

The ending of the Cold War, and the emergence of an ever increasing number of ethnic and internal conflicts, provide opportunities for a significant expansion in the use of mediation as an instrument of conflict resolution. The old techniques of power and deterrence seem increasingly less relevant to the problems and conflicts we face in the 21st century. Mediation may well offer a coherent and effective response to these problems. To ensure that it can also be successful, we need to develop a better understanding of the process, and offer consistent guidelines to guide the involvement of international actors in mediation. This effort is still in its infancy, and many, from different fields and disciplines, can contribute to it. Jeffrey Rubin took the first steps in this direction (1981), here I hope to follow in his footsteps.

References

Adcock, F. E. and Mosley, D. (1975) *Diplomacy in Ancient Greece*, New York: St. Martin's Press – now Palgrave Macmillan.

Bercovitch, J. (1984) *Social Conflict and Third Parties*, Boulder, Co.: Westview Press.

Bercovitch, J. (1986) 'International Mediation: A Study of the Incidence and Strategies of Successful Outcomes', *Cooperation and Conflict*, 21: 155–68.

Bercovitch, J. (1989) 'International Dispute Mediation', in Pruitt, D.G. and Kressel, K. (eds), *Mediation Research*, San Francisco: Jossey-Bass.

Bercovitch, J. (1997) 'Mediation in International Conflict', in I. W. Zartman and L. Rasmussen (eds), *Peacemaking in International Conflict*, Washington, DC: US Institute of Peace Press.

Bercovitch, J. and A. Houston (1993) 'Influence of Mediator Characteristics and Behavior on the Success of Mediation', *International Journal of Conflict Management*, 4: 297–321.

Bercovitch, J. and J. Langley (1993) 'The Nature of the Dispute and the Effectiveness of International Mediation', *Journal of Conflict Resolution*, 37: 670–91.

Bingham, G. (1985) *Resolving Environmental Disputes*. Washington, DC: The Conservation Foundation.

Blake, R. A. and J. S. Mouton (1985) *Solving Costly Organizational Conflicts*. San Francisco: Jossey-Bass.

Brown, D. (1982) 'Divorce and Family Mediation: History, Review and Future Directions', *Conciliation Courts Review*, 20: 1–34.

Burton, J. W. (1969) *Conflict and Communication*. London: Macmillan – now Palgrave Macmillan.

Carnevale, P. (1986) 'Strategic Choice in Mediation', *Negotiation Journal*, 2: 41–56.

Cohen, R. and R. Westbrook (eds) (2000) *Amarna Diplomacy: The Beginning of International Relations*. Baltimore: The Johns Hopkins University Press.

Folberg, J. and A. Taylor (1984) *Mediation*. San Francisco: Jossey-Bass.

Haass, R. (1990) *Conflict Unending*. New Haven, Conn.: Yale University Press.

Hiltrop, J. (1989) 'Factors Affected with Successful Labor Mediation', in K. Kressel and D. G. Pruitt (eds), *Mediation research*. San Francisco: Jossey-Bass.

Jabri, V. (1990) *Mediating Conflict: Decision-Making and Western Intervention in Namibia*. Manchester: Manchester University Press.

Kelman, H. C. (2000) 'The Role of the Scholar-Practitioner in International Conflict Resolution', *International Studies Perspective*, 1: 273–88.

Kolb, D. (1983) 'Strategy and Tactics of Mediation', *Human Relations*, 36: 247–68.

Kressel, K. (1972) *Labor Mediation: An Exploratory Survey*. New York: Association of Labor Mediation Agencies.

Mitchell, C. R. (1981) *The Structure of International Conflict*. London: Macmillan – now Palgrave Macmillan.

Moore, C. W. (1986) *The Mediation Process: Practical Strategies for Resolving Conflict*. San Francisco: Jossey-Bass.

Princen, T. (1992) *Intermediaries in International Conflict*. Princeton, NJ: Princeton University Press.

Rubin, J. Z. (ed.) (1981) *Dynamics of Third Party Intervention: Kissinger in the Middle East*. New York: Praeger.

Rubin, J. Z. (1992) 'International Mediation in Context', in J. Bercovitch and J. Z. Rubin (eds), *Mediation in International Relations*. London: Macmillan – now Palgrave Macmillan.

Schelling, T. C. (1960) *The Strategy of Conflict*. Cambridge, Mass.: Harvard University Press.

Singer, L. R. (1990) *Settling Disputes*. Boulder, Co.: Westview Press.

Slim, R. (1992) 'Small-State Mediation in International Relations', in J. Bercovitch and J. Z. Rubin (eds), *Mediation in International Relations*. London: Macmillan – now Palgrave Macmillan.

Spencer, D. E. and H. Yang (1993) 'Lessons from the Field of International Conflict Resolution', *Notre Dame Law Review*, 67: 1495–512.

Stein, J. G. (1985) 'Structure, Strategies and Tactics of Mediation', *Negotiation Journal*, 1: 331–47.

Stevens, C. M. (1963) *Strategy and Collective Bargaining Negotiations*. New York: McGraw-Hill.

Stulberg, J. (1987) *Taking Charge/Managing Conflict*. Lexington, Mass.: D. C. Heath.

Susskind, L. and J. Cruikshank (1987) *Breaking the Impasse*. New York: Basic Books.

Touval, S. (1992) 'The Superpowers as Mediators', in J. Bercovitch and J. Z. Rubin (eds), op.cit.

Touval, S. and I. W. Zartman (eds) (1985) *International Mediation in Theory and Practice*. Boulder, Co.: Westview Press.

Wall, J. A. (1981) 'Mediation: An Analysis, Review and Proposed Research', *Journal of Conflict Resolution*, 25: 157–80.

Wall, J. A., J. B. Stark and R. L. Standifer (2001) 'Mediation: A Current Review and Theory Development', *Journal of Conflict Resolution*, 45: 370–91.

Yarrow, C. H. (1978) *Quaker Experiences in International Conciliation*. New Haven, Conn.: Yale University Press.

Young, O. R. (1967) *Intermediaries: Third Parties in International Crises*. Princeton, NJ: Princeton University Press.

Zartman, I. W. (1985) *Ripe for Resolution: Conflict and Intervention in Africa*, 2nd edn. New York: Oxford University Press.

2
Mediating from Strength

Peter J. Carnevale

'You can get a lot more done with a kind word and a gun than with a kind word alone.'

Introduction

It was the gangster Al Capone who allegedly made that statement (Safire, 1998, p. 28), and we might ask if it applies to mediation. Can a mediator get more done when mediating from strength? The question has a parallel in negotiation. The idea of 'Negotiating from strength' was popularized in the 1950s by Dean Acheson (then US Secretary of State) and Winston Churchill (then Leader of the Opposition) (Bell, 1962), and the idea is simple: strength provides the basis for agreement on favorable terms and lessens the likelihood of being exploited. Applied to mediation, the idea is also simple: strength can hasten agreement, in particular one that the mediator likes, and it may lessen the mediator's trouble in getting an agreement.

But the doctrine of negotiating from strength is not without critics: Kenneth Boulding, for example, stated '...one does not compromise with a man with a gun, and getting a gun oneself does not assist the process of compromise either. One does not negotiate from strength; one may dictate from strength, but one does not negotiate' (1962, p. 323). This criticism is justified if the goal of negotiation is a mutually acceptable agreement; a mutually acceptable agreement is unlikely if one side imposes its will on the other. Bell (1962) noted that 'There are two possible reasons for not negotiating: because one is weak and cannot afford to, or because one is strong and does not need to' (p. 213).

Mediating from strength can be criticized on similar grounds. If the goal of mediation is mutually acceptable agreement, how likely is this achieved with a strong mediator, especially one with some interest in the character of the agreement? Will the strong mediator work hard to find an agreement that satisfies the parties' underlying interests? In social influence, the weak often decry the strong, and we might expect the same in mediation. William Shakespeare put it this way, in *Measure for Measure*:

> O! it is excellent
> To have a giant's strength; but it is tyrannous
> To use it like a giant.

Was it tyrannous for Henry Kissinger, in mediating in the Middle East, to threaten a military embargo on Israel (Sheehan, 1976, p. 260)? Was strength at play in Argentina and Chile's dispute over the Beagle Channel, when the Pope, as mediator, stated '... the mediator, after having asked God for enlightenment, presents suggestions to the Parties with the purpose of carrying out his work of rapprochement ...' (cited in Princen, 1987, p. 350). What about mediation done by the leopard-skin chief of the Nuer, who threatens an intransigent party with a curse (Merry, 1989)?

Without some strength, how can mediators encourage intransigent disputants to solve their problems or reach agreement? Is strength a component of all mediation, given that the basis of mediation is influence (Kressel, 1972; Zartman and Touval, 1985; Kressel and Pruitt, 1989; Bercovitch, 1992; Carnevale and Arad, 1996; Wall *et al.*, 2001)? Touval (1992) notes that US mediation of international disputes covers the full gamut 'from minimal intercession in the performance of good offices, to the wielding of powerful inducements – offers of massive economic and military aid on some occasions, and brutal arm-twisting on others' (p. 241). A central issue is how the various aspects of strength in mediation relate to one another and to the outcomes of mediation.

A real problem is that the concept of strength is ambiguous in mediation. There are many related concepts – power, influence, control, leverage – a plethora of meanings and uses. To assess whether or not mediating from strength is a desirable position whence to mediate, we need an agreeable definition of the concept.

The central questions of this paper include the following: What is strength in mediation? What aspects of strength enable the mediator to move the disputant in the direction that the mediator intends? What behaviors and resources are exercised in what manner to afford an effect in mediation? Is strength anathema to mediation? Is it desirable to 'strengthen' mediation (cf. Ury, 1987)?

In this chapter, a definition of mediating strength is proposed that rests on a distinction between two basic forms of strength: strategic strength and tactical strength. This distinction has its foundation in analyses of negotiation by Schelling (1960) and Stevens (1963), and in the analysis of power in mediation by Zartman and Touval (1985). The major proposition is thus that there are two forms of strength in mediation. An aspect of this is that some forms of mediating strength, in some circumstances, may be counterproductive.

The shape of mediation

Mediation can take on a variety of shapes and forms. Like negotiation, a mediator's decisions and inferences are often made in context of complex social, organizational, and cultural systems that have legal constraints and historical underpinnings (Touzard, 1977). A central feature of mediation is that the negotiation continues but is helped along by the third party. Mediation preserves the voluntary, joint decision features of negotiation – the disputants retain the right to accept or reject any suggestion made by the mediator. Hence mediation can be seen as a special case of negotiation.

Mediation in international settings is done in a variety of forms by a wide variety of actors: private individuals, academic scholars, non-government organizations, government representatives, regional organizations, regional and international organizations, or one of the 190 or so states in the international system (Zartman and Touval, 1985; Bercovitch, 1992). Mediation has always been important in intergroup relations: the earliest known writings of conflict, from more than four thousand years ago, were about a Summarian ruler who helped to avert a war between neighboring groups and to develop an agreement in a dispute over land (Kramer, 1963).

The concept of mediating strength

Mediating strength is a reflection of social power, which is defined as one party's ability and willingness to influence another party to achieve a goal. In negotiation, power will often have a goal founded in self-interest; in mediation, that self-interest may be less discernible. But mediation is goal directed behavior, and it is a matter of influencing other's behavior, and hence a matter of power. Moreover, especially in political contexts, mediators can have interests that can rival those of the disputants (Touval, 1985).

In mediation, the concept of power is usually derived from the types of social power developed by French and Raven (1959) and Raven and Kruglanski (1970) (see Bercovitch, 1992, p. 19). Most analyses of social power suggest a positive correlation between strength and power, as in Thibaut and Kelley's (1959) notions of dependence, as well as Emerson's (1962), and March (1955). The notion of dependence indicates that the key source of strength in mediation comes from the disputants' need for the mediator's involvement in finding solutions to their problems (Zartman and Touval, 1985; Touval, 1992). This source of strength is exercised when the mediator threatens to terminate mediation.

But the standard conceptions of strength fail to consider two additional essential ingredients: will and skill. Stevens (1963) made this point in arguing that the standard form of social power – resource based – is one of two forms. Using a game matrix notation, he argued that social power is represented by the a priori values in the matrix. The other form is about behavior, about advantages gained via moves in the game.

This relates to Schelling's (1960) argument that having financial resources, or physical strength, or military potency, or the ability to withstand losses, are in some cases a disadvantage. Via the exercise of certain tactics, a weak party can do quite well by fooling, bluffing, or making relational commitments appear credible. Making such commitments may force the stronger party to choose between that position over no agreement, thus favoring the weaker party. Komorita (1977) labeled the social power aspect of strength 'strategic power' and the tactical, process aspect of strength 'tactical advantage'. These terms are also reflected in Lawler's distinction between 'power capability' and 'power-use (i.e. action)' (Lawler, 1992, p. 21).

The resource-based aspect of social power, referred to here as 'strategic strength', has a straightforward extension to mediation. The behavioral, tactical aspects of mediation, referred to here as 'tactical strength', is about the moves in the mediation game. However, it does not necessitate fooling, bluffing, concealing, or anything underhanded. Rather, it entails the mediator's adroit handling of the negotiation process, to affect it. In other words, strategic strength in mediation refers to what the mediator has, to what the mediator brings to the negotiation table; tactical strength refers to what the mediator does at the negotiation table.

Strategic strength in mediation

When a resource is identified as strategic, as with the statement 'Copper is a strategic material', the resource is located in a broad framework of potential application and use. For mediation, the central question is, What are the strategic materials of mediation? Strategic strength in mediation is the aspect of social power that relate to the resources and relationships that the mediator brings to the conflict (Carnevale, 1986; Rubin, 1992). This includes the types of social power identified by French and Raven (1959; Raven and Kruglanski, 1970) – legitimate, informational, expert, referent, coercive, and reward. In addition, it includes relational power, a unique source of strength in mediation.

Legitimate power

In mediation, this is influence driven by the belief that the mediator has the right to prescribe behavior, and derives from a norm that has been accepted by the disputants. For example, mediation by the Pope, in some places (e.g. the Beagle Channel dispute), may carry with it a norm of obligation to comply with the Pope's requests. Influence here rests on a judgment of how one *should* act, and the authority determines the standard. Sometimes a mediation identified as an international organization is seen as more legitimate, and carries with it greater weight than one identified as a US mediation (Touval, 1992, p. 244).

Informational power

The mediator may provide information that makes compliance with the mediator's request seem rational. This often requires an understanding of the values and priorities of the parties, because the information and its associated persuasive appeal must link the desired behavior to these values. For example, Sheehan (1976, p. 13) wrote about Henry Kissinger that his 'great function – he has said so many times – was to explain persuasively to each party the constraints upon the other'.

The information aspect of mediation is represented in the 'communicator' and in the 'formulator' roles defined by Zartman and Touval (1985). In communicator roles, mediators serve as a channel of information between disputants; in formulator roles, mediators rely on innovative thinking to merge the disputants' basic interests into mutually agreeable solutions. This involves efforts to find a solution that satisfies both parties' limits or major aspirations. An example can be found in Ralph Bunche's mediation in the Syria–Israel negotiations of 1949 when he proposed that Syrian troops withdraw and that certain areas along the border be demilitarized – a proposal that eventually led to an armistice agreement (Touval, 1982).

Expert power

The mediator may have impact that derives from special knowledge, or their reputation for having that knowledge.

Referent power

Mediators may gain strength by their status and prestige, as well as charisma, all which may enhance their ability to persuade.

Coercive power

This reflects the 'sticks' in the 'carrots and sticks' of mediation (Zartman and Touval, 1985). In mediation, Carnevale (1986) referred to coercive power as mediator 'pressure', which involves efforts to reduce the parties' limits or aspirations. It was seen when Henry Kissinger threatened a military embargo on Israel (Rubin, 1992). Another example was seen when the Soviet Foreign Minister Andrei Gromyko hinted to India that if India refused to remove troops from Pakistan territory, the Soviet Union would not protect India with its veto in the UN Security Council (Touval, 1992). Merry (1989) noted pressure can even be supernatural.

Reward power

The 'carrots' of mediation, Carnevale (1986) called it 'compensation', which involves mediator provision of rewards or benefits in exchange for agreement or compromise. A classic example was seen in 1954 when Italy and Yugoslavia quarreled over territory at the northern end of the Adriatic Sea. One concern of Yugoslavia was giving up the port city of Trieste; in its mediation effort, the US promised economic aid in developing a new port city for Yugoslavia.

Zartman and Touval (1985) refer to mediators who press and compensate as in 'manipulator' roles. Manipulator roles involve exercising 'leverage' in adding inducements that make alternatives agreeable or disagreeable.

Relational power

This refers to the structural role that transforms the two-party dispute into one that is 'triangular', with the mediator positioned in a way to take advantage of possible coalitions, or the threat of a coalition, with one side (Zartman and Touval, 1985, p. 39). This position helps move the parties to a mediated agreement, and away from one side's victory. It is the essence of Zartman and Touval's (1985) power politics model of mediation, where preservation of the mediator role has a high value.

Relational power can be gained in mediation by the mediator's pre-existing relationship – or lack of relationship, with the parties (Carnevale and Arad, 1996). Sometimes, mediator bias plays an important role in influence. The mediator's closer relationship with one side than the other can add to the mediator's capacity and desire to influence. A mediator with close ties to one side may have access to that side, and the potential to deliver concessions and agreements. For example, the Algerian mediators in the Iran Hostage crisis had 'the required revolutionary credentials and the necessary international connections needed for the job' (Slim, 1992, p. 228).

In other cases, relational power is driven by impartiality, which becomes the main source of the mediator's influence. The mediator is more likely to be accepted, more effective in eliciting information, and the mediator's suggestions are compelling, to the extent that the mediator is untainted by any affinity with the opposing side. A suggestion from an impartial mediator is imbued with fairness. This, together with the idea that perceived fairness and trust in the mediator are good predictors of settlement in mediation (Carnevale and Pruitt, 1992), indicates that the impartial mediator in some cases has an influence advantage.

Tactical strength in mediation

Tactical strength in mediation refers to what the mediator does at the negotiating table. It is about adroit maneuvering, technique, and procedure. Most discussions of mediation turn to descriptions of tactical strength in mediation. For example, Moore (1986) outlines numerous means in which the mediator exercises influence in mediation, such as controlling the communication process (e.g. determining the agenda). Indeed, almost anything a mediator does may be construed as influential, including simply being there (Pruitt and Carnevale, 1993).

In the sections below, several key categories of tactical strength are defined. Each of these is described in terms of the tactics of process control exercised by the mediator. In general, mediators have a variety of tactics at their disposal to affect the disputants' moods, motivations, and beliefs.

Communication tactics

Mediators can have an effect by controlling communication, and thereby the information that is available to the parties. These tactics also provide the opportunity to control emotion. A key tactic here is separating the parties, and shuttling back and forth between them. Communication control provides a basis for helping the parties resolve internal group disagreements especially with constituents, control expressions of anger, clarify interests, and provides the foundation for exchanging concessions. Hiltrop (1989) found that mediators can control the communication between the parties and help the parties to understand one another's positions, and such efforts were positively related to settlement.

Image tactics

Mediators can affect the image that the parties have of one another by clarifying and interpreting events, and helping them 'save face' when making concessions by sponsoring concession exchanges. In one of the first laboratory studies of mediation, Pruitt and Johnson (1970) reported that a mediator's suggestion, when combined with time pressure on the negotiators and a hostile setting, produced the greatest concession making but at the same time preserved the negotiator's face, i.e. their sense of self-worth.

Momentum tactics

These tactics create momentum, which is early success in cooperation that can enhance the viability of later cooperation. This includes control of the agenda, efforts to build trust between the parties, and developing a framework of the issues, and early agreement on a framework for agreement. Lim and Carnevale (1990) found that mediator efforts to structure an agenda increase the chances of success in mediation.

Relational tactics

These tactics pertain to the relationship between the mediator and the parties, and modifying this relationship to enhance the success of mediation. In some cases, the mediator needs to steer a precise course between the disputants lest they alienate one side and lose their credibility and acceptability. Here, the mediator manages their relational power, via their behavior, and is the tactical aspect of relational power and of what

Zartman and Touval (1985) call 'three cornered bargaining', where the prospect of siding with one party is an element of the mediator's strength.

Sometimes the exercise of relational tactics entails deliberate efforts to show evenhandedness, which in some contexts, can enhance the mediator's strength. This was seen in the 1966 mediation of the India/Pakistan conflict over Kashmir at Tashkent, where Aleksei Kosygin, premier of the Soviet Union, stressed his evenhandedness despite stronger ties to India. Signs of this included his efforts to maintain balanced press coverage of both sides, balanced references to each side in Soviet speeches, and even ritualistic alternation of whose name was mentioned first (Thornton, 1985, p. 156).

Another example is the United States mediation in the early stages of the dispute between Great Britain and Argentina over the Falkland Islands. Despite more substantial ties to Britain, the US presented a neutral front and made such statements to the point that the British feared an unfavorable mediated agreement. It has been suggested that the US wanted to preserve relations with both sides (Purcell, 1982). This is a 'juggling of partialities' (Tome, 1992), so that the mediator maintains credibility with all sides.

Strategic strength versus tactical strength

Schelling (1960) noted that having strategic, resource-based power can add to the possible set of moves or tactics that are available. This suggests that strategic strength and tactical strength are related. For example, some combinations of strategic and tactical strength are optimal. Consider, as an example, the use of compensation. A mediator who offers one side in a dispute compensation (e.g. economic assistance) in exchange for a concession in the negotiation, might best do that in private, without the other side hearing. The reason is that the other side may develop a desire for similar compensation. This suggests that controlling communication may facilitate the success of a compensation strategy. The point is that tactical strength – controlling communication – interacts with strategic strength – the ability to provide compensation, to produce an effective mediation effort. The same applies with other mediator strategies, such as pressure.

In some cases, the mediator with strategic strength may rely just on it, and have less need for tactical strength. And the less-rich mediator may be especially adroit at exercising aspects of tactical strength. But a key issue is how the mediator who has strategic strength can be encouraged to develop skills in tactical strength.

Research by Carnevale *et al.* (1989) suggests that strategic strength is more often exercised the longer a dispute progresses, and under high time pressure. And a laboratory study by Conlon *et al.* (1994) suggests that mediators will rely on strategic strength when they have few incentives to seek a mutually acceptable agreement, and when hostility is high. These findings are consistent with the predictions of the strategic choice model of mediation (Carnevale, 1986).

The distinction between strategic and tactical strength helps us understand better how some variables in mediation interact. Consider, as an example, the matter of mediator bias. Carnevale and Arad (1996) identified two forms of mediator bias: (1) alignment, which refers to the general closeness of the mediator to one side or the other (in economic, cultural, or political terms), and (2) overt behavior, which refers to the character of the mediator's efforts in the negotiation. These two forms interact to have unique effects. For example, a mediator who is seen as biased in favor of the opponent at the outset was seen in a very favorable light if that mediator went out of their way to act in an even-handed manner – even more favorable than a mediator who initially was impartial.

This means the analysis of the two forms of strength in mediation provide a basis for separating effects in mediation due to behavior (tactics), and effects due to structure (strategic strength), and the unique aspects of how these variables interact.

Implications for effectiveness in mediation

The issue of what to do, and when to do it, is a central concern in mediation. There is little to go on for guidance, in particular with regard to the interaction of timing, tactics, and contexts. No doubt there are more questions than clear-cut answers in the matter of what is effective in mediation.

Power is the centerpiece of mediation. There is a lot to recommend power. Powerful mediators are more likely to have greater access to influential decision makers. Merry's (1989) study of mediation in nonindustrial societies shows that it is usually done by a community leader, older, more powerful, more prestigeful members of the collective. Studies of international conflict also suggest that mediators from powerful countries, and with high positions in their countries, gain more acceptance as mediators and are more likely to succeed (Frei, 1976; Bercovitch, Anagnoson *et al.*, 1991; Bercovitch, 1992). Welton and Pruitt (1987) found that disputants who dealt with low power mediators were more accepting of the mediator and behaved less contentiously, but they were also less influenced by the mediator.

In a study of community mediation, mediation was shown to be more effective when arbitration was threatened as a next step. McGillicuddy *et al.* (1987) compared mediation to two forms of mediation–arbitration: (1) med-arb(same), where the mediator becomes an arbitrator and issues a binding decision if agreement is not reached during mediation, and (2) med-arb(diff), where a fourth party, not present during mediation, becomes an arbitrator. The results indicated that the med-arb(same) condition produced the highest levels of problem solving and the lowest levels of hostility.

There is evidence that direct, forceful mediator intervention is effective when the conflict between the disputants is so intense that they are unable to engage in joint problem solving. But such intervention is counter-productive when the disputants are capable of talking things over themselves (Carnevale and Pruitt, 1992).

However, power in mediation can corrupt: the powerful mediator may be tempted to dictate terms of agreement, terms that are not acceptable to the parties. Power has been found to encourage mediators to use more forceful tactics. For example, community mediators who had the capacity to arbitrate were especially likely to use threats and heavy advocacy (McGillicuddy *et al.*, 1987). This is consistent with the finding that judges who mediate often use strong-arm tactics (Wall and Rude, 1989).

Laboratory research indicates that mediators who can impose an outcome will tend to ignore the underlying interests of the parties (Conlon *et al.*, 1994). Mediators who could impose an outcome were more likely than mediators to use forceful, pressure tactics, and also were more confident and saw themselves as more influential. Powerful mediators imposed outcomes in 66 per cent of the cases, but more when they viewed the disputants as uncooperative than cooperative. Only 44 per cent of the imposed outcomes reflected the disputants' underlying interests, and this was much lower when the powerful mediator had low compared to high concern for the disputants' aspirations. To counteract this effect, mediation may require surveillance and accountability, which is easier done in some contexts than others.

Mayer (1987) argued that the type of power exercised by a mediator may be inappropriate or even incongruent, and this may interfere with the development of integrative agreements. Pruitt (1981) provided an even more pessimistic view of the long-term impact of strategic strength in mediation – in particular the use of compensation – arguing that it can create problems in the later relationship between the parties and the mediator. It can create:

> (a) dependence on the mediator for further compensation in later negotiations, and (b) development of a tripartite negotiation system is which much of the bargaining takes place between the mediator and the two principals with the aim of establishing a price to be paid by the mediator for each concession (p. 145).

In other words, mediator compensation can exacerbate conflict in the sense that the disputants sometimes will be intransigent as a stratagem to extract rewards and benefits from the mediator who has interests to protect or extend. Laboratory work described in Carnevale *et al.* (1989) indicates that the power to reward diminished respect for the mediator and reduced concession making, in an apparent effort to extract the reward from the mediator, something that Zartman and Touval (1985) warned of in international mediation.

However, the mediator's power to punish the disputants – coercive power – encouraged respect for the mediator and greater cooperation in concession making (Carnevale *et al.*, 1989). These findings suggest the following generalizations: (1) Mediator power to punish has a positive impact because disputants try to avoid the punishment by moving toward agreement and because they respect the mediator more; (2) Mediator power to reward has a positive impact only if it is mobilized in the form of reinforcement of concessions or new ideas or promises such reinforcement.

Of course, use of such power can be very costly to the mediator, as shown by the US mediation of the Egypt–Israel conflict (Pruitt, 1981). It is important to distinguish between the power to reward and the power to punish, with the reward case encouraging disputants to wait for the mediator to provide *quid pro quo*.

Rubin (1981) noted that if the mediator makes a threat and then it fails to elicit compliance, and the threat is not carried out, the mediator's credibility is likely to diminish. Of course, both coercive and reward power depend on the needs and values of the disputants, having greater potency to the extent they intersect with a party's strongest needs and values (Pruitt, 1976).

Questions and conclusions

The central thesis of this chapter is that strength in mediation can be separated into two components, strategic strength and tactical strength. Hence there are two ways in which strength in mediation can be increased. It can be increased by creating a larger resource base for the mediator, or by improving the mediator's tactical skills. Ury's (1987) call to strengthen mediation is about how to add to both strategic and tactical strength. This includes informal methods to support and supplement formal mediation, that entail, for example, monitoring conflict hot spots and providing support services and expert advice.

In this chapter, mediation is treated as a general social phenomenon that occurs in a variety of conflict contexts – international, organizational, interpersonal. It does appear that mediator strength operates the same way in a variety of cultural contexts (Merry, 1989). However, there are important differences across mediation contexts in the forms of mediation strength. For example, compensation is often unlikely in labor mediation, as well as divorce mediation. Perhaps some mediation contexts more than others engender reliance on tactical strength in mediation.

Of course, mediator strength can be multi-dimensional, with the full-spectrum mediator having the capacity to exercise all forms of tactical strength in mediation and the capacity for all forms of strategic strength.

This mediator might be most effective. However, in some cases, when, for example, a go-between is all that is important, one to just pass messages or offer just a modicum of interpretation and clarification, the full-strength mediator may in fact be too much chef for the kitchen.

A central question for further work is, when is the full-strength mediator most effective? What forms of strength in mediation are best suited for what types of situations? These questions are, once again, about contingencies in mediation (cf. Lim and Carnevale, 1990).

It may be that tactical strength requires the greatest dexterity and finesse in mediation. Knowing what to do and when, with the appropriate touch, often borne of years of training and experience, is what makes the 'art' side of mediation so salient. But dexterity applies to both strategic and tactical strength. This is made clear when one looks closely at the difference between the use and anticipation of strength, in particular the use of rewards. Wall (1979) tested the effects of mediator rewards on concession making in negotiation. The mediator gave negotiators money after each concession, with the effect that the rewards resulted in larger negotiator total concessions, more agreements, and higher joint outcomes.

But a very different picture emerges when one looks at the anticipation of rewards. Carnevale *et al.* (1989) reported research on mediators who could reward or punish the negotiators in the future. In an analysis of the negotiator's offers and concessions, the greatest concessions were made when the negotiators believed the mediator had little concern for their aspirations, could apply pressure, and could not offer rewards. The fewest concessions were made when the negotiators believed the mediators had something at stake in the outcome, had no ability to punish, and had rewards to offer. Moreover, the negotiators saw the mediator who could apply pressure as the better mediator than the one who could only apply rewards, because this kind of mediator was more successful in moving the negotiators to agreement.

Other laboratory work on the impact of mediation raises questions about power and the face-saving function of mediation. As mentioned earlier, a mediator's suggestion can help, in some cases – as when the disputants face pressures to make concessions and concerns about losing face, the negotiators make a concession yet preserve face, that is, maintain their image of personal strength in negotiation (Pruitt and Johnson, 1970). It may be that a powerful mediator may even be better at this than a not-so-powerful mediator.

Another question is under what conditions should the mediator's strength match the disputants' strength. In mediating a dispute between 'two men with guns', is it advantageous for the mediator to have a larger gun than both? Does mediator strength interact with the relative and absolute power of the disputants? It seems reasonable to suppose that most disputes are not between equals, or at least, not between equals on every dimension on which power can be compared. There is evidence, in community and organizational contexts, that mediators will tend to side with the weaker party, and also will side with the party who they see as having the more legitimate position (Ippolito and Pruitt, 1990; Laskewitz *et al.*, 1994). Another set of questions is about whether or not the relative power of the parties makes a difference in mediation. Young (1972), for example, argued that the smaller the power difference between the two parties, the more successful will be the mediator.

An interesting set of questions arise when the relationship between power capability and power use is considered in the context of the actual influence that occurs (Lawler, 1992). Komorita (1977) has argued that the nonuse of power is equivalent to its nonexistence. This idea has not been tested in controlled studies of mediation. Will a mediator who has heavy coercive capabilities have the same impact as one who does not, if that coercion is never exercised?

Since tactical strength in some cases may require concealment and adroitness, it may be more likely to produce distrust in the mediator than strategic strength. For example, mediators need to be concerned that, in meeting privately with one side, that the other side not grow suspicious of collusion in this meeting.

In answer to the question posed above – Is mediating strength anathema to mediation? – the answer is: All mediation entails some form of strength. It is either strategic or tactical, and it all rests on the parties' need for something that the mediator can provide, which, in the model case, may be a mutually acceptable agreement. Moreover, strategic and tactical capabilities can distinguish the character of mediation of even large nation states; compared to the US, it is evident that the former Soviet Union had less of both (Touval, 1992).

Nevertheless, there is a downside to mediator strength, again captured in William Shakespeare's *Measure for Measure*:

> ... authority, though it err like others,
> Hath yet a kind of medicine in itself
> That skins the vice o' the top.

Even in mediation, the strong mediator may be prone to superficial treatment of the problem. This was in part Fisher's criticism of Henry Kissinger's mediation in the Middle East, in 1973:

> To be so concerned with the power that comes from success is to be too little concerned with making the world a better place ... Kissinger's insistence on the appearance of success precluded the possibility that his efforts would lead to a real settlement of the region's problems (Fisher, 1981, pp. 102, 121).

In a similar vein, Walton (1969) wrote that strong third-party intervention is not likely to produce long-lasting agreement and an improvement in attitudes.

And here, Jeff Rubin (1980) has the last word, in reporting that strong third-party intervention in some cases will exacerbate conflict. And this is perhaps the greatest danger of strength in mediation, that its exercise will have lasting effects worse than the conflict itself.

References

Bell, C. (1962) *Negotiating from Strength*. London: Chatto & Windus.

Bercovitch, J. (1992) 'The structure and diversity of mediation in international relations'. In J. Bercovitch and J. Z. Rubin (eds), *Mediation in International Relations*. New York: St. Martin's Press.

Bercovitch, J., Anagnoson, J. and Wille, D. (1991) 'Some conceptual issues and empirical trends in the study of successful mediation in international relations'. *Journal of Peace Research*, 28, 7–17.

Boulding, K. E. (1962) *Conflict and Defense*. New York: Harper & Row.

Carnevale, P. J. (1986) 'Strategic choice in mediation'. *Negotiation Journal*, 2, 41–56.

Carnevale, P. J. and Arad, S. (1996) 'Bias and impartiality in international mediation'. In J. Bercovitch (ed.), *Resolving International Conflicts: The Theory and Practice of Mediation*, pp. 39–53. Boulder, CO: Lynne Rienner.

Carnevale, P. J. and Pruitt, D. G. (1992) 'Negotiation and mediation'. *Annual Review of Psychology*, 43, 531–82.

Carnevale, P. J., Conlon, D., Hanisch, K. and Harris, K. (1989) 'Experimental research on the strategic choice model of mediation'. In K. Kressel and D. G. Pruitt (eds), *Mediation Research: The Process and Effectiveness of Third Party Intervention*. San Francisco: Jossey-Bass, Inc.

Conlon, D. E., Carnevale, P. J. and Murnighan, K. (1994) 'Intravention: Third-party intervention with clout'. *Organizational Behavior and Human Decision Processes*, 57, 387–410.

Emerson, R. M. (1962) 'Power-dependence relations'. *American Sociological Review*, 27, 31–41.

Fisher, R. (1981) 'Playing the wrong game?'. In J. Z. Rubin (ed.), *Dynamics of Third Party Intervention*, pp. 95–121. New York: Praeger.

Frei, D. (1976) 'Conditions affecting the effectiveness of international mediation'. *Papers, Peace Science Society (International)*, 26, 67–84.

French, J. and Raven, B. (1959) 'The bases of social power'. In D. Cartwright (ed.), *Studies in Social Power*, pp. 150–68. Ann Arbor, Michigan: Institute for Social Research.

Hiltrop, J. M. (1989) 'Factors associated with successful labor mediation'. In K. Kressel and D. G. Pruitt (eds), *Mediation Research*, pp. 241–62. San Francisco: Jossey-Bass.

Ippolito, C. A. and Pruitt, D. G. (1990) 'Power balancing in mediation: Outcomes and implications of mediator intervention'. *The International Journal of Conflict Management*, 1, 341–55.

Komorita, S. S. (1977) 'Negotiating from strength and the concept of bargaining strength'. *Journal for the Theory of Social Behavior*, 7, 65–79.

Kramer, S. (1963) *The Summarians: Their History, Culture, and Character*. Chicago: University of Chicago Press.

Kressel, K. (1972) *Labor Mediation: An Exploratory Survey*. Albany, NY: Association of Labor Mediation Agencies.

Kressel, K. and Pruitt, D. G. (1989) 'Conclusion: A research perspective on the mediation of social conflict'. In K. Kressel and D. G. Pruitt (eds), *Mediation Research: the Process and Effectiveness of Third Party Intervention*, pp. 394–435. San Francisco: Jossey-Bass.

Laskewitz, P., van de Vliert, E. and de Dreu, C. (1994) 'Organizational mediators siding with or against the powerful party'. *Journal of Applied Social Psychology*, 24, 176–88.

Lawler, E. J. (1992) 'Power processes in bargaining'. *The Sociological Quarterly*, 33, 17–34.

Lim, R. and Carnevale, P. J. (1990) 'Contingencies in the mediation of disputes'. *Journal of Personality and Social Psychology*, 58, 259–72.

March, J. G. (1955) 'An introduction to the theory and measurement of influence'. *American Political Science Review*, 49, 431–51.

Mayer, B. (1987) 'The dynamics of power in mediation and negotiation'. *Mediation Quarterly*, no. 16, 75–86.

McGillicuddy, N. B., Welton, G. L. and Pruitt, D. G. (1987) 'Third party intervention: a field experiment comparing three different models'. *Journal of Personality and Social Psychology*, 53, 104–12.

Merry, S. E. (1989) 'Mediation in nonindustrial societies'. In K. Kressel and D.G. Pruitt (eds), *Mediation Research*, pp. 68–90. San Francisco: Jossey-Bass.

Moore, C. W. (1986) *The Mediation Process: Practical Strategies for Resolving Conflicts*. San Francisco: Jossey-Bass.

Princen, T. (1987) 'International mediation – the view from the Vatican: Lessons from mediating the Beagle Channel Dispute'. *Negotiation Journal*, 3, 347–66.

Pruitt, D. G. (1976) 'Power and bargaining'. In B. Seidenberg and A. Snadowsky (eds), *Social Psychology: A Textbook*. New York: Free Press.

Pruitt, D. G. (1981) 'Kissinger as a traditional mediator with power'. In J. Z. Rubin (ed.), *Dynamics of Third Party Intervention*, pp. 136–47. New York: Praeger.

Pruitt, D. G. and Carnevale, P. J. (1993) *Negotiation in Social Conflict*. Pacific Grove: Brooks/Cole.

Pruitt, D. G. and Johnson, D. F. (1970) 'Mediation as an aid to face-saving in negotiation'. *Journal of Personality and Social Psychology*, 14, 239–46.

Purcell, S. K. (1982) 'War and debt in South America'. *Foreign Affairs*, 61, 660–74.

Raven, B. H. and Kruglanski, A. W. (1970) 'Conflict and power'. In P. Swingle (ed.), *The Structure of Conflict*. New York: Academic Press.

Rubin, J. Z. (1980) 'Experimental research on third-party intervention in conflict: toward some generalizations'. *Psychological Bulletin*, 87, 379–91.

Rubin, J. Z. (1981) 'Introduction'. In J. Z. Rubin (ed.), *Dynamics of Third Party Intervention*. New York: Praeger.

Rubin, J. Z. (1992) 'Conclusion: International mediation in context'. In J. Bercovitch and J. Z. Rubin (eds), *Mediation in International Relations*. New York: St. Martin's Press.

Safire, W. (1998) 'On language'. *The New York Times Magazine*, 8 March, p. 28.

Schelling, T. C. (1960) *The Strategy of Conflict*. Cambridge, Mass.: Harvard University Press.

Sheehan, E. R. F. (1976) 'How Kissinger did it: Step by step in the Middle East'. *Foreign Policy*, 22, 3–70.

Slim, R. (1992) 'Small-state mediation in international relations: The Algerian mediation of the Iranian Hostage Crisis'. In J. Bercovitch and J. Z. Rubin (eds), *Mediation in International Relations*. New York: St. Martin's Press.

Stevens, C. M. (1963) *Strategy and Collective Bargaining Negotiations*. New York: McGraw-Hill.

Thibaut, J. W. and Kelley, H. H. (1959) *The Social Psychology of Groups*. New York: Wiley.

Thornton, T. P. (1985) 'The Indo-Pakistani conflict: Soviet mediation, Tashkent, 1966'. In S. Touval and I. W. Zartman (eds), *International Mediation in Theory and Practice*. Boulder, Co.: Westview Press.

Tome, V. (1992) 'Maintaining credibility as a partial mediator: United States mediation in Southern Africa, 1981–1988'. *Negotiation Journal*, 8, 273–89.

Touval, S. (1982) *The Peace Brokers: Mediation in the Arab–Israeli Conflict, 1948–1979*. Princeton, NJ: Princeton University Press.

Touval, S. (1985) 'The context of mediation'. *Negotiation Journal*, 1, 373–8.

Touval, S. (1992) 'The superpowers as mediators'. In J. Bercovitch and J. Z. Rubin (eds), *Mediation in International Relations*, pp. 232–48. New York: St. Martin's Press.

Touzard, H. (1977) *La mediation et la resolution des conflicts* [Mediation and the Resolution of Conflicts]. Paris: PUF.

Ury, W. 'Strengthening international mediation'. (1987) *Negotiation Journal*, 3, 225–9.

Wall, J. A. Jr (1979) 'The effects of mediator rewards and suggestions upon negotiations'. *Journal of Personality and Social Psychology*, 37, 1554–60.

Wall, J. A. Jr, Stark, J. B. and Standifer, R. L. (2001) 'Mediation: a current review'. *Journal of Conflict Resolution*, 45, 370–91.

Wall, J. A. Jr and Rude, D. E. (1989) 'Judicial mediation of settlement negotiations'. In K. Kressel and D. G. Pruitt (eds), *Mediation Research*, pp. 190–212. San Francisco: Jossey-Bass.

Walton, R. E. (1969) *Interpersonal Peacemaking: Confrontations and Third-party Consultation*. Reading, MA: Addison-Wesley.

Welton, G. L. and Pruitt, D. G. (1987) 'The mediation process: the effects of mediator bias and disputant power'. *Personality and Social Psychology Bulletin*, 13, 123–33.

Young, O. R. (1972) 'Intermediaries: Additional thoughts on third parties'. *Journal of Conflict Resolution*, 16, 51–65.

Zartman, I. W. and Touval, S. (1985) 'International mediation: Conflict resolution and power politics'. *Journal of Social Issues*, 41, 27–45.

3
Mediator Behavior and Success in Mediation

Dean G. Pruitt

Introduction

This chapter assumes that mediation is a general phenomenon, with many similarities from setting to setting, as well as some orderly differences. This implies two things: One is that it will often be possible to generalize what is known about other kinds of mediation to international mediation. Such generalizations must remain speculative until tested in the international realm, but informed speculation should be welcome in any field. The other implication is that it will eventually be possible to develop a general theory of mediation.

A general theory of mediation should have two parts. One part should deal with effects that are universal. For example, Susskind and Babbitt assert that international mediation is more likely to succeed if parties associated with the disputants 'exert pressure for resolution' (1992: 34), a point that is as applicable to married couples and labor and management as it is to nations. The other part of a general theory should identify orderly differences between various types of mediation and between various types of settings. This will produce some strange bedfellows, classifying together phenomena that look quite different. Consider, for example, the distinction between emergent mediation, in which the mediator is an associate of the disputants who volunteers for the role, and contractual mediation, in which the mediator is a professional who specializes in the role (Pruitt and Carnevale, 1993: 166–8). Interpersonal and international mediation, though quite different in surface appearance, are usually of the emergent sort, in contrast to community mediation and labor–management mediation. Hence Touval's observation that the United States government often mediates so as to 'avoid siding with one of its friends against the other' (1992: 237) applies equally well to interpersonal mediation.

The chapter is divided into three sections. The first section deals with disputant behavior during conflict resolution, which is a necessary prelude to understanding mediator behavior. The second examines mediator behavior itself. And the third is concerned with the conditions that foster acceptance of and success in mediation.

Conflict resolution by disputants

The job of the mediator is to assist disputants in their efforts at conflict resolution and to supplement these efforts if they are unsuccessful. Hence, we first look at how disputants must behave – the way they must negotiate – if they are to resolve the conflicts they face.

Most conflicts are resolved by disputant yielding and problem solving. By 'yielding' is meant reducing aspirations. By 'problem-solving' (also called 'integrative bargaining' and 'mutual gains bargaining') is meant seeking integrative solutions, that is, solutions that satisfy both parties' current aspirations (Pruitt and Carnevale, 1993: 3; Rubin *et al.*, 1994: 4). Yielding and problem-solving must go hand in hand, because there is no point in trying to find solutions for unrealistic aspirations. Nevertheless there is a tension between these strategies, because effective problem-solving requires holding one's aspirations firm for a time while vigorously seeking a way to achieve them in the context of the other party's aspirations. Too much yielding runs the risk of failing to find mutually beneficial solutions that would otherwise be available, yet too little yielding runs the risk of failing to reach agreement.

Structuring integrative solutions

There is a common misunderstanding that problem-solving and integrative solutions always involve the development of totally new ideas. We also have problem-solving when an old idea is found that satisfies both parties' aspirations. In longstanding conflicts, there are usually many old ideas, and it is no small task to winnow them down to the few that are viable and adjust these few to current circumstances.

Five basic types of integrative solutions can be distinguished (Pruitt and Carnevale, 1993: 36–7; Rubin *et al.*, 1994: 173–9): (1) expanding the pie, which involves augmenting a scarce resource; (2) logrolling, in which each party concedes on issues that are of low priority to itself and high priority to the other party; (3) cost cutting, in which one party gets what it wants while the other's costs are reduced or eliminated; (4) compensation, in which one party gets what it wants while the other is repaid in an unrelated coin; and (5) bridging, in which a way is found to satisfy the most important interests underlying the two parties' current demands.

Specialized information is needed to locate most of these types of integrative solution. Thus for logrolling, one must know the parties' priorities among the issues under discussion – which issues are more and which less important for each party. Cost cutting and compensation rely on knowledge about one of the parties' costs or needs. For bridging, it is essential to discover the most important interests underlying the parties' demands – the unexpressed needs that give rise to the positions they are taking.

Some issues lend themselves to one type of integrative solution and some to another. But there is usually no way to tell ahead of time which type will be appropriate. Hence, when negotiators and mediators are engaged in problem-solving, they need to search the environment for all five types of solution and to collect all of the kinds of information just described.

Problem-solving is sometimes portrayed as taking place in a single creative leap producing a formula whose details can be worked out later (Zartman, 1977). But formula-building is more often a sequential matter involving a slow, and sometimes partially recursive, piling up of subagreements. Thus a logrolling agreement often results from a series of 'ratcheted trade-offs, in which each concession both responds to and calls for concessions from the other side, until … the two "piles" of concessions are equalized' (Zartman, 1997). The result may nevertheless be a formula requiring further elaboration.

Effective problem-solving behavior

Effective problem-solving has a number of standard elements; and a major role of the mediator is to encourage, or substituting for the absence of, these elements. The following six guidelines are a useful summary of these elements (Pruitt, 1993; Lewicki *et al.*, 1994).

First, effective problem-solving requires firm flexibility – firmness about fundamental ends coupled with flexibility about the means to these ends. One must be firm about one's basic interests, unless or until these prove to be unattainable, yet at the same time perceptive of and concerned about the other party's interests and flexible enough to seek and adopt proposals that benefit both sides.

Secondly, the negotiators should establish a good working relationship. They need to emphasize what they have in common and establish a solidarity of basic purpose without, of course, losing sight of their separate missions. An informal, friendly, humorous atmosphere should develop, along with a common understanding of the issues, and a common vocabulary. Each side needs to achieve an understanding of the other's history and culture. Above all, there is a need for *working trust* – a belief, on both sides, that the other side is willing to make substantial concessions to achieve a peaceful settlement. Working trust is a narrowly defined concept. It does not mean a belief that the other side has one's interests at heart but only that the other is ready to take risks and make sacrifices in order to achieve a settlement. It is important to note that negotiation may fail because of the absence of working trust even when the two sides are highly motivated to achieve a settlement.

The third guideline for effective problem-solving is full information exchange (Walton and McKersie, 1965: 137). The parties need to inform each other about their priorities among the issues, the interests underlying their positions, and their priorities among these interests. This makes it possible to discover logrolling, cost cutting, and bridging solutions.

The fourth guideline entails flexible reframing (reconceptualization) of the issues. The parties need to be able to reframe their objectives in ways that take the other's objectives into consideration. For example, after analysing the underlying issues in a negotiation, a party that started asking 'How can we retain governance of such-and-such buffer zone when the population of the zone is determined to have autonomy?' might now ask 'How can we achieve our security needs while allowing the population of this zone to run certain basic institutions of their own?'. Reframing of this kind should facilitate development of a bridging solution.

The fifth guideline involves 'no-fault' brainstorming. The parties need to be able to throw out ideas for solving jointly understood problems on a tentative basis, without committing themselves. They should also be able to make comments about one another's proposals without being later accused of having accepted or rejected them. Such a tentative, non-committing discussion maximizes the number of ideas that will be introduced and deeply discussed.

Privacy is the sixth and last guideline. Negotiations are most successful when held away from the press and from each side's constituents. Otherwise one gets grandstanding and constituent interference with the process of negotiation, both of which lead to rigidity of positions – an unwillingness to entertain new ideas. US President Woodrow Wilson argued that negotiations should involve open agreements openly reached. But a better strategy is to have open agreements covertly reached, in locations that are out of the public eye.

Sometimes adequate privacy can be achieved without secrecy, as in the 1978 Camp David negotiations between Israel and Egypt. But when either side contains militant factions that oppose negotiation or insist on mutually incompatible positions, secrecy may also be needed, as in the 1993 Oslo negotiations that led to the establishment of the Palestinian Authority. There is a tradeoff with secrecy. It facilitates reaching agreement but may make it difficult to sell the agreement to constituents because they were unable to introduce their views into the discussions.

Back channels and chains

Because of the value of privacy and secrecy, back channel and sidebar negotiations are often required to unstick difficult negotiations (Rubin *et al.*, 1994: 188–9). These occur out of the sight of, and often unbeknownst to most of the negotiators. Only a small number of people are involved in such meetings, often only one from each side. Back channels are particularly useful when they occur in the context of formal negotiations that are understood to be the proper place to present official proposals and reach official agreements. The existence of formal negotiations serves to empha-size the unofficial status of statements made in the back channels, which increases the frankness and flexibility of discussions in these channels.

When negotiations are between organizations, as in international rela-tions, each negotiator is typically linked to one or more stakeholders through communication chains of intermediaries (Pruitt, 1994). For yield-ing to take place and new proposals to be accepted, the stakeholders must be persuaded by these intermediaries. Furthermore, a good deal of the problem-solving may take place in discussions between adjacent members of these chains. This means that for negotiators to be flexible enough to reach agreement, these chains must function well. People who are side-by-side in a chain must trust each other and be able to talk effectively, or it must be possible to erect alternative communication channels around these people. Flexibility is also enhanced by the capacity to hold meetings that span larger sections of the chain. In short, negotiator flexibility is largely a function of communication flexibility within the organizations involved in the negotiation (Pruitt, 1995a).

Mediator behavior

Mediators can often be useful when negotiations flounder. But mediation is no magic bullet. 'Intensely conflicted disputes involving parties of widely disparate power, with low motivation to settle, fighting about matters of principle, suffering from discord or ambivalence within their own camps, and negotiating over (exceedingly) scarce resources are likely to defeat even the most adroit mediators' (Kressel and Pruitt, 1989: 405). Mediators have scores of tactics available to encourage or supplement the disputant processes described in the prior section. Good mediators use most of these tactics contingently, depending on the nature of the situation (Pruitt and Carnevale, 1993: 175; Bercovitch and Houston, 1996: 15).

Mediators often structure the situation to improve the chances for agree-ment. For example, remote locations such as Camp David or the country-side near Oslo enhance privacy and thus increase intimacy and flexibility. Furthermore, holding the sessions on the mediator's own territory, rather than the territory of one of the disputants, has been shown to increase the likelihood of agreement (Bercovitch and Houston, 1996: 29).

Structuring the situation often extends to efforts to encourage the devel-opment of working relationships. Thus in the Oslo talks, the Norwegian mediators made every effort to encourage friendly, intimate interaction between members of the Israeli and PLO delegations. The delegates took meals together and shared recreational activities (Corbin, 1994: 60, 87, 111; Makovsky, 1996: 22). The result was that the 'participants felt free to listen to each other, to enter each other's perspective, to re-examine difficult issues over time, and to develop a mutually reassuring language' though these personal relationships '(did) not in any way dispense with the difficult political issues that (had to) be negotiated and resolved at their own level' (Kelman, 1997: 190).

Most mediators spend some time alone with each delegation, shuttling between them. This 'shuttle diplomacy' (also called 'caucusing') is essential when the parties are unwilling or unable to meet, as was true in 1973, when US Secretary of State Henry Kissinger flew back and forth between the capitals of Israel and Egypt (Rubin, 1981). When the antagonists occupy totally separate worlds, shuttle diplomacy may require a chain of mediators, because there is no single mediator that has access to both sides and can adequately interpret each side to the other. For example, Kraslow and Loory (1968) report that during the Vietnam War, a mediation chain went from the US Government through officials in Great Britain to officials in eastern Europe and finally to the government of North Vietnam.

Separate meetings ('caucus sessions') with disputants are also advisable when the parties are very hostile toward each other or are making no progress in their joint discussions. Research on community mediation reveals that with the antagonist out of the room, negotiators tend to become less emotional, they feel freer to provide intimate information that permits finding integrative solutions, and they are more willing to reveal flaws in their case and to discuss possible concessions and compromises without fear of weakening their official position (Pruitt, 1995b: 370). In caucus sessions, mediators often try to establish working trust by portraying the adversaries as reasonable people who are interested in settlement. They also commonly seek to undermine the parties' aspirations so as to encourage concession making (Colosi, 1983: 233, 243–4).

Virtually all mediators gather information about the priorities and underlying interests of the disputants. Such information is essential to the development of most kinds of integrative agreements. Being more neutral than the disputants, they are more likely to get an undistorted picture by listening to what the disputants say.

Other very useful services have to do with reframing the issues so as to make them more amenable to solution and urging the parties to develop new ideas. These mediator tactics have been shown to encourage the development of mutually beneficial settlements in both domestic (Lim and Carnevale, 1990; Zubek et al., 1992) and international (Bercovitch, 1997) mediation.

If the parties are incapable of effective brainstorming in joint sessions, a mediator can engage in idea-generating discussions with each of them separately. If the mediator detects a mutually acceptable solution during a caucus session, he or she can present it as a way out in the next joint session. In doing so, the mediator may be compensating for an absence of working trust. Without working trust, disputants tend to be reluctant to concede because of fear that the other side will not reciprocate. The way around this is for the mediator to present a proposal involving simultaneous concessions that both parties have said they are willing to make.

If viable alternatives are not generated in caucus sessions, mediators can come up with their own solutions and suggest them to the disputants. One common variant of this tactic is the single text procedure (see Fisher *et al.*, 1991: 112–16; Antrim and Sebenius, 1992: 117–18). After gathering information, the mediator draws up a tentative draft agreement and meets separately with each side to get reactions. The draft is changed in response to these reactions and floated again and again until an acceptable version has been produced. Mediator generated solutions have the advantage over disputant generated solutions of not producing reactive devaluation, the common tendency to discredit all suggestions that come from the other side (see Ross and Stillinger, 1991: 394–5).

Often the difficulty encountered by a mediator lies not with the negotiators but with their constituents, up the communication chain, who seem unsupportive of the negotiations or are unwilling to make the concessions deemed necessary by the mediator. Some mediators respond to this difficulty by going to the source of the problem. For example, during a crisis in the Oslo talks, Norwegian Foreign Minister Johan Jorgen Holst visited PLO Chairman Yasser Arafat to assure him that the Israelis remained interested in a negotiated settlement and to urge him to make a key concession (Abbas, 1995: 106–9; Makovsky, 1996: 60–1). Creative mediation may also involve organizing meetings of officials from different parts of the communication chain who are having difficulty coordinating their decision-making.

Finally, when mediators are convinced that a solution is in sight, they can attempt to precipitate agreement by setting a deadline after which they will leave. US President Jimmy Carter used this tactic toward the end of the 1978 Camp David talks between Israel's Prime Minister Menachem Begin and Egypt's President Anwar Sadat (Rubin *et al.*, 1994: 206).

Research on domestic mediation supports a key contingent guideline which undoubtedly applies to the international realm as well: Mediators should stay out of the discussion when disputants are engaged in effective problem-solving, but they should intervene when the talks are not going well and should take more vigorous action the greater the impasse or level of hostility (Hiltrop, 1985, 1989; Donohue, 1989; Lim and Carnevale, 1990; Zubek *et al.*, 1992).

Disputant acceptance of and progress in mediation

This section concerns the conditions that determine whether disputants will seek or accept mediation and whether the mediation will move toward agreement. A theory of readiness to settle the controversy is presented (Pruitt, 1997a), which is inspired by, but somewhat broader than, Zartman's ripeness theory (Zartman, 1989, 1996).

Readiness theory

For disputants to accept mediation and move toward agreement, they must be (a) motivated to settle their dispute and (b) optimistic about reaching a mutually acceptable and binding agreement. Both motivation to settle and optimism – the two components of readiness – are viewed as variables. The stronger they are, the more willing a party will be to: (a) negotiate or accept mediation, (b) devote scarce human resources to the negotiation, and (c) make deep concessions of the kind that make agreement possible. Motivation to settle the dispute is assumed to be the driving force behind conciliatory behavior, while optimism is a 'gating' variable that determines the extent to which this motivation will affect behavior. The stronger a party's optimism, the farther open will be the 'gate' between its motivation and its behavior, in other words, the more fully will it act on its motivation. Without optimism, no conciliatory action will be taken, however strong the motivation to settle the dispute.

Motivation to settle

Motivation to settle develops either because the existing conflict has become unbearable or because major benefits seem to be associated with settlement. Conflict can become unbearable because of excessive costs or undue risks. For the US, the costs of the Vietnam War became unbearable after the TET offensive. For the Soviet Union, the risks of continuing to build missiles in Cuba became unbearable when the US discovered what they were doing during the Cuban Missile Crisis.

Costs and risks associated with conflict can sometimes produce the exact opposite of the motivation to settle – further escalation aimed at victory over the adversary. Thus, in 1968, the Mexico City police, faced with a student rebellion that threatened the forthcoming Olympic games, decided to escalate and shot a lot of students on the Plaza of the Three Cultures. There are three conditions under which unacceptable costs or risks are likely to lead to a desire for settlement rather than further escalation:

- *Victory seems unlikely.* Thus, after the TET offensive, further US escalation in Vietnam was ruled out because sufficient numbers of Americans concluded that victory was unlikely. This is the kind of thinking that occurs on both sides during what Zartman (1996: 276) has called a 'mutually hurting stalemate' and may be the reason why mediation tends to be 'more effective when it follows, rather than precedes, some "test of strength" between the disputants' (Bercovitch and Houston, 1996: 23). By contrast, victory was possible for the Mexico City police.
- *Further escalation seems likely to increase the already unacceptable costs and risks.* Such was the case for both the Soviet Union and the US during the Cuban Missile crisis. After a period of mutual escalation, both sides concluded that the risks associated with further escalation

were far too great. Such risks were apparently not seen by the Mexico City police.

- *The other party's existence or voluntary cooperation is needed to overcome the costs or avert the risks.* A well known instance of this is when a common enemy threatens to overwhelm both sides if they do not support each other. Such was the case for both the Israel and the PLO after the election of Yitzhak Rabin as prime minister of Israel in 1992. Both feared the rise of Hamas, a rival Palestinian political group with a philosophy of militant Islam (Corbin, 1994: 36; Makovsky, 1996: 113). The PLO needed Israel's cooperation to give it enough political power to counter Hamas, and Israel needed the PLO's existence and cooperation for the same reason. The police were not dependent on student cooperation in Mexico City.

Most mediators have limited tools for strengthening the motivation to settle. They can point out the dangers of continuing the conflict, paint a rosy picture of a peaceful future, or threaten to leave if the parties do not make progress toward agreement. But such moves have limited impact. Mediators with the power to influence the disputants' outcomes are more effective in this regard. Thus, it has been found in domestic mediation that when mediators have the power to arbitrate (med/arb), disputants tend to be more motivated to resolve their controversies (Pruitt, 1995b: 366–7). This is where the capacity for 'mediation with muscle' is useful. Large states mediating conflicts between smaller states can employ threats or promises that increase the costs and risks of continuing the conflict or that compensate the disputants for reaching agreement. According to Touval (1997), this includes 'promising a favorable decision or warning of an unfavorable decision by the UN Security Council or some other international organization ... promising a broad cooperative relationship ... threatening a "reassessment" of relations ... (and) manipulating a party's environment such as encouraging other states to play a role or form a supportive or opposing coalition'. Touval argues that combinations of threats and promises are usually more effective than promises alone.

Optimism

Optimism about reaching a mutually acceptable and binding agreement is partly a function of working trust, a belief that the other party is ready for settlement. It is also a function of perceived common ground, the perception that a mutually acceptable formula is probably available (see Rubin *et al.*, 1994: 38–40). The latter means that optimism will be greater the closer the positions of the parties are to each other and the more flexible the parties seem to be. Optimism is also a function of the perception that one is negotiating with a valid spokesperson – a person who can commit the other side in a binding way.

In highly escalated relationships, there tends to be little optimism about reaching a mutually acceptable solution to the conflict. Furthermore, communication is typically broken off and the parties often develop highly distorted, uncomplimentary views of each other (Rubin *et al.*, 1994). Hence, it is often quite difficult for them to resolve the controversy on their own, even if both sides become highly motivated to settle. This is where mediators excel (Kressel and Pruitt, 1989: 402–3).

The entry of a mediator into a conflict or negotiation can serve to encourage optimism, especially if that mediator seems to have access to key players on the other side and can thus 'persuade the other side to accept a compromise' (Touval, 1997). One strategy often available to mediators is to structure the agenda to put easily solvable issues at the beginning of the agenda. Success on these issues tends to encourage optimism and, hence, a willingness to make concessions when the really tough issues arrive (Pruitt, 1997b: 483).

Mediators are well advised to time their entry into a conflict at a point when the parties are maximally motivated to settle but are having difficulty meeting or moving forward – when they are fed up with the conflict but unable to escape it (see Touval and Zartman, 1985: 16). Under such circumstances, mediators can encourage an incremental process in which working trust and faith in the negotiation grow steadily to a point where the disputants are ready to invest major human resources in the negotiation and to make large enough concessions to reach agreement.

A case in point is the role of the Norwegian mediators during the Oslo negotiations. The instigator of the Oslo process, Terje Larsen, recognized in 1992 that there was high motivation for settlement in both the Israeli Labor government and the PLO leadership. Having good ties with both sides and with the Norwegian government, he offered mediation services. A series of 12 secret meetings were held in out-of-the-way locations in Norway. The Norwegians housed and fed the delegates and made elaborate efforts to ensure secrecy. They encouraged fellowship and cooperation, and helped with communication between meetings. From time to time, they also encouraged working trust by assuring each side that the other side was serious.

An incremental process ensued, which involved growing optimism on both sides about the possibility of reaching an acceptable and binding agreement (Pruitt, 1997a). Working trust flowered, in the sense that each side became increasingly convinced that the other was genuinely interested in settlement. Furthermore, Israeli leaders became progressively more certain that the chief Arab negotiator, Abu Ala, was a valid spokesman who could commit both the PLO and the Palestinians. This led them to increase the rank, and hence the validity, of the spokesmen they sent. The result was an unprecedented breakthrough in what had looked like an intractable conflict.

Mediator power and status

Readiness theory helps understand the effect of mediator power on the success of mediation. A mediator's power usually derives from the organization (e.g. the state) he or she represents. Strong mediators like those from the US are needed when the parties lack sufficient motivation to settle, when 'rearranging pay-offs (is) needed to tip the cost-benefit calculations of each side' (Princen, 1992: 171). By contrast, weak mediators excel when the parties are motivated to settle but lack the necessary optimism or communication facilities to move forward. When disputants are fed up with or frightened about their conflict, even lowly newsmen (e.g. John Scali during the Cuban Missile Crisis) or representatives of church-based organizations (e.g. the Vatican or the Quakers) can sometimes bring messages about sentiments for peace on the other side that produce peace feelers in return (Hare, 1992). Norway's success in the Oslo negotiations is another case in point.

The weak mediator's main tools are in the realm of communication and formulation rather than manipulation, to use terms developed by Touval and Zartman (1985: 12). They include the capacity to transmit and interpret messages, to bring realism into the parties' conceptions of each other, to reframe the issues, and to make suggestions for settlement. When the motivation to settle is secure on both sides, weak mediators like Norway are often superior to strong mediators like the US, for several reasons: international reporters are less attentive to the weak than the strong, making it easier for them to assure secrecy to the disputants; weak mediator are less often biased by their own interests; and disputants sometimes find it easier to agree to a weak mediator's suggestions, because it is less likely to be viewed as giving in to superior power.

Mediator status also contributes to mediator effectiveness. Status can derive from the standing of the organization (e.g. the state) with which the mediator is affiliated or from the mediator's position or former position in that organization. The impact of status is somewhat different depending on whether the mediator represents a powerful or weak organization. Having a high status position in a powerful organization contributes to the credibility of threats and promises made by a mediator (Kleiboer, 1996). High status helps weak mediators by giving them easier access to key decision makers. For example, in 1994, Former President Jimmy Carter (who represented nobody but himself) gained access to the top leadership of North Korea and sent a message to US President William Clinton about their readiness to negotiate (Smith and Devroy, 1994). This message averted a major international crisis. High status mediators also offer disputants a face-saving excuse for conceding, because disputants can assert that they yielded to a suggestion from a highly esteemed source. High status mediators can, in addition, encourage citizen support for a leader who wishes to move in a peaceful direction.

There is one problem with high status mediators, they are usually in short supply. Hence, low status mediators are more likely to be available for protracted efforts that take place over a long period of time.

Since different advantages are associated with strong and weak mediators and with high and low status mediators, it makes sense to employ a mix of several kinds in complicated controversies (Putnam and Carcasson, 1997). Such a mix was seen in the Oslo talks. A high status mediator, Norwegian Foreign Minister Johan Jorgen Holst, took charge of delicate interactions with high level officials such as PLO Chairman Yasser Arafat and Israeli Foreign Minister Shimon Peres; while two lower status mediators, social scientist Terje Larsen and foreign service officer Mona Juul, had responsibility for the day-to-day success of the talks between the delegates.

Conclusions

The focus of this chapter has been on the processes that occur in conflict management: problem-solving, back channel conversations, mediator behavior, and disputant motivation and optimism. This emphasis on process should not be surprising, in that the author is a social psychologist. But a question must still be raised about whether it is important to do such a microanalysis. Are not broader analyses of economic, political, and military conditions sufficient to explain most instances of conflict resolution? Can we not, for instance, adequately explain the success of the 1993 Oslo negotiations in terms of such events as the disintegration of the Soviet Union, which was providing political and economic backing to the PLO?

The author has no quarrel with the examination of broader economic, political, and military conditions. Rather, he argues that to fully understand how these conditions operate, one must look at the kinds of processes described in this chapter, which often mediate the impact of these conditions on disputant behavior and the status of a conflict. He also argues that knowledge of these microprocesses is heuristic, in the sense of aiding in the search for broader conditions. In short, a sophisticated approach to explanation and prediction in any field requires a grasp of several levels of analysis.

References

Abbas, M. (1995) *Through Secret Channels*. Reading, Berkshire: Garnet.

Antrim, L. N. and Sebenius, J. K. (1992) 'Formal Individual Mediation and the Negotiators' Dilemma: Tommy Koh at the Law of the Sea Conference', in J. Bercovitch and J. Z. Rubin (eds), *Mediation in International Relations*. New York: St. Martin's Press – now Palgrave Macmillan.

Bercovitch, J. (1997) 'Conflict Management and the Oslo Experience: Assessing the Success of Israeli Palestinian Peacemaking', *International Negotiation*, 2: 217–35.

Bercovitch, J. and Houston, A. (1996) 'The Study of International Mediation: Theoretical Issues and Empirical Evidence', in J. Bercovitch (ed.), *Resolving International Conflicts: The Theory and Practice of Mediation*. Boulder, CO: Lynne Rienner.

Colosi, T. (1983) 'Negotiation in the Public and Private Sectors: A Core Model', *American Behavioral Scientist*, 27, 229–53.

Corbin, J. (1994) *Gaza First: The Secret Norway Channel to Peace between Israel and the PLO*. London: Bloomsbury; New York: Atlantic Monthly Press.

Donohue, W. A. (1989) 'Communicative Competence in Mediators', in K. Kressel and D. G. Pruitt (eds), *Mediation Research*. San Francisco, CA: Jossey-Bass.

Fisher, R., Ury, W. and Patton, B. (1991) *Getting to Yes: Negotiating Agreement without Giving In*, 2nd edn. Boston: Houghton-Mifflin.

Hare, A. P. (1992) 'Informal Mediation by Private Individuals', in J. Bercovitch and J. Z. Rubin (eds), *Mediation in International Relations*. New York: St. Martin's Press – now Palgrave Macmillan.

Hiltrop, J. M. (1985) 'Mediator Behavior and the Settlement of Collective Bargaining Disputes in Britain', *Journal of Social Issues*, 41, 83–99.

Hiltrop, J. M. (1989) 'Factors Associated with Successful Labor Mediation', in K. Kressel and D. G. Pruitt (eds), *Mediation Research*. San Francisco, CA: Jossey-Bass.

Kelman, H. C. (1997) 'Some Determinants of the Oslo Breakthrough', *International Negotiation*, 2, 183–94.

Kleiboer, M. (1996) 'Understanding Success and Failure of International Mediation', *Journal of Conflict Resolution*, 40, 360–89.

Kraslow, D. and Loory, S. H. (1968) *The Secret Search for Peace in Vietnam*. New York: Vintage.

Kressel, K. and Pruitt, D. G. (1989) 'Conclusion: A Research Perspective on the Mediation of Social Conflict', in Kenneth Kressel and Dean G. Pruitt (eds), *Mediation Research*. San Francisco, CA: Jossey-Bass.

Lewicki, R. J., Litterer, J. A., Minton, J. W. and Saunders, D. M. (1993) *Negotiation*, 2nd edn. Burr Ridge, IL: Irwin.

Lim, R. and Carnevale, P. J. (1990) 'Contingencies in the Mediation of Disputes', *Journal of Personality and Social Psychology*, 58, 259–72.

Makovsky, D. (1996) *Making Peace with the PLO: The Rabin Government's Road to the Oslo Accord*. Boulder, CO: Westview.

Princen, T. (1992) 'Mediation by a Transnational Organization: The Case of the Vatican', in J. Bercovitch and J. Z. Rubin (eds), *Mediation in International Relations*. New York: St. Martin's Press – now Palgrave Macmillan.

Pruitt, D. G. (1993) 'Problem-Solving Negotiation in Escalated Conflict', in R. Twite and T. Hermann (eds), *The Arab-Israeli Negotiations*. Tel Aviv, Israel: Papyrus.

Pruitt, D. G. (1994) 'Negotiation between Organizations: A Branching Chain Model', *Negotiation Journal*, 10, 217–30.

Pruitt, D. G. (1995a) 'Flexibility in Conflict Episodes', *Annals of the American Academy of Political and Social Science*, 542, 100–15.

Pruitt, D. G. (1995b) 'Process and Outcome in Community Mediation', *Negotiation Journal*, 11, 365–77.

Pruitt, D. G. (1997a) 'Ripeness Theory and the Oslo Talks', *International Negotiation*, 2, 91–104.

Pruitt, D. G. (1997b) 'Social Conflict', in D. Gilbert, S. T. Fiske and G. Lindzey (eds), *Handbook of Social Psychology*, 4th edn. New York: McGraw-Hill.

Pruitt, D. G. and Carnevale, P. J. (1993) *Negotiation in Social Conflict*. Buckinghamshire: Open University Press; Pacific Grove, CA: Brooks/Cole.

Putnam, L. L. and Carcasson, M. (1997) 'Communication and the Oslo Negotiation: Contacts, Patterns, and Modes', *International Negotiation*, 2: 251–78.

Ross, L. and Stillinger, C. (1991) 'Barriers to Conflict Resolution', *Negotiation Journal*, 7, 389–404.

Rubin, J. Z. (1981) *Dynamics of Third Party Intervention: Kissinger in the Middle East.* New York: Praeger.

Rubin, J. Z., Pruitt, D. G. and Kim, S. H. (1994) *Social Conflict: Escalation, Stalemate, and Settlement,* 2nd edn. New York: McGraw-Hill.

Smith, R. J. and Devroy, A. (1994) 'Carter's Call from N. Korea Looms Large', *Washington Post,* p. A1, 26 June.

Susskind, L. and Babbitt, E. (1992) 'Overcoming the Obstacles to Effective Mediation of International Disputes', in J. Bercovitch and J. Z. Rubin (eds), *Mediation in International Relations.* New York: St. Martin's Press – now Palgrave Macmillan.

Touval, S. (1992) 'The Superpowers as Mediators', in J. Bercovitch and J. Z. Rubin (eds), *Mediation in International Relations.* New York: St. Martin's Press – now Palgrave Macmillan.

Touval, S. (1997) 'Mediators' Leverage', study prepared for the National Research Council (unpublished).

Touval, S. and Zartman, I. W. (1985) *International Mediation in Theory and Practice.* Boulder, CO: Westview.

Walton, R. E. and McKersie, R. B. (1965) *A Behavioral Theory of Labor Negotiations.* New York: McGraw-Hill.

Zartman, I. W. (1977) 'Negotiation as a Joint Decision-making Process', *Journal of Conflict Resolution,* 21, 619–38.

Zartman, I. W. (1989) *Ripe for Resolution: Conflict Resolution in Africa,* 2nd edn. New York: Oxford.

Zartman, I. W. (1996) 'Bargaining and Conflict Resolution', in E. A. Kolodziej and R. E. Kanet (eds), *Coping with Conflict after the Cold War.* Baltimore, MD: Johns Hopkins Press.

Zartman, I. W. (1997) 'Explaining Oslo', *International Negotiation,* 2: 195–215.

Zubek, J. M., Pruitt, D. G., McGillicuddy, N. B., Peirce, R. S. and Syna, H. (1992) 'Short-term Success in Mediation: Its Relationship to Disputant and Mediator Behaviors and Prior Conditions', *Journal of Conflict Resolution,* 36, 546–72.

Part II
The Range of Mediation Experience

4
Quasi-Informal Mediation in the Oslo Channel: Larsen and Holst as Individual Mediators

Karin Aggestam

> My people are hoping that this agreement…marks the beginning of the end of a chapter of pain and suffering which has lasted throughout this century. My people are hoping that this agreement…will usher in an age of peace, coexistence and equal rights.
>
> Yasir Arafat, PLO Chairman, on signing the DOP in Washington 1993 (Institute for Palestine Studies, 1994: 138)

> We wish to open a new chapter in the sad book of our lives together, a chapter of mutual recognition, of neighborliness, of mutual respect, of understanding.
>
> Yitzhak Rabin, Israeli Prime Minister, on signing the DOP in Washington 1993 (Institute for Palestine Studies, 1994: 137)

Introduction

In September 1993 Israel and the PLO signed a Declaration of Principles. The now famous handshake between Yasir Arafat and Yitzhak Rabin raised many questions as to how the parties were able to reach an agreement and why, after almost a century of conflict, they decided to recognize each other. The US played a critical role in many phases of the negotiation process, including hosting the signing ceremony in Washington. Yet, it was in Norway that the conflicting parties negotiated and reached a DOP under the auspices of the Norwegian Foreign Office and FAFO (a Norwegian research institute for Applied Social Science).

It is the aim of this chapter first, to critically examine and analyse the Norwegian 'quasi-informal' mediation.[1] The term 'quasi-informal' has been selected as the Norwegian mediation cannot be described as a strict formal nor an informal process but as a combination of both. How are we to conceptualize this type of *interplay* within theories of international mediation? What kind of resources may a small country like Norway use? Who are the individuals involved and, what mediation strategies do they utilize? Secondly, how can we evaluate and assess the Norwegian mediation in regards to success and failure in theories of international mediation? What theoretical and empirical insights may this particular case of mediation provide?

In the first part of the chapter, two strands of international mediation will be discussed. In the second part, the Norwegian mediation is contextualized and analysed. Four roles, combining formal and informal processes of mediation are identified: a facilitator, a communicator, a formulator, and a psychoanalyst. The chapter concludes with a discussion of the *problematique* to evaluate the success and failure in international mediation in general, and the outcome(s) of the Norwegian mediation in particular.

Theories of international mediation

International mediation takes place within a complex process of both conflictual and cooperative elements. Thus, I favour an inclusive and comprehensive definition adopted from Bercovitch (1997: 130) where international mediation is understood 'as a process of conflict management, related to but distinct from the parties' own negotiations, where those in conflict seek the assistance of, or accept an offer of help from, an outsider (whether an individual, an organization, a group, or a state) to change their perceptions or behavior, and to do so without resorting to physical force or invoking the authority of law'.

Theories of international mediation have brought great insights to conflict management and specially to the roles, functions and strategies of mediators. However, theorizing about international mediation has not always presented a uniform picture on the contents of the research. Scholars frame and conceptualize international conflict from various theoretical traditions, and evaluations of the outcomes of mediation are therefore diverse and sometimes even contradictory (see further, Bloomfield, 1997: 67–95; Kleiboer and t'Hart, 1995).

Two tracks of mediation

Within theories of international mediation we may delineate two tracks of mediation – one emphasizing the formal and official dimension, and another stressing the informal and unofficial setting of mediation (see, for example, Bercovitch, 1992: 15; Rubin, 1992: 257–60; Botes and Mitchell, 1995: 175–83; Fisher, 1995: 45–9; Rouhana, 1995: 263). The two tracks of mediation have several connotations as to who mediates, the specific strategies utilized, and underlying assumptions about the purpose of mediation.

Track one mediation has gained most attention in theory since this is the traditional kind of mediation. This type of mediation is commonly pursued by states or intergovernmental organizations, like the UN or regional organizations, and is characterized by formal and official structures. These formal structures may, however, inhibit flexibility since mediators have to consider not only the interests of the conflicting parties but also other constituents as well (Botes and Mitchell, 1995: 177). For example, when American officials are mediating the Israeli–Palestinian conflict they have to think simultaneously about the interests of the conflicting parties as well as other actors, such as allies in the region and domestic interest groups at home. Yet, this limitation in flexibility should be weighted against the power bases (political, military and economic), which formal mediators may utilize as a state or an organization. These power bases can be used as rewards ('carrots') or punishment ('sticks') in order to influence the parties' preferences of the feasibility and benefits of an agreement (see, for example, Rubin, 1992: 255–6; Zartman and Touval, 1996: 455–7).

Track two mediation is contrasted with the former in that the unofficial and informal dimension is emphasized (see further, McDonald and Bendahmane, 1987). This type of mediation, or what Fisher and Keashly (1988) prefer to call 'consultation', is often pursued in a so-called 'prenegotiation' phase (Stein, 1989; Rothman, 1990). Actors practicing informal mediation are often referred to as private individuals, frequently with links to Non-Governmental Organizations (NGOs), or scholars facilitating problem-solving workshops. Associations of private individuals are, for example, the Quakers, who have been particularly active in the Middle East and in Africa.

In problem-solving workshops, scholars invite representatives among the conflicting parties to participate. Scholars acting as facilitators help the parties to address analytically their conflicting perceptions and encourage them to present new ideas within a supportive and nonthreatening framework (see, for example, Kelman, 1992; Värynen, 1995).

As opposed to the first track, the second track of mediation often lacks an explicit mandate to intervene but acts on the motivation of the parties to settle the conflict and to finally resolve it (Hoffman, 1995). These kinds of mediators have limited options to use political, economic or political leverage. However, they gain greater flexibility to mediate since they do not represent any other groups than themselves and can therefore devote their time and energy to the conflicting parties (Botes and Mitchell, 1995: 180–2). In addition, the informality and unofficial setting of mediation is generally seen as promoting trust between antagonists which should be contrasted with official negotiation where there is a 'tendency of parties to use the negotiating process as a forum for publicity and point-scoring against each other' (Rupesinghe, 1996: 165).

Yet, there is a recognition also within track one mediation that there are times when privacy is essential, particularly in resolving deep-rooted conflict where the adversaries are experiencing a high degree of mistrust and suspicion (see, for example, Thompson, 1965: 403; Eban, 1983: 346–7). Back channels have become an important feature of and supplement to international negotiation in which secret mediation may take place parallel to official negotiation. It is therefore important to highlight the interplay between secret and official negotiations (Zartman and Berman, 1982: 219–20; Colosi, 1986; Klieman, 1988).

To conclude, there is an inclination within mediation theories to focus on a multitude of dichotomies (formal/informal, official/unofficial, public/private, states/individuals, active/passive), which tends to overemphasize the distinction between track one and track two mediation and to ignore the importance of the *interplay* between the two tracks of negotiation (Kriesberg, 1991, 1996a; Rouhana, 1995: 263; Aggestam, 1996). We shall therefore turn to see what theoretical and empirical insights the secret negotiations between Israel and the PLO in 1992–93 may provide.

The Norwegian case: a combination of formal and informal processes of mediation

Since international mediation is part of a wider process of negotiation it is important to underline the context of mediation. In this section, we will first discuss the context of and the secret negotiation process in the Oslo channel (cf. Aggestam, 1996: 1999). We will then identify and analyse the various roles played by mediators in order to further our understanding of the Norwegian quasi-informal mediation process.

The context of Oslo: why a secret channel?

After the Gulf War in 1991 the American administration identified a 'window of opportunity' and consequently attempted to initiate an official negotiation process (Baker, 1995: 412–15, 443–69). Yet, this 'window of opportunity' was not entirely shared by the conflicting parties. The Americans had to use a great deal of manipulation to receive the consent of both Palestinians and Israelis to a negotiation process co-chaired by the United States and the Soviet Union.

Manipulation strategies are often applied in conflicts where the need for a settlement is seen as less urgent by the parties. Mediators intend, by the use of power, to affect the parties' way of framing their gains and losses. Rewards ('carrots') and punishments ('sticks') are applied as a method to bring the opposing sides towards a negotiated settlement. These side-payments may motivate the parties to reframe losses and gains, thereby increasing the prospects of a conflict settlement (Zartman and Touval, 1989: 125–6). These kinds of manipulating strategies were used by the American administration. For instance, an Israeli compliance to a freeze on building new settlements in the occupied territories became a precondition for obtaining loan guarantees. Before attending the Madrid conference the United States also provided the Israeli and Palestinian delegation 'Letters of Assurances' (Institute for Palestine Studies, 1994: 5–11) on negotiation procedures, which was essential as the parties exhibit a deep mistrust concerning the sincerity of the other. Massalha (1994: 54) has depicted this particular mediation as 'constructive ambiguity' in that the Americans managed to temporarily transform major obstacles to procedural matters.

Still, the bilateral negotiation process in Washington was from the beginning plagued with obstacles, originating in the composition of the Palestinian delegation and the negotiation context. The composition of the Palestinian delegation had been determined by Israel's insistence that no PLO officials and no Palestinians from East Jerusalem could participate in the negotiations. The PLO had given the delegation a reluctant mandate to pursue the negotiations, because 'the peace process was a compulsory track' for the political survival of the PLO (Ashrawi, 1995: 184). Behind the scenes, however, the PLO unofficially controlled and instructed the Palestinian delegation. The negotiations clearly posed a dilemma for the PLO. If progress was made in the negotiations, the 'inside' leadership would become the major player and the control of the PLO would decline. At the same time, if there was no progress there was a risk that the Hamas would take over and undermine the legitimacy of the PLO. Hence, the PLO never clearly defined the objectives of the negotiations and the delegation lacked any real decision-making capacity (Hirschfeld, 1994: 105; Ashrawi, 1995: 58, 139, 241; Inbar, 1996: 183).

Both the Israeli and Palestinian delegations have attributed the failure of the Washington negotiations to the high degree of publicity and the complete lack of confidentiality between the opposing parties. The negotiations were hampered by constant leaks as well as press conferences in which the parties justified their positions. This publicity prevented flexibility and the negotiation positions became so rigid that concessions were impossible. For some observers, 'the "klieg lights" of the media had reduced the talks to public posturing' (Makovsky, 1996: 13) and as a 'PR-campaign' (Peres, 1994; Larsen, 1995; Hirschfeld, 1994; Abu Ala, 1997).

Furthermore, in contrast to the prenegotiation phase, the Americans did not at first actively participate in the official negotiations. They assumed that once the parties began to negotiate, they would gain an interest to see them succeed (Perry, 1994: 95). However, with constant deadlocks and with a new American administration headed by President Clinton, the United States augmented its role as a 'principal mediator' by initiating separate negotiations with the Israeli and the Palestinian delegation. But the Palestinian delegation described this mediating strategy as a 'non-starter' deriving from a pro-Israeli stance (Shaath, 1993: 6; Ashrawi, 1994; Pundak, 1995). Moreover, the Israelis viewed the Americans as becoming too preoccupied with their own formulae (Peres, 1993: 10).

The negotiation process: from a back to a front channel

In May 1992, the Israeli election brought the Labor party to power on a political platform that included negotiating a Palestinian autonomy plan within nine months. It was expected that the new Israeli government would give new vitality and impetus to the official negotiations as the former Premier, Yitshak Shamir, never had a real commitment to the negotiation process (Bergqvist, 1993: 151; Baker, 1995: 556). However, the negotiations reached a complete deadlock when Israel decided to deport 413 suspected Islamic activists to Lebanon. The PLO was also intentionally blocking these negotiations so to leave Israel no alternative to direct talks with the PLO. Moreover, both parties shared a mutual perception that the official negotiations were unworkable in their present form and setting 'due to their character as open propaganda diplomacy' (Østerud, 1995: 1). A secret back channel in Norway was therefore established after a year of official negotiations in Washington.

The first session took place on 20–22 January 1993, at Sarpsborg in Norway and included the chief Palestinian negotiator Abu Ala,[2] Maher Al-Kurd (formerly economic adviser to Abu Ala) and Hassan Asfour (secretary of the negotiation committee in Washington) as representatives of the PLO, and an Israeli professor Yair Hirschfeld[3] and Dr Ron Pundak (a close associate of Hirschfeld) representing the Israeli side. In the first meeting, the parties presented ideas and recognized common ground. Furthermore, it was decided that substance rather than procedures should take precedence, which included negotiating without protocols and set agendas. The intention to establish a secret back channel was to try out new ideas and make tentative concessions. It was also agreed that the role of the PLO would become public years later. This meant that an Israeli recognition of the PLO was *not* considered when these secret negotiations were initiated. Thus, results concluded in Norway were to be transferred back to the official negotiations in Washington and the channel was to be permanently secret (Aas, 1994; Beilin, 1994; Savir, 1994; Abu Ala, 1997).

As early as the first meeting Abu Ala presented the idea of Gaza first (an Israeli withdrawal from the Gaza Strip as a first step – an idea that had been extensively discussed within the Israeli Labor Party). He also stressed the importance of economic cooperation in the region. The principle of gradualism, based on a DOP, was brought forward by the Israelis, which was to be understood as an ongoing process of negotiations, a step-by-step approach (Hirschfeld, 1994; Abbas, 1995: 115–26). However, in this session and the one that followed, the Palestinian negotiators were constantly raising the question in what way Hirschfeld and Pundak represented the Israeli government and if ideas agreed upon in Norway would be promoted in Israel. The Palestinians wanted to be sure of the 'political relevance' of the negotiations and that these negotiations were not just an academic exercise. The two Israelis acknowledged that they did not have a clear mandate to negotiate since they did not represent an official body. However, they indicated links to various Israeli officials (Hirschfeld, 1994; Abbas, 1995: 127; Pundak, 1995; Abu Ala, 1997).

Several meetings took place in Norway during February to April and a first preliminary DOP was drafted. At this stage both parties recognized the potential to conclude a DOP and became hesitant to bring the principles agreed upon in Norway into the official negotiations, as they feared that parts of the agreement could be exposed before being finally concluded. In such circumstances, domestic opposition to the agreement could be mobilized and would threaten the continuation of the negotiations (Juul, 1994). Also the question remained of whether the back channel should be upgraded to an official level on the Israeli side. Aware that Rabin and Peres were old political rivals, the Palestinians wanted to know if the channel had Rabin's support and threatened to end the talks if the Israeli negotiators were not upgraded (Abbas, 1995: 128–35; Abu Ala, 1997).

At the sixth meeting in May, Director General Uri Savir of the Israeli Foreign Ministry was sent to Norway, but under two conditions: (1) that the back channel was to remain in total secrecy, and (2) that the PLO would agree that it could not participate in the official negotiations. In addition, Savir was in Norway to verify the information received from Hirschfeld and Pundak and to underline to the Palestinian negotiators a number of issues: (a) that the Oslo channel was no substitute for the official negotiations; (b) Israel had its 'redlines', including no concessions on the status of Jerusalem; (c) Israeli settlements were at this stage not negotiable; and (d) the talks should center on an interim agreement, including the concept of Gaza–Jericho first (Savir, 1994).

Notwithstanding the Israeli upgrading of the delegation by including Savir, who was a close associate of Peres, Savir's presence confirmed the Palestinian suspicion that Rabin was still not completely involved in the back channel. It was therefore significant that at the next session the legal adviser for the Foreign Ministry, Joel Singer (also known as an associate to Rabin), participated in the Israeli delegation. Singer's purpose was to evaluate the back channel and judge whether the concessions offered by the PLO were sincere and credible. After the session, Singer concluded in a report to Rabin that the PLO was prepared to reach an agreement and recommended that the negotiations should proceed (Singer, 1994).

In July, the parties experienced a deep crisis and both sides threatened to break off the negotiations. However, with the facilitation of the Norwegians, the parties were able to overcome most of the differences. On the remaining issues in dispute, the negotiators would try to convince their decision-makers back home to compromise. At this meeting, the Israeli negotiators also presented their suggestion of a mutual recognition by Israel and the PLO which would enable the PLO to become Israel's official and public negotiating partner (Savir, 1994).

In August 1993, the Israeli Foreign Minister Shimon Peres was on an official visit in Stockholm. He asked the Norwegian Foreign Minister Johan Jørgen Holst to join him in Stockholm and to help the parties overcoming the remaining obstacles via telephone between Stockholm and Tunis. During seven hours of negotiations, the last issues of dispute were resolved and a DOP between Israel and the PLO was finally concluded 18 August 1993 (Savir, 1994; Singer, 1994; Abbas, 1995: 168–75). Negotiations on mutual recognition between Israel and the PLO continued in Paris via an intensive Norwegian shuttle between Tunis and Jerusalem. The letters confirming mutual recognition were signed and exchanged between Arafat and Rabin on 9 September 1993.

Four roles of mediation

In the Oslo channel we can distinguish four roles of mediation: a facilitator, a communicator, a formulator and a psychoanalyst.[4] Before elaborating further on these various roles, we will first identify the actors behind the Norwegian mediation.

Identifying the mediators

Three different actors as mediators are frequently cited in the literature: states, organizations and individuals (Bercovitch, 1992: 10–14; Rubin, 1992: 257–68; Zartman and Touval, 1996: 446–50). These categories relate to the resources and skills that these actors may possess and utilize for mediation purposes.

A common distinction of *states* is between small states and great/superpowers. Small states are assumed to have less influence in world politics and therefore lack a direct interest in international conflict. Moreover, small states tend to practice what Fisher (1995: 41) calls 'pure mediation' or what Princen (1992: 24) views as 'neutral mediation'. Pure or neutral mediation is understood as a noncoercive form of mediation, characterized by impartiality and on improving communication and interaction between the conflicting parties. Great and superpowers, in contrast, are assumed to have global objectives and therefore at least an indirect interest in international conflict. Great and particularly superpowers are thus inclined to intervene by using 'power' or 'principal' mediation (Princen, 1992: 24; Fisher, 1995: 41). Power mediation is a coercive form of direct bargaining with the conflicting parties which includes making threats and offering rewards.

Norway is a small and nonthreatening country that enjoys good relations with both Israelis and Palestinians. The close relation with Israel dates back to 1948 when Israel was declared a state, while relations with the PLO are more recent. It was not until 1978 that a Norwegian official, namely Defence Minister Johan Jørgen Holst, met with PLO Chairman

Arafat. Since then both Foreign Minister Thorvald Stoltenberg and Holst improved their personal ties to the leadership of the PLO, although being sensitive to the implications on relations with Israel[5] (Østerud, 1995: 5; Stoltenberg, 1996).

Seeking a negotiation context worked by secrecy and confidentiality, Norway was considered ideal and as Rubin (1992: 267) points out, 'small states may be particularly well suited for intervention in disputes between states of unequal power – trustworthy by the weaker state, while being considered non-threatening by the powerful'.

Another category of mediators is *organization* which includes both inter-governmental (IGO), such as, the UN and the OAU, as well as NGO, like the Quakers and the IRC. Most organizations lack any real coercive power and are therefore inclined to utilize pure mediation with some form of informational and expertise power (Rubin, 1992: 265). IGOs regularly have a formal mandate to intervene, while mediation efforts by NGOs often are informal, that is, without a special mandate or detailed instructions on how to pursue mediation.

The Norwegian institute, FAFO, provided an excellent cover and 'smoke-screen' for the parties in case of a leak. FAFO had an ongoing research project directed by Larsen in the Gaza Strip on Palestinian living conditions. Thus the Norwegians had both expertise and informational power with linkages to a variety of people and organizations such as the Israeli organization ECF (Economic Cooperation Foundation) headed by Yossi Beilin and Yair Hirschfeld.

Finally, *individuals* are sometimes mentioned as a separate category, even though '*all* mediation entails the work of individuals' (Rubin, 1992: 260). As mentioned, a common distinction is made between informal mediators (private individuals/scholars) and formal mediators (official individuals).

The Norwegian Foreign Office, particularly the Director General Jan Egeland with the backing of then Foreign Minister Stoltenberg was involved in the initial stages offering to facilitate a secret back channel. In later phases of negotiation, Mona Juul, a career diplomat, played an important role together with Terje Rød Larsen, the director for FAFO. Juul's presence gave a 'political relevance' to the process when the Israeli negotiators were represented as unofficials. She together with Jan Egeland and later also Holst reported back to Yossi Beilin (who informed Peres), and to Dan Kurtzner, an official at the American State Department (who briefed US Secretary of State Warren Christopher) (Beilin, 1994; Pedersen, 1994).[6] However, it was the sociologist Larsen and the new Norwegian Foreign Minister Holst – each in their own capacity as an informal and formal mediator – who in a decisive way influenced the negotiation process. When the secret channel turned from a back to a front channel and with the prospect to conclude a DOP, Holst augmented his role as a mediator. Larsen played a significant role in improving communication and facilitating a supportive negotiation milieu. Assisting Larsen with practicalities such as arranging tickets, accommodation, and transportation, were Even Aas and Geir Pedersen, both researchers at FAFO.

Below, these roles of mediation will be elaborated further and how various dimensions of formal and informal mediation were combined will be discussed.

The facilitator: providing secrecy and deniability

Conflicting parties in protracted conflicts often experience great difficulties to establish a first contact of negotiation. Several mediators have therefore attempted to facilitate prenegotiation and to establish official negotiation. Facilitation may include arranging interaction, communication and ultimately to construct a milieu promoting negotiation.

The Norwegian role as a facilitator has been underlined by the Israeli and Palestinian negotiators. As Hirschfeld (1994) states 'we could not have started without anyone to help us'. So, how did the Norwegians establish and facilitate negotiations between Israel and the PLO?

Shortly before the Israeli election, Beilin from the Israeli Labor party met with Larsen. Larsen together with Egeland expressed their willingness to facilitate a back channel between Israel and the PLO. Immediately after the Israeli election, a meeting was arranged by Larsen, in which Hirschfeld, Beilin, and Faisal Husseini (a Palestinian leader from Jerusalem, and the head of the Palestinian delegation in Washington) further explored the possibilities of setting up a secret back channel (Beilin, 1994; Hirschfeld, 1994; Larsen, 1995).

The first meeting took place in London on 4 December 1992. Meanwhile, the multilateral talks were being held in London and Larsen, Beilin, Hirschfeld, and Abu Ala, were all in London for these negotiations. Before Hirschfeld held his first meeting with Abu Ala, Larsen mentioned that FAFO was arranging a seminar on human resources in January 1993, an 'academic gathering' which could provide a *cover* for the next meeting (Beilin, 1994; Abbas, 1995: 112; Larsen, 1995).

The context of secrecy and 'deniability' of the negotiations were considered a precondition because, as noted, at the time of negotiation Israel had a law against its citizens meeting with PLO officials. According to Savir (1994), the parties 'were hysterical about leaks' and thus, a confidential networking between the Norwegian Foreign Office and FAFO was established.[7] If there would be any leaks, the parties could refer to 'academic activities' pursued by NGOs which included FAFO and the Israeli ECF. Any direct links to the Israeli government and the PLO leadership could thereby be denied. Conversely, the Norwegian Foreign Office provided a 'political relevance' which the Palestinian negotiators sought since Hirschfeld and Pundak were unofficial Israeli diplomats.

The facilitation included arranging when and where subsequent meetings would take place and in times of crisis Larsen was able to persuade the parties to return to the negotiation by suggesting a 'non-meeting' to discuss the issues they disagreed on (Juul, 1994). Moreover, the secrecy and the supportive milieu and atmosphere in Norway allowed the parties, in contrast to the official negotiations in Washington, 'to think loud' (Aas, 1994) and to talk frankly, which promoted greater knowledge about the other party (Beilin, 1994).

The communicator: supplying information and carrying messages

A common problem to conflict settlement is how to keep communication channels open, ongoing, and undistorted between two mistrusting parties. In these situations, mediators may for instance act as a 'go-between', supply with additional information, and identify common problems that may inhibit deadlocks and enhance communication. As Princen has stated (1992: 8), a mediator gathers necessary information and 'serves as a regime surrogate in disputes where institutionalization is impractical'.

Larsen and Holst played an essential role as communicators in between the negotiation sessions since at that time there were no direct telephone links between Israel and Tunisia. Thus, the Norwegians became the 'go-between' with extensive telephone contacts, especially Larsen, who had daily contacts with Abu Ala and Savir. Moreover, there were times when the parties preferred to communicate their opinions indirectly via the Norwegians which gave them a certain kind of influence in that they could phrase some issues a bit differently and put them in a context less fraught with rhetoric (Hirschfeld, 1994; Pedersen, 1994; Larsen, 1995).

The role as a communicator was enlarged by the active involvement of Holst. His role became decisive in times of crisis, particularly in July when the parties exhibit great difficulties to resolve the last 16 issues of dispute. At that time, Holst, Larsen and Juul travelled to Tunisia and Israel in order to reassure, communicate, and convince each party that the other side was indeed negotiating in good faith. The role as a communicator was vital since the Israeli and Palestinian political leadership never met face-to-face before the signing ceremony in Washington. Holst in particular became influential (and later also as a formulator) as he structured and arranged meetings and discussions in an attempt to reconcile disparate positions (Corbin, 1994: 122–5; Savir, 1994; Abbas, 1995: 107–8; Peres, 1995: 341–3).

The formulator: finding acceptable formulae

When the parties are at the negotiation table, they may need assistance of a formulator to conclude an agreement. A formulator attempts to influence and persuade the parties of more conciliatory strategies by presenting a formula, or encourage them to use the technique of a Single Negotiating

Text (SNT),[8] which may help the parties to recognize common interests. Moreover, the parties' need for a solution and their own inability to proceed with negotiations without third party intervention gives a formulator some additional leverage.

In the Oslo channel, the role as a formulator was first assumed in later stages of negotiation. However, both negotiation teams emphasize that this particular assistance was only accepted since the credibility of Norway had greatly increased during previous phases, in which the Norwegians never attempted to negotiate directly with the parties (Juul, 1994; Singer, 1994; Abbas, 1995: 104–5).

As mentioned, Holst became active as a communicator and later as a formulator.[9] During the decisive meeting in Stockholm, Holst acted as the middleman during seven hours of negotiations via telephone between Peres (in Stockholm) and Arafat (in Tunis) in order to settle the remaining points of dispute. Holst helped the parties with some formulation, specific sentences and presented his own views and analysis about what issues may pose obstacles and what may be feasible. Similarly, during the intensive shuttle exchanging letters of mutual recognition between Israel and the PLO, Holst was able to reconcile viewpoints[10] without forceful interference (Corbin, 1994: 157; Perry, 1994: 303–7; Savir, 1994; Abbas, 1995: 104–8).[11]

According to several observers, Holst's role as a formulator constituted of an ability to communicate in a credible manner the position of each side; to analytically identify mutual ground; to assess the situation and concurrently being optimistic about reaching a mutually satisfying formula (Pedersen, 1994; Abbas, 1995: 104; Larsen, 1995; Peres, 1995: 343).

The psychoanalyst: confronting self- and enemy images

Many scholars emphasize the need for mediators to possess content and process skills (see, for example, Bercovitch, 1992: 16; Rubin, 1992: 252) but a psychoanalytical role is less mentioned in traditional theories of international mediation. This role, however, shares many aspects of an interactive problem-solving approach (see further, Kelman, 1997) and thus, accentuates similar psychological features of conflict, such as the importance to address stereotyped enemy images and to develop trust between conflicting parties.

The psychological dimension of negotiation and the role of Larsen as a 'psychoanalyst' has been underlined by the negotiators. In the Oslo channel, Palestinians and Israelis were able to reframe the conflict by confronting old enemy images in a nonthreatening and supportive framework. Larsen underlines two components in the negotiations: (a) the *cognitive* element (images and perceptions) which played an important part in the 'telephone arena'; and (b) the *emotive* factor (feelings and emotions) which was primarily present in the 'meeting arena' (in face-to-face negotiation). By being sensitive to these two components, the Norwegians were able to confront problems of suspicion and lack of confidence between the parties.

To address enemy images[12] Larsen (1995) insisted on a 'small group setting'. In this setting, the Norwegians were 'monitoring from a distance, trying to look on the psychological balance' (Savir, 1994). Larsen, in particular, was managing the frequent tension and suspicion, and acted as a 'punching bag' (Savir, 1994) and as 'a shock-absorber for both sides' (Singer, 1994). Each party had to listen to the concern of the other and thus, came to understand their basic interest – the importance of security for Israelis and the recognition of the national rights for the Palestinian people (Abu Ala, 1997).

Moreover, Larsen (1995) insisted that the parties should negotiate directly without Norwegian interference. According to him, there would otherwise be a risk that the parties would blame the Norwegians for failures to reach result. Savir (1994) agrees with this view and states that 'they [the Norwegians] became what you rarely have in negotiations – a facilitator rather than a mediator which creates a much bigger credibility and therefore a much stronger emotional outlet simply than just juggle with words'. Both the Israeli and Palestinian negotiators frequently came to the Norwegians asking questions about the other party: 'are they playing games; are they serious; do you believe in this; why are they doing this; how did it sound; are you one of us' (Larsen, 1995). Thus, the Norwegians were able to provide assurances that the other side was indeed negotiating in good faith and according to Abu Ala (1997) this was the 'secret of Oslo'. Abbas agrees (1995: 105): '[w]ithout a doubt, a thorough understanding of the psychology of negotiation contributed to the success of the mission undertaken by the Norwegian team'.

The Oslo channel: a successful case of mediation?

How to evaluate success and failure in mediation has been approached in several ways. The concepts of timing and ripeness are often mentioned in regards to the effectiveness of mediation. This approach emphasizes favoring conditions for successful mediation and particularly how mediation is interrelated to a ripe moment.[13] However, a more fundamental question is how we understand and define success in international mediation. In this last section, we will elaborate on these two aspects, and how to evaluate the outcome(s) of the Norwegian case of mediation.

The right time to mediate an end to conflict?

The notion of timing has become a disputed topic within the research field of mediation. As Cohen (1996: 119) underlines, 'the concept of time is among the most insidious. It is ever-present, unconscious, and formative' and the entry of mediators is conditional on a variety of factors, including both the context and the processes of conflict.

Pathbreaking research on ripeness was initiated by Zartman (1986, 1989) who states that a ripe moment is a 'mutually hurting stalemate'. A mutually hurting stalemate is characterized by a deadlock where the parties have recognized the limits of unilateral strategies and therefore perceive a nego-tiated settlement as the only way to de-escalate the conflict.

Several researchers have attempted to refine Zartman's notion of ripeness and a whole range of prerequisites for effective mediation have been pre-sented (Haass, 1990; Stedman, 1991; Kleiboer, 1994; Mitchell, 1995; Pruitt, 1997): a hurting stalemate, an enticing opportunity, the existence of a peaceful way to de-escalate the conflict, willingness to compromise, accept-able negotiation procedures and changes in leadership – only to mention a few. However, despite the number of studies conducted in this area, the concept of ripeness continues to be associated with several conceptual and methodological problems, for instance, its applicability of prerequisites to different conflicts; the operationalization of the concept and the risk of tautology; and the dilemma to identify a mutually hurting stalemate in internal conflict (see, for example, Stedman, 1991: 26–7; Rubin, 1991: 238; Zartman, 1995: 8; Hampson, 1996: 211).

Recognizing the importance of conducive factors in the domestic, regional and international contexts, one may conclude that the degree of ripeness is still conditional on how the adversaries perceive the conflict. Pruitt (1997: 239) has elaborated further on the perceptual dimension and refined ripeness theory. He makes a useful distinction between *motivational* ripeness (motivation to avoid further conflict escalation) and *optimism* about reaching an agreement (optimism that the other party responds pos-itively towards cooperative behavior). 'Full readiness for conflict resolution is attained when the situation is symmetrical, such that *both* parties are motivated to achieve de-escalation and *both* are optimistic about reaching an agreement' (Pruitt, 1997: 239). Thus, a refined concept of ripeness that focuses on the perceptions of the parties is useful when assessing a conflict.

A contingency approach attempts to relate mediation strategy with a particular phase of conflict (see, for example, Bercovitch and Houston, 1996; Keashley and Fisher, 1996). 'The basic rationale of the contingency approach is to intervene with the most appropriate methods at the relevant stages in order to de-escalate the conflict down through the stages' (Fisher, 1995: 50). Accordingly, success or failure of mediation is contingent upon a particular phase of conflict, and by the specific mediation strategy applied. However, criticism has also been directed towards a contingency approach, primarily towards its oversimplification of conflict into a few stages[14] and by framing conflict as one-dimensional and linear therewith ignoring the dynamic and complexity within each phase (Webb with Koutrakou and Walters, 1996: 171–3; Bloomfield, 1997: 79–95).

If we turn to the Israeli–Palestinian conflict, the question is if the conflict was ripe and the parties ready for conflict settlement? Many explanations offered to the breakthrough between Israel and the PLO relate to contextual features constituting a 'window of opportunity', for instance, the impact of the *intifada*, the Gulf War and the end of the Cold War.[15] However, despite these favoring contextual conditions the parties only reluctantly agreed to negotiate.[16] With a new Israeli government in 1992, the motivation on the Israeli side became stronger, yet the PLO was still excluded from the official process which inhibited any progress in the negotiations. It was first in the Oslo channel, during exploratory negotiations between PLO officials and unofficial Israeli diplomats, that 'full readiness' for conflict settlement envelop (see also, Pruitt, 1997: 248; Zartman, 1997: 198). At this time, both sides agreed that there was no alternative to negotiation, only unacceptable costs of a non-agreement (Abu Ala, 1997).

A contingency approach highlights the success of American power mediation in the prenegotiaton phase, that is, getting the parties to the table. Yet, in later stages of the official negotiations the American mediation became counterproductive. After experiencing a learning process in Washington, the parties had a desire to meet face-to-face to identify mutual ground, to break deadlocks and enhance the negotiation process. The Norwegian mediation was successful in that they provided the parties with what they required at that specific time, that is, impartial facilitation of direct negotiations – the first ever between Israel and the PLO.

Assessing mediation objectively and subjectively

A comprehensive assessment of international mediation is a challenging task which 'poses serious conceptual and methodological problem' (Bercovitch, 1997: 147). For instance, how can we isolate and evaluate a specific effort of mediation from the overall process of conflict settlement? Moreover, how is a contested concept such as 'success' conceptualized and understood?

Mediation may be evaluated either subjectively or objectively (Bercovitch, 1997: 147–8). A subjective evaluation is based on how the mediators and the parties perceive and assess the mediation effort (e.g. expressing contentment, fairness, efficiency), whereas an objective evaluation is founded on specific indicators that can be observed empirically (e.g. outcomes resulting in a cessation of violence or in a partial/comprehensive agreement).

Using an objective perspective, we can conclude that the Norwegian mediation is generally considered a success due to the fact that Israel and the PLO agreed to a 'Declaration of Principles on Interim Self-Government Arrangements'. Moreover, the letters of mutual recognition between Israel and the PLO indeed changed the pattern of conflict behavior. However, several reservations towards the 'success' may also be raised. For instance, an objective perspective does not elaborate on the durability and the implementation of an agreement and thus, may limit the explanation of 'success' over time. The DOP signed by Israel and the PLO was not a peace accord, but an interim agreement on how and when to proceed in the coming stages of negotiations. Moreover, the agreement did not address the core issues of conflict (such as, the status of Jerusalem, Israeli borders, the final status of the occupied territories, Palestinian refugees and Jewish settlements) since the parties, at that time, did not view them as 'ripe' for negotiation. Since the signing of the agreement, we can notice an increase of violence and terrorism posing great obstacles to the implementation of agreements reached (see further, Aggestam and Jönsson, 1997).

From a subjective perspective, based on an evaluation of the parties and the mediators involved, the Norwegian mediation was viewed as a success. However, it should be pointed out that the Palestinian and Israeli negotiators prefer a minimalist and restricted definition of mediation, that is, power mediation (a definition presumably interrelated with American power mediation). Consequently, they prefer the concept of facilitation rather than mediation when depicting the Norwegian intervention (Beilin, 1994; Juul, 1994; Singer, 1994; Larsen, 1995; Abu Ala, 1997).

A subjective perspective has its limits as well since a subjective evaluation is based solely on the assessment of the leadership of the conflicting parties. For instance, even if the negotiators in the Oslo channel redefined their images of each other, and the Israeli and Palestinian leadership exchanged letters of recognition, this reframing process was not paralleled on the ground. Many Israeli and Palestinian groups vehemently opposed the DOP and the mutual recognition. These opposition groups did not frame the outcome as a success but rather as a 'national disaster' (see, for example, Said, 1995; Kass and O'Neill, 1997; Wolfsfeld, 1997: 104–23).

Accordingly, the evaluation of an outcome of mediation is contingent on what we define as success, that is, the aim and purpose of mediation. As discussed in the first part of this chapter, we may delineate in theory two divergent approaches to mediation. These two approaches assume distinct mediation activities and different aims and purpose of mediation. The first approach strives towards conflict *settlement*, that is, some kind of 'pragmatic' approach aimed at reaching an agreement to de-escalate a conflict, although, without ambitions to resolve all issues of dispute. The second approach emphasizes *resolution*, that is, the causes to conflict, including human needs and psychological factors (Bloomfield, 1997: 67–71). This division between the two approaches has caused a debate of what constitute successful and effective mediation (manipulation–power vs communication–facilitation) and at length what we define as mediation. This polarization may be traced to the difference in ontology and epistemology among scholars, that is, how they view and conceptualize the origin and the nature of conflict (Kleiboer and t'Hart, 1995; Bloomfield, 1997; Kleiboer, 1997). As Groom (1988: 114) states 'what we think causes conflict determines what we think we can do about it'.

As a result, there has been a tendency to ignore the interplay and coordination of various mediation attempts by formal and informal mediators. Moreover, these various strands of mediation are not mutually exclusive but interrelated. For instance, track two mediation may facilitate prenegotiation and pave the way for track one mediation resulting in a conflict settlement and resolution (see also, Kelman, 1997: 202–8; Rasmussen, 1997: 42–5). In the Norwegian case, the coordination of informal and formal processes of mediation might be the most important insight from this empirical case. The complementary mediation effort provided the parties with a secret context, a political relevance, a supportive negotiation milieu, communication channels and various formulae.

Conclusion

After several years since the signing of a DOP, Israel and the PLO are still in an intricate transition from war to peace, in which mediation constitutes one part of a larger process. To analyse and evaluate international mediation is contingent on many contextual factors (e.g. the underlying causes to and duration of a particular conflict). To prescribe and predict about international mediation is therefore 'tempered by the constraints of a complex reality' (Bercovitch, 1997: 148). Yet, we may gain greater understanding from diverse in-depth cases which may facilitate cumulative knowledge about the contents, scope and boundaries of international mediation.

The success of the Norwegian mediation was contingent on several processes preceding the Oslo channel. First, different secret channels and meetings have been held for the last decade between Israelis and Palestinians that paved the way for the breakthrough (see, for example, Abbas, 1995; Kelman, 1995; Heikal, 1996). Secondly, the American mediation pursued in the prenegotiation phase was considered a success in itself, since the Americans were able to get the parties – for the first time – to the official negotiation table. Thirdly, the willingness and determination of the parties to conclude an agreement in the Oslo channel was probably *the* decisive factor why an agreement, notwithstanding its major weaknesses, was reached.[17]

In this chapter, we have examined and analysed the Norwegian quasi-informal mediation pursued primarily by Larsen and Holst. Four roles of mediation were identified: a facilitator, a communicator, a psychoanalyst, and a formulator. These roles reveal how formal and informal mediators may combine and complement each other in an effort to mediate.

As an informal mediator, Larsen emphasized the psychological and social context of negotiation – an approach that shares several aspects of an interactive problem-solving approach (e.g. the role as a facilitator, addressing enemy images). As a result, both the Israeli and Palestinian negotiation team came to view the Norwegians as sincere, impartial and trustworthy, a kind of 'leverage' or *referent power* that the Norwegians later were able to use in specific situations.

Holst added a political relevance to the negotiations with his involvement as a formal mediator – representing a small country with excellent relations with both parties and lacking a direct interest in the conflict.

With analytical and persuasive but yet impartial skills, Holst was able to act forcefully as a formulator. Moreover, with optimism and sincerity, Holst together with Larsen exercised *informational power* in the role as a go-between – transmitting and exchanging messages between the parties.

In sum, the Oslo channel was based on a close professional and personal networking between officials at the Norwegian Foreign Office and academics from NGOs. This networking provided a flexible negotiation milieu based primarily on the parties' shifting preferences and requirements. With an increasing number of nonstate actors in international politics, the Norwegian model of collaboration between formal and informal mediators constitutes an innovation in the practice of modern diplomacy.

Notes

1. The informal dimension is emphasized since the establishment of the Oslo channel was largely informal and unofficial.
2. Abu Ala (Ahmad Qrei) was the principal Palestinian negotiator during the entire process. At the time of negotiation, Abu Ala was the PLO's finance minister and leading the multilaterals on economic cooperation (today the speaker of the Palestinian parliament). Abu Ala received instructions mainly from Abu Abbas (Abu Mazen) head of the PLO's Department of International Relations and a close aide to Yasir Arafat.
3. Hirschfeld has close links to the Labor party and particularly to Yossi Beilin, the then Deputy Foreign Minister.
4. Three roles of mediation are frequently mentioned in the literature, that is, a manipulator, a formulator and a communicator–facilitator (see further, Zartman and Touval, 1989: 126–9; Bercovitch, 1992: 17). On the Oslo channel, see also, Putnam and Carcasson, 1997: 251–78.
5. Compare when Sweden developed closer ties with the PLO, which Israel viewed as impairing on its relation with Sweden.
6. Albeit these briefings, the Americans never took the channel seriously. However, the American administration was not fully informed of the progress in later stages of negotiation (Juul, 1994).
7. The informal networking between the Foreign Office and FAFO was also built on close personal and professional relations between the Norwegians. Stoltenberg together with Egeland initiated the first contact with the parties. Holst, married to Stoltenberg's daughter, Marianne Heiberg, replaced Stoltenberg as a Foreign Minister in 1993. Heiberg works as a researcher at FAFO and was at the time of the Oslo channel included in the same research project on Palestinian living conditions as Larsen. Larsen, the director of FAFO is married to Juul who works as a career diplomat at the Foreign Office.
8. The first outline of an agreement is usually drafted by the mediators and presented to the parties for criticism. However, the parties are not forced to accept or make concessions. By redrafting the proposal several times, the mediators improve the text and finally submit it to the parties. The advantages of SNT are that it identifies the differences between the parties. Through a joint process of improvements, the parties may gain a greater understanding of their differences and the bargaining range. The negotiation technique of SNT was, for instance,

successfully used during the Camp David negotiations in 1978 (see, for example, Raiffa, 1982: 220; Lax and Sebenius, 1986: 176–8).

9. When Holst augmented his role as a formulator, there were some discussions among the Norwegians how it may impair on the Norwegian role as an impartial facilitator (Pedersen, 1994).

10. Disagreements included expressions and contested issues such as annulling the PLO covenant, statement to end violence, willingness to normalize relations, and activities of Palestinian institutions in East Jerusalem.

11. Simultaneously to and as a supplement to the Oslo channel another secret channel was operating between Ahmad Tibi (adviser to Arafat) and Haim Ramon (close aide to Rabin) to double check concessions offered (Abbas, 1995: 74–8; Inbar, 1996: 212–15).

12. Acting as a psychoanalyst, Larsen constantly posed questions to the negotiators about themselves and their stereotyped enemy images.

13. A great deal of attention has been given to favoring conditions, however, less to what pose as obstacles to and failure of conflict settlement (see further Arrow *et al.*, 1995).

14. Fisher (1995: 51) categorizes conflict into four phases: discussion, polarization, segregation and destruction. Rubin (1992: 270) relates effectiveness of various mediators to the following stages: conflict escalation, stalemate, conflict settlement. Kriesberg (1996b: 227–30) presents a third variant: de-escalation, preparation, initiation, negotiation and implementation.

15. The *intifada* had a direct and significant impact on both parties. Over four years, Israel attempted all kinds of strategies to end the *intifada* without success and Israel's international reputation was suffering, due to the actions taken against the Palestinian population under occupation. For the Palestinians, the *intifada* activated the struggle for independence in the occupied territories and strengthened the 'inside' leadership, who wanted a two state solution. The process culminated in 1988 when the PLO implicitly recognized Israel and declared a Palestinian state in the West Bank and the Gaza Strip with East Jerusalem as its capital. After the Gulf War, the PLO found itself in political and economic isolation as a consequence of its actions taken during the war. For Israel, the Gulf War demonstrated that the United States did not necessarily regard Israel as a 'strategic asset' in the region. With the end of the Cold War, the United States was now able to build regional alliances with other Arab states, including Syria. A greater pragmatism towards the Arab–Israeli conflict was also discernible among Arab regimes. This encouraged the United States to assume an active mediating approach to the Arab–Israeli conflict aimed at facilitating a peace process (see, for example, Massalha, 1994: 27; Rubin *et al.*, 1994; Perry, 1994: 113–15; Abbas, 1995: 18).

16. According to Zartman (1997: 196–7) there was no mutually hurting stalemate in 1991 and thus, no ripe moment.

17. According to Singer (1994) this was the least bad solution, that is, the only formula that the parties could agree on.

References

Aas, E. (1994) Interview. Oslo, 18 May.

Abbas, M. (1995) *Through Secret Channels – The Road to Oslo: Senior PLO Leader Abu Mazen's Revealing Story of the Negotiations with Israel*. Reading, Berkshire: Garnet.

Aggestam, K. (1996) 'Two-Track Diplomacy: Negotiations Between Israel and the PLO Through Open and Secret Channels'. *Davis Papers on Israel's Foreign Policy*, No. 53.

Aggestam, K. (1999) *Reframing and Resolving Conflict: Israeli–Palestinian Negotiations, 1988–1998*. Lund: Lund University Press.

Aggestam, K. and Jönsson, C. (1997) '(Un)Ending Conflict: Challenges in Post-War Bargaining'. *Millennium: Journal of International Studies*, Vol. 26, No. 3, pp. 771–93.

Ala, A. (1997) Interview. Jerusalem, 23 May.

Arrow, K., Mnookin, R. H., Ross, L., Tversky, A. and Wilson, R. (eds) (1995) *Barriers to Conflict Resolution*. New York: W. W. Norton & Co.

Ashrawi, H. (1994) Interview. Jerusalem, 19 July.

Ashrawi, H. (1995) *This Side of Peace: A Personal Account*. New York: Simon & Schuster.

Baker, J. (1995) *The Politics of Diplomacy: Revolution, War and Peace, 1989–1992*. New York: Putnam's.

Beilin, Y. (1994) Interview. Jerusalem, 28 June.

Bergqvist, M. (1993) *Konflikt utan Ände?* Stockholm: Norstedts Juridik.

Bercovitch, J. (1992) 'The Structure and Diversity of Mediation in International Relations'. In Bercovitch, J. and Rubin, J. Z. *Mediation in International Relations: Multiple Approaches to Conflict Management*. New York: St. Martin's Press – now Palgrave Macmillan.

Bercovitch, J. (1997) 'Mediation in International Conflict: An Overview of Theory, A Review of Practice'. In Zartman, I. W. and Rasmussen, L. J. (eds), *Peacemaking in International Conflict: Methods & Techniques*. Washington: United States Institute of Peace.

Bercovitch, J. and Houston, A. (1996) 'The Study of International Mediation: Theoretical Issues and Empirical Evidence'. In Bercovitch, J. (ed.), *Resolving International Conflicts: The Theory and Practice of Mediation*. London: Lynne Rienner Publishers.

Bloomfield, D. (1997) *Peacemaking Strategies in Northern Ireland: Building Complementarity in Conflict Management Theory*. London: Macmillan Press – now Palgrave Macmillan.

Botes, J. and Mitchell, C. (1995) 'Constraints on Third Party Flexibility'. *The Annals of the American Academy of Political and Social Science*, Vol. 542, pp. 168–84.

Cohen, R. (1996) 'Cultural Aspects of International Mediation'. In Bercovitch, J. (ed.), *Resolving International Conflicts: The Theory and Practice of Mediation*. London: Lynne Rienner Publishers.

Colosi, T. (1986) 'The Iceberg Principle: Secrecy in Negotiation'. In Bendahmane, D. and McDonald, J. (eds), *Perspectives on Negotiation: Four Case Studies and Interpretations*. Washington, DC: Center for the Study of Foreign Affairs.

Corbin, J. (1994) *Gaza First: The Secret Norway Channel to Peace Between Israel and the PLO*. London: Bloomsbury.

Eban, A. (1983) *The New Diplomacy – International Affairs in the Modern Age*. New York: Random House.

Fisher, R. (1995) 'Pacific, Impartial Third-Party Intervention in International Conflict: A Review and an Analysis'. In Vasquez, J. A., Johnson, J. T., Jaffe, S. and Stamato, L., *Beyond Confrontation: Learning Conflict Resolution in the Post-Cold War Era*. The University of Michigan Press.

Fisher, R. J. and Keashly, L. (1988) 'Third Party Interventions in Intergroup Conflict: Consultation is Not Mediation'. *Negotiation Journal*, Vol. 4, pp. 381–93.

Groom, A. J. R. (1988) 'Paradigms in Conflict: The Strategist, the Conflict Researcher and the Peace Researcher'. *Review of International Studies*, Vol. 14, pp. 97–115.

Hampson, F. O. (1996) *Nurturing Peace: Why Peace Settlements Succeed or Fail.* Washington, DC: The United States Institute of Peace Press.

Haass, R. (1990) *Conflict Unending.* New Haven, Conn.: Yale University Press.

Heikal, M. (1996) *Secret Channels.* London: Harper Collins.

Hirschfeld, Y. (1994) Interview. Haifa, Ramat Yishay, 4 July.

Hoffman, M. (1995) 'Defining and Evaluating Success: Facilitative Problem-Solving Workshops in an Interconnected Context'. *Paradigm: The Kent Journal of International Relations*, Vol. 2, pp. 150–67.

Inbar, P. (1996) *The Palestinians Between Terrorism and Statehood.* Brighton: Sussex Academic Press.

Institute for Palestine Studies (1994) *The Palestinian–Israeli Peace Agreement: A Documentary Record.* Washington, DC: Institute for Palestine Studies.

Juul, M. (1994) Interview. Oslo, 19 May.

Kass, I. and O'Neill, B. (1997) *The Deadly Embrace: The Impact of Israeli and Palestinian Rejectionism on the Peace Process.* Lanham: University Press of America.

Keashley, L. and Fisher, R. J. (1996) 'A Contingency Perspective on Conflict Interventions: Theoretical and Practical Considerations. In Bercovitch, J. (ed.), *Resolving International Conflicts: The Theory and Practice of Mediation.* Boulder and London: Lynne Rienner Publishers.

Kelman, H. (1992) 'Informal Mediation by the Scholar/Practitioner'. In Bercovitch, J. and Rubin, J. Z., *Mediation in International Relations: Multiple Approaches to Conflict Management.* New York: St. Martin's Press – now Palgrave Macmillan.

Kelman, H. (1995) 'Contributions of an Unofficial Conflict Resolution Effort to the Israeli–Palestinian Breakthrough'. *Negotiation Journal*, Vol. 11, pp. 19–27.

Kelman, H. (1997) 'Social–Psychological Dimensions of International Conflict'. In Zartman, I. W. and Rasmussen, J. L. (eds), *Peacemaking in International Conflict: Methods & Techniques.* Washington, DC: United States Institute of Peace.

Kleiboer, M. (1994) 'Ripeness of Conflict: A Fruitful Notion?'. *Journal of Peace Research*, Vol. 31, pp. 109–16.

Kleiboer, M. (1997) *International Mediation: The Multiple Realities of Third-Party Intervention.* London: Lynne Rienner Publishers.

Kleiboer, M. and t'Hart, P. (1995) 'Time to Talk? Multiple Perspectives on Timing of International Mediation'. *Cooperation and Conflict*, Vol. 30, No. 3, pp. 307–48.

Klieman, A. (1988) *Statecraft in the Dark: Israel's Practice of Quiet Diplomacy.* Tel Aviv: Jaffee Center for Strategic Studies.

Kriesberg, L. (1991) 'Formal and Quasi-Mediators in International Disputes: An Exploratory Analysis'. *Journal of Peace Research*, Vol. 28, pp. 19–27.

Kriesberg, L. (1996a) 'Coordinating Intermediary Peace Efforts'. *Negotiation Journal*, Vol. 12, No. 4, pp. 341–51.

Kriesberg, L. (1996b) 'Varieties of Mediating Activities and Mediators in International Relations'. In Bercovitch, J. (ed.), *Resolving International Conflicts: The Theory and Practice of Mediation.* London: Lynne Rienner Publishers.

Larsen, T. (1995) Interview. Jerusalem, 7 June.

Lax, D. and Sebenius, J. (1986) *The Manager as Negotiator: Bargaining for Cooperation and Competitive Gain.* New York: The Free Press.

Makovsky, D. (1996) *Making Peace with the PLO: The Rabin Government's Road to the Oslo Accord.* Boulder, CO and Oxford: Westview Press.

Massalha, O. (1994) *Towards the Long-Promised Peace.* London: Saqi Books.

McDonald, J. and Bendahmane, D. (1987) *Conflict Resolution: Track Two Diplomacy.* Washington, DC: Center for the Study of Foreign Affairs, Foreign Service Institute.

Mitchell, C. (1995) 'The Right Moment: Notes on Four Models of Ripeness'. *Paradigm: The Kent Journal of International Relations*, Vol. 2, pp. 35–52.

Pedersen, G. (1994) Interview. Oslo, 19 May.

Peres, S. (1994) Interview. Jerusalem, 17 July.

Peres, S. (1995) *Battling for Peace – Memoirs*. London: Weidenfeld & Nicolson.

Perry, M. (1994) *A Fire in Zion: The Israeli–Palestinian Search for Peace*. New York: William Morrow and Co.

Princen, T. (1992) *Intermediaries in International Conflict*. Princeton: Princeton University Press.

Pruitt, D. (1997) 'Ripeness Theory and the Oslo Talks'. *International Negotiation*, Vol. 2, No. 2.

Pundak, R. (1995) Interview. Tel Aviv, 8 June.

Putnam, L. L. and Carcasson, M. (1997) 'Communication and the Oslo Negotiation: Contacts, Patterns, and Modes'. *International Negotiation: A Journal of Theory and Practice*, Vol. 2, No. 2, pp. 251–78.

Raiffa, H. (1982) *The Art and Science of Negotiation*. Cambridge, MA: Harvard University Press.

Rasmussen, J. L. (1997) 'Peacemaking in the Twenty-First Century: New Rules, New Roles, New Actors'. In Zartman, I. W. and Rasmussen, J. L. (eds), *Peacemaking in International Conflict: Methods & Techniques*. Washington, DC: United States Institute of Peace.

Rothman, J. (1990) 'A Pre-Negotiation Model: Theory & Training-Project on Pre-Negotiation Summary'. *Policy Studies. Leonard Davis Institute*. No. 40.

Rouhana, N. (1995) 'Unofficial Third-Party Intervention in International Conflict: Between Legitimacy and Disarray'. *Negotiation Journal*, Vol. 11, pp. 255–70.

Rubin, B., Ginat, J. and Ma'oz, M. (1994) *From War to Peace: Arab–Israeli Relations 1973–1993*. Brighton: Sussex Academic Press.

Rubin, J. Z. (1991) 'The Timing of Ripeness and the Ripeness of Timing'. In Kriesberg, L. and Thorson, S. T. (eds), *Timing the De-Escalation of International Conflicts*. Syracuse: Syracuse University Press.

Rubin, J. Z. (1992) 'Conclusion: International Mediation in Context'. In Bercovitch, J. and Rubin, J. Z., *Mediation in International Relations: Multiple Approaches to Conflict Management*. New York: St. Martin's Press – now Palgrave Macmillan.

Rupesinghe, K. (1996) 'Mediation in Internal Conflicts: Lessons from Sri Lanka'. In Bercovitch, J. (ed.), *Resolving International Conflicts: The Theory and Practice of Mediation*. London: Lynne Rienner Publishers.

Said, E. (1995) *Peace & Its Discontents. Gaza–Jericho 1993–1995*. London: Vintage.

Savir, U. (1994) Interview. Jerusalem, 3 July.

Shaath, N. (1993) 'The Oslo Agreement: A Interview with Nabil Shaath'. *Journal of Palestinian Studies*, Vol. 23, No. 1, pp. 5–13.

Singer, J. (1994) Interview. Jerusalem, 30 June.

Stedman, S. (1991) *Peacemaking in Civil War: International Mediation in Zimbabwe 1974–1980*. London: Lynne Rienner Publishers.

Stein, J. (ed.) (1989) *Getting to the Table: The Processes of International Prenegotiation*. Baltimore: The Johns Hopkins University Press.

Stenelo, L.-G. (1972) *Mediation in International Negotiations*. Lund: Studentlitteratur.

Stoltenberg, T. (1996) Interview. Lund, 20 November.

Thompson, K. W. (1965) 'The New Diplomacy and the Quest for Peace'. *International Organization*, Vol. 19, pp. 394–409.

Webb, K., Koutrakou, V. and Walters, M. (1996) 'The Yugoslavian Conflict, European Mediation, and the Contingency Model: A Critical Perspective'. In Bercovitch, J. (ed.), *Resolving International Conflicts: The Theory and Practice of Mediation*. London: Lynne Rienner Publishers.

Wolfsfeld, G. (1997) *Media and Political Conflict: News From the Middle East*. Cambridge: Cambridge University Press.

Värynen, T. (1995) 'Going Beyond Similarity: The Role of the Facilitator in Problem-Solving Workshop Conflict Resolution'. *Paradigm: The Kent Journal of International Relations*, Vol. 2, pp. 71–85.

Zartman, I. W. (1986) 'Ripening Conflict, Ripe Moment, Formula, and Mediation'. In Bendahmane, D. and McDonald, J. (eds), *Perspectives on Negotiation: Four Case Studies and Interpretations*. Washington, DC: Center for the Study of Foreign Affairs.

Zartman, I. W. (1989) *Ripe for Resolution*. New York: Oxford University Press.

Zartman, I. W. (ed.) (1995) *Elusive Peace: Negotiating an End to Civil Wars*. Washington, DC: The Brookings Institution.

Zartman, I. W. (1997) 'Explaining Oslo'. *International Negotiation: A Journal of Theory and Practice*, Vol. 2, No. 2, pp. 195–215.

Zartman, I. W. and Berman, M. (1982) *The Practical Negotiator*. New Haven, CT: Yale University Press.

Zartman, I. W. and Touval, S. (1989) 'Mediation in International Conflicts'. In Kressel, K., Pruitt, D. G. and Associates (eds), *Mediation Research: The Process and Effectiveness of Third Party Intervention*. San Francisco: Jossey-Bass Publishers.

Zartman, I. W. and Touval, S. (1996) 'International Mediation in the Post-Cold War Era'. In Crocker, C. A., Hampson, F. O. and All, P. (eds), *Managing Global Chaos: Sources and Responses to International Conflict*. Washington, DC: United States Institute of Peace Press.

Østerud, Ø. (1995) 'Between Realism and Crusader Diplomacy – Correlates of the Norwegian Channel to Jericho'. Working Paper 02. Department of Political Science, University of Oslo.

5
Mediation by Regional Organizations: the OAU in Chad and Congo

I. William Zartman[1]

Introduction

Regional organizations are in a difficult position in regard to the mediation of disputes among their members. While they are collective defense organizations toward the outside world, they are also collective security institutions within their own membership (Wolfers, 1962). In both areas, they operate with the broad authority of the collectivity, mobilizing the community of their members in dealing with conflict according to norms that all have adopted. But this characteristic also creates an important ambiguity. In disputes within the community, member-states have a primary interest in capturing its flag for their side of the dispute. Since such organizations are above all meeting places for sovereign states, and much less corporate entities in their own right, they are under pressure from their own members to endorse rather than to mediate. Thus, the conflict management activities of a regional organization embody all the contradictory elements of the current debate over the role of institutions in the anarchic world of international politics (Kratochwil and Ruggie, 1986; Rochester, 1986; Keohane, 1998).

This situation has important implications. It means that the basic questions of interest and leverage which are the key to the understanding and the practice of mediation have to be answered in terms of the member states, not in terms of an organization (Touval and Zartman, 1985, 1989, 2001). It also means that the question of *whether* to mediate becomes more important than the question of *how* to mediate. Members of the organization continue to have two prior questions to decide: whether to take sides, as the contesting parties clamor for it to do, and then, if they decide not to take sides, whether to bid the organization to sit it out on the sidelines in safe neutrality or to intervene actively as a mediator.

In addition, the latter decision is further complicated by another role of regional organizations, that of enunciating norms and principles which will help define stable outcomes, a role that is often halfway between partisanship and neutrality (Thompson and Zartman, 1975; Foltz and Widner, 1984; Zartman, 1991). International organizations to structure the relations among newly sovereign states in the developing regions of the world tend to find an important part of their *raison d'être* in the establishment of principles such as sovereign equality, frontier inviolability (*uti possidetis juris*), non-interference in internal affairs, and non-condemnation of fellow members, leaving the individual states to use these principles to justify their own particular positions in a dispute. These norms then form the basis for both endorsement and mediation, often giving ambiguous guidance between the two.

Mediation takes place when it is perceived by both the mediator and the disputants to be in their respective interests, and then when the mediator is able to generate a prospective outcome that is both relatively and absolutely attractive to the parties, that is, that is more attractive than the perceived stalemate in which they find themselves and attractive enough to meet their minimum or redefined goals (Freeman, 1997: 163–70). Regional organizations undertake to mediate when their members see it in their interest to do so rather than taking sides or staying neutral; it must be remembered that 'regional organizations' means 'the individual sovereign state members acting to authorize regional organizations'. Thus, the decision will be based on the sum of the *members'* self-interests combined with their judgment between two conflicting interests for the self-preservation of the organization: whether reconciling parties to a conflict is worth the risk of offending conflicting members of the organization. When so authorized to act, institutions do matter, since they can then – but only then – mobilize impressive moral pressure and political skill.

Parties' interest in being reconciled, in turn, depends on the attractiveness of the proposed solution but also on the importance of relations with the mediator. The second is an important ingredient in the mediation calculation and one that has only recently been given attention (Touval and Zartman, 1985; Mitchell, 1988). It is also an element in the mediator's leverage. Unfortunately (for mediation), this element of interest is not very compelling in the case of regional organizations. The mediator is more interested in the continued support of the parties, on which its existence depends, as already noted, than the parties are in the organization's good will, a concept that has little meaning. Only when the individual members, either of the whole organization or of its mediation committee, put their own relations with the conflicting parties on the line, is there an interest factor pulling the parties to accept mediation.

Similarly, the sources of leverage of a regional organization are limited. Such sources are four: the ability to provide a solution, shifting weight (relations with the parties), persuasion, and side payments (Zartman and Touval, 2001). The first two have been discussed. Persuasion is a function of the communications skills of the mediating individuals and hence is quite independent of the organization itself. Side payments are generally prohibited by both the regulations and the budget of the organization. Thus, except for the general stamp of approval that the organization brings, if its members decide to launch it on the mediating course, the regional organization has little to bring to mediation that a group of member states cannot do, acting on their own.

The following chapter will examine one such organization – the OAU – operating in two cases – the rebellion in Chad, a member state, and the associated territorial dispute with Libya, another member state, from 1977 to 1986, and the electoral violence in Congo–Brazzaville, which also involved neighboring states, in 1993–94 and 1997. Not all the details of the larger or smaller case will be applicable to all other regional organizations and their own mediation efforts, of course, but the African case in its broad outlines and in many specific characteristics is a relevant subject for analysis and lessons (see also Bipoun-Woum, 1984; Pittman, 1984; Wiseman, 1984; Zartman, 1985; Zartman and Vogeli, 2000).

Mediation in the OAU

The OAU was essentially created as a security community designed to enhance the maintenance of non-violent relations within the African region and thereby protect each state from the other. The compromise which resulted in the founding of the OAU in 1963 largely favored the 'statists' over the 'unionists', and the principles which evolved consecrated the primacy of independence over unity as an African value (Cervenka, 1969; Woronoff, 1970; Wolfers, 1976; Zartman, 1987: ch. 1; Pondi, 1990). The first five of the seven OAU principles are devoted to the sanctity and the preservation of state sovereignty and independence. In pursuit of conditions of peace and security, the Charter of the OAU imposes on member states the adherence to the principle of 'peaceful settlement of disputes by negotiation, mediation, conciliation or arbitration'. The Charter further establishes a 'Commission of Mediation, Conciliation and Arbitration' to resolve interstate disputes in Africa as one of the four principal institutions of the OAU alongside the Assembly of Heads of State and Government, the Council of Ministers and the General Secretariat (Elias, 1964; Amate, 1986: ch. 5). The OAU is therefore entrusted with the primary and explicit mandate to eliminate, reduce or control conflict among its members, and this mandate constitutes one of the members' interests in the organization.

The emphasis on the critical norms of sovereignty and independence, however, also imposed limitations on constitutional power for the organization's intervention in regional conflicts. The very principle which the OAU is created to defend – the sovereignty of its members – prevents it from conducting that defense effectively. The organization is devoid of any coercive powers for conflict management and the maintenance of peaceful interstate relations. Although Article VI of the Charter provides that member states pledge themselves to observe scrupulously the OAU norms, the Charter is silent on what happens should any of the provisions of this pledge be flouted by a member state. There is no mention of collective measures against an offending state and, only in the late 1990s, suspended the voting rights of members deeply in arrears with their dues. The OAU is even denied the ultimate sanction of expelling a recalcitrant member.

The supreme organ of the OAU, the Assembly of Heads of State and Government (the Summit) has the primary responsibility and the ultimate authority to resolve disputes and conflicts which threaten the peace and security of the region. The Commission of Mediation, Conciliation and Arbitration established in a separate protocol at its first summit in Cairo in July 1964 in consequence of Article XIX was never staffed and never functioned, and was eventually replaced by *ad hoc* mediation committees from among the Assembly's membership, as allowed by Rule 37 of the Assembly's rules of procedure. An initiative in the late 1970s to revive the Commission collapsed as well (Amate, 1986: 163ff; Kanto, 1990: 40f). Twenty years after the founding of the Organization, a new 14-member Mechanism was established to take decisions between summits on issues of conflict and intervention (Amoo, 1994). Between 1999 and 2002, the OAU converted itself into an African Union (AU) with basically the same institutions, including a peace and security council to replace the Mechanism.

In addition to establishing *ad hoc* mediatory bodies, the Assembly (now Conference of Head of States) plays important roles in the management of regional conflicts. The Body's formal role usually begins at its summits where an aggrieved state, party or an ally would lodge a complaint against a member state and lobby for its inclusion in the summit's agenda. This is usually followed by a debate in the plenary which almost always circumvents the merits of the respective positions of the parties, and thereby avoids the need to apportion blame or identify the guilty party. The summit concludes the debate with a resolution which represents the general consensus, and enunciates principles of legitimate behavior in a particular conflict situation.

Its ruling on what is legitimate or otherwise in these circumstances may have three identifiable results (Snyder, 1972: 221; Butterworth, 1978: 6; Touval, 1982: 8): (1) it narrows the area of uncertainty in disputes which may precipitate conflicts; (2) it influences in a predictable and positive manner the behavior of the parties in the conflict environment; and (3) it helps clarify the general bargaining setting and, consequently, facilitates the negotiation process.

The Assembly is often more effective in managing regional conflicts through a process described by Alger (1961) as the non-resolution consequences of international organization. The Assembly's regular sessions furnish opportunities for heads of state (or their representatives) in conflict to meet without loss of face or bargaining position. The presence of other heads of state means that there are numerous potentially helpful third parties readily available to assist in bringing conflicting colleagues together (Meyers, 1974). The summits also foster a congenial atmosphere for communication and legitimize individual mediators in regional conflicts. The sense of solidarity and the fraternal atmosphere which usually prevail at summits also constitute a catalyst which helps conflicting parties to justify concessions and rationalize retreat – 'in the spirit of African solidarity and unity'. The convention of off-the-record intervisitation among heads of state and delegation at summits, in camera meetings and numerous social gatherings where the news media are barred, are all propitious for conflict management.

In Africa as in most of the developing world where rule tends to be personalized, foreign policy is more often a function of individual leadership than institutions or national interests. Interstate conflicts may result from personal antagonism between leaders and competition on the African or subregional political scene. The Assembly's summits offer an ideal venue for such privately motivated interstate conflicts to be resolved. By extension, they also empower the Secretary General and his special representative or heads of state – especially the OAU President of the year – to perform personal diplomacy between sessions.

OAU mediation in the Libya/Chad conflict

Libya had designs on Chad well before Qadhdhafi thrust himself onto the African political scene and attempted to absorb his southern neighbor. (See Decalo, 1980; Thompson and Adloff, 1981; Neuberger, 1982; Pittman, 1984; Zartman, 1986.) At the beginning of the twentieth century Ottoman and later Italian rulers attempted to enlarge their sphere of influence southward; Italy obtained the 3,700-square-mile Aouzou strip from northern Chad in a 1935 treaty, but it was never ratified and the current boundary was reaffirmed upon Libyan independence in 1951. In 1954, the troops of King Idris Sanusi attempted to occupy the Aouzou strip but were repulsed by French troops.

From the late 1960s onward, two sets of developments facilitated and intensified Libyan threat to absorb Chad. The first occurred within Chad. The French withdrew their administrators from the north region, Boukou–Ennedi–Tibetsi (BET) only in 1965, five years after independence, to be replaced by ill-trained Chadian administrators from the southern Sara tribe, and the resultant northern rebellion and civil war led to implosion, disintegration and state collapse. The second set of developments was presented by the arrival of a new Libyan leadership with revolutionary zeal, ambitions and resources to pursue them. Qadhdhafi's pan-Islamic vision to consolidate political power under Libya's guidance in the Muslim Sahel belt of Africa, his hopes of gaining access to the uranium deposits in northern Chad, and his ambition to turn Libya into a major regional power using Chad in central Africa as a stepping stone to the heart of the continent set up the conflict. The Libya/Chad conflict was thus a product of the convergence of geopolitical opportunity and ambition.

After 1966 under Idris and after 1969 under Qadhdhafi, Libya was the major supporter of Chad's Muslim rebels, furnishing the latter with money, arms, sanctuaries and staging areas. Following an attempted coup against Tombalbaye in 1971, Chad promptly severed diplomatic relations with Libya. In retaliation, Libya officially recognized the National Liberation Front of Chad (FroLiNaT) in September 1971 as the 'only legitimate representative of the people of Chad', allowed FroLiNaT to open offices in Tripoli, and built FroLiNaT's army into a large well-equipped force, and then occupied the Aouzou strip in 1973. In April 1975, Tombalbaye was ousted in a coup d'etat and replaced by a Sara General Felix Malloum, who vehemently denounced Libya's annexation of the Aouzou strip and its support to the FroLiNaT, particularly the faction under Goukouni Weddeye. With Libyan troops and armored units, Goukouni's faction trounced the Chadian national army and captured most of the BET region in July 1977. Malloum for the first time lodged a complaint against Libya with the OAU at the Libreville summit in July 1977. The summit's response was to appoint an Ad Hoc Committee (comprising Gabon, Algeria, Mozambique, Nigeria, Senegal and Cameroon) to mediate the conflict. The only action taken by the Committee was a recommendation in Libreville on 10 August 1977 counselling moderation by the two parties.

By the beginning of 1978, FroLiNaT with open and massive Libyan support captured Faya Largeau, capital of the BET, and pushed south. Chad complained of Libya's aggression to the United Nation Security Council on 6 February 1978. Within a few days, however, confronted with an imminent defeat of his army, Malloum withdrew his complaint from the UN, and succumbed to 'mediation' by Libya and Sudan, in two peace conferences between FroLiNaT leaders and Malloum in Sebha and Benghazi in February and March 1978. The Benghazi Accords of 27 March 1978 stipulated withdrawal of all French forces; formal recognition of FroLiNaT; immediate ceasefire to be supervised by officers from Libya and Niger; appointment of Niger, Sudan, and Libya as guarantors of the agreement; Libyan promises of a financial aid to Chad; and Libyan readiness to initiate negotiations on the border issue. The Benghazi accords amounted to Chadian submission to Libya as a satellite state, legitimizing Libyan military presence in Chad as a guarantor of the accords.

The Benghazi accords, however, collapsed within a month. The conflict was again on the agenda for the next OAU summit held in Khartoum in mid-July 1978, where a new Ad Hoc Committee (Sudan, Cameroon, Niger and Nigeria) continued its mediation. No blame was apportioned, no party was condemned. The situation changed in February 1979 by the defeat of Malloum's regime by the FroLiNaT faction led by Hissene Habre, Goukouni's longstanding rival, transforming the conflict from a north–south dispute into a struggle for power among the Muslim leaders from the north.

From 1979 onward, Nigeria took over the OAU initiatives which were legitimized, in turn, because they were pursued in the framework of the OAU mediation. From March to August 1979, Nigeria hosted four reconciliatory conferences on Chad under the auspices of the OAU. Libya attended all the four conferences as part of the OAU mediatory team which included members of the Ad Hoc Committee and the neighboring countries of Chad. From the collapse of Malloum's regime in 1979 till the establishment of the northern regime under Habre in June 1982, the OAU largely treated the Chadian conflict as a civil war and pursued its regional intervention accordingly. The Libya/Chad issue took a backstage. Chad had collapsed as a state, there was no effective government, and Qadhdhafi had in fact become a kingmaker among the Chadian factions.

Qadhdhafi, however, eventually overplayed his hand. The OAU-sponsored peace conferences among the factions and the paper agreements which the conferences spawned failed to produce any movement toward the solution of the civil war. The conflict in fact continued to deteriorate as Weddeye and Habre waged a bitter war for the capital, N'Djamena. Toward the end of 1980, Qadhdhafi's troops mounted a large-scale intervention in support of Goukouni. In a concerted anti-Habre campaign, Libya and its clients put Habre's troops to rout from N'Djamena by the end of December 1980. The Libyan intervention intensified ideological cleavages within the OAU. Fourteen African countries suspended normal diplomatic relations with Libya because of the latter's subversive activities in the region.

Against this background, a conference was organized by the OAU Ad Hoc Committee in Lagos on 23–24 December 1980. Participants were sharply divided over how to handle Libya's intervention in Chad; in the end some refused to sign the final communique because it did not go far enough in condemning Libya's involvement. Instead, on 6 January 1981, Libya and Chad announced their decision for a merger of the two countries, immediately incurring the furor of most African states. Presidents of 12 African states met in Lome on 14 January 1981, under the chairmanship of Sierra Leonean President Siaka Stevens, the current president of the OAU, to conclude on a nine-point communique strongly condemning the Libya/Chad merger and calling on Libya to withdraw all its forces from Chad (Report of the Secretary General on Chad, 6–11 June 1983; OAU Document AHG/109 [XIX]).

Galvanized by Libya's intervention, African leaders resolved at their 18th Summit in Nairobi in June 1981 to implement their decision taken at the

Lagos peace conference on Chad two years earlier to send in peacekeeping forces. The two conditions they demanded for the dispatch of OAU forces were formal invitation from Weddeye's government and withdrawal of Libyan troops. Under strong pressure from the OAU, Weddeye requested that Libya withdraw its troops from N'Djamena and surrounding areas immediately, and from the rest of Chadian territory by the end of 1981. Qadhdhafi, unwilling to jeopardize his chances of becoming the next president of the OAU, decided to withdraw from the entire territory by November. By 8 January 1982, the OAU had deployed its peacekeeping troops in Chad with a Nigerian General, Geoffrey Ejiga, as force commander (Pelkovits, 1983; Wiseman, 1984).

As soon as the peacekeeping mission became operational it encountered immense problems. The first was logistic and financial. The transportation and general logistics for the Senegalese contingent of the Force were borne by France, and the US committed $12 million for logistic help to the Zairian and Nigerian contingents. But this assistance amounted to a pittance in relation to the estimated cost of $192 million for the first year of operations. There was no way the OAU could finance a project of such magnitude given the Organization's perennial financial problems (Report of the External Auditors on the Accounts of the OAU for the 1985 Financial Year, February 1986, OAU Document CM/1408 [XLV]). A request to the UN Security Council for financial, material and technical assistance for the peacekeeping mission only elicited a Security Council resolution (UNSC/R 504, 30 April 1982) calling for voluntary contributions.

The second set of problems encountered by the peacekeeping mission was the lack of cooperation from the Chadian factions. They failed to appreciate the neutral interpository role of the peacekeeping force and were uninterested in a negotiated settlement. Habre routed Goukouni's force from N'Djamena on 7 June 1982, and set up a new Chadian government, while Goukouni fled to Cameroon. In spite of Habre's request to the OAU to maintain its peacekeeping mission in Chad and pursue its original mandate, President Arap Moi of Kenya, the current president of the OAU, ordered the immediate termination of the mission and withdrawal of troops by 30 June 1982.

There was not, however, a complete return to peace in Chad. Qadhdhafi, rebuffed by the OAU's denial of its presidency, embarked on a renewed military campaign in Chad, using GouKouni as a proxy. Habre's government complained both to the UN Security Council and the OAU about Libya's aggression against Chad and its occupation of the Aouzou Strip. The OAU responded with the reactivation of its Ad Hoc Committee on the Chad/ Libya dispute, whose call for a ceasefire in August 1983 was rejected by Chad. Successive OAU presidents rose to mediate. First, Ethiopian president Mengistu Haile Miriam called a meeting of 'all factions' in December 1983, later changed to a meeting between 'Government and opposition leaders' in January 1984, but Habre boycotted when Goukouni was received with too much status in Ethiopia. Then, Congolese president Sassou Nguesso, ideologically a bit more neutral than Mengistu, was entrusted by the OAU with mediation on behalf of the Ad Hoc Committee in two meetings in Brazzaville in 1984 and a third in Loubomo in March 1986 in the presence of the new OAU president, Senegalese president Abdou Diouf; all three were abortive. At the 1986 summit, Nguesso became OAU president and he took up the Chadian problem with increased authority, but to no avail. The Ad Hoc Committee was newly chaired by President Omar Bongo of Gabon (who had been converted to Islam by Qadhdhafi), but he resigned when Qadhdhafi refused to attend a reconciliation meeting. Habre, in the meantime, had negotiated the return of many of Goukouni's allies, often making them ministers in his government. Goukouni himself developed a spat with Qadhdhafi, left Libya, and began wandering around Africa, seeking a return to Chad but never able to find acceptable conditions for it, despite the efforts of nearly a dozen heads of state as mediators, each seeking to improve slightly on the deal that another had proposed (Zartman, 1989b: 13f).

The 1986 Summit also heard the proposal that the Aouzou Strip issue be taken to the World Court, a proposition echoed by the Ad Hoc Committee but rejected by many heads of state who saw a political reconciliation as the only way to a solution. When the Chadian army siezed the offensive in 1987, pushed the Libyans out of Chad and even momentarily retook the Aouzou Strip, the current OAU president, Kenneth Kaunda of Zambia, arranged a ceasefire on 11 September 1987. Qadhdhafi offered a peace treaty, a mediation of the dispute between Habre and Goukouni, and a renewal of diplomatic relations, at the 1988 OAU Summit, with an agreement that if the political reconciliation did not resolve the Aouzou dispute after a year, the issue would be taken to the International Court of Justice. All of these eventualities took place; and the Court upheld the Chadian position in 1994. The ironic turn of a truly Byzantine conflict is that the inclusion of all factions in the Chadian government proved too much for the political system to handled with rewards, and a tribal plot in April 1989 was played out to a eventual overthrow of Habre in December 1990, with Libyan support.

OAU mediation in the Congo–Brazzaville conflicts

Since its independence in 1960, despite a quarter-century of Marxist single party rule under the Congolese Workers' Party (PCT), Congo suffered almost biennial coup attempts, five of them successful, and bloody retribution followed afterward. The fifth successful coup brought authoritarian stability from 1979 to 1991 under Denis Sassou Nguesso. When the single-party rule collapsed at the beginning of the 1990s, the violence in Congo was over big stakes – control of the new competitive pluralist political system that emerged (on this case, see Zartman and Vogeli, 2000).

The wave of democratizations sweeping through French-speaking Africa was spearheaded by sovereign national conferences (CNS) in which civil society seized sovereignty and reorganized government; Congo opened its own CNS in March–June 1991 to end the power monopoly of the PCT. A new constitution was adopted by referendum on 15 March 1992, followed by five rounds of elections, beginning at the municipal level in May. These elections, however, were stained with fraud and violent protests and were marked by the transformation of the new multiparty system into ethnoregional parties. The two rounds of the national assembly elections in June and July produced no clear majority and a need for government by coalition. In between the two rounds, the opposition again claimed fraud and called for civil disobedience.

The two rounds of presidential elections in August brought a clear victory for Pascal Lissouba in the first round over past president Sassou Nguesso and in the runoffs over perennial opponent Bernard Kolelas. Within weeks, the alliance between Lissouba's Pan-African Union for Social Democracy (UPADS) and Sassou's PCT fell apart over the allocation of cabinet seats, and the PCT joined forces with its old enemy, Kolelas, to form an opposition majority. Faced with a vote of no-confidence in his government, Lissouba dissolved the assembly on 17 November and called new elections.

Robbed of its parliament and in danger of losing its majority, the opposition again called for popular resistance and took to the streets. The new general elections of May and June 1993 produced the same violent reaction from the opposition, particularly since the results showed them to be losing their majority; international observers were much more positive about the free and fair quality of the elections, showing that the electoral mores and practices had improved over the year of democratization.

At this point, an array of national and international mediators swung into action. On the request of the new prime minister, Gen. Joachim Yhombi-Opango, Congo turned in July to the OAU, where Secretary-General Salim Ahmed Salim proposed to test the newly authorized Mechanism for Conflict Prevention, Management and Resolution by nominating a personal representative and sending three names to the Congolese principals. Both sides unanimously chose former OAU deputy secretary-general Mohammed Sahnoun, who then invited neighboring Gabonese president Omar Bongo – member of the same tribe as Lissouba and father-in-law of Sasso – to become involved, as the only figure with enough authority and close ties to both sides to bring them together. Bongo invited the parties to meet under the auspices of the OAU in Libreville, where a Franco-African conference of foreign ministers was taking place.

At the same time, local mediator Gen. Damase NGollo was able to secure a ceasefire between the presidential and opposition groups, who finally signed a communiqué pledging to dismantle barricades, disarm and disband militias, and end looting and property destruction. They then boarded Bongo's plane and arrived in Libreville on 29 July. There Sahnoun shuttled back and forth between the two groups in different hotels, while Bongo and French Minister Michel Roussin and their teams offered good offices. After a week of tough proximity talks, the Libreville Accord was finally signed on 4 August 1993.

The conflicting groups agreed to submit the contentious election results from the first round for arbitration by an international jury of seven judges – three from Europe named by the European Union and by France, and three from Africa, named by the OAU and Gabon, and headed by Sikhe Camara, representing the OAU. The second round of elections was to be held again, under the supervision of an international election committee chaired by Mamadou Ba as the representative of the OAU. Except for the contested districts, the results of the first round of the elections were ratified. The OAU and its new Mechanism for the Prevention, Management and Resolution of Conflicts in Africa were reinforced and created a precedent for future involvement in intra-state conflicts; in turn they gave the Libreville Accord a broader legitimacy.

Bongo and Sahnoun complemented each other, with the president's family ties and presidential prestige fitting well with envoy's diplomatic skill and institutional prestige, and French pressure backing them both. In sum, the successful mediation appears to have had three components: a large supporting nest of international efforts to convince the parties that violent confrontation had reached a point of diminishing returns, specific proposals and persuasive arguments by a few key actors, and an independent realization by the parties that they had more to gain by reconciling and cooperating than by fighting for total control.

But the peace of 1994 was not to last. The next presidential elections were to take place on 27 July 1997, with the same principal candidates as five years previous. Sassou Nguesso had been biding his time, building support for a return, while Lissouba enjoyed the advantage of incumbency and the frustration of having seen two of his five years in office wasted in conflict. But the conflict was larger than the egos of the contenders, for its real dynamic came from the uncontrolled groups of followers, the militia, who were not disbanded as the 1994 agreement had required. Violence on the campaign trail in early June 1997 sparked open civil war in the capital.

International and national mediation efforts joined together in Libreville under the auspices of Bongo on 15 June. Joined again by Sahnoun, then the special representative of the UN and OAU secretaries-general for the region, Bongo arranged terms including prolongation of a ceasefire, joint patrols and progressive removal of barricades. The mediators held nine hours of proximity talks in Libreville on 16 June, but when the departure of the French forces evacuating foreign nationals from the airport was announced, the same day, the parties left Libreville to continue the combat.

Operation Pelican flew away on 16–21 June, its evacuation mission completed, despite requests to the contrary by the mediators.

The battle for the airport and competing domestic mediations continued and then slowly stalled, while Bongo and Sahnoun pursued their efforts. The operative element to an agreement remained a 1,000–2,000-man peace-keeping force which the mediators proposed to the UN Security Council, with support on 21 June from UN Secretary-General Kofi Annan; African states (Niger, Senegal, Togo) plus Bangladesh pledged their military participation. Meeting on 3 July, the Security Council hesitated, asking for a further report from the special representative.

Bongo and Sahnoun obtained another ceasefire on 5 July, and again on 14 July; negotiations progressed, turning to the details of the new elections before the end of August but stumbling on the designation of a prime minister. With signatures on a ceasefire but uncontrolled militias continuing sporadic shelling across an unmoving battle line, the mediators and parties agreed that an interposition force placed in time between the ceasefire and the general peace agreement was the key to a settlement. The new Libreville proposal was for an Inter-African Force of 700 men for six months, costing only $15 million; Bongo obtained a promise from Senegal of 500 men and the commanding officer, while Botswana and Namibia pledged the remainder of the force. Former French Prime Minister Michel Rocard, member of the European Parliament, called in by Bongo, obtained pledges of financing from various members of the European Union, but the European Council of Ministers on 23 July ran up against the need for UN Security Council authorization for an international peacekeeping force.

Instead, the Security Council rebuffed the Inter-African proposal. While the parties were straining at their ceasefire, marking time and awaiting a UN decision, the mediators were told by US representatives that the cost was out of the question, and the Security Council on 8 August finally decided that neither a peacekeeping force nor lesser measures were 'viable options' at that time. Both Rocard and Sahnoun have indicated that the time was ripe and the stalemated parties ready, and that a small force at a tiny cost (in international terms) would have ended the conflict.

Mediation by Bongo and Sahnoun continued, however, despite the fact that it was hard to keep Lissouba's attention with the distraction of a potential and more favorable mediator in the person of Laurent Kabila in Kinshasa. On 20 August the fourth peace plan was issued from Libreville. Lissouba rejected it, and instead formed his own new government of national unity with Kolelas as prime minister. At the beginning of September, he traveled to France, only to be refused audience by the French president, premier, foreign minister and cooperation minister, and in a telephone conversation with President Chirac was advised to take on Sasso Nguesso as prime minister.

Continuing the mediation and to counter Kinshasa, a regional summit was held in Libreville on 14 September with the heads of state with close relations with France, from Togo, Benin, Central Africa, Chad and Cameroun, along with Bongo and Sahnoun, to establish a new ceasefire and peace plan. Instead of attending, Lissouba visited Kabila, but with neither diplomatic nor military results. On the ground, the fighting stalemated again, with the more populous South in government hands and the North consolidated under Sasso's control.

With extraordinary tenacity, equalled only by the persistence of the blocked but bloody shelling, Bongo and Sahnoun continued to work on a peace plan and ceasefire. On 26 September, Sahnoun again asked for a peacekeeping force as the last chance, only to be told that a permanent ceasefire was a necessary precondition and the US would not support any expenditures for the purpose. The new peace proposal was delivered to the rivals the next day, and Lissouba found its proposals for a presidential council and multiparty technical commissions acceptable. On 9 October Sasso Nguesso initialed the peace plan and ceasefire, finally bringing both parties into agreement to end the conflict.

Preventive diplomacy was at the end of its rope, however, cut off by new developments on the battlefield. The day after bilateral agreement on the peace plan, Sasso's 'Cobras' broke the four months' military deadlock in Brazzaville and took the presidential palace. On 14 October, as the 'Cobras' completed the takeover of Brazzaville, they were joined by Angolan troops in an attack on the main cities at the mouth of the river and Pointe Noire, the oil capital. The operation was completed in two days. International intervention had indeed ended the fighting, but by providing a victory for the challenger over the elected president, not as a mediation.

Conclusions

The OAU's interventions in the Libya/Chad and Congo events are instructive because they touch so many facets of conflict – interstate, interethnic, interfactional, with the three impinging on each other. It is this multiplicity of conflicts in single cases that is perhaps their most striking characteristic, since the common belief, enhanced by the myths of the organizations themselves, is that regional organizations' mediation never dares reach inside the state and touch internal affairs. Regional organizations, in their manner, can mediation any type of dispute, as long as the mediation is useful to the parties looking for some acceptable way out of their conflict. And that is the basic element of any mediator's leverage (Zartman and Touval, 2001).

The second element of success in any type of mediation is the parties' perception of a mutually hurting stalemate, which makes it possible for the mediator to be welcome with his offer of a way out of the conflict (Zartman, 1989a: ch. 6). Such a stalemate was not clearly present in the Chadian conflict. It was present on a number of occasions in 1993 and 1997 in Congo, so that the unwillingness of the UN Security Council to take advantage of it was particularly irresponsible. Without the objective evidence of a stalemate that is uncomfortable to both sides, mediation is doomed. Even with objective evidence, the mediator's job is to bring the parties to perceive realities. Both elements are necessary, neither is sufficient: Stalemate makes mediation possible, mediation makes stalemate fruitful.

The third element is support from the outside community of states. The agents of regional organizations have limited resources for mediation and their fragile exercise relies on supplemental assistance from other actors within the organization and from external actors as well. Their work can be undone from a number of sides: from competing mediators offering a slightly better deal, from potential holders of the peace who do not reinforce a ceasefire when necessary, and from external sources of power who tip the delicate balance between the parties during the negotiations. Against such interferences in its work the regional organization and its agents are powerless, despite their dedicated energies, and they can only watch their efforts unravel before their eyes.

The two cases demonstrate the strengths and weaknesses of the OAU/AU as a mediator in regional conflicts, attributes that are typical of any regional organization. The body's major strengths lie in its moral authority and regional salience. The inclusive membership of the OAU, the ethos of Pan-Africanism, the reaction against a common history of exploitation, and the normative principle of African solidarity give the organization the prominence and uniqueness which make it the natural place toward which African states turn in times of conflict.

But what they find is an organization that is unable to resolve their conflicts because instead they have asked it to preserve their independence against any conceivable threats, even its own. Yet the same members have a strong interest in keeping the organization alive, for that same reason. Therefore, acting as individuals in the name of member states, they pick up the mediation function which was assigned to the organization but without any of the sources of leverage that a more collective approach would afford them. The most institutionalized form the OAU can produce is a powerless *ad hoc* committee and a prestigious but weak annual president, to which has been added in the 1990s a special representative of the active but circumscribed secretary-general. These agencies are left with only the raw rhetoric of persuasion at their disposal, the other sources of leverage in mediation being absent. They are also dependent in their operations on the interest-determined position of the individual states and their presidents, which gives them entry but which also makes them dependent on particularistic rather than on collective interests. Since the potential mediators are also interested parties in the conflict, it is their interests rather than the interests of the conflicted area that will predominate in a mediation.

The particularistic nature of the OAU's mediation efforts also raises the problem of coordination, so well illustrated by the two cases. In the mediations over Goukouni's and other dissidents' return, African heads of state stumbled all over each other in providing good offices, to the point where they continually undercut each other's efforts. The result was failure. In the second Congolese affair, the special representative's efforts were undercut by the parties' search for alternative support, either as competing mediation or as destructive intervention. *Ad hoc* committees work to some extent to mitigate this problem, since the chairman or a few members end up speaking for and with the authority of the committee and ultimately the organization. But coordination remains a problem inherent in the OAU's *modus operandi*.

African mediators tend to come from neighboring states or at least states of the same region, and from states with the same colonial background as the disputants when they are both English- or French-speaking. Mediators are also most successful if, serving as a sanctuary for an insurgency against a neighboring state, they are able to use their privileged relations to deliver the agreement of their hosted insurgents (Zartman, 1999: 520–4, 530–2). When *ad hoc* commissions are constituted, all these criteria for membership find their representation, plus the need to have other members from outside the geographic and ex-colonial region to establish a balance and maintain an entree to all the parties (Amate, 1986: esp. 18f, 164). Affinity, supply, experience, friendships and alliances combine to dictate the selection of six to eight member states who will make up the commission.

The OAU's establishment and maintenance of norms of interstate relations, and the enunciation of the principles pertinent in the negotiated settlement of a particular conflict situation help in clarifying the issues involved and the legitimacy of the positions of the parties. Libya's occupation of the Aouzou Strip contravened the regional principle of the inviolability of the borders inherited at the time of independence. In accordance with the organizational principle of respect for the sovereignty and the territorial integrity of member states, the OAU successfully reacted against external threat to Chad's existence and was part of a situation which induced strong government to appear. Unfortunately, Sasso Nguesso's challenge and ultimate seizure of power did not run up against as strongly enunciated a principle of electoral legitimacy, largely because the organization has not been as clear and outspoken about internal norms as about interstate norms. As a result, the mediation came to a crashing failure. It is hard to mediate when the underlying norms are not clear and firm.

OAU summits and other organizational meetings facilitate the patching up of disputes by fellow heads of state using their informal good offices. The successful role of Bongo in the first Congolese affair and his partial success in the second are telling examples. Most susceptible to this kind of treatment are personal squabbles, slights and problems either liable to a simple solution or requiring an initial contact to start more sustained and detailed discussions. A large number of African disputes can be reduced to these types, others cannot. The OAU is weakest when it intervenes in conflicts which demand complex negotiations and solutions, an autonomous mediating body, an effective executing agency, a collective authority and a source of deployable resources (Zartman, 1985: 20f). The Libyan/Chad and particularly the second Congolese conflicts were of the type that demanded such resources, and they were beyond the capability of the organization.

The OAU's frustrations in the Chadian and Congolese conflicts underscore the paradox which confronts regional organizations. They have the regional salience to intervene in regional conflicts, but lack the requisite broad-based political will to sustain conflict management endeavors because they are not a corporate actor. They also lack the logistical and financial resources required for intensive and effective intervention in regional conflicts. Their members are interest-driven parties to the very conflicts the organization is asked to resolve. And they can only be effective where they operate on a clear and firm normative base, which is still absent in the area of domestic conflict into which they are increasingly drawn.

Note

1. I am grateful for the collaboration of Samuel Amoo in writing the Chad case.

References

Alger, C. (1961) 'Non-Resolution Consequences of the United Nations and their Effect on International Conflicts', *Journal of Conflict Resolution*, 2: 128–45.

Amate, C. O. C. (1986) *Inside the OAU*. New York: St. Martin's Press – now Palgrave Macmillan.

Andemichael, B. (1972) *Peaceful Settlement among African States*. New York: UNITAR.

Babu-Zalé, R., Sala, K., Mye-Kulemba, J. and Malumeka, R. (1996) *Le Congo de Pascal Lissouba*. Paris: L'Harmattan.

Bercovitch, J. (1997) 'Mediation in International Conflict', in I. W. Zartman and L. Rasmussen (eds), *Peacemaking in International Conflict*. Washington, DC: US Institute of Peace.

Bipoun-Woum, J.-M. (1984) 'Role de l'OUA dans la solution des conflicts', in Association des Juristes Africains, *L'Afrique, L'OUA, et le Nouvel Ordre Juridique*. Libreville: Actes de la rencontre international de mai.

Butterworth, R. L. (1978) *Moderation from Management; International Organizations and Peace*. Pittsburgh: University of Pittsburgh Center for International Studies.

Cervenka, Z. (1969) *The Organization of African Unity and Its Charter*. New York: Praeger.

Clark, J. F. (1996) 'Transition and the Struggle to Consolidate', in J. Clark and D. Gardinier (eds), *Political Reform in Francophone Africa*. Boulder, CO: Westview Press.

Clark, J. F. (1993) 'Socio-Political Change in the Republic of Congo: Political Dilemmas of Economic Reform', *Journal of Third World Studies*, 1: 52–77 (Spring).

Clark, J. F. (1994) 'Elections, Leadership and Democracy in Congo', *Africa Today*, 3: 41–60.

Decalo, S. (1980) 'Regionalism, Political Decay and Civil Strife in Chad', *Journal of Modern African Studies*, 1: 23–56.

Elias, T. O. (1964) 'The Commission of Mediation, Conciliation and Arbitration', *British Yearbook of International Law*, 60, 336–54.

Elias, T. O. (1965) 'The Charter of the OAU', *American Journal of International Law*, 59, 2: 243–67.

El-Ayouty, Y. (ed.) (1975) *The OAU after Ten Years*. New York: Praeger.

El-Ayouty, Y. and Zartman, I. W. (eds) (1984) *The OAU after Twenty Years*. New York: Praeger.

Foltz, W. and Widner, J. (1984) 'The OAU and Southern African Liberation', in El-Ayouty and Zartman (eds) ibid.

Freeman, C. W. (ed.) (1997) *The Diplomat's Dictionary*. Washington, DC: US Institute of Peace.

Friedman, K. E. (1994) *Den magiska världsbilden: on statens frigörelse från folket i Folkrepubliken Kongo*. Stockholm: Carlssons Bokförlag.

Friedman, K. E. and Sundberg, A. (1994) 'Ethnic war and ethnic cleansing in Brazzaville'. Lund: University Dept of Social Anthropology.

Kanto, M. (1990) 'Les mutations institutionnelles de l'OUA', & 'La dynamique normative dans le cadre de l'OUA', in Kanto, Maurice et al., *L'OUA: Retrospective et Perspectives africaines*. Paris: Economica.

Keohane, R. O. (1998) 'International Institutions: Can Interdependence Work?', *Foreign Policy*, 110: 82–95 (Spring).

Kratochwil, F. and Ruggie, J. G. (1986) 'IO as an Art of the State', *International Organization*, 40, 4: 753–76 (Autumn).

Meyers, D. (1974) 'Intraregional Conflict Management by the OAU', *International Organization*, 28, 2: 345–73.

Mitchell, C. (1988) 'Motives for Mediation', in Mitchell, C. R. and Webb, K. (eds), *New Approaches to International Mediation*. New York: Greenwood.

Mokoko, J.-M. M. (1994) *Congo: Le temps du devoir*. Paris: L'Harmattan.

Neuberger, B. (1982) *Involvement, Invasion and Withdrawal: Qadhdhafi's Libya and Chad 1969–81*. Tel Aviv: Shiloah Center Studies.

Pelkovits, N. (1983) 'Peacekeeping: The African Experience', in H. Wiseman (ed.), *Peacekeeping: Appraisals and Proposals*. New York: Pergamon Press.

Pittman, D. (1984) 'The OAU in Chad', in El-Ayouty and Zartman (eds), op.cit.

Pondi, J.-E. (1990) 'L'evolution de l'ideal panafricaniste sur le continent depuis 1963', in Kanto, op.cit.

Rochester, J. M. (1986) 'The Rise and Fall of International Organization', *International Organization*, 40, 4: 777–814 (Autumn).

Snyder, G. H. (1972) 'Crisis Bargaining', in Hermann, Charles (ed.), *International Crises: Insights from Behavioral Research*. New York: Free Press.

Stremlau, J. (1977) *The International Politics of the Nigerian Civil War*. Princeton: Princeton University Press.

Thompson, V. and Adloff, R. (1981) *Conflict in Chad*. Berkeley: University of California Press.

Thompson, S. and Zartman, I. W. (1975) 'The Development of Norms in the African System', in El-Ayouty, op.cit.

Touval, S. (1972) *The Boundary Politics of Independent Africa*. Cambridge, MA: Harvard University Press.

Touval, S. (1982) *The Peace Brokers*. Princeton: Princeton University Press.

Touval, S. and Zartman, I. W. (1985) *International Mediation in Theory and Practice*. Boulder, CO: Westview Press.

Touval, S. and Zartman, I. W. (1989) 'Mediation in International Conflicts', in Kressel, K. and Pruitt, D. (eds), *Mediation Research*. San Francisco: Jossey-Bass.

Touval, S. and Zartman, I. W. (2001) 'Interventions in the Post-Cold War Era', in Crocker, C. A., Hampson, F. and Hall, P. (eds), *Turbulent Peace*. Washington, DC: United States Institute of Peace.

Wiseman, H. (1984) 'The OAU: Peacekeeping and Conflict Resolution', in El-Ayouty and Zartman, op.cit.

Wolfers, A. (1962) *Discord and Collaboration*. Baltimore: The Johns Hopkins University Press.

Wolfers, M. (1976) *Politics in the OAU*. London: Methuen.

Wolfers, M. (1984) 'The OAU as Mediator', in Touval and Zartman, op.cit.

Woronoff, J. (1970) *Organization of African Unity*. Metachen: Scarecrow.

Yengo, P. (ed.) (1997) *Identités et démocratie*. Paris: L'Harmattan.

Yengo, Patrice *et al.* (1997) *Brazzaville des Violences, Rupture*, no. 10.

Zartman, I. W. (1985) 'Strengthening the OAU', in Onwuka, Ralph *et al.* (eds), *African Development*. Lawrenceville: Brunswick Publishing Co.

Zartman, I. W. (1986) 'Conflict in Chad', in Day, A. and Boyle, M. (eds), *Escalation and Intervention*. Boulder, CO: Westview Press.

Zartman, I. W. (1987) *International Relations of the New Africa*, 2nd edn. Lanham: University Press of America.

Zartman, I. William (1989a) *Ripe for Resolution: Conflict and Intervention in Africa*, 2nd edn. New York: Oxford.

Zartman, I. W. (1989b) 'African Insurgencies: Negotiations and Mediation', Washington, DC: US State Department Intelligence Research Report no. 206.

Zartman, I. W. (1991) 'Conflict in Africa: Prevention, Management, Resolution', in F. Deng and I. W. Zartman (eds), *Conflict Management in Africa*. Washington, DC: Brookings Institute.

Zartman, I. W. (1999) 'Inter-African Negotiations', in Harbeson, J. and Rothchild, D. (eds), *Africa in World Politics*. Boulder, CO: Westview Press.

Zartman, I. W. and Vogeli, K. R. (2000) 'Prevention Gained and Prevention Lost: Collapse, Competition and Coup in Congo', in Gentleson, B., *Opportunities Missed, Opportunities Seized*. Lanham, MD: Rowman and Littlefeld.

6

International Organizations and Conflict Management: the United Nations and the Mediation of International Conflicts

Judith Fretter

Introduction

The United Nations (UN) is a unique actor in the field of international conflict management. The UN has been successful in utilizing its skills in some of the most intense conflicts this century, and it does this without many of the advantages enjoyed by other conflict managers. So, how does the UN manage conflicts? The organization is without the leverage and resources possessed by individual member states, making its success in the field of international conflict management even more remarkable. When it enters a conflict, it relies on its international status as a global organization, the legitimacy it acquires from this status, its credibility as an international actor, the cohesiveness of its members, and its mediators' experience and persuasiveness. To what extent do the organization's characteristics enhance or inhibit its success? With little resources of its own, the organization is limited in its ability to offer inducements or threaten penalties. The UN is reliant on its international status to give its resolutions the impetus to be taken seriously. Having no standing army of its own to engage in conflict management strategies, the UN must rely solely on the support of its members to give its resolutions credibility and its actions strength. This chapter examines how the UN mediates; what it is expected to do and what it achieves; the constraints under which it operates; the mechanisms and tools it employs; the innovations it has made in the field; and briefly summarizes the characteristics of the conflicts the UN seeks to resolve.

The UN's role is a particularly important factor in the overall management of international conflicts. The international community intervenes in conflicts through multilateral channels provided by an international organization such as the UN, or a regional organization or, on occasions, a single state can act alone in pursuit of a resolution, on a unilateral basis. An intervention can reflect the intensity of the international community's reaction to events, and their commitment to resolve a perceived problem. In its own right, the UN is an effective conflict manager, but in the international arena it also performs a legitimizing function for unilateral conflict management attempts undertaken by state actors or individuals (Rubin, 1992). Where the UN has not intervened itself, it has set standards in the engagement of international conflict management strategies, standards of impartiality and fairness. The expectations of impartiality and fairness are qualities disputants seek when enlisting the UN as a conflict manager.

On the international scene, the UN is one of several conflict management actors trying to pre-empt protracted conflict and find solutions for states already in the throes of conflict. Regional organizations such as the OAU, Organization of American States (OAS) and The League of Arab States, have had some success with interstate conflict resolution: the OAU in the conflict between Tanzania and Uganda; the OAS in a Nicaraguan conflict; and the Arab League, Islamic Conference and Algeria in the Iran–Iraq war. Unilateral attempts can also boast some successes: the United Kingdom in the Rhodesian–Zimbabwe conflict; New Zealand in the Papua New Guinea conflict; the Contadora Group in Central America; and the United States in the Middle East. Various NGOs have also achieved successes: the Vatican, mediating between Chile and Argentina in the Beagle Channel conflict; the Quakers, in numerous lower profile cases; and the mediation of The Carter Center in the conflict between Ethiopia and Eritrea (Evans, 1994). The EU and the Organization for Security and Cooperation in Europe (OSCE), the newer European mechanisms for conflict management, have both shown considerable involvement in regional conflicts in the last decade as witnessed by their efforts in the former Yugoslavia.

With the end of the Cold War, the UN is perceived as more impartial. After the thaw of relations between the USA and the Soviet Union, the Security Council is no longer hamstrung by the superpower rivalry that scarred many of its earlier conflict management decisions. Increasingly, the UN has been able to act more decisively, without vetoes regularly hindering the implementation of its conflict management resolutions. In addition to this substantial systemic change, the nature of international conflict has also been transformed. Over the period from 1945 to 1989, international conflicts could generally be categorized as traditional interstate rivalries, arising from issues of territorial sovereignty, resource ownership and economic rivalry (Bercovitch, 1996). Following the dissolution of the Soviet Union in 1989, the global conflict landscape is very different. The UN has had to adapt to this changing conflict environment. Its efforts now concentrate on intrastate conflicts, those originating from ethnic and religious rivalries. These types of conflicts are fuelled by a desire for ethnic independence and equal secular representation. Fortunately, for the UN, intrastate conflicts are no longer exacerbated by superpower rivalry. However, the prolonged nature and intensity of recent intrastate conflicts, such as those in Rwanda and Yugoslavia, has seen the UN intervene more often than any other conflict manager. In this altering conflict environment, the UN's most frequently utilized conflict management strategy is that of mediation.

UN mediation

Mediation is just one of the peaceful and diplomatic initiatives used by the UN to facilitate rather than force a solution on the disputants. Responding to international conflict, the UN can intervene using three different levels of conflict management:

> (1) violence and coercion which can extend to both physical and psychological manifestations; (2) direct or indirect negotiation in its many forms (bargaining between the disputants); (3) the binding (e.g. adjudication) or non-binding (e.g. mediation) intervention of a third party. (Bercovitch *et al.*, 1991: 7)

All of these levels of conflict intervention are utilized by the UN, though a response entailing a use of force is used only as a last resort, and coercive measures are mainly exercized in the form of sanctions and blockades. The more customary role of the UN as a third party can include: enforcing a physical separation of the disputing parties; observing, monitoring and maintaining ceasefire agreements between the parties; encouraging an environment more conducive to achieving a settlement and a lasting resolution (Bercovitch, 1985):

> These third party activities, ranging from a passive to a more active involvement, are traditionally described as *fact finding* or inquiry (providing an impartial determination of the facts in conflict), *good offices* (acting as a go-between, transmitting messages and information between the protagonists), and *mediation* (aiding or influencing the adversaries to find a solution). (Bercovitch, 1989: 285)

Mediation is selected on its appropriateness and its ability to achieve certain objectives in the conflict environment. At an international level, conflict management by a third party aims to achieve five main objectives: to limit the spread or escalation of the conflict; to achieve an early resolution of the conflict; to minimize human suffering; to uphold international laws; and to promote an environment for better future relations between the disputants (Bercovitch, 1996). The UN is seen as the bastion of international morality, and so has greater pressure placed on it to pursue these objectives. Individual state actors, on the other hand, have less pressure on them to pursue altruistic objectives and are usually only concerned with managing conflicts that will affect them to some degree. The UN mediates to limit the spread of conflict and pre-empt hostilities more often than it engages in mediation on humanitarian grounds. Prolonged conflicts, such as those in Angola, Somalia, Afghanistan and Cambodia, are just a few instances where UN missions have gradually become more focused on the pursuit of humanitarian objectives. All of these operations have involved the UN in its mediation capacity, but these intense conflicts presented some of the most difficult conflict conditions for the mediators.

Since 1945, the effectiveness of UN mediation has been observed closely. In 1966, Holsti found that the UN and various regional organizations were managing to forge agreements in 37 per cent of cases where they used more active mediation strategies, proposing terms of agreement or initiating procedures of settlement. Interestingly, he concluded that although the UN's intervention had often led 'to a stalemate between two countries or between two warring factions within a country, such an arrangement may eventually lead to 'passive' settlements or to formal agreements, while unilateral intervention by outside powers usually has the purpose of gaining a clear victory for one side' (Holsti, 1966: 288). A subsequent study by Levine identified 388 mediation attempts and revealed just how frequently mediation was utilized in international conflicts between 1816 and 1960 (Levine, 1971). 'On average mediation attempts occurred about every 4.5 months over the period' (Bercovitch, 1985: 741). Butterworth's assessment of *Do Conflict Managers Matter?*, joined Holsti's 1966 study, in analysing institutionalized conflict management (Butterworth, 1978). He reviewed 255 interstate conflict management attempts over a 29-year period, from 1945 to 1974. Of these 255 attempts, the UN and regional organizations accounted for 71 per cent (181 attempts) of all management efforts (Butterworth, 1978). These studies highlight the role of international conflict managers and the need for developing efficient methods of conflict management.

Over the period from 1945 to 1995, from a total count of 295 international conflicts, the UN has been involved in 86 conflicts in varying capacities, a significant 29 per cent of the total number of international conflicts. No other organization, regional or global, has attempted the number of interventions, nor has been expected to achieve more resolutions than the UN. To put the UN's attempts into a broader perspective, the UN has performed approximately 23 per cent (615 attempts) of the total recorded formal international mediation attempts (1,485 attempts) initiated globally over a 50-year period. Mediation attempts by other conflict managers over the period have been recorded, including: state mediators 47 per cent; regional organizations 11 per cent; mixed mediators 9 per cent; non-governmental organizations 6 per cent; and individual mediators at 4 per cent. In Bercovitch's study the percentage of cases in which the UN intervened indicates that it is a substantial conflict manager, over-shadowing its regional competition in the field (Bercovitch, 1996). The figures presented here are drawn from Bercovitch's extensive data set of approximately 1,500 formal mediation attempts in the period 1945–95. Each of the mediation attempts were coded for particular contextual factors and mediation characteristics. Analysis of this data allows us to identify some of the characteristics of UN conflict mediation and examine where, when, and how effective UN interventions have been since 1945.

Engagement of UN mediation can occur because either one, or both, of the disputants request the assistance of the UN or appeal to one of its organs, the Security Council, the General Assembly or the Secretary-General. The disputants may prefer to have their dispute aired in a more impartial UN forum rather than have a particular state or regional organization intervene (Touval, 1994). On occasion, the UN also initiates its own involvement by offering to assist the disputants in restoring dialogue, though this is not always accepted. The initial offer of assistance comes in the form of an offer to use the good offices of the Secretary-General. Mediation generally occurs when an international conflict is long and drawn out, when the parties have come to an impasse, when the parties do not want to escalate the conflict further, and when the parties are prepared to participate in dialogue to achieve a settlement (Bercovitch, 1989). The tasks before the third party can include efforts to: promote the conditions required for a settlement; arrange meetings or maintain a distance between the disputants; organize appropriate settings for talks; sustain ceasefire conditions; and produce information required by the disputants for informed decision making.

In addition to the facilitative role of the UN Secretary-General and the provision of 'good offices', mediation is utilized to complement the strategies of peacekeeping, peacebuilding, observer missions and preventive diplomacy. The UN has utilized formal mediation as a free standing strategy during all phases of the conflict cycle where it is perceived that a conducive environment for mediation existed. The UN mediator's role ostensibly epitomizes the organizations' struggle as a conflict manager. Acting on behalf of the organization, the UN mediator operates only with a semblance of leverage, leverage that is imbued on their position as a representative of the international organization. Skill and expertise, honed by experience, are the only 'swords' used by the mediator in a conflict. Often the mediator relies on sheer moral persuasion and the reinforcement of international norms to reason with the disputants, as the organization itself has few resources of its own to enhance the mediator's position.

The UN's level of resources and organizational capabilities determine whether or not it is able to apply a particular strategy. Limited resources may govern many UN decisions. The UN is reliant on its member states for logistical and financial support, and for the experienced mediators employed in its missions. The speed of intervention depends on the

Security Council or Secretary-General's perception of the potentiality for conflict escalation. With the lengthy periods of involvement commonly expected with the use of peacekeeping and conflict management strategies, costs can amount to a substantial burden on contributing member states. UN members are becoming reluctant to commit to an intrastate conflict, because of the perceived complexity associated with intrastate conflicts. Despite growing reluctance to become involved in these types of intractable conflicts, the frequency of UN mediation has increased in recent years, though its involvement has been limited to fewer conflicts. In Table 6.1 data shows the lower frequency of conflicts and increased number of UN mediation attempts indicate the changing nature of UN involvement in intractable intrastate conflicts.

Interstate conflicts stem from conflicting interests between states and may involve issues of military power, economic power, territory or resource issues. 'Ideological tensions and misperceptions can exacerbate conflicts, but seldom cause them. In intrastate conflicts, interests and instrumental objectives also matter, but they are often intertwined with conflicting identities' (Leatherman and Vayrynen, 1995: 56). The UN has often seen the involvement in the more intractable intrastate conflicts as a necessary, lesser of two evils. Intrastate conflicts have proved to be the most difficult to manage. These conflicts are characteristically like the civil war conflicts in Bosnia, Liberia, Cambodia, Somalia, Ethiopia, Zaire and Georgia, and the former Yugoslavia. UN resolutions and actions dealing with these intrastate conflicts were severely impeded by the complex nature of the conflicts (Helman and Ratner, 1992). UN mediation has been used to enhance and complement peacekeeping and peacebuilding activities and to assist in the containment of these conflicts, rather than act in any preventive capacity. Regardless of whether UN mediation complements another strategy or stands alone in the conflict, it must still contend with several operational constraints.

Table 6.1   Frequency of conflicts and UN mediation attempts, 1945–95

System era	Total no. of conflicts	No. of conflicts involving the UN	UN mediation attempts	Frequency of attempts after fatalities of 10,000+
1945–55	41	14	72	27
1956–65	69	25	75	43
1966–75	50	16	132	88
1976–85	73	17	135	125
1986–95	62	14	201	168
Total	295 conflicts	86 conflicts	615 attempts	451 attempts

Operating under constraints

As an international third party, the UN operates under a number of constraints that affect its role as a mediator, more so than any other state actor, regional organization or NGO. These constraints come partly from the UN's composition as a truly international organization and partly from its member states' level of commitment to its consensual and collective procedures. The UN operates under certain limitations: the voluntary nature of its membership; the diversity and level of cohesion amongst its members; the reliance of the organization on its membership's funding and resources; the binding principles of the organization, as set out in the UN Charter; and the basic principles of state sovereignty and non-interference.

The most intrinsic element of the UN's operation is the fact that the participation by states is voluntary. States can choose to participate or refuse to participate. As there is no means by which the international organization can force its members to participate, this voluntary element of the organization presents the first major stumbling block for conflict management efforts. Fluctuations in the state system have impacted on the development of a conflict management role for the UN. The support and level of agreement of the two major powers has been shown to be a factor affecting the success of UN mediation attempts (Tunnicliff, 1984; Haas, 1986, 1987). An organization based principally on the cooperation of its members can only reflect the nature of fluctuating relationships among its membership. Adapting to cope with these fluctuations has proved both challenging and costly for the organization's credibility.

Many of the criticisms of the UN lie not with the organization itself but with the nature of its membership. 'It is commonly said that the UN is nothing more than the sum of its members – those 185 sovereign states of which it is composed' (Roberts and Kingsbury, 1988: 4). Often it is the level of their commitment and their interactions in the decision-making process which decrease the possible effectiveness of any conflict management intervention. The use of the veto in the Security Council has been identified as an indicator of the UN's resolve to deal with conflicts. The impression of organizational cohesiveness is important to enhance the basis of UN leverage. Early on in its operation the UN had to contend with strategic voting within the two voting bodies (Kim and Russett, 1996). Shifting levels of cooperation and compromise in the Security Council and the General Assembly, have proved to be the bane of decisive conflict management leadership in the UN.

One of the basic problems facing the UN's mediators stems from a lack of cohesion in its membership. From this comes the criticisms of budget allocation, the non-committal attitude towards the escalating conflicts brought before it, and the criticisms of the lack of democracy in decisions. Vague objectives at the Secretariat level sometimes result in a lack of policy clarity and insubstantially defined resolution goals.

With its haziness of outline, 'the UN' becomes an irresistible target for blame when something goes wrong. Since the organization is, in a sense, everybody, it is also always somebody else. ... The UN has no anthem to sing and although it does have a flag – a map of the world – at its centre lies the North Pole, where no one lives'. (Hall, 1994: 20)

For mediation to have a chance of being effective the UN must be seen as being representative of a global body, a cohesive entity or, at least, an organization in one voice in its resolutions (Touval, 1994). The Secretary-General, who is ultimately constrained by the will of the Security Council, performs more successfully when he has the full support of the Security Council (Tunnicliff, 1984).

The UN has a distinctly universal composition, with a complete membership of 185 countries. Ironically, it is often the same universal nature of the UN's membership that can either enhance or diminish the organization's level of legitimacy in the conduct of its mediation role. The support of its membership is essential for the running of missions and for enhancing the perceived legitimacy of UN mandates. In recent times there has been a growing reluctance by members to become committed to situations that appear to be progressing to an increasingly intractable situation. In mediation 'some of the UN leverage derives from its institutional standing and the kind of norms it exemplifies, but beyond that UN mediation is hampered considerably by lack of resources' (Bercovitch, 1996: 86). The USA for example, is the UN's biggest financial contributor as well as its biggest debtor (Thakur, 1996: 19). As of September 1998, the USA owes the UN $1.6 billion toward its regular running costs and peacekeeping budget. The total running costs of the organization amounts to $2.5 billion in 1998 (UN, 1998a). Other members are also reluctant to provide their annual financial contributions and the military force and resources that give credibility to the otherwise symbolic resolve of Security Council mandates. As Russell pointed out in 1970, 'the United Nations financial crisis is not primarily a result of *incapacity* of the members to pay but a result of their *unwillingness* to do so' (Bennett, 1988: 94). The UN manages to survive as an organization with relatively meager resources of its own. It operates with a skeletal staff of approximately 52,280 globally, and this staff total includes the Secretariat and twenty-nine other UN agencies (UN, 1998b). So, without the resource commitment and support from its members for mandated actions, the UN's ability to implement decisions and its credibility are seriously compromised.

Despite the possible consequences of abandoning this international safety-valve for global conflict, the UN's membership appears reluctant to finance its conflict management efforts in a *carte blanche* fashion any longer. Calls for budget constraints and a general pruning of what some depict as a bloated bureaucracy are but more of the problems facing the organization in the 1990's. The USA has been a particularly vocal advocate of UN reforms. The cost of long-term peacekeeping missions, some $1.3 billion in 1997, seems a lot but it only equates to 0.2 per cent of global military spending (UN, 1998b). A withdrawal from the facilities available through the UN, a reluctance to fund the organization, and a general diminished level of confidence in the UN, has led to a growth in an alternative avenue of international conflict management; that of multilateralism.

The nature of the international system, with the sovereignty of the nation-state an unwritten but binding convention, often sees conflicts becoming well-entrenched before international assistance is sought or internationally condoned. The recognition of sovereignty and the conventions of international interaction can act as a major impediment to earlier intervention by an international organization. It is obvious that the early detection of a potential conflict has not necessarily meant that early intervention in the conflict was equally as possible. More accurately though, Evans points out that the UN's indecision over intervention in Bosnia, Haiti, Somalia and Rwanda was mainly due to a lack of political will in the Security Council rather than any systemic constraints (Evans, 1994: 8).

The UN's recent troubles have not just been caused by the difficulties associated with intervening in intrastate conflicts. Hindrances to more rapid interventions have been exacerbated by membership commitment levels, budget blowouts, the organization's bureaucratic process, and a general reluctance from UN membership to become involved in already entrenched conflicts. Slow reaction, low commitment, poor early recognition of a potential conflict, and the difficulty in pin-pointing a moment of 'ripeness' for an intervention, all contribute to the ineffectiveness of an intervention. Knowing when mediation is able to achieve a quicker, inexpensive resolution would definitely prove worthwhile for the UN and the parties in conflict. Developing some criteria for the appropriate engagement of UN mediation may increase its overall effectiveness and prevent member states from selectively engaging mediation based on their state-centric motivations.

Multilateral and unilateral action, conducted under the auspices of the UN, can lead to a conflict of interest for member states in the UN. The possible prioritizing of state issues, protecting national interests over participation in a UN directive, merely highlights the awkward nature of the UN as an organization. So far the UN Security Council has approved several multilateral actions conducted by member states. Multilateral military operations after Iraq's invasion of Kuwait, and efforts in Somalia, Rwanda and Haiti have all received endorsement from the Security Council (UN, 1998b). A growing UN reliance on multilateral operations though can seriously undermine the organization's international credibility. 'If the major powers employ international organizations chiefly as public relations vehicles and fail to supply them with the means to get the job done, then the credibility of those organizations, and that of collective norms and decisions, will suffer' (Luck, 1992: 148). The credibility of the UN is essential to maintain its leverage as a mediator in international conflicts.

Constraints and contextual problems have prompted the UN to be innovative and flexible in its approach to conflict management. There are six recognizable operational constraints that the UN contends with on a regular basis in its mediation role:

1. *The commitment level of its membership*: Membership commitment affects the level of financial support, and personnel and equipment availability. The perceived level of commitment aids the perception of UN strength and leverage in mediation situations. The UN generally lacks resources of its own and so gains credibility for its actions through the support of its members.
2. *The level of cooperation and consensus of its membership*: Disagreement can promote inaction, ineffectual actions being too late to have the desired impact. A lack of consensus can be viewed as disunity within the organization and can work against a mediator who is assigned to represent the organization as a mouthpiece, a spokesperson who acts in accordance with the full backing of the world body. The mediator's position can be undermined if the weight of the organization's support is not seen to be fully behind the mediation effort. UN cohesion enhances the leverage position of the UN mediator.
3. *The constraints of operating within an international system*: The principles of state sovereignty, the presence of state interests and motivations and state alignments.
4. *The voluntary nature of UN participation*: A state only participates as much as it is willing.
5. *The explicit operating principles set out in the UN Charter*: The Charter's binding prescriptions and procedures denote the UN's international position and primary responsibility. The Charter sets out restrictions on the UN's use of force and expresses its obligation to use peaceful means of conflict settlement, where possible, before forceful measures are engaged.
6. *The decision-making procedures of the organization*: The UN system is based on consensual decision-making. Achieving the required vote approval and just the general bureaucratic process can hinder a quick response in a crisis situation.

In summary, it is clear that the UN is as equally enhanced by its international status as it is impaired. Considering these operational constraints with the nature of the mediation attempt itself, the equation for successful mediation becomes even more complex. The process of the mediation effort; the perception of mediator impartiality and experience; the rank of the mediator; the mediation strategy used; and the perception of mediator leverage, all affect the UN's ability to mediate successfully. With operational constraints and procedural factors impinging on the mediation attempt itself, it is natural to ask how the UN mediates successfully at all? How does it engage in mediation? Who mediates and what techniques are used by the mediator? The UN mechanisms of mediation, the Security Council, the General Assembly and the offices of the Secretary-General, accentuate the need for adaptability, flexibility and innovation, as they also operate under considerable organizational constraints of their own.

Mechanisms of UN mediation

The UN Security Council and the General Assembly

The Security Council determines 'the existence of any threat to the peace, breach of the peace, or act of aggression' (Article 39) and must then decide what measures to take to maintain or restore international peace and security (Articles 41 and 42). The Security Council, under Article 34, has the mandate 'to investigate any conflict or any situation which may lead to international friction or give rise to a conflict, in order to determine whether the continuance of the conflict or situation is likely to endanger the maintenance of international peace and security' (Article 34). Indeed, the achievement of the Charter's aims and the organization's progression in the area of conflict management has been consistently hampered by global circumstances the UN could not hope to control.

Traditionally, any intervention or interference in the internal domestic affairs or external affairs of another state is deemed a violation of that state's independence and sovereignty, and is considered to be a breach of international law:

> A state may justify an act of intervention where it has a treaty right to interfere in the external affairs of one of its protected states; where it interferes to protect one of its citizens; where it invades in self-defence; where it joins with other members of the United Nations to restrain a state which disturbs world peace by resorting to war; and in certain other cases. (Elliot and Summerskill, 1964: 185)

Such definitions can assist in the process of international legitimation where intervention is concerned, but the unwritten norms of behavior in the international political system still apply. Dithering reactions in recent conflicts in Bosnia, Haiti, Somalia and Rwanda do not reflect the organization's inability to determine or agree on issues of international law, nor on the constraints posed by any binding law, but more it reflects the organization's lack of decisive will in the Security Council to follow through with the resources for such ventures (Evans, 1994).

Like the Security Council, the General Assembly provides disputants with a forum in which to air their grievances. Although the General Assembly has no mechanism for mediation, it often requests that the Security Council or the Secretary-General initiate a process of mediation either through the Secretary-General's good offices, or by establishing a specialized mission. The General Assembly can also authorize further action in a conflict if the Security Council has become deadlocked on the matter. The main role of the General Assembly in the UN's management of conflicts is its legitimization function (Riggs and Plano, 1989). Hearing a conflict in this forum gives the conflict international recognition and legitimizes the concerns of the disputants. Sometimes the mere airing of a conflict in this international forum, or in the Security Council as a referral, is sufficient to create the desired effect of prompting the disputants to resume dialogue and resolve their conflict without further international concern.

The UN is not a typical bureaucracy or organization, being more akin to a parliamentary voting style system in its decision-making processes. As an international governmental organization, the UN 'operates at a level of consent, recommendation, and cooperation rather than through compulsion or enforcement' (Bennett, 1988: 2–3). Willetts identifies the UN as a political sub-system, where applying a 'bureaucratic politics approach to the UN shows that states cannot be considered to be coherent actors in the system. The consideration of how delegates work shows that there are many pressures upon them, in addition to those from their home country....' (Willetts, 1988: 35–6). It is evident that much like a parliamentary style system, the voting behavior of the member states takes on some pattern of alignment within the voting body. The General Assembly reflected this shift in the distribution of voting power. 'Voting patterns in the General Assembly help to illuminate the influences on state alignment in other UN bodies, most notably in the Security Council' (Kim and Russett, 1996: 649). Non-alignment, Third World development and regionalization have exerted a major impact on the voting patterns within the UN organs, especially during the Cold War years.

Clearly, occasions of greater cooperation within the Security Council have existed between 1964 and 1975. Evidence of this can be seen in the consensual authorization of the UN peacekeeping mission to Cyprus (UNICYP) in 1964, the UNEF II mission (Emergency Force supervising a cease-fire between Egyptian and Israeli forces) in 1973, and the joint endorsement of UNDOF (a Disengagement Observer Force stationed in the Syrian Golan Heights) in 1974. (Vayrynen, 1985: 157–8) The shaky foundations of the *détente* relationship were already doubted by the US government as early as 1973, when conditions in the Middle East deteriorated due to the Soviet failure to control Arab allies within its influence. Over this period of *détente*, the Security Council facilitated a number of summit meetings under the auspices of the UN. This may have assisted later

UN-initiated summit discussions on conflict issues, in that the initiation of top-level meetings at the UN headquarters in New York and Geneva was a familiar process in international relations.

The Secretary-General and the use of good offices

The Secretary-General personally conducted a total of 103 mediation efforts between 1945 and 1995, accounting for 17 per cent of all UN mediation attempts. The position of the Secretary-General has provided a useful medium for mediation, in the use of 'good offices', but has varied in its effectiveness over the years. The inconsistency in this role depends a lot on the person who holds the office. It relies a great deal on the disputants' perception of the Secretary-General, both as a representative of the organization and the reputation of the individual (Tunnicliff, 1984; Skjelsbaek, 1991). Skill in this position as a mediator definitely contributes to success, but a number of other factors also have an impact such as: experience; flexibility; the mediator's previous relations with the disputant; diplomatic skill; the credibility of the official position and the individual; the knowledge of the conflict and disputants; the level of impartiality; and well-developed personable skills which help to establish a level of trust and confidence in their involvement (Young, 1967, 1972; Ott, 1972; Wehr, 1979; Touval and Zartman, 1985; Bercovitch, 1986; Bercovitch *et al.*, 1991; Brouillet, 1988; Carnevale *et al.*, 1989; Touval, 1995). A mediator's experience has been seen as a large determinant of mediation success (Kolb, 1983, 1985; Carnevale and Pegnetter, 1985).

In the case of the Secretary-General, many critics argue the effectiveness of the role has declined. The Secretary-General's organizational position is a political role, involving administrative responsibility as well as diplomacy. According to Tunnicliff (1984) and Skjelsbaek (1991), the dual responsibilities of the position have hindered the performance of the Secretary-General's mediation duties. It requires more skill balancing the pressures of administration, financial constraints and organizational bureaucracy and allows less time to be spent conducting mediation and performing the tasks involved with good offices, a function that requires visible involvement. An increased lack of consensus has also been seen as an impediment to the successful employment of good offices:

> The potential scope of mediation by the Secretary-General depends very much on what he is permitted to do by the major powers. ... The main weakness of the Secretary-General is that he cannot apply sanctions, but the members of the Security Council can strengthen his position by endorsing his endeavors and by exerting bilateral pressure on the parties to a conflict'. (Skjelsbaek and Fermann, 1996: 99)

As a figurehead of the organization, the Secretary-General's position is supposed to epitomize the unified voice of the organization it represents.

Kolb points out that where some mediator's authority is derived referentially, others derive theirs from expertise, and some even use themselves and their reputation as recommendation for the role (Kolb, 1985). The Secretary-General's position carries with it the aura of legitimacy, the support and authority of the UN organization and usually some recognition of the personal attributes and diplomatic expertise of the appointed Secretary-General. Unfortunately, any lack of consensus about the Secretary-General's involvement severely undermines the perceived legitimacy of the position (Tunnicliff, 1984). Indecision on the part of the Security Council or even the semblance of disunity appears to filter into the perceptions of the disputants in the mediation process. When the Security Council or General Assembly prefers to leave a conflict off the main UN agenda, the Secretary-General can work at a discretionary level alone, using good offices and appointing a representative (Skjelsbaek and Fermann, 1996).

The use of the good offices is one of the methods of diplomatic conflict management. Good offices is a passive form of mediation. It does not allow the mediator to employ the full range of active mediation techniques such as persuasion, pressing, and directive strategies that can be used to induce the disputants to a resolution. Though not listed in Article 33 of the Charter, with the other seven methods of conflict management, good offices is another traditional and frequently used strategy. In this technique the third party offers to facilitate a channel of communications, supplies information or arranges facilities for the disputants. By strict definition, the use of good offices does not allow the third party to offer suggestions for the terms of settlement. 'By providing a neutral ground for the negotiation or by offering to carry messages between the disputants, the third party displays a friendly desire to promote a settlement without getting involved in the issues at stake' (Bennett, 1988: 102).

Usually a strategy employed by the Secretary-General, good offices involves the third party as a facilitator or go-between and can be utilized in conjunction with all of the other non-binding diplomatic strategies. Fetherston describes this possible exchange and flexibility between strategies as a potential of complementarity (Fetherston, 1994). There is a great potential for complementarity between these passive and active mediation roles and other methods of conflict management. This UN role has all of the characteristics of good old-fashioned diplomacy in definition, however, roles can and do merge occasionally, and it would not be unusual for a UN good offices role to expand into the wider techniques and broader mediation role for subsequent attempts. In fact, the most frequently utilized strategy by the Secretary-General and the other UN mediators is that of *communication–facilitation*.

Communication–facilitation describes a strategy involving the mediator in a facilitation role, promoting a resumption of dialog between the disputants by supplying information and acting as a go-between. This role is the most passive of the mediator's functions in comparison to *procedural* and *directive* strategies. *Procedural* strategies entrust much of the logistical arrangements of the meeting to the mediator's care. This role sees the mediator in an organizational role, appointing the size and seating of the meeting, preparing agendas, ensuring that the disputants have the information they need and the resources they require. The last of these strategies is the most active role for the UN mediator. A *directive* strategy allows the mediator to apply more leverage in meetings, pressing the disputants with penalties ('sticks') or inducements ('carrots') (Bercovitch and Houston, 1996). During the mediation attempt a mediator tries to build up a rapport with the disputants and often this has worked best for the Secretary-General's Special Envoys. For instance, Alioune Blondin returned to mediate in Angola on 23 occasions; Diego Cordovez mediated nineteen times in Afghanistan; and in Yugoslavia, Cyrus Vance and Thorvald Stoltenberg mediated 46 times between them. Each of these mediators had the chance to build rapport with the disputants over successive contacts and were subsequently able to develop the disputants' trust and confidence in their continued involvement.

Crisis situations often require quick thinking, initiative, flexibility and adaptability from the UN representatives. Rigidity of roles, within the confinement of strict definitions, may work well in some circumstances and not in others. A mediator's initiative and adaptability is imperative considering the evolving nature of a conflict. The use of good offices can be an effective means of intervention and is often a stepping stone in the foundations for further talks and mediation attempts. The use of the Secretary-General's good offices as a mediating strategy is more recognized because of its visibility as the highest level interaction between state officials and the UN.

The Secretary-General performs a valuable function within the organization itself, acting as a bridge between the Security Council, the General Assembly and the disputants. The position provides for a flexible intermediary, one able to act independently from the Security Council and the General Assembly, and one that can readily meet with the disputants on their own turf. The capability of acting independently of other executive organs, makes intervention by the Secretary-General more affable to the disputants. As well, there are benefits from the position, being more logistically accessible to the disputants during the course of the conflict. The Secretary-General can initiate mediation after receiving an appeal from one of the parties, a request from the Security Council or the General Assembly, or he can initiate an intermediary action based on his own assessment of the situation (Article 98). The Secretary-General's efforts in the Falkland Islands and Kashmir for instance, occurred before Security Council resolutions were even passed (Merrills, 1991). Being able to mediate in a conflict using his own initiative has distinct advantages and allows the Secretary-General the freedom to act on a situation without delay.

Where the Secretary-General does not personally mediate in a conflict, he may appoint a Special Envoy or Personal Representative to assist the disputants in reaching a peaceful settlement. The functions of the Secretary-General's Special Envoy can range from the mere reporting of events in the conflict, to the arrangement of meetings between the disputants, and to the direct mediation of the conflict. Special Envoys were appointed by the Secretary-General in 30 conflicts, over the course of the 86 UN-mediated conflicts. Often the Envoy's task was to establish a clear line of dialog between the disputants and maintain a UN presence during the disputants' meetings. Olof Palme's mediation efforts during the conflict between Iraq and Iran (1980–89), helped to maintain an open line of communication between the disputants and paved the way for later successful mediation efforts conducted by the Secretary-General. In El Salvador, Special Envoy Alvaro de Soto mediated successfully on four occasions, achieving a ceasefire and several partial agreements on certain issues between the disputants. Whether the Envoy's involvement is passive, passing information on to the disputants, or active, pressing for a settlement, the most important function of the Envoy is to bridge the gap between the disputants and the Secretary-General. The supply of information to the Secretary-General is vital for the formulation of UN policy and the Secretary-General makes recommendations to the Security Council based on these field reports. Overall, the Special Envoys mediated on 206 occasions over this time, amounting to 34 per cent of all UN mediation attempts made from 1945 to 1995. The constraints on the application of mediation techniques are much the same for both the Secretary-General and his appointed representatives (Merrills, 1991). The main differences lie in the Secretary-General's experience, rank and international status, attributes that enhance his overall legitimacy.

Rank and leverage

Much of the leverage a UN mediator possesses is derived from the organization's power and preparedness to act. Leverage is an important asset that can enhance a mediator's position. Looking at mediation in general, Zartman and Touval recognized three sources of leverage. Firstly, leverage emanates from the disputants' desire for the mediator to come up with an acceptable solution to their problems. The second point of leverage comes from the disputants' susceptibility to 'pressing' strategies employed by the mediator. The third source of leverage really relies on the resources the mediator commands for it depends on the disputants' interest in bargaining for incentive offers and concessions ('carrots') or the withholding of such incentives if the disputants are unwilling to cooperate ('sticks') (Zartman and Touval, 1985). The use of the third strategy weighs even more heavily on the attractiveness of a proposal and the added resource incentives the mediator can offer with the proposal. A UN mediator's leverage is limited by the fact that they can offer very little.

Unlike its members, the UN organization has no 'carrots' of its own and has no 'sticks' to wield. The UN derives its leverage from its universality and from its membership's support and cohesiveness. UN mediators derive leverage from their position as an official organizational representative and from their experience. In the case of the UN mediator, rank, position and status in the organization enhance the disputants' perceptions of the mediator, and subsequently the level of mediation success. High-ranking mediators may be preceded by a reputation. They can exude an air of confidence in their approach, an aura of experience and can knowledgeably make offers or exert political influence to the decision-making process with an element of credibility. Whereas, lower ranking mediators, coming to the table with a less visible position and possibly without a recognized diplomatic reputation, can be perceived by the disputants as carrying less authority and weight in the mediation attempt.

To what extent does the mediator's authority, rank and position, affect the outcome of the mediation attempt? Kolb proffers that 'what authority mediators do have emanates from their person, their behavior and skill, and the parties' ongoing assessment of them during a case' (Kolb, 1985: 11). Previous studies have shown that the high rank mediator has a better chance of achieving a successful outcome (Bercovitch, 1986). The high ranking mediators are those who have the greater prestige, accessibility to leverage 'carrots' and organizational backing to add weight to their involvement and to their 'sticks'. The high ranking UN mediators experience a similar result, even though they do not have direct access to the 'carrot and stick' tactics available to state mediators.

Rank is an important aspect of any mediator's level of credibility and can indirectly affect the outcome. 'Much of their influence stems from the expressive management of their expertise, their rapport with the parties, and the parties' perceptions of their contributions to progress and settlement in the current case and in others external to it' (Kolb, 1985: 23). The rank of the mediator is considered by the disputants to equate, to a degree, to the mediator's level of experience:

> Kessler asserts that an experienced mediator is likely to facilitate a settlement between the disputants than is an inexperienced mediator. Her argument is that experienced mediators tend to be perceived as credible and to instil trust. (Zubek *et al.*, 1992: 551)

The disputants' perceptions of the mediator's experience and authority are all important in the acceptance and credibility of the mediator's efforts.

In this study, UN mediators have been identified according to their position and rank in nine categories:

1. *Organization mediator*: This mediator was identified as a UN mediator but the details of identity and rank remained unspecified.
2. *Secretary-General of the organization*: The executive position of authority in the Secretariat of the United Nations. The Secretary-General's mediation can be requested by the Security Council or the General Assembly or equally can be offered by the Secretary-General himself.
3. *Security Council of the organization*: Mediation by the Security Council is usually made in the form of a referral, by one or both of the disputants. The referral places the disputants' issue on the international agenda and poses the possibility of international intervention.
4. *Organization's structural committee or body*: These committees are specifically tasked to deal with the pacific settlement of conflict, e.g. Good Offices Committee.
5. *Commission or special mission or task force*: The Special Mission can be established by the Security Council to manage this particular conflict. The Secretary-General is usually kept informed of the Mission's progress and reports are made to the Security Council on the Mission's progress in the field.
6. *Special Envoy or Special Representative of the Secretary-General*: Appointed by the Secretary-General, this representative usually represents the Secretary-General when the situation is too controversial for the Secretary-General to mediate personally.
7. *Field Commander/high rank military mediator*: This category relates to high-ranking military personnel stationed in the field, generally the Head or Commander of a UN mission or task force.
8. *Appointed high-ranking mediator*: Formerly a high-ranking official, diplomat or dignitary of a member nation, this mediator has been selected to represent the UN and mediate individually or in a group of representatives.
9. *Appointed low-ranking mediator*: This UN mediator can be categorized as a low ranking representative or official, with no former diplomatic experience stipulated.

The performance of the Secretary-General and the Secretary-General's Special Envoy outflanked by the success of the Field Commander/high rank military mediator, the high rank/ex-diplomat mediator and the Security Council. By far, most mediation attempts were conducted by a Special Representative of the Secretary-General or Special Envoy of the Secretary-General, some 206 (33 per cent) attempts in all. The relative rate of success, considering the percentage of successful attempts against the overall

number of attempts by the specific mediator, shows the success of the
Good Offices Committee (75 per cent) as the most successful, though it
intervenes in only a small percentage of attempts (see Table 6.2).

The comparative success of the Field Commander and the Security
Council are important in that the two positions have a differing level of
proximity to the conflict. Where the Field Commander is immersed in the
day to day disputant interactions, the Security Council involvement is
quite detached from the actual situation. UN mediation can result in varying disputant responses, ranging from complete disagreement to the more
successful results where the parties agree to further talks, reach a partial
settlement or a ceasefire, or ultimately reach a full settlement. The higher

Table 6.2 Characteristics of mediator rank and performance

UN Mediator rank	Frequency of attempts	Most utilized strategy	No. of successful attempts	Raw success rate
Unspecified UN mediator	69	Procedural 23	36	36/69 (52%)
Secretary-General	103	Communication–facilitation 36	29	29/103 (28%)
Security Council	74	Security Council referral 47	23	23/74 (31%)
UN Good Offices Committee	4	Communication–facilitation 2	3	3/4 (75%)
UN Commission or special Mission	50	Communication–facilitation 17	13	13/50 (26%)
Secretary-General Special Representative	206	Communication–facilitation 89	58	58/206 (28%)
Field Commander or high military rank	40	Communication–facilitation 16	23	23/40 (58%)
High rank UN mediator	55	Communication–facilitation 21	20	20/55 (36%)
Low rank UN mediator	14	Communication–facilitation 8	3	3/14 (21%)
Total	615 (100%)		208 (33.8%)	

ranked mediators have achieved the most success overall considering how many mediation attempts they were engaged in. The Field Commanders and high ranked military officers in the field appear to have the best success rate overall considering that the UN no longer engages the use of a Good Offices Committee. The Good Offices Committee was an early mode of operations in the field for the UN and only intervened in the Netherlands/Indonesia Conflict, 1945–49. Subsequent mediation committees have engaged in other strategies other than the use of 'good offices'.

UN mediation often operates in conjunction with a number of other strategies, though the Secretary-General can mediate alone at any time. The whole process of attaining a peaceful settlement is an incremental process involving one or more mediation attempts in succession, or a combination of mediation and other UN conflict management strategies, to achieve a successful result. The complementarity of mediation to other strategies of peacekeeping, observing, and inquiry, often sees mediation used in different phases of a conflict.

UN innovations in the peaceful settlement of conflict

The UN has been instrumental in the development of some significant practices in international conflict mediation. The UN utilizes the flexible position of the Secretary-General, the leverage of the Security Council and expertise of 'in-the-field' representatives to engage the parties in mediation. But, the UN has had to be innovative in its methods of conflict management, developing new theories and practices in the field, etching newer roles for the peacekeeper and the Secretary-General's facilitative use of 'good-offices'. A new approach in the field of international conflict management puts a greater emphasis on a preventive measures. The UN often sustains harsh criticism for its inconsistency in early recognition of conflicts, despite the fact that the involvement of UN mediation is often a last-ditched method of conflict management. Yet, if the current emphasis on preventive methods and early intervention are to become more effective, offering mediation in earlier conflict phases becomes crucial.

Mediation is more an incremental process of attaining a long-term resolution and often involves multiple mediation attempts. It is inappropriate to view a single mediation effort in isolation, without the perspective of previous attempts. When the initial strategy has failed to bring about resolution, there remains a residual effect on which subsequent conflict management attempts must compete. A mediator can achieve a degree of change in the disputants perceptions in basically three ways: 'by supplying information (factual or normative); by transferring information among the disputants and by altering procedures of the negotiation process, including the physical environment in which negotiation takes place' (Kaufman and Duncan, 1992: 690). The progressive nature of these processes, the incremental nature of mediation attempts and the dependence on the evolution of conflict conditions make the actual timing of the mediation attempt crucial (Hiltrop, 1985). Unfortunately, for UN mediators, they start off at a disadvantage in most conflicts; being called upon to engage in mediation efforts when the conflict is intense and the relationship between the disputants has already reached its lowest ebb.

Much of the UN mediator's function is to facilitate discussion or bring about a resumption of dialogue between the disputants. The Security Council though often uses directive strategies, in the form of referrals, in its mediation role. The use of referrals by the UN is an interesting mediation technique. Referrals have had an amazing success rate after their application considering what they entail. Of the total number of referrals to international, regional or independent mediators from 295 conflicts, the UN has had 47 (70 per cent) referrals out of the 67 total. The success of referrals as a method of conflict management is interesting because the disputing parties are not compelled to engage in a face-to-face negotiating situation.

A referral brings the conflict to the Security Council's attention and places it on the agenda as a matter of international importance. Referrals here are treated as another mediation strategy. It falls within the spectrum of techniques available to mediators which ranges from the ostensibly passive role, such as acting as a go-between, to the more active role, where mediators can impart persuasive techniques and offer settlement incentives to disputants (Bercovitch, 1996). From the data, successful referrals account for 27 per cent of the 47 referrals initiated. Referrals are the most common method of conflict management over the earlier stages of the conflict. Attempts in the early phases of the conflict, during the first six months, total 94, of these referrals 30 were successful. It is evident that the timing of a referral is best suited to early intervention and this is when it is most frequently utilized and most successful. However, most UN mediation attempts are undertaken in the later stages of conflict when hostilities are well entrenched. With a total of 74 attempts, the Security Council achieved success in 23 of its attempts (31 per cent). The earlier timing of this intervention strategy appears to correspond with the level of success it achieves.

It appears that mediators do not apply strategies in an *ad hoc* fashion, but instead weigh up the situation, consider the issues in conflict, the disputants and the resources at their disposal when intervening: 'Mediator behavior is less reactive and more pro-active and systematic than popularly thought...mediators are skilled practitioners of a learned craft – not innately intuitive artists' (Shapiro *et al.*, 1985: 101). The rational evaluation done by the mediator involves a great deal of psychological processing, but we can assume that the mediator is a rational actor, balancing the costs and benefits of various strategies in their selection process. Bercovitch and Wells also made this connection saying that 'it seems reasonable to suggest that, in any one conflict, their choice of a strategy, or mode of behavior, depends on (a) the kind of actors they are and (b) the kind of conflict they intervene in' (1993: 4). The rational choice of a mediation strategy is based on objective factors that are contingent on the nature of the conflict, the disputants, and a consideration of the mediator's previous relationship with the parties. The UN mediator's choice is restricted by the availability of resources and by the mediator's rank and level of experience, but frequently the choice is also limited by the disputants' level of cooperation during the mediation process, and the contextual characteristics of the conflict itself.

Contextual factors affecting UN mediation success

The conflict conditions in which the UN mediator operates also make their experience different from that of other international conflict mediators. Beyond their reliance on experience, leverage and organizational legitimacy, the UN mediator intervenes in the most intense conflict situations. Frequently, UN mediation is employed far too late in the process, long after the hostilities have already increased antagonism and distrust between the parties to such an extent that they disregard meetings or dialog as a means to achieving their objectives. In addition to the incidence of these contextual factors, the data shows that the UN made 401 (65 per cent) mediation attempts after 36 months of hostilities had already elapsed. It is evident that the UN intervenes in the most complex of intrastate conflicts, the majority of which have a high degree of active hostilities, substantial counts of human loss, and a record of prolonged conflict. A total of 451 mediation attempts were made after fatality levels exceeded 10,000. Indeed, the UN generally acts when the parties have reached a stalemate in their own efforts.

The UN relies on the support of its most powerful member states to give weight to its resolutions. Large states wield the most powerful carrots and sticks through their political influence and resource capabilities. Consequently, UN mediation relies not only on legitimization from the general membership but on the power conferred on the UN's involvement by the superpowers (Rubin, 1992). The UN cannot offer rewards or threaten coercive measures but the level of superpower commitment to resolving a conflict acts as an important motivator to the disputants. A UN mediator's authority is given more credibility by the agreement of the superpowers (Tunnicliff, 1984).

Beyond the influences of credibility and leverage, a UN mediation effort is not isolated or immune to the context in which it occurs (Zartman and Touval, 1985). The dynamics of this contextual environment are described in Figure 6.1. The mediator's role is dependent on the evolution of the disputant relationship and the conditions of the conflict, making a mediator's

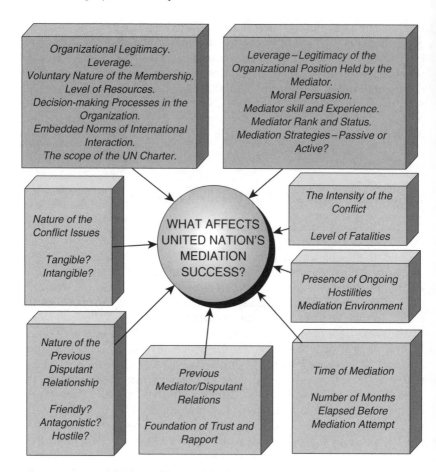

Figure 6.1   Contextual factors affecting UN mediation success

flexibility, adaptability and intuition for the developing situation essential attributes. The conflicts that typify the situations in which the UN has predominantly mediated can be summarized by looking at the frequency of many of the preconditions of the conflict and the contextual factors of the nature of the conflict:

1. The majority of mediation attempts occur between disputants that have had no pre-recorded conflict between them. ($N = 382$; 62 per cent.)
2. The disputants have already engaged in hostilities prior to the UN intervention and hostilities are, more than likely, ongoing during the course of the intervention. ($N = 409$; 67 per cent.)
3. The majority of the issues at the heart of the conflict are of an intangible nature. ($N = 367$; 60 per cent.)

4. An overwhelming number of UN mediation attempts occur after fatalities have already risen over 10000. ($N = 451$; 73 per cent.)
5. The UN has generally mediated in conflicts which have exceeded 36 months duration, ample time for hostilities and antagonisms to become socially entrenched and make the conflicts more difficult to settle. ($N = 416$, 68 per cent.)

The nature of the issues involved, the presence of ongoing hostilities between the disputants, the number of fatalities and the duration of the conflict all have an impact on the success rate of UN mediation attempts. The most significant findings in these results are seen in the success rate of mediation attempts during conflicts where a high rate of fatalities has occurred, where the issues involved are intangible and where the duration of the conflict has long surpassed a 36-month period of hostilities.

Over different system eras the frequency of UN mediation has increased even though the number of conflicts involving the UN has fallen. This increase is indicative of the growing recognition given to mediation as an effective method of preventive conflict management and the UN's heavier involvement in serious intrastate conflicts. 'Since 1948, the UN has carried out more than 40 peacekeeping operations – 30 of them since 1988' (UN, 1998: 2). The nature of international conflicts emerging has also had a fundamental impact on the level of UN mediation. Encountering more intractable conflicts, those with a higher intensity and fatality level, has become commonplace. For example, in 1994, 25 out of 42 international conflicts could be considered major armed conflicts (Wallensteen and Sollenberg, 1995). Since its involvement in the earlier eras 1945–55 and 1956–65, the UN has mediated more frequently and its involvement has concentrated on fewer conflicts after 1986. With the complexity of intractable conflict, the UN has engaged more frequently in mediation attempts than ever before and expectations of its success are also higher.

Pressure to perform successfully in the rising number of protracted intrastate conflicts severely challenges the UN's credibility because these types of conflicts are usually the most difficult to resolve. The conflicts of an ethnic, religious or ideological ilk are on the increase in a global conflict profile. 'Of 33 major conflicts that occurred in 1992, only one was an interstate conflict, and all the 34 major conflicts that occurred in 1993 were intrastate conflicts' (Bercovitch, 1996: 75). Under the strains of resource availability and budget allocation, the UN is expected to intervene in intrastate conflicts yet little credit is given to the successful completion of its mandates. Lt General Sir Michael Rose, former UN military commander in Bosnia, points out that:

> amidst all the distortion and misunderstanding surrounding the UN mission in Bosnia, it is often forgotten that its mandate is simply to sustain the people of that country in the midst of civil war, and to try and

bring about the conditions necessary for a peaceful resolution of that war ... that mandate by the end of 1994 had, by and large, been fulfilled. (Rose, 1996: 170)

Indeed, judgement of the organization's performance as an international conflict mediator needs to be viewed in the wider context and some consideration given to the organization's original objectives before final criticism is cast.

Conclusion

The UN's role as a mediator has been critically described as largely ineffectual. As Touval puts it, fleeting earlier successes have led to expectations above and beyond the UN's current capabilities. He cites many of the organizational characteristics of the UN as inherent constraints on its ability to perform as an effective mediator (Touval, 1994). Based on this summary one could assume that the UN has little going for it as an international mediator. Admittedly, there are a number of constraints that lower the consistency of UN mediation success, but as an international organization its continued success in the field, though less dramatic after the demise of the Cold War era, is solid evidence of its capabilities in mediation. The UN, as Touval concludes: 'should draw lessons from its more successful mediating efforts to develop mechanisms for an efficient division of labor between member states and the organization, allowing each to contribute what it does best' (Touval, 1994: 55). Touval's summation expresses many of the concerns we ourselves have for this international organization.

For the organization to operate fluidly in the international system, cooperation between its members is not essential as such but definitely beneficial. The perception of legitimacy for UN actions is essential and with this perception comes some leverage and power from its status as an international organization, so long as the action is condoned and supported by its membership. Some of the success of UN mediation attempts can be attributed, in part, to the position of the international organization and its international backing. What is clear is that UN objectives must be laid out plainly and coherently in order to enable intervention using the most appropriate intervention strategy. Touval suggests that 'decentralizing mediation efforts by making greater use of regional organizations might ease the plight of the overburdened UN Security Council and Secretariat', and ponders a reversal of roles where the UN encourages or charges a state with the responsibility to mediate in an associated conflict (Touval, 1994).

The systemic development, bloc alignments and disagreement have had a direct impact on the development of UN conflict management responses. Mediation on an international level relies heavily on the leverage of the third party and its ability to persuade the disputants to come to some compromise or settlement. When any collective action has been implemented by the UN this leverage comes into play, thus allowing the UN a strong position for bargaining amongst the disputants. Unfortunately though, any collective action that is still in dispute by some of the member states tends to lower the organization's initial position of leverage. Early in its development 'the permanent members of the Security Council had to sanction all action; their failure to agree meant inaction' (Haas, 1986: 5–6). Inaction caused by internal disagreement has been equally as costly to the UN's leverage in conflict management as it has to its reputation as an ineffective conflict manager. Due to continuing dissension between the two voting bodies and between the leading members of the Security Council itself, the UN is seen to have 'failed, or rather the nations composing it have failed, to create a framework of international security' (Howard, 1988: 44).

High expectations of this truly international organization and its mediators, should first be grounded by the realities of its operating environment, the constraints, the resource limitations, and the increased intensity of recent conflicts. Secretary-General Boutros Boutros-Ghali emphasized the need to pre-empt conflict situations before they escalate to an intractable 'phase' (Boutros-Ghali, 1993). With the increasing emphasis on preventive UN strategies, there are higher expectations being placed on the organization's mediators than ever before. UN mediation has the flexibility to be applied during all phases of a conflict, the accessibility to be the perfect complement to other diplomatic initiatives, and enough perceived impartiality to be accepted by the disputants. It relies heavily on the voluntary support, participation and resources of its members. The UN's mediation efforts are only enhanced by the organization's cohesiveness, decisiveness and preparedness to act, all of which in turn bolster its mediator's credibility. In the mediation attempt itself, the UN mediator relies on the perception of legitimacy conferred on their position, on their expertise and experience, on their raw powers of persuasion, and ultimately, on the disputants' determination to resolve the conflict.

References

Bennett, P. G. (1988) *International Organizations – Principles and Issues*, 4th edn, Prentice Hall, Englewood Cliffs, NJ.

Bercovitch, J. (1985) 'Third Parties in Conflict Management: The Structure and Conditions of Effective Mediation in International Relations', *International Journal*, 40: 4: 736–52.

Bercovitch, J. (1986) 'International Mediation: A Study of Incidence, Strategies and Conditions of Successful Outcomes', *Cooperation and Conflict*, 21: 3: 155–68.

Bercovitch, J. (1989) 'International Dispute Mediation: A Comparative Empirical Analysis', *Mediation Research – The Process and Effectiveness of Third Party Intervention*, in Kressel, K., Pruitt, D. G. and Associates (eds), Jossey-Bass Inc., San Francisco, CA, 284–99.

Bercovitch, J. (1996) 'The United Nations and the Mediation of International Disputes', *The United Nations at Fifty – Retrospect and Prospect*, Thakur, R. (ed.), Otago Foreign Policy School Symposium, Otago University Press, Dunedin, New Zealand, pp. 73–87.

Bercovitch, J. and Houston, A. (1996) 'The Study of International Mediation: Theoretical Issues and Empirical Evidence', in Bercovitch, J. (ed.), *Resolving International Conflicts – the Theory and Practice of Mediation*, Lynne and Rienner Publishers, Boulder, CO, pp. 11–35.

Bercovitch, J., Anagnoson, J. T. and Wille, D. L. (1991) 'Some Conceptual Issues and Empirical Trends in the Study of Successful Mediation in International Relations', *Journal of Peace Research*, 28: 1: 7–17.

Bercovitch, J. and Wells, R. (1993) 'Evaluating Mediation Strategies – a Theoretical and Empirical Analysis', *Peace & Change*, 18: 1: 3–25.

Boutros-Ghali, B. (1993) *An Agenda For Peace*, United Nations Department of Public Information, New York.

Brouillet, A. (1988) 'Mediation as a Technique of Dispute Settlement: Appraisal and Prospects', *International Conflict Resolution*, Thakur, R. (ed.), Westview Press, Boulder, CO.

Butterworth, R. L. (1978) 'Do Conflict Managers Matter? An Empirical Assessment of Interstate Security Disputes and Resolution Efforts, 1945–1974', *International Studies Quarterly*, 22: 2: 195–214.

Carnevale, P. J. D. and Pegnetter, R. (1985) 'The Selection of Mediation Tactics in Public Sector Disputes: A Contingency Analysis', *Journal of Social Issues*, 41: 65–81.

Carnevale, P. J. D., Lim, R. G. and McLaughlin, M. E. (1989) 'Contingent Mediator Behaviour and Its Effectiveness', *Mediation Research – the Process and Effectiveness of Third Party Intervention*, Kressel, K., Pruitt, D. G. and Associates (eds), Jossey-Bass, San Francisco, CA, pp. 213–40.

Elliot, F. and Summerskill, M. (1964) *A Dictionary of Politics*, 4th edn, Penguin Harmondsworth, Middx.

Evans, G. (1994) *Cooperating for Peace – the Global Agenda for the 1990's and Beyond*, Allen Unwin, St Leonards, New South Wales, Australia.

Fetherston, A. B. (1994) *Towards a Theory of United Nations Peacekeeping*, St. Martin's Press, NY and Macmillan Press – now Palgrave Macmillan – London.

Haas, E. B. (1986) *Why We Still Need the United Nations – the Collective Management of International Conflict, 1945–1984*, Policy Papers in International Affairs No. 26, Institute of International Studies, University of California, Berkeley, pp. 1–104.

Haas, E. B. (1987) 'The Collective Management of International Conflict, 1945–1984', *The United Nations and the Maintenance of International Peace and Security*, United Nations Institute for Training and Research, Martinus Nijhoff Publishers, Dordrecht, The Netherlands, pp. 3–69.

Hall, B. (1994) 'Blue Helmets, Empty Guns', *The New York Times*, Late Edition, Sunday, 2 January, Section 6, 20.

Helman, G. B. and Ratner, S. R. (1992) 'Saving Failed States', *Foreign Policy*, 89: 3–20.

Hiltrop, J. M. (1985) 'Mediator Behaviour and the Settlement of Collective Bargaining Disputes in Britain', *Journal of Social Issues*, 41: 2: 83–99.

Holsti, K. J. (1966) 'Resolving International Conflicts: A Taxonomy of Behaviour and Some Figures on Procedures', *Conflict Resolution*, 10: 3: 272–96.

Howard, M. (1988) 'The United Nations and International Security', in Roberts, A and Kingsbury, B. (eds), *United Nations in a Divided World – The UN's Role in International Relations*, Clarendon Press, Oxford.

Kaufman, S. and Duncan, G. T. (1992) 'A Formal Framework for Mediator Mechanisms and Motivations', *Journal of Conflict Resolution*, 36: 4: 688–708.

Kim, S. Y. and Russett, B. (1996) 'The New Politics of Voting Alignments in the United Nations General Assembly', *International Organization*, 50: 4: 629–52.

Kolb, D. M. (1983) 'Strategy and Tactics of Mediation', *Human Relations*, 36: 247–68.

Kolb, D. M. (1985) 'To Be a Mediator: Expressive Tactics in Mediation', *Journal of Social Issues*, 41: 11–26.

Leatherman, J. and Vayrynen, R. (1995) 'Conflict Theory and Conflict Resolution – New Directions for Collaborative Research Policy', *Cooperation and Conflict*, 30: 1: 53–82.

Levine, E. (1971) 'Mediation in International Politics: A Universe and Some Observations', *Peace Science Society Papers*, 13: 23–43.

Luck, E. C. (1992) 'Making Peace', *Foreign Policy*, 89: 137–55.

Merrills, J. G. (1991) *International Dispute Settlement*, 2nd edn, Grotius Publications, Cambridge.

Ott, M. C. (1972) 'Mediation as a Method of Conflict Resolution: Two Cases', *International Organization*, 26: 4: 595–618.

Riggs, R. E. and Plano, J. C. (1989) *The United Nations – International Organization and World Politics*, The Dorsey Press, Chicago, Illinois.

Roberts, A. and Kingsbury, B. (eds) (1988) *United Nations in a Divided World – the UN's Role in International Relations*, Clarendon Press, Oxford.

Rose, Lt Gen. Sir Michael, (1996) 'The Bosnia Experience', *The United Nations at Fifty – Retrospect and Prospect*, R. Thakur (ed.), Otago Foreign Policy School Symposium, Otago University Press, Dunedin, New Zealand, pp. 167–78.

Rubin, J. Z. (1992) 'Conclusion: International Mediation in Context', *Mediation in International Relations: Multiple Approaches to Conflict Management*, in Bercovitch, J. and Rubin, J. Z. (eds), St. Martin's Press, New York.

Shapiro, D., Drieghe, R. and Brett, J. (1985) 'Mediator Behaviour and the Outcome of Mediation', *Journal of Social Issues*, 41: 2: 101–14.

Skjelsbaek, K. (1991) 'The UN Secretary-General and the Mediation of International Disputes', *Journal of Peace Research*, 28: 1: 99–115.

Skjelsbaek, K. and Fermann, G. (1996) 'The UN Secretary-General and the Mediation of International Disputes', *Resolving International Conflicts – the Theory and the Practice of Mediation*, in Bercovitch, J. (ed.), Lynne Rienner Publishers Inc., Boulder, CO, pp. 75–104.

Thakur, R. (ed.) (1996) 'Past Imperfect, Future Uncertain', in *The United Nations at Fifty – Retrospect and Prospect*, University of Otago Press, Dunedin, New Zealand, pp. 1–32.

Touval, S. and Zartman, I. W. (eds) (1985) *International Mediation in Theory and Practice*, Westview Press, Boulder, CO.

Touval, S. (1994) 'Why the UN Fails', *Foreign Affairs*, 73: 5: 44–57.

Touval, S. (1995) 'Mediator's Flexibility and the UN Security Council', *The Annals of the American Academy of Political and Social Science*, 542: 116–30.

Tunnicliff, K. H. (1984) 'The United Nations and the Mediation of International Conflict', PhD Dissertation presented to the University of Iowa, University Microfilms International, Michigan, USA, reprinted 1987.

UN (1998a) 'Setting the Record Straight – the UN Financial Crisis', UN Internet Homepage, http://www.un.org/News/facts/finance.htm.

UN (1998b) 'The UN in Brief', UN Internet Homepage, http://www.un.org/Overview/brief.html.

Vayrynen, R. (1985) 'The United Nations and the Resolution of International Conflicts', *Cooperation and Conflict*, 20: 141–71.

Wallensteen, P. and Sollenberg, M. (1995) 'After the Cold War: Emerging Patterns of Armed Conflict (1989–94) *Journal of Peace Research*, 32, 3: 345–60.

Wehr, P. (1979) *Conflict Regulation*, Westview Press, Boulder, CO.

Willets, P. (1988) 'The United Nations Political System', *International Institutions at Work*, Taylor, P. and Groom, A. J. R. (eds), Pinter, London pp. 21–38.

Young, O. R. (1967) *The Intermediaries: Third Parties in International Crises*, Princeton University Press, Princeton, NJ.

Young, O. R. (1972) 'Intermediaries: Additional Thoughts on Third Parties', *Journal of Conflict Resolution*, 16: 51–65.

Zartman, I. W. and Touval, S. (1985) 'International Mediation: Conflict Resolution and Power Politics', *Journal of Social Issues*, 41: 2: 27–45.

Zubek, J. M., Pruitt, D. G., Peirce, R. S., McGillicuddy, N. B. and Syna, H. (1992) 'Disputant and Mediator Behaviours Affecting Short-Term Success in Mediation', *Journal of Conflict Resolution*, 36: 3: 546–72.

7

Great Power Mediation: Using Leverage to Make Peace?[1]

Marieke Kleiboer

Introduction

'What we lack is clout', EU mediator David Owen muttered in a 1992 television documentary. He clearly saw the lack of great power backing as one of the prime reasons why his collaborative mediation efforts with UN representative Cyrus Vance failed to bring peace in the former Yugoslavia. He seemed to be right. The subsequent series of peace plans put forward by various mediators were rejected immediately by the warring parties (Atiyas, 1995). It took a bloody Serbian invasion of the UN-protected 'safe haven' Srebrenica in the summer of 1995 before the United States decided to increase its involvement. Backed up by American political muscle, and a new and more elaborate campaign of NATO air strikes, US mediator Richard Holbrooke succeeded in getting the parties to come to a set of agreements on 21 November 1995.

Holbrooke's efforts in Yugoslavia add to the nearly hundred cases in which the US has mediated since World War II (Touval, 1992: 235). Great powers, such as the US, are assumed to be particularly well suited for a role as mediator because they possess leverage *vis-à-vis* the parties in conflict. Leverage entails both a mediator's ability to become a relevant player in the conflict as well as to put pressure on one or more of the conflicting parties to accept a proposed settlement. This assumes a mediator has resources (e.g. military, economic, political) that can be brought to bear on the parties. It is not clear, though, which resources are crucial for gaining and exploiting leverage. Analysts distinguish between the ability to use 'sticks' (negative sanctions) and 'carrots' (positive sanctions) (Touval and Zartman, 1985: 13), and between material (e.g. withholding or supplying economic aid) and immaterial (using moral or psychological pressure) dimensions of leverage (Princen, 1992: 167). Moreover, leverage does not only depend on resources alone but also on the *willingness* of the mediator to deploy them, and the *skill* with which this is done.

In this chapter, I will argue that although leverage is often necessary to become involved as a mediator in conflicts where the conflicting parties are still determined to dominate one another, it is not a sufficient condition for achieving successful outcomes. It would be more accurate to state that the role of power in mediation, even by important states, is contingent: not only are many other variables in play (Kleiboer, 1996), there are also important constraints at work that prevent great powers from effectively employing their potential leverage. The next section briefly outlines neorealist theory on international relations and considers some *international* constraints upon great power mediation. The black box of policy-making will be opened on when international constraints upon using leverage will be analysed from a domestic politics perspective. Next the concept of mediator leverage in a more fundamental way is considered. Taking what I have called a humanist perspective on international mediation, the very notion of mediation success and the role of leverage as a critical condition for achieving it are critiqued.

Throughout, the argument will be illustrated with a case study of US mediation efforts in the Falklands conflict. This involves a long-standing dispute between Great Britain and Argentina about a group of some 200 little islands in the South Atlantic. After a long 'incubation period' featured by a mix of routine bilateral negotiations and occasional flare ups of tensions, the conflict rapidly escalated in the spring of 1982. A crisis situation occurred at the beginning of April when Argentine forces occupied the Falkland Islands which had been under British rule for nearly 150 years. The ruling Argentinean military Junta had initiated the occupation as a means to force Britain's hand at the bargaining table. The act generated a strong and uncompromising response from the Thatcher government, and the parties moved towards military confrontation. It was in this period that Ronald Reagan's Secretary of State, Alexander Haig, became involved in the conflict as a mediator. Nearly three weeks of intensive mediation followed. On 30 April 1982, however, Haig announced that the US mediation had failed. War soon broke out and was concluded several weeks later when British forces recaptured the Islands.

Using leverage: international constraints

The prevalent way to explain the role of leverage in international mediation is offered by a neorealist perspective on international relations. In this research tradition, international politics is characterized as essentially conflictual, with state interests clashing as a result of a competition for scarce resources such as security, territory, status and access to raw materials. Conflict is considered a threat to the international order, particularly so when it has the potential of escalating into military confrontation between the great powers in the international system. Conflicts of this kind should therefore be kept in check. Since conflict is seen as endemic in the anarchic structure of the international system, which lacks authoritative political institutions wielding a monopoly of power, comprehensive conflict prevention is deemed impossible. Conflict management therefore boils down to achieving *settlements*, where parties arrive at a negotiated compromise that reduces the intensity of the conflict below escalation thresholds and maintains the stability of the international system.

In neorealist thought, the crucial resource for a mediator stepping in to help settling a conflict is leverage to pressure the parties to make concessions and to ensure that disputants adhere to the agreements they have entered into (Brookmire and Sistrunk, 1980: 326; Bercovitch *et al.*, 1991: 15; Touval, 1992: 233). Great powers are therefore considered the most likely candidates for a role as mediator. They bring a higher degree of authority to the mediation process, since it is much more perilous to alienate a great power than less powerful international actors. Furthermore, great powers can wield far more and more diverse sticks and carrots which each party believes will help to achieve its objectives or minimize its losses. Thirdly, great powers have the ability to compensate parties making concessions. They can participate in a triangular negotiation process, in which they actually pay the price for some of the concessions made by the two sides (Touval, 1982: 327). Finally, great powers are often the only ones that can guarantee that a negotiated agreement will be implemented.

Nevertheless, their leverage does not guarantee that great powers are always successful mediators. From a neorealist perspective two important constraints may prevent major powers from using their leverage effectively. Both of these constraints have to be viewed against the neorealist portrayal of the international system as characterized by interstate rivalry and competition for hegemony among great powers. One refers to the position of the mediator *vis-à-vis* other great powers in the international system. The second refers to the trade-offs that may occur in the relationship between the great power mediator and the conflicting parties. The first cut on the Falklands case illuminates both constraints.

A neorealist account of Haig's mediation: systemic constraints

Superpower rivalry

From a neorealist perspective, Haig's mediation effort is a paradigm case of a great power's attempt to manage a conflict between two allies against the backdrop of heightened global superpower rivalry. During the 1960s and 1970s, the Soviet Union and the United States built more and better weapons largely for the purpose of neutralizing the other's nuclear arsenal and maintaining some sort of strategic balance of power between them. This nuclear gamesmanship and the extraordinary importance the two superpowers attached to recruiting new allies and keeping old ones inside the fold, became a recurrent source of tensions and instability during the Cold War.

At the end of the 1970s, when tensions between Great Britain and Argentina built up, superpower rivalry also intensified. Especially the Soviet invasion of Afghanistan at the end of 1979 signalled the end of attempts at *détente* in East–West relations. Speaking about the 'evil empire' when referring to the Soviet Union, incoming US President Reagan demonstrated firm anti-communist resolve. He articulated a new US policy towards the Western hemisphere, generally called the 'Reagan Doctrine', which involved that the United States should support all friendly, anti-communist regimes in the hemisphere, irrespective whether they were democratic or authoritarian (Kaufmann, 1994: 3).

In Europe, this implied that the United States maintained a large army as hostage to its commitment that the American 'nuclear umbrella' would be opened to defend European countries against a possible Soviet attack. In Latin America, an area of primary influence that was seen as 'weakened' in balance-of-power terms during the Carter Administration (Gamba, 1987: 72), the United States needed to re-establish its influence. As a response to a communist guerrilla insurgency in El Salvador and the Sandinista takeover in Nicaragua, the Reagan administration increased its economic and military aid to beleaguered regimes in Central America, hoping to enlist the assistance of sympathetic governments in South America in its worldwide struggle against communism. In a significant departure from the Carter administration's policy, the Reagan Government directed its criticism of human rights violations on the continent mainly at left-wing regimes, and much less at friendly right-wing governments.

US relations with Britain and Argentina

With respect to the Falkland Islands conflict, the United States had traditionally adopted a neutral stance, not committing itself to the sovereignty claims of either Britain or Argentina. During the 1960s and 1970s, it had also avoided direct involvement in the negotiations on the Islands' status. Hence in 1982 the US Government reacted with dismay and grave concern to the invasion. Although it was not interested in any way in the Falklands themselves – Reagan referred to them as 'that little ice-cold bunch of land down there' (Freedman, 1988: 14) – the crisis posed a threat to US policy in that it caused regional instability. In particular, the impending crisis forced the United States to take a stance in the conflict between two of its Cold War allies.

Balanced on the one side was the relationship with the United Kingdom. The Anglo-American tie is special and has deep historical backgrounds. Rooted in shared language, cultural and legal traditions, it was reinforced during two world wars. Moreover, the Thatcher Government had recently supported the United States on contentious NATO issues, such as the deadlocked negotiations over intermediate nuclear forces (INF), US attempts to block construction of a Russian natural-gas pipeline to Europe, and the deployment of US cruise missiles in Europe. In fact, in 1981–82, Britain was a key factor to the viability of the American missile deployment plan. The Reagan administration was depending upon Britain (together with four other nations) to allow a new generation of intermediate-range nuclear missiles to be placed on its soil.

Reagan's courtship of Argentina was also based on a combination of ideological and geopolitical reasons. In Washington, the right-wing, anti-communist junta led by General Galtieri was judged to represent the accept-able face of military dictatorship. During 1981, the Reagan administration relaxed the Carter arms embargo for human rights violations, which further improved American–Argentine relationships. Both governments shared a concern for suppressing the expansion of communism, and began to coop-erate closely on military and intelligence issues. The junta bolstered US pol-icy by providing military advisors and aid to El Salvador, Honduras and the Nicaraguan contras – help that was particularly welcome because of con-gressional restrictions on US activities in these hotbeds of Central America. Since no other Latin American country was willing or able to provide com-parable levels of support, the administration came to regard Argentina as its most reliable ally in the hemisphere (Lippincot and Treverton, 1994: 3).

Impact on US mediation

For a neorealist perspective, the trade-off for Haig was sharp: on the one side was the special relationship with the United Kingdom, one of the oldest US allies and a major NATO country; on the other, friendly and increasingly important relations with Argentina, just improving during the Reagan admin-istration. On balance, however, the relationship with the British counted more to US policy-makers. As the former director of the Department's Office of Regional Security Affairs Richard Haass expressed it:

> we felt that Mrs. Thatcher had placed a lot of her eggs in the Falklands basket. What we saw at stake was not simply the policy of the Thatcher government towards the missiles, but really Britain's role in the world.... And we were very worried about American interests in Europe and the East–West relationships if Britain were no longer an active player in the Atlantic alliance. How the Falklands crisis was resolved would have major implications for British – and indirectly for the US – foreign policy world-wide. (cited in Lippincot and Treverton, 1994: 3)

To put real pressure on Britain with the risk of breaking off good relationships was therefore impossible.

At the same time, a public tilt towards the British and supporting them or forcing Argentina to withdraw from the Falkland Islands was also a risky strategy for the United States. In particular, as a strong anti-communist one of Haig's major concerns was that if the United States would pressure the right-wing junta, it would – in desperation – be tempted to seek or accept material aid from the Soviet Union or their proxies in Cuba (Gamba, 1987: 153). This was a real option, as the Soviet Union already had a privileged place in trade relations with Argentina.[2] Also, the Soviet Union needed grain from Argentina at a time of American embargo following Soviet's invasion in Afghanistan. During Haig's first visit to Buenos Aires, President Galtieri already mentioned that the Soviets – through the Cuban ambassador – had begun to offer material and intelligence assistance to the junta (Haig, 1984: 278). Haig took the possibilities of the Soviet Union to become involved seriously in case the Argentineans lost trust in the United States (Haig, 1984: 278).

If the United States supported Britain, not only would it lose a valuable hemisphere ally, it would possibly damage its general political standing in Latin America. Thus, the United States was confronted with a dilemma: '[s]upport for either disputant would risk damaging US ties with the s[other], possibly irreparably' (Kaufmann, 1994: 1–2). As one US politician expressed it:

> The risks for us, if we had chosen to do nothing, were very substantial. If we had just sat back and let the situation unfold, we would have had to make an immediate decision about our attitude towards the British invasion force. Were we going to try to restrain them? Have another Suez? Well, we clearly couldn't do that, though we knew the Argentines would be pressuring us to try to restrain the British. We knew we couldn't ask the British to be restrained. Could we just take no position at all? That was kind of difficult because, in fact, we did have a position. I mean, we weren't neutral and evenhanded, even though a couple of people made some remarks to that effect very early on. We weren't. You just don't invade disputed territory. You settle the dispute by peaceful means, or not at all. So we weren't neutral on the merits of the issue. The British were going to be after us for support, clearly. We'd be forced to make a choice. So the idea was, if we put ourselves in a negotiating role, we might be able to avert the war and also, avoid having to make the trade-off. (cited in Lippincot and Treverton, 1994: 9–10)

Thus, the United States procrastinated on a solution so as not to internationalize the conflict, see it escalate and undermine US credibility in balance of power considerations *vis-à-vis* the Soviet Union and Central America (Gamba, 1987: 163). Mediation without pressuring any party, in fact, offered Haig two ways of extracting the United States from its predicament. Ideally, a peaceful settlement would obviate the need to choose between the two allies while denying the Soviet Union any chance of establishing influence with a South American regime. Should mediation fail, however, Haig would be better placed to overcome those in the administration who valued hemispheric goals more than alliance solidarity. The administration could then be united in support of its most important ally, as well as in defense of principles which it had always professed (Dillon, 1989: 142).

In sum, in the context of renewed East–West tensions at the beginning of the 1980s, it was not in the national interest of the United States to use its power and break off relationships with either Britain or Argentina. This implied that the only option left was to mediate, but without the use of the full range of its great power resources, thereby effectively reducing its leverage. Since from a realist perspective high leverage is an essential incentive for parties to find some sort of settlement between them, Haig was doomed to fail.

Using leverage: domestic constraints

According to political–psychological approaches, the neorealist 'billiard-ball' representation of international politics which tends to 'black-box' the decision-making process is considered to obscure international relations far more than it illuminates. To make sense of international events the domestic politics approach focuses on the policy-making process within states as well as within non-state institutions. Rather than being homogenous and unitary, actors in the international system tend to be complex entities consisting of different parties who often disagree among themselves about the definition of their national or organizational interests and how these can be best promoted in a particular situation. Moreover, this approach suggests we need to study how and why key leaders and agencies that formulate and implement the actor's policies perceive their situation, reach decisions, and take action. Finally, foreign policy-making is considered a process of 'double-edged diplomacy' (Evans *et al.*, 1993): international interaction is influenced by psychological, organizational and political factors at the domestic level while at the same time domestic politics is affected by what goes on at the international level.

Given this interpretation of international politics, conflict that arises between states is considered a contingent result of psycho-political dynamics in the interplay between various foreign policy actors, acting on behalf of states. In particular, misperceptions and distrust between political and bureaucratic elites and institutions are often seen as a source of conflict. Conflict, in other words, is socially constructed, and so this is so there is no *prima facie* reason why a complete *resolution* of conflict – taken to be a fundamental change of attitudes and behavior of parties resulting in a trust-based peaceful and stable interstate relationship – should be impossible.

The key challenge to conflict management is therefore more ambitious than neorealists allow for: it is to prevent conflict spirals from occurring, or to effectively transform them into spirals of de-escalation. In this process, other assets besides leverage are crucial. These include: information, analytical and communication skills, a commitment to peace, and an astute awareness of the political environment in which parties operate and its impact upon their behavior.

Below, I will return to Haig's mediation in the Falklands crisis and demonstrate that even if the US had been willing to use more leverage to pressure Argentina into compliance, domestic organizational and political disputes about Haig's mission further compromised United States effectiveness as an international power broker.

A domestic politics account of the Falklands case

State versus staff

Haig's position in the Reagan administration was controversial. When Haig was appointed as Secretary of State in 1981 and presented himself as the general manager of American diplomacy, his authority came under strong attack from conservative allies of the president and from key members of the White House staff. The criticisms of Haig were two-fold (Kaufmann, 1994: 4). At an organizational level, the White House chief of staff Baker and his associates believed Haig's 'take-charge' administrative style tended to antagonize other government officials by failing to acknowledge their responsibilities and expertise. Ideologically, the president's 'New Right' supporters, such as UN Ambassador Kirkpatrick, accused the moderate Haig of betraying Reagan's mandate to combat communism worldwide. Haig's opponents won a major victory in January 1982, when Haig's ally, National Security Adviser Richard Allen was replaced by William Clark, a Reagan loyalist.

In the spring of 1982 when the crisis over the Falklands erupted, Haig knew his position had become delicate and that a failure could bring him down (Haig, 1984: 76–86). From Haig's point of view, therefore, taking center stage as mediator in the Falkland crisis was a major, high-risk policy gamble. He was aware:

> that there were men and women around the President who would urge my departure. "If the situation cannot be saved, and this is very possible," I told my wife, "then whatever I do will be seen as a failure, even if it is a success in larger terms than the conflict itself. I'm going to take this on because I have to, but it may turn out to be my Waterloo". (Haig, 1984: 272)

When Haig suggested to Reagan that he might attempt to mediate, Haig's opponents were equally worried, not only that he would fail, but also that he would succeed. As Richard Haass, former director of the State Department's Office of Regional Security Affairs, explained:

> [T]he former might hurt the president in obvious ways unless it could be pinned on Haig; the latter might make it impossible to get rid of Haig, something quite a few people sought. (cited in Lippincot and Treverton, 1994: 9)

Haig, therefore, felt he had to watch his back all the time when manoeuvring as a mediator. This limited his flexibility. For one thing, it made him hasty: he wanted a quick success, knowing that his critics would gain strength the more they could depict him as ineffectual (Haig, 1984: 271).

'Latin Americanists' versus 'Europeanists'

The bureaucratic politics surrounding Haig's mediation effort were not merely about his organizational position and power. They were also driven by political differences. When the National Security Council (NSC) met in the beginning of April to discuss Haig's proposal to mediate, conflict emerged between factions supporting Argentina versus factions favoring Britain. The pro-Argentine faction was centered around the State Department's Bureau of Inter-American Affairs, headed by Assistant Secretary Thomas Enders and UN Ambassador Kirkpatrick. These 'Latin Americanists', supported by Pentagon officers and civilians, stressed the anti-colonialist dimension of Argentine claims and the importance of US relations with Argentina.

The pro-British faction, including Haig himself, was concentrated in the State's Bureau of European and Political–Military Affairs, and represented by Undersecretary for Political Affairs Lawrence Eagleburger. The 'Europeanists' found support from Secretary of Defense Caspar Weinberger. They focused on Argentina's unprovoked aggression and the need for the United States to preserve its special relationship with Britain. Depicting the junta's action as analogous to Hitler's, they saw the junta as a 'militarized, authoritarian, xenophobic' regime that had miscalculated behavior of democracies such as Britain and the United States (Haig, 1984: 267). Moreover, these 'Europeanists' did not want to lose British support during a particularly sensitive and contentious episode in NATO alliance. Their strong preference, therefore, was for Argentina to withdraw from the Falklands as soon as possible, and settle the issue by piecemeal negotiations.

Since both factions were represented in Haig's mediation team, Haig felt he could not afford to dismiss the Latin Americanists. Consequently, he tried to accommodate both his opponents and his supporters by emphasizing his evenhandedness in the mediation process. At the same time, however, he would not suppress his personal commitment to an Argentine withdrawal as a precondition for talks on sovereignty. This resulted in an ambiguous strategy, frustrating both Britain and Argentina. Britain, on the one hand, expected an unequivocal statement of support from the United States. It considered itself the aggrieved party in the dispute and a long-term special ally, and became increasingly irritated watching 'a display of American evenhandedness between aggressor and aggrieved' (Freedman, 1988: 43). The Argentine Junta, on the other hand, which had been counting on a neutral if not supportive US stance, quickly lost faith in Haig's mediation efforts when it sensed that Haig was on the British side.

Consequently, both Britain and Argentina came to view the mediation merely as a symbolic act of the United States, initiated mainly for US domestic reasons. Nevertheless, both went along with the mediation initiative for their own political purposes. The British acceptance of Haig's mediation can be understood as an attempt to secure vital diplomatic and military help from the United States. As the British saw it, this could only be achieved if they would agree to engage in mediation. Only by doing so could Britain demonstrate its reasonableness, and encourage the United States to make its assistance available at a speed and a degree that would ensure the success of the Task Force (Dillon, 1989: 141). The Argentineans, on their part, accepted Haig as a means to transfer blame for a military confrontation to the British side. Showing a willingness to solve the dispute through diplomatic channels, they could point at the British Task Force as the initiator of a military showdown that Argentina had never sought.

In sum, Haig's hastiness to score political points as a peacemaker in Latin America before his opponents in the Reagan administration would have an opportunity to floor him, his ambiguous mediation strategy in an attempt to please both Latin Americanists and Europeanists back home seriously compromised his mediation effort. This alternative interpretation of the Falklands case highlights the political complexities that great power mediators may have to deal with in their own back yard. The effective use of leverage presupposes that mediators are able to muster full and continuous support at home for their interventions abroad. When this is lacking, their chances of being successful decrease considerably.

Using leverage: a normative critique

The first two models of international relations presented here portray the conventional wisdom about mediator leverage: they focus particularly on the political influence and the vast material capabilities of mediators to reward or punish (e.g. coerce) parties to accept a proposed solution – often one that is to the mediator's liking (Touval, 1992; 268). Both emphasize the importance of mediator resources significantly surpassing those of the parties in conflict. In short, conflict management is a top-down process, in which exerting power is one of the most important mechanisms for achieving successful outcomes (e.g. maintaining the current stability of the international system).

The third, humanist approach to international relations launches a normative attack on the role of power in mediation based on a divergent perspective on the nature of conflict. Instead of accepting the existing international order and considering conflict an undesirable disturbance to be checked by the great powers, this approach questions the prevailing institutional arrangements of international politics. Taking a bottom-up view, it sees conflict as a result of frustration, suppression, and denial of basic human needs (i.e. identity, security, effective participation in social, economic, and political systems, a sense of control in the pursuit of one's goals) (Azar *et al.*, 1990). This manifests itself in unequal, unjust, or illegitimate institutional arrangements. Conflict, in other words, is an opportunity to transform the political arena in such a way as to increase the need satisfaction of all social groups, not just ruling elites.

This divergent view on the origins of conflict also implies an alternative philosophy of conflict management. It ought to move beyond the mere settlement of conflict in which its negative side effects are kept in check and the *status quo* in international relations is restored. Instead, conflict management should probe beneath the surface of manifest conflict behavior. Underlying issues must be uncovered, which usually remains hidden in power bargaining and adversary behavior. Put differently, a *resolution* of the underlying roots of conflict rather than a pragmatic political settlement is aimed for.

Secondly, accepting conflict to be a call for social change, the task of conflict management is to help set the conditions for a more consensual process dealing with differences and contending claims. Unlike a change imposed by coercion and force, the consensual approach seeks to get parties face up to the need for change, with both of them being conscious of the outcomes and not just instinctively fearing and rejecting them. Social change in this way entails more than a mere substitution of one ruling elite for another.

In this alternative philosophy of conflict management, a mediator plays a crucial yet different role than in the previous models of international relations. In particular, the humanist approach turns the role of power and the meaning of leverage upside down. Rather than the power of the mediator to impose solutions on the conflicting parties, it is the task of the mediator to empower them, especially the weaker party, to resolve their own problems. The mediator's role is primarily facilitative. To be able to do so, mediation needs to move away from the usual high politics bargaining arena to a more informal workshop setting. This setting will have to enable parties to explore their conflict freely, without commitment, without implied obligations to arrive at quick solutions, and probably without giving up any military or bargaining position they may hold. Three clusters of factors are important in creating such a setting: (1) The mediator should be a nonpolitical figure committed to social change whose main asset is expertise and experience in the analysis and resolution of conflict; (2) The exploratory discussions, aimed at defining the problem and clarifying parties' attitudes, should take place in a more or less private setting; and (3) Parties should be people who are not personally in a position of authority, yet influential and preferably close to the policy-makers. The mediation process is more successful the more it leads to a durable social change supported by all parties.

A humanist account of Haig's mediation: limits of a principal great power mediator

Seen from the third perspective on international mediation, Haig's intervention was a typical example of a *status-quo* oriented superpower representative jumping into the conflict when it has reached an international crisis point, acting first and foremost on its own agenda by seeking the prevention of war between two US allies. In addition, in line with the US role as guardian of the rules of interaction in the international system, Haig sought to give a signal to the international community at large that the United States would not tolerate what it saw as 'aggressive behavior'.

Yet the *status-quo post bellum* advanced by the United States would imply a return to precisely the situation that had prompted the Argentine mission in the first place, namely a freeze in the sovereignty conflict and the establishment of a permanent fleet in the South Atlantic. In other words, Haig's effort to impose a solution heavily biased towards one of the disputants, forced Argentina into an underdog position it was unwilling to accept. As Argentine demands escalated, the expected recognition as an equal standing party never came and successive mediation proposals were perceived as 'more of the same'. Thus, as Gamba (1987: 186) concludes: 'the issue still lies in the grey area between a changed *status quo* and an international crisis'.

In short, the Haig mediation effort was a typical example of the wrong party, acting at the wrong time, taking the wrong approach. Arriving on the scene when the conflict had already escalated to a major test of wills, there was not enough time to redefine the stakes, penetrate the community relations on the Islands, and work towards a more durable solution.

Conclusion

David Owen's call for clout may have been appropriate in the Yugoslav conflict, as great powers are better able than small states and other nonpowerful third parties to create opportunities for intervention and be taken seriously as mediators. But once involved, leverage does not guarantee successful mediation outcomes. This is, as we have seen in this chapter, largely dependent upon the context within which mediations operate. More specifically, different theoretical approaches to international mediation highlight different elements of this context as constraints on mediator leverage. Neorealism focuses on the relations between great power states and how these effect the national interests of them as mediators. Both can prevent a powerful mediator from being willing to use its resources to put pressure on conflicting parties. The domestic politics approach emphasizes international constraints on the use of mediator leverage. Foreign politics is considered a source of domestic political disputes, both in parliamentary and bureaucratic arenas, transforming mediation into a double-edged bargaining game. Whether or not a mediator can use its great power resources depends upon the outcome of this game. Finally, the humanist approach turns the leverage issue upside down and points to the importance of neutral power*less* mediators in *empowering* conflicting parties. It raises doubts whether a 'forced agreement' equals 'peace'. Again Yugoslavia can serve as an example: three years after the US-brokered Dayton agreements, the situation continues to be volatile with a serious potential of renewed violence.

Note

1. I am grateful to the Swedish Institute of International Affairs for their financial and hospitable support during my stay in Stockholm. Large parts of this analysis are based on Kleiboer (1998).
2. Argentina's exports to the Soviet Union increased from 5.7 per cent of total exports during the period 1975–79 to 33.7 per cent in 1981 (Moneta, 1984: 313). Thus the anti-communist regime in Argentina had a very opportunistic approach as far as economic trade is concerned. This approach overcame the contradictions arising between ideological demands and economic requirements, and was not basically the consequence of a sophisticated exercise in the formulation of foreign policy. It was to a large extent imposed by circumstances (e.g. the high degree of protectionism and loss of traditional markets in Western Europe).

References

Atiyas, N. B. (1995) 'Mediating Regional Conflicts and Negotiating Flexibility: Peace Efforts in Bosnia-Herzegovina', in D. Druckman and C. R. Mitchell (eds), *Flexibility in International Negotiation and Mediation. The Annals of the American Academy of Political and Social Science*, pp. 185–201.

Azar, E. E., J. L. Davies, A. F. Pickering and H. A. Shahbazi. (1990) 'Track Two Diplomacy: process and Critique', in J.B. Gittler (eds), *The Annual Review of Conflict Knowledge and Conflict Resolution*, vol. 2. New York: Garland Publishing, pp. 296–303.

Bercovitch, J., J. T. Anagnoson and D. Wille. (1991) 'Some Conceptual Issues and Empirical Trends in the Study of Successful Mediation in International Relations', *Journal of Peace Research*, 28, pp. 7–17.

Brookmire, D. and F. Sistrunk. (1980) 'The Effects of Perceived Ability and Impartiality of Mediator and Time Pressure on Negotiation', *Journal of Conflict Resolution*, 24, pp. 311–27.

Dillon, G. M. (1989) *The Falklands, Politics and War*. London: Macmillan – now Palgrave Macmillan.

Evans, P. B., H. K. Jacobson and R. D. Putnam (eds) (1993) *Double-Edged Diplomacy: International Bargaining and Domestic Politics*. Berkeley, CA University of California Press.

Freedman, L. (1988) *Britain and the Falklands War*. Oxford: Blackwell.

Gamba, V. (1987) *The Falklands/Malvinas War: a Model for North–South Crisis Prevention*. London: Allen and Unwin.

Haig, A. L. (1984) *Caveat: Realism, Reagan and Foreign Policy*. New York: Macmillan – now Palgrave Macmillan.

Kaufmann, C. D. (1994) 'U.S. Mediation in the Falklands/Malvinas Crisis', Pew Case Studies in International Affairs, Instructor Copy 431, Washington, DC: Georgetown University.

Kleiboer, M. A. (1996) 'Understanding Success and Failure of International Mediation', *Journal of Conflict Resolution*, 41, pp. 360–89.

Kleiboer, M. A. (1998) *The Multiple Realities of International Mediation*. Boulder, CO: Lynne Rienner.

Lippincot, D. and G. F. Treverton. (1994) Falklands/Malvinas: the Haig Mediation Effort, Pew Case Studies in International Affairs, Instructor Copy 406, Washington, DC: Georgetown University.

Moneta, C. J. (1984) 'The Malvinas Conflict: Some Elements for an Analysis of the Argentine Military Regime's Decision-making Process, 1976–82', *Millennium: Journal of International Studies*, 13, pp. 311–24.

Princen, T. (1992) 'Mediation by a Transnational Organization: the Case of the Vatican', in J. Bercovitch and J.Z. Rubin (eds), *Mediation in International Relations: Multiple Approaches to Conflict Management*. New York: St. Martin's Press, pp. 149–75.

Touval, S. (1982) *The Peace Brokers: Mediators in the Arab-Israeli Conflict 1948–1979*. Princeton: Princeton University Press.

Touval, S. (1992) 'The Superpowers as Mediators', in J. Bercovitch and J.Z. Rubin (eds), *Mediation in International Relations: Multiple Approaches to Conflict Management*. New York: St. Martin's Press, pp. 232–47.

Touval, S. and I. W. Zartman. (1985) 'Introduction: Mediation in Theory', in S. Touval and I. W. Zartman (eds), *International Mediation in Theory and Practice*. Boulder, CO: Westview Press, pp. 7–17.

8
Mediation by International Peacekeepers

James A. Wall, Daniel Druckman and Paul F. Diehl

Introduction

With the end of the Soviet–US rivalry ushering in what may be termed a new world disorder, international peacekeeping has climbed to the top of the agenda of the United Nations and many national governments. Yet, despite the increasing resort to peacekeeping, there is little systematic understanding of its appropriate application. Progress depends on advances in conceptualization and analysis.

To improve the conceptualization, we provide a three-dimensional taxonomy for framing the various peacekeeping missions. And to improve the analysis, we link the literature on mediation (and related forms of conflict management) to that reflecting recent developments in the theory and practice of peacekeeping.

As we think about mediation in the context of peacekeeping operations, we are drawn by the earlier literature to a conception that emphasizes the control of conflict. (See Fetherston, 1994, for a review of this literature.) Traditional peacekeeping consists of the stationing of neutral, lightly armed troops, usually with the permission of the host state, as an interposition force following a cease fire to separate the combatants. Examples are the deployment of UN peacekeeping troops to Cyprus beginning in 1964 and in southern Lebanon in 1978 (Diehl, 1994). In these operations, the peacekeeper relies on leverage to coerce a settlement. However, as Fetherston notes, a shift in perception from control to management is needed 'because it not only legitimizes (conflict-management) activities but shows that peacekeeping without peacemaking and peacebuilding, especially in protracted social conflict situations, will be ineffective in the long term, and possibly also in the short term' (1994: 157). The challenging question is whether peacekeeping can contribute to the long-term resolution of conflicts. By placing peacekeeping in a conflict resolution framework, we can improve our understanding of how this might be accomplished.

Dimensions of peacekeeping

Recent changes in the functions of peacekeeping have indeed altered our conception of the intervention from an emphasis on control to a concern for managing or resolving conflicts. In pursuit of this general goal, peacekeepers have undertaken a wide variety of missions. In our recent taxonomic analysis, we distinguished among 16 types of military peace operations in terms of 11 general characteristics (Diehl *et al.*, 1998). As can be noted in Table 8.1, examples of operations are collective enforcement, preventive deployment, humanitarian assistance, and intervention in support of democracy. Among the characteristics of the peace operations that we considered are the clarity of relationships with the host country, the clarity of procedures, goals, and desired outcomes, the extent of control over the conflict, the ease of exit from the mission, the possibility of mission creep, and the extent to which various constituencies are tolerant of the costs borne by the mission.

The results of a scaling exercise showed that 16 operations could be organized in terms of two dimensions, (a) the role of the peacekeeper

Table 8.1   Types of peacekeeping missions

1. Traditional peacekeeping: stationing troops in an area after the ceasefire in order to keep combatants separate
2. Observation: collecting information and monitoring activities
3. Collective enforcement (e.g. Kuwait): a large-scale operation to defeat an aggressor
4. Election supervision: monitoring an election after a peace agreement
5. Humanitarian assistance during conflict: transportation and distribution of life-sustaining food and medical supplies
6. Disaster relief: assistance following natural disasters
7. State/nation building: restoration of law and order in the absence of government authority (i.e. failed states)
8. Pacification: quelling civil disturbances and defeating local armed groups
9. Preventive deployment: stationing tripwire troops between two combatants to deter the onset or prevent the spread of war
10. Arms control verification: inspection of military facilities, supervision of troop withdrawals, etc. as part of an arms control agreement
11. Protective services: establishment of safe havens, 'no fly' zones, etc.
12. Drug eradication: destruction of vegetation and monitoring of international drug trafficking
13. Anti-terrorism: Supplementing and replacing traditional civilian forces
14. Intervention in support of democracy: overthrowing existing leaders and supporting freely elected government officials
15. Sanctions enforcement: use of military troops to enforce sanctions (e.g. banned arms trading) defined by the international community
16. Aid to domestic, civilian populations: using military forces to enhance the well-being of the population (e.g. public health assistance in Michigan)

(as primary or third party) and (b) the conflict management process (as distributive or integrative). We also noted (c) that the peacekeeper's operations can vary in terms of the ratio of 'combat' (fighting) activities to those of 'contact' (communicating, negotiating, etc.) These dimensions are represented in Figure 8.1.

Briefly consider each of the dimensions; first, the primary/third-party axis. With regard to this dimension, peacekeepers do not always function in third-party roles. In some situations they are actually part of the conflict, invited by (or choosing to align with) one or another party as a member of a coalition in which they are a combatant or negotiating party with clear interests in the outcome. In other situations, they are invited by a host country as a third party to deal with a crisis or resolve an ongoing dispute. In addition, peacekeepers may not retain the same role throughout

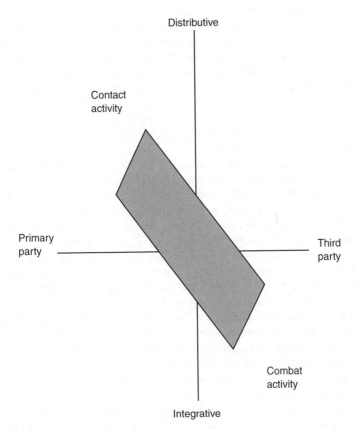

Figure 8.1 Dimensions of peacekeeping operations

their deployment. In some situations, the peacekeeper's third-party role shifts to that of a primary party in the conflict. In Somalia, for example, as a result of deaths to their peacekeepers, the US switched from a third-party humanitarian role to that of primary-party combatant before exiting from the situation.

With regard to the distributive/integrative dimension, the distinction between the two processes was made originally by Walton and McKersie (1965) in labor–management negotiations. Distributive interactions are those in which the parties attempt to increase their own outcomes (usually money, territory, positions, or power) at the other's expense. In integrative interactions, the parties attempt to achieve mutually beneficial (win–win) solutions to a problem. Usually parties in an integrative interaction also seek to improve their relationship and to hammer out enduring solutions.

Finally, as for the third dimension, peacekeepers find that their missions vary in terms of the ratio of combat (fighting) to contact (communicating) activities engaged in by peacekeepers; for example, contrast collective enforcement (higher combat than contact) with election supervision (higher contact than combat). This ratio has been shown to have implications for the likelihood of mediator effectiveness in the sense of settling or resolving the conflict. Mediators are more likely to be effective in missions involving contact or communication activities or those that are less intense in terms of number of fatalities (Kressel and Pruitt, 1989; see also Bercovitch *et al.*, 1991; Bercovitch and Langley, 1993). They are also more likely to be effective in less complex conflicts of relatively short duration (Bercovitch and Langley, 1993).

How are the various missions arranged on these three-dimensional axes? In the primary party-distribution arena, peacekeepers find themselves in missions such as collective enforcement and integrations in support of democracy. They are third parties in such distributive conflicts as preventive deployment and humanitarian assistance during conflict. Operations involving disaster relief or sanctions enforcement cast the peacekeeper in a primary-party role confronted by a situation that can be regarded as being integrative in the sense of searching for joint gains through problem-solving. And they are third parties in such integrative situations as election supervision, observation, and arms control verification.

Turning to the final dimension, we find that restoration, emergency, and monitoring interventions are examples of missions involving more contact than combat activities. And the collective enforcement mission usually entails a high level of combat activity.

As they fulfill their multi-faceted roles (with primary/third party, distributive/integrative, and contract/combat activities) peacekeepers need to think strategically in making decisions. In the sections to follow, we (a) describe a decision model of mediation that shows how a peacekeeper in a third-party role chooses tactics and implements a plan, (b) provide evidence to the

third-party peacekeeper based on our analysis, and (c) develop some implications for other mediation settings.

Peacekeeper decision-making

In the various missions, the peacekeeper targets and attempts to improve
the relationship between the disputing parties. Doing so requires the peacekeeper to develop and implement a strategy or plan. Figure 8.2 gives a con-
cise representation of the strategy development. Initially, the peacekeeper
sets goals, analyses the situation, and develops/chooses the appropriate
strategy and tactics that will move him toward the goal. With the strategy
and tactics in mind, the peacekeeper maneuvers and implements the
strategies.

The feedback arrows in Figure 8.2 simply indicate that the goal-setting,
strategy-development sequence is an ongoing interactive process in which
the peacekeeper modifies his or her behavior based on experience. For example, goals are lowered if the strategy is put into effect and fails; likewise
tactics are modified as the peacekeeper discovers new approaches.

Goal-setting

When setting goals, the peacekeeper must consider the goals of all parties.
He or she might seek to maximize the joint payoffs to all parties, or he or
she can opt for maximization of the disputants' payoffs, at a major sacrifice
to his own. For example, US peacekeepers sacrificed the morale of their

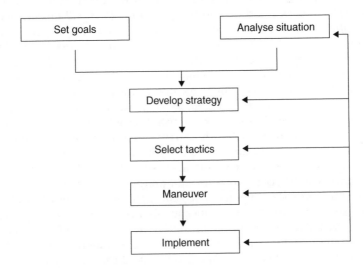

Figure 8.2 Strategy development

troops – and some argue, their combat effectiveness – in Bosnia for the benefit of the Muslims, Serbs, and Croats in that region (Hedges, 1997).

Theoretically, but not practically, peacekeepers can set a goal of maximizing their own outcomes and those accruing to their constituency. Or they may ignore the concrete, short-term outcomes to concentrate upon improvement of the relationships among the parties. For example, this seems to be the goal of the peacekeepers in Cyprus. With the relationship between the Greek and Turkish inhabitants rather stabilized, the peacekeepers choose activities such as jointly installing a sewage system (a superordinate task) not so much for the outcomes they yield but for the improvement of the relationships between the communities.

Situation analysis

When analysing the situation, the peacekeeper must first determine if there is a conflict between the disputing parties. Typically there is, and the peacekeeper must develop skills in analysing the causes and issues of the conflict.

Causes are often distinct from the issues, and many of the causes lie within the parties themselves (Augsburger, 1992), in their perceptions of each other, their communications, past interactions, and structural relationships (Putnam and Wilson, 1982). A disputing party may have the goal of hurting the other or may simply be angry. Such feelings will generate conflict. With regard to perceptions, conflict is likely to occur whenever one party perceives the other side's interactions to be harmful or unfair. Interpersonal communication leads to conflict (Putnam and Poole, 1987) when it entails insults or intentions to harm the other. Structured interdependence between parties who have opposite goals will quickly engender conflict. Because conflict has so many causes, the peacekeeper must become adept at identifying the genesis of the current dispute and determining which ones can be addressed.

Peacekeepers must also understand the issues that are generating problems. When parties interact and come into conflict, it is usually over issues that are either large or small, simple or complex, emotional or substantive (Walton, 1987). Certain issue characteristics have been shown to generate conflict and thereby merit the third-party's attention. One is complexity. Complex issues are more apt to lead to conflict than simple ones. Multiple (versus a few) issues also more often spawn conflict. The explanation in both cases is rather clear: complex and multiple issues are more likely to generate misunderstanding, tap divergent interests, and unearth dissimilar goals. Issues of principle or nonnegotiable needs also generate conflicts (Fisher, 1994; Rouhana and Kelman, 1994). On these types of issues, parties become emotionally bonded to their positions and find that trades – reciprocal give-and-take – are quite difficult. Broad or intangible issues are another source of conflict and are less amenable to conflict resolution

(Vasquez, 1983; Diehl, 1992). Because such issues entail high stakes and are often indivisible, the parties hold strongly to their positions and move toward conflict (Albin, 1993). Once in the conflict, the all-or-nothing characteristic of the issue makes palatable, face-saving, piecemeal trades quite difficult to settle (Zechmeister and Druckman, 1973).

The peacekeeper should address issues and causes that are of low cost to deal with and about which one has some knowledge. Peacekeepers should work with the disputing parties to solve complex issues, multiple issues, and issues of principle. Issues and causes that are intractable and minor should be ignored as long as possible. Also, the agenda should be arranged so that early agreement on simple issues and successful elimination of minor causes of conflict produce momentum for improved relations (Fisher, 1964; Pruitt and Rubin, 1986).

Tactics

Having defined the overall goals for the mission and analysed the situation, the peacekeeper begins to develop a strategy and to select tactics. The literature on third-party processes reveals that the line between strategy and tactics is blurred (Carnevale and Pruitt, 1992) and that third parties (even when placed in primary-party roles), for the most part, rely on sets of tactics rather than major strategies to improve the disputing parties' interactions. This being the case, we discuss tactics first, turning subsequently to strategies.

When managing the conflict, the peacekeeper has three targets for tactical behavior: (1) the disputing parties themselves, (2) the interparty relationship, and (3) the peacekeeper–party relationship (Wall, 1981). Each is discussed in turn.

Disputing parties

In general, a peacekeeper can take steps to move the parties off their current positions and to nudge them toward positions that are more agreeable to the other side. Such steps include:

- help the parties save face when making concessions (Stevens, 1963; Podell and Knapp, 1969; Pruitt and Johnson, 1970);
- help the sides resolve internal disagreements (Lim and Carnevale, 1990);
- help them deal with constituents (Wall, 1981);
- add incentives or payoffs for agreements and concessions (Kissinger, 1979);
- apply negative sanctions, threats, or arguments (Kissinger, 1979);
- propose agreement points that were not recognized by either side (Douglas, 1972); and
- expand the agenda to find a larger arena in which rewards will be higher and costs lower to both sides (Lall, 1966; Pruitt and Rubin, 1986).

Interparty relationship

As the peacekeeper targets the parties, its primary concerns must be on the interparty relationship and the agreement that will be implemented. In seeking these goals, the peacekeeper may follow many routes. One is setting up the interaction: often the peacekeeper discovers that the parties are fighting but not talking; there might be a stalemate in which there is neither talking nor fighting; or there could be an absence of interaction because some other third party has separated the parties and prevented their interaction (as in the case of traditional peacekeeping). In such situations, the peacekeeper must often establish a negotiation relationship between the parties and stabilize the process. Doing so may require that the third party identify the membership of the opposing groups or their leaders and then bring them to the bargaining table.

Having established the interaction and identified the disputing parties, the peacekeeper next faces the task of enticing them to negotiate. Often this is a difficult task, because the parties do not like the negotiation format, they feel – especially after open fighting – that negotiating is a sign of weakness, they believe negotiation gives some legitimacy to the opponent, or they believe negotiation puts them at risk in some way (Pruitt and Rubin, 1986). To overcome these obstacles, the peacekeeper must discover the parties' objections, then discount or reduce them. Also, the outcomes from negotiating or interacting peacefully may be increased or the costs for refusing to negotiate raised, and at times the peacekeeper must protect some of the negotiators.

After initiating interactions, the peacekeeper can establish the protocol for the negotiation process by suggesting and enforcing mechanisms through which the interaction will be conducted. These can be formal, specific agendas or somewhat more informal ones. In addition, he can inform each party as to what behaviors can be expected from the other side and advise each side on its own initial and responsive actions.

When establishing the protocol, the peacekeeper can provide evaluations of the situation. In joint or separate meetings, he can enumerate and describe the important issues, interpret their complexity (or simplicity), note how similar problems have been handled, and provide data as to the costs of continued disputing (Lim and Carnevale, 1990).

Once the interaction is under way, the peacekeeper should channel the initial discussion toward an area in which she believes the parties can agree (Maggiolo, 1971). As both sides discuss this arena, the mediator needs to expand the agenda to bring in additional issues. When doing so he or she should set up trades in which one disputant gives in on issues that are of low value to it but of high value to the opposing side. As he or she facilitates such trades, the peacekeeper must maintain the integrity of the interaction channel, enforce the protocol rules, and proscribe such behaviors as retracting offers previously made or threatening the other side.

At times, the peacekeeper will find it necessary to separate the disputing parties (Pruitt, 1971). This separation allows a peacekeeper to sever, relay, or modify communications for the sake of productive negotiations. Peacekeepers might reopen the channels and bring the parties together if this is useful, forbid their interaction if it seems likely to incite antagonism, or create a formal schedule of meetings if such a mechanism proves helpful.

As the peacekeeper severs and reconstructs the interactions, the parties' power relationship is thereby managed – a relationship that is of great importance to both the peacekeeper and the parties. Typically, the mediator should strike a balance between the parties' total power positions. Doing so lowers the probability that the stronger side will attempt to exploit the weaker and that the weaker will break off the relationship or seek to undermine the stronger's position (Thibaut, 1968). If the power relationship cannot be balanced, the peacekeeper must bargain with or use force against the stronger side to constrain the exercise of its power. As an example, NATO forces in the fall of 1995 carried out intensive artillery bombardments and air strikes against the Serbs in Bosnia. These strikes seriously reduced their power and constrained them from using it in future hostilities (Wall and Stark, 1996).

Peacekeeper–party relationship

To be successful in interactions with the parties, the peacekeeper must gain their trust and confidence. Tactics with these goals are typically labeled 'reflexive' (Kressel and Pruitt, 1985, 1989) and include: appearing neutral, not taking sides on important issues, letting the parties blow off steam, using humor to lighten the atmosphere, attempting to speak the parties' language, expressing pleasure at progress in the negotiation or conflict resolution, keeping the parties focused on the issues, offering new points of view, bringing in relevant information, and correcting one party's misperceptions.

When utilizing these tactics – as well as many of the preceding ones – peacekeepers may find that they sacrifice the image of neutrality. This is not a major obstacle if they demonstrate trustworthiness and effectiveness or if the parties feel that the intervention provides more benefits than costs.

Strategy

Currently, the literature does not provide adequate descriptions or prescriptions for mediation strategies. A strategy, in mediation as well as in warfare, football, chess, bridge, and organizational policy, is a broad plan of action for attaining some goal. For example, in a retreat-and-flank battle strategy, an army retreats when the enemy attacks in force. Once the enemy has extended itself, the army flanks the enemy, striking at one or more vulnerable points. Or in a simpler strategy, the football team for one quarter might establish a running attack and then shift to a mix of running and passing. Note the ingredients in each of these strategies: goals, actions, and timing. Presently, the literature deals adequately with the goals and action components of third-party strategies but ignores the last element.

In this literature, one group of researchers (e.g. Kressel, 1972; Kressel and Pruitt, 1985, 1989; van de Vliert, 1985; Carnevale, 1986; Carnevale and Henry, 1989) describes third-party strategies as techniques that are oriented toward a similar goal. Specifically, Kressel and Pruitt (1985, 1989) hold that a reflexive strategy consists of techniques that orient the third party to the dispute and establish the ground work for later activities. A substantive strategy includes techniques that deal directly with the issues and actively promotes settlement, whereas contextual tactics alter the climate or conditions between the disputants.

A second group of scholars in the literature (e.g. Touval and Zartman, 1985; Silbey and Merry, 1986; Kolb, 1987; McLaughlin *et al.*, 1991; Carnevale and Pruitt, 1992) have taken a different tack, combining techniques that share conceptual or operational similarities (other than goal). For example, Silbey and Merry's (1986) typology contains four principal categories: (1) the third party's presentation of self and program, (2) its control of the mediation process, (3) control over the substantive issues, and (4) activation of commitments and norms. In a similar fashion, Kolb (1987), after in-depth interviews, laid out alternative strategies or postures that the third party assumed. She distinguished between helping and fact-finding corporate ombudsman roles: the helper invents individualized solutions to the problems people present, whereas the fact-finder investigates whether proper procedures were followed and if there are plausible explanations for a complaint.

A third group of researchers (Lewicki and Sheppard, 1985; Elangovan, 1995) classify the third-party's techniques into strategies according to the target for control. In the group, Sheppard (1984) maintains that third-party strategic behaviors differ along two principal lines: decision control and process control. A third-party's decision control is the management of the outcomes of the dispute. By contrast, process control entails control over the presentation and interpretation of evidence in the dispute. Elangovan (1995), relying heavily on Sheppard's concepts, generates five strategies:

- Means control strategy: the third party influences the process of resolution.
- Ends control strategy: the third party influences the outcomes.
- Full control strategy: the third party influences both.
- Low control strategy: the third party influences neither outcomes nor process.
- Part control strategy: the third party shares both controls with the disputants.

Finally, another group of investigators (e.g. Wall and Rude, 1985; Karambayya and Brett, 1989; Lim and Carnevale, 1990; Wall and Blum, 1991; Kim *et al.*, 1993) has defined strategies as techniques that are used together by third parties when they deal with disputes. For example Kim *et al.* (1993), relying on a factor analysis, found techniques used together in four strategic combinations: reconciliation, dependence, analysis, and data gathering. In the 'analysis' strategy, third parties were found to rely on the techniques of getting a grasp of the situation, analysing the parties, and capping the agreement with a handshake, meal, or drink.

The above four approaches deal quite adequately with the goals and action components of third-party strategies. And some of the literature (Elangovan, 1995) deals creatively with the contingencies under which the various strategies are or should be applied. However, none of the approaches deals with the timing aspect of strategies. This omission is unfortunate, because timing is an essential element in any strategy. In a retreat-and-flank battle strategy, for example, *when* the army flanks and attacks is essential. If it is either too early or too late, the strategy is a failure. Likewise, *when* a third party uses various sets of techniques is quite important.

Maneuvering

The peacekeepers' options for maneuvering are manifold. Specifically, they can increase their own strength, reducing that of the parties, or leveraging them. If the peacekeepers attempt to weaken either or both parties, perhaps by closing off some of their options or by preventing them from forming coalitions, they risk generating resentment. Possibly one or both parties' retaliation may convert the initial third-party relationship into an adversarial primary-party affair.

Under some circumstances, the peacekeeper might try leveraging the parties, that is, bring her own strength to bear at a time or place that is advantageous. For example, Secretary of State Henry Kissinger in the Yom Kippur war of 1973 delayed munitions shipments to the Israelis until they had only a one-day supply. Nevertheless, this approach also risks their resentment and encourages retaliation.

Implementation

We propose a simple contingency approach for implementing peacekeeping tactics and strategies. Such an approach is based on two observations: (1) The effectiveness of most tactics are contingent on the situation, and (2) we know more about what a peacekeeper can do than we do about what is effective, at least given the current state of research findings.

The first observation dictates that the peacekeeper should choose tactics that fit the situation. To date, we know that the following behaviors are likely to be effective in a wide range of situations:

- separating aggressive opponents (Pruitt, 1971);
- controlling the agenda and helping the sides to establish priorities among the issues (Lim and Carnevale, 1990);
- adding control to the process (Prein, 1984); and
- being friendly to both sides (Ross *et al.*, 1990).

Other behaviors or tactics are more likely to be effective in some situations. Humor might be used when the peacekeeper detects hostility (Harbottle, 1992). If there are many issues, the peacekeeper should simplify the agenda and suggest trade-offs. When the disputing parties lack bargaining experience, the peacekeeper should educate them or note procedures that have been used in the past. And when the parties are able to resolve their own problems, the third party for the most part should not intrude (Lederach, 1995).

The second observation suggests that peacekeepers should adopt a pragmatic approach. They should first try techniques that seem reasonable. If none of these works, then they should try a different set. Again, if there is failure, a new set should be put in place and the failure noted.

This approach should be continued until the relationship and the outcomes between the parties improve. Most important, the peacekeeper, in this process, must be diagnostic, remembering what failed and what was successful for each episode; this is consistent with the experiential learning model discussed above. He or she should also use feedback in the process of evaluating and modifying the goals, tactics, and maneuvers.

Feedback

As noted earlier, the feedback arrows in Figure 8.2 indicate that goals, tactics, and strategies are modified as the peacekeeper/mediator gains experience. For example, goals are usually lowered when a strategy fails; likewise, tactics are modified as the peacekeeper discovers new approaches.

While the feedback adjustments are manifold in any mediation, the most important ones for the peacekeepers are those involving goals. When establishing and adjusting his goals, the mediator must continually make trade-offs between micro-level effectiveness – the effective performance of specific military duties – and macro-level effectiveness – was the mission successful? A very specific example is that of a peacekeeper who refrains from killing snipers – a choice not to pursue the micro-goal of self defense – so as to improve the chances that the leaders from the two sides will meet and make concessions at the bargaining table, a sign of success at the macro-level. Or a peacekeeper might violate the macro-goal of neutrality in order to protect civilians in a 'safe haven' under her command.

The cultural environment

When they mediate – setting goals, analysing the situation, developing and implementing strategies – peacekeepers interface with two cultures, a civilian culture and that of the nation to which they are posted.

Civilian culture

The first, perhaps alien, culture is that of civilians. Peacekeepers usually are soldiers who have operated for an extensive period within a military culture, and who are accustomed to taking orders and conforming. They are healthy, well fed, well clothed, and regularly well paid. In short, they exist in a protective, orderly environment that has a great deal of structure. The civilian culture, especially that to which the peacekeeper is likely to be posted, is quite different. It is frequently disorderly, and life for many civilians is very tentative; they are often sick, ill-clothed, and paid erratically. Furthermore, civilians, for the most part, do not like being ordered about, especially by military personnel.

The impact of the military–civilian divide is multifaceted, with one critical aspect being differences in goals. The peacekeeper's goal (Figure 8.2) of keeping the peace differs from the civilian's goal of staying alive and earning a living, and the simultaneous pursuit of these may generate conflict rather than peace. For example, roadblocks might be set up to keep one militant faction from having access to and attacking the other. The goal from a peacekeeper's – traditional soldier's – perspective is to minimize conflicts, which will result in civilian, as well as military, casualties. This is a legitimate goal, but the farmer's goals might be more pragmatic – to get to his fields without waiting and to gain access to markets on the other side of the dividing line.

Another impact is that civilians often tend to dislike or distrust soldiers; therefore, peacekeepers must vigilantly monitor civilians' reactions to their presence and behavior. Often the most straightforward, nonassertive tactics can be misunderstood and resented. (For example, asking a civilian family to get out of a car is many times seen as a prelude to looting it.)

Indigenous culture

The second culture encountered is that endemic to the disputing country/ies. Seldom is the peacekeeper given a mission within his own country. Rather, he is often posted to countries which (a) perceive conflict differently, (b) have different social structures, and (c) have different norms concerning interpersonal relations.

Consider first the perception of conflict. People from many non-industrialized cultures think of conflict as the normal way of interacting. From childhood, they are taught to settle differences by fighting (Merry, 1989). Therefore they tend to accept and rely on conflict (somewhat as an alcoholic relies on alcohol for life-sustaining calories). That is, conflict has a 'win–win' appeal. In most Western cultures (i.e. the peacekeeper's culture), conflict is often viewed as one person's opposing or negatively affecting another person's interests (Pruitt and Rubin, 1986; Putnam and Poole, 1987; Donohue and Kolt, 1992; Thomas, 1992) – that is, conflict is perceived as having a 'win–lose' effect on the parties.

From a different perspective, Polynesians and several other agricultural-based societies view conflict as a mutual entanglement that is detrimental to both parties (Wall and Callister, 1995) – that is, the situation is 'lose– lose'. For Koreans and residents of other Asian counties with a strong Confucian underpinning, conflict is viewed as a mutual disruption of society's harmony (Hahn, 1986; Augsburger, 1992). These societies feel that the character and impact of conflict on the disputants is irrelevant, although it is 'lose–lose'. The major negative impact is the disruption of the larger community and the violation of its norms.

The second cultural factor is the structure of society and the resultant perceptions. Cultures in the West, for the most part, are rather egalitarian and do not have a strong ingroup–outgroup orientation. Other cultures – such as the Muslims and the Japanese – have this orientation. Also consider that within many cultures – mid-African and Polynesian – family and clan structures prevail.

Norms

Finally, a major cultural impact comes from the society's norms; even casual observations reveal that these vary from culture to culture. One widely accepted norm is reciprocity (Gouldner, 1960). In Western societies (Homans, 1961) and in Japan (Goldman, 1994), people feel that an outcome given to one individual or group obligates that person, in return, to give an outcome (repayment) in some form to the other person. Similarly, a cost imposed on a person permits, even obligates, him or her to retaliate against the person imposing that cost. Although many cultures abide by this norm, others do not. Rather, they perceive that an outcome given by one party to another is a sign of weakness or deference. Thereby, it does not obligate the recipient to reciprocate; instead, it raises the expectation that the original party should deliver an additional outcome.

Because the reciprocity norm has a strong impact on an individual's behaviors, the peacekeeper needs to know if that norm exists in the culture to which he or she is posted. For example, in cultures with strong hierarchial structures, reciprocity is not a societal norm. There will be some reciprocity within levels, but not between them. Typically, the higher-level person does not initially make a concession to a lower-level person, because that would be incongruous with his or her status. And when receiving a concession from a lower-level person, the higher-level person does not reciprocate, because he or she considers it a gift to which a high-level person is entitled (Augsburger, 1992).

Advice for peacekeepers

Two of our primary goals in this chapter were to improve the conceptualization of peacekeeping and to enhance its analysis. By delineating the 16 peacekeeping missions (Table 8.1) and framing them with a three-dimensional paradigm (Figure 8.1), we hope we have accomplished our first goal. And by utilizing a simple decision model to link the peacekeeping and mediation/conflict management literature, we have provided some insight into the peacekeeping process.

In addition to these contributions, our paradigms enable us to tender some prescriptions for peacekeepers and, conversely, to present some novel insights into mediation research.

Distributive versus integrative processes

The distinction between integrative and distributive encounters has a major relevance for the peacekeeping roles. Namely, different tactics are suited for the two situations. In an integrative situation, the peacekeeper should adopt a problem-solving approach (Kressel *et al.*, 1994). This approach is characterized by persistent question-asking intended to achieve an understanding of the causes of the conflict. The peacekeeper should be willing to depart from strict neutrality, especially when the conflict is being fueled by one of the parties. By doing so, however, the peacekeeper runs the risk of becoming a primary party in the conflict. It is a more demanding challenge than a settlement-oriented approach (discussed below), and its effectiveness depends on the extent to which the peacekeeper is flexible and the disputing parties are not eager to reach quick settlements as when, for example, time pressures are low and alternatives are attractive.

By contrast, distributive conflicts are often approached with a settlement orientation (Kressel *et al.*, 1994). That is, peacekeepers are primarily concerned with getting a settlement. They remain neutral and do not question the disputing parties about the underlying issues in their conflict. This approach is efficient and may be beneficial if the parties are strongly motivated to end their dispute as when, for example, they are faced with time pressure or have unattractive alternatives. The settlements may, however, be less durable and the approach can produce unfavorable attitudes toward the peacekeeper.

Several other tactics, discussed earlier, can also be used in distributive situations. They support or enhance the peacekeeper's leverage over the disputants in order to attain a settlement that works for the parties and is acceptable to the peacekeeper and his constituents. Examples are managing the parties' power relationship, managing the interaction through a schedule or agenda, channeling the discussion, separating the parties when necessary, and closing off some options. While appearing neutral with regard to desired outcomes, the peacekeeper attempts to exert considerable control over the process – referred to above as a *means control strategy*. It has the advantage of providing a structure for discussing and settling contentious issues. It has the disadvantage of creating resentment toward the peacekeeper as well as jeopardizing future interactions between the parties.

The tactics used by peacekeepers to settle distributive conflicts are not unlike those used by the bargainers themselves. They focus somewhat narrowly on interests, compete with each other for control over the process, and attempt to win in the sense of maximizing relative gains in the outcome. This kind of competitive bargaining is typical of parties in the sorts of antagonistic relationships that exist between them in the conflict zones where peacekeepers are deployed (Druckman, 1980). It has been shown to perpetuate or hinder future relations between those parties (Druckman *et al.*, 1988). A major challenge for peacekeepers in distributive settings is to change the way the parties perceive their conflict.

In order to change distributive perceptions, the mediator must, first, persuade the parties that their conflict is fueled by misunderstandings that may polarize the differences between them on interests or values. Second, she must offer the possibility that solutions can be found that do not require concessions from either party. The parties' orientations must be changed from maximizing relative gains to seeking joint gains. Third, the parties must be encouraged to engage in a strenuous process that includes the sharing of information about interests and needs. Developing trust in the peacekeeper is essential; the parties must believe that the peacekeeper is committed to searching for the best solution. Fourth, the peacekeeper must help the parties develop a view of the dispute in terms of implications of any agreement for their long-term relationship. Exposing them to arguments about the importance of relationships in negotiation (Fisher and Brown, 1988) and in post-Cold War international relations (Saunders, 1991; Stern and Druckman, 1995) may contribute to the changes of perspective needed to be effective.

Contact and combat activities

Having offered some prescriptives for distributive versus integrative disputes we now shift focus to the contact/combat facet. Here the bottom line is unequivocal: Peacekeepers need to be trained for both contact and combat activities. In the highly charged conflict situations that they often face, they at times must resort to using coercive tactics in order to prevent further escalations in the interactions or simply to protect themselves against attacks launched by one or the other party.

Even though there has been a change in the purpose of peacekeeping operations – from conflict control to management – there is still a large amount of combat-related activity in many types of missions. Based on their survey of Canadian soldiers serving in Bosnia ($N = 197$) and Croatia ($N = 185$), Last and Eyre (1995) reported that an average of about 25 per cent of peacekeepers' time is spent in combat-related work. The most frequent combat experiences reported were being a target for rocks thrown, encountering mines, coming under small arms' fire, being restrained, and being held at gun point. The most frequent *contact* experiences were working with interpreters, negotiating with civilian police and belligerent factions, and interacting with local civilians.

Instructive results were obtained when the data were broken down by ranks. Combat activities occurred with roughly equal frequency at all levels (enlisted, senior NCOs, officers), but contact activities were considerably more frequent among officers; the officers reported about twice as many contact (about 40 per cent) as combat (about 20 per cent) activities in the Bosnian operation and almost three times as many contact (40 versus 15 per cent) activities in the Croatian operation.

With regard to activities involving negotiation, almost all officers and many senior NCOs reported having had these experiences with a soldier or officer of one of the warring factions; only 29 per cent of the enlisted group reported having these experiences. Similarly, more officers (60 per cent) reported negotiating with civilian leaders of one of the factions than the enlisted group (about 15 per cent). With regard to mediation or conciliation, about 50 per cent of the officers and NCOs reported that they had these experiences while only about 10 per cent of the enlisted officers had performed mediative functions.

These findings support the observation that modern military peacekeepers are involved in managing or resolving conflicts (i.e. contact activity), particularly at the level of officers. For this reason it is important that they be trained to develop negotiation and mediation skills. This is also the case for junior officers and enlisted personnel who are often, even if less frequently, confronted by situations in which they must deal directly with interpersonal or intergroup conflicts. However, the extent to which these skills are needed depends, to a large extent, on the type of mission. The Canadian survey documents soldiers' activities in one type of operation, which they refer to as 'limiting damage'. This type of mission may consist of more combat activities than monitoring missions and more contact than missions involving collective enforcement. Contact skills are also less important when peacekeepers are stationed as part of an interposition force in an area of low population density such as the Sinai Desert than when they are assigned to such missions as election supervision or humanitarian assistance where they must interact on a daily basis with the local population.

Clearly, peacekeepers must learn to move between roles, sometimes being combat-ready and at other times being sensitive to the sources of conflict and issues in the role of a third party. To do this effectively, they need to be trained in a variety of relevant skills so that they can handle the changes that occur within missions as well as assignments to different types of missions. This is best done through practice exercises that anticipate the variability that exists in the setting where they must perform (see chapter 3 of Druckman and Bjork, 1994). We have proposed elsewhere a confidence-building approach to mediation skills acquisition based on this principle and taking into account the possible incompatibilities of skills needed for different activities and missions. (The details are discussed in chapter 7 of Druckman *et al.*, 1997.)

Primary- and third-party roles

As noted above, peacekeepers must learn to shift roles, sometimes using combat skills and at other times, relying upon contact proficiencies. Such flexibility is also necessary for their primary- and third-party roles.

In theory, the distinction between primary- or third-party roles is rather clear. For primary-party missions (e.g. disaster relief, collective enforcement), the peacekeeper must control or modify the other parties' behavior in some fashion. A simple example is having civilians in a disaster relief mission to line up for water allocations; a more complex example is forcing a hostile army to withdraw from occupied territory (Abizaid, 1993).

By contrast, in third-party missions, the peacekeeper for the most part controls the relationship between two other groups who are really disputants. The activities and skills are quite different from those needed in the primary-party role; namely, they are more likened to mediation and arbitration activities – albeit perhaps rather forceful ones – than to negotiation and one-on-one confrontation activities of the primary party.

In practice, however, the distinction between the two roles blurs as the peacekeepers play them concomitantly. They may be perceived as playing a role that is different than the one intended, or they shift roles in or between missions. Perhaps simultaneous role fulfillment is the most prevalent of these obfuscations. In Somalia, for example, the Indian peacekeepers were officially on a humanitarian assistance (primary-party) mission to deliver life-sustaining food to the population. Since rival factions and clans vied for control of many areas in which the food was to be delivered, the peacekeepers frequently had to broker peace between/among the factions as they were delivering the aid.

This blurring and shifting of roles spawns a prescription somewhat analogous to that proffered for the contact/combat activities: peacekeepers must be trained for both primary- and third-party activities. In addition, they must learn when and when not to shift from one role to another.

Conclusion: implications for civilian mediation

Having drawn prescriptions for peacekeepers from the analyses, we now shift our focus to draw insights from our peacekeeping observations that could prove useful for describing mediation in other settings. The first step in our extrapolations is to emphasize that peacekeeping entails the management of intense conflicts; therefore, our observations are most relevant to the mediation of other intense conflicts.

One insight is spawned by the primary/third-party axis in Figure 8.1. This axis, in tandem with our earlier discussion, reveals that a mediator may become a primary party in an intensive dispute even though she intended to play, or previously served in, a third-party role. For example, such a shift was reported recently in a Chinese community mediation. Initially, the street committee mediator served as a third party, mediating between two neighbors over the punishment for one son's vandalism. When he was threatened by the son (with some family backing) and consequently had him jailed by the police, the street committee shifted to a primary-party role.

This example also indicates that mediators outside of the peacekeeping arena also can shift from contact to combat roles. Admittedly the shifts to more forceful techniques made by hostage negotiations, industrial mediators, community mediators, or marriage counselors are not as drastic or potent as those taken by peacekeepers. Yet they do entail a progression from contact to combat tactics. Such a movement is seen in an example of a strong-arm mediation by two Malaysian policemen: A citizen had reported to them that he had been swindled by a local con-man. When the police brought the victim and con-man together to settle the problem, charges and counter charges followed. Knowing the reputation of the con-man, the police beat him, returned the money to its rightful owner, and wrote up the case as 'unsolvable'.

Having considered the axes in Figure 8.1 separately, we turn to a combination, noting that a mediator's adoption of more forceful techniques (i.e. a choice of forceful tactics in Figure 8.2 and a movement toward the combat end of the contact–combat axis in Figure 8.1) often is accompanied by a shift to a primary-party (versus a third-party) role. Such a shift is noted in peacekeeping: when a Dutch peacekeeper comes under fire while he mans a roadblock, it is very difficult for him to act as a third party, to feel like a third party, or be perceived as a third party when he returns fire. Likewise it is quite difficult for a mediator in a labor–management dispute to remain perceived as a third party when it threatens one side or points out illegal activities. The threatening labor–management mediator must realize, like the Dutch peacekeeper who is returning fire, that he/she has shifted to the 'combat-primary party' arena and must adjust his/her strategy and tactics accordingly.

We close with a conclusion about which we have mixed feelings: In the mediation of intense conflict by peacekeepers as well as by civilians, we are able to evaluate the mediation when it fails. However, it is very difficult to evaluate when it is not a failure. Seldom is any intense conflict – in peacekeeping or civilian sectors – totally resolved by mediation. Rather, it tends to improve; it does not escalate; or it diminishes over the long run. We are pleased to be able to extrapolate confidently from one setting to another. Yet, we are dissatisfied that giving mediation 'two thumbs up' is as difficult in civilian settings as it is in peacekeeping.

References

Abizaid, J. (1993) 'Lessons for Peacekeeping', *Military Review*, March, pp. 11–19.

Albin, C. (1993) 'The role of fairness in negotiation', *Negotiation Journal*, 9: 223–44.

Augsburger, D. W. (1992) *Conflict Mediation Across Cultures: Pathways and patterns*. Louisville, KY: Westminster, John Knox.

Bercovitch, J. and J. Langley. (1993) 'The nature of the dispute and the effectiveness of international mediation', *Journal of Conflict Resolution*, 37: 670–91.

Bercovitch, J. J. Anagnoson and D. Wille. (1991) 'Some conceptual issues and empirical trends in the study of successful mediation in international relations', *Journal of Peace Research*, 28: 7–17.

Carnevale, P. and R. Henry. (1989) 'Determinants of mediation tactics in public sector disputes: A contingency analysis', *Journal of Applied Social Psychology*, 19: 469–88.

Carnevale, P. J. D. (1986) 'Mediating disputes and decisions in organizations', *Research on* 1: 251–69.

Carnevale, P. J. D. and D. G. Pruitt. (1992) 'Negotiation and mediation', *Annual Review of Psychology*, 43: 531–82.

Diehl, P. (1992) 'What are they fighting for? The importance of issues in international conflict research', *Journal of Peace Research*, 29: 333–44.

Diehl, P. (1994) *International Peacekeeping*. Baltimore, MD: Johns Hopkins University Press.

Diehl, P., D. Druckman, and J. Wall. (1998) 'International peacekeeping and conflict resolution: a taxonomic analysis with implications', *Journal of Conflict Resolution*, 42: 33–55.

Donohue, W. A. and R. Kolt. (1992) *Managing Interpersonal Conflict*. Newbury Park. CA: Sage.

Douglas, A. (1972) *Industrial Peacekeeping*. New York: Columbia University Press.

Druckman, D. (1980) 'Social–psychological factors in regional politics', in *Comparative Regional Systems*, W. J. Feld and G. Boyd (eds). New York: Pergamon.

Druckman, D. and R. A. Bjork (eds), (1994) *Learning, Remembering, Believing: Enhancing Human Performance*. Washington, DC: National Academy Press.

Druckman, D. B. Broome and S. H. Korper. (1988) 'Value differences and conflict resolution: Facilitation or delinking?', *Journal of Conflict Resolution*, 32: 473–88.

Druckman, D. J. Singer and H. VanCott (eds) (1997) *Enhancing Organizational performance*. Washington, DC: National Academy Press.

Elangovan, A. R. 1995 'Managerial third-party dispute intervention: a prescriptive model of strategy selection', *Academy of Management Review*, 20: 800–30.

Fetherston, A. B. (1994) *Toward a Theory of United Nations Peacekeeping*. New York: St. Martin's Press – now Palgrave Macmillan.

Fisher, R. (1964) 'Fractionating conflict', in *International Conflict and Behavioral Science: The Craigville Papers*, R. Fisher (ed.). New York: Basic Books.

Fisher, R. and S. Brown. (1988) *Getting Together*. Boston: Houghton Mifflin.

Fisher, R. J. (1994) 'Generic principles for resolving intergroup conflict', *Journal of Social Issues*, 50: 47–66.

Goldman, A. (1994) 'The centrality of "Ningensei" to Japanese negotiating and inter-personal relationships: Implications for U.S.–Japanese communication', *International Journal of Intercultural Relations*, 18: 29–54.

Gouldner, A. W. (1960) 'The norm of reciprocity: A preliminary statement', *American Sociological Review*, 25: 161–78.

Hahn, P. C. (1986) *Korean Jurisprudence. Politics and Culture.* Seoul, Korea: Yonsei University Press.

Harbottle, M. (1992) 'What is proper soldiering?', Report from the Centre for International Peacebuilding, Oxford, England.

Hedges, C. (1997) 'Studying Bosnia's U.S. prisoners of war', Sunday, 30 March, *New York Times*, p. 6Y.

Homans, G. C. (1961) *Social Behavior: Its Elementary Forms.* New York: Harcourt, Brace and World.

Karambayya, R. and J. M. Brett. (1989) 'Managers handling disputes: third-party roles and perceptions of fairness', *Academy of Management Journal*, 32: 687–704.

Kim, N. H., J. A. Wall, D. W. Solm and J. S. Kim. (1993) 'Community and industrial mediation in South Korea', *Journal of Conflict Resolution*, 37: 361–81.

Kissinger. H. (1979) *White House Years.* Boston: Little, Brown.

Kolb, D. M. (1987) 'Corporate ombudsman and organizational conflict', *Journal of Conflict Resolution*, 31: 673–92.

Kressel, K. (1972) 'Labor Mediation: An Exploratory Survey'. Albany, NY: Association of Labor Mediation Agencies.

Kressel, K. and D. Pruitt. (1985) 'Themes in the mediation of social conflict', *Journal of Social Issues*, 41: 179–96.

Kressel, K. and D. G. Pruitt. (1989) 'Conclusion: a research perspective on the media-tion of social conflict', in K. Kressel and D.G. Pruitt (eds), *Mediation Research*. San Francisco: Jossey-Bass.

Kressel, K., E. A. Frontera, S. Forlenza, F. Butler and L. Fish. (1994) 'The settlement orientation vs. the problem-solving style in custody mediation', *Journal of Social Issues*, 50: 67–84.

Lall, A. (1966) *Modern International Negotiation: Principles and Practice.* New York: Columbia University Press.

Last, D. and K. C. Eyre. (1995) 'Combat and contact skill in peacekeeping: Surveying recent Canadian experience in UNPROFOR', Unpublished manuscript, The Lester B. Pearson Canadian International Peacekeeping Training Centre.

Lederach, J. P. (1995) *Beyond Prescription: Perspectives on Conflict, Culture, and Training.* Syracuse, NY: Syracuse University Press.

Lewicki, R. and B. Sheppard. (1985) 'Choosing how to intervene: Factors affecting the use of process and outcome control in third party dispute resolution', *Journal of Occupational Behavior*, 6: 49–64.

Lim, R. and P. Carnevale. (1990) 'Contingencies in the mediation of disputes', *Journal of Personality and Social Psychology*, 58: 259–72.

Maggiolo, W. A. (1971) *Techniques of Mediation in Labor Disputes.* Dobbs Ferry, NY: Oceana.

McLaughlin, M. E., P. Carnevale and R. G. Lim. (1991) 'Professional mediators' judgements of mediation tactics: multidimensional scaling and cluster analysis', *Journal of Applied Psychology*, 76: 465–72.

Merry, S. (1989) 'Mediation in non-industrial societies', in *Mediation Research*, K. Kressel and D. G. Pruitt (eds). San Francisco: Jossey-Bass.

Podell, J. E. and W. M. Knapp. (1969) 'The effect of mediation on the perceived firmness of the opponent', *Journal of Conflict Resolution*, 13: 511–20.

Prein, H. (1984) 'A contingency approach to conflict resolution', *Group and Organizational Studies*, 9: 81–102.

Pruitt, D. G. (1971) 'Indirect communication and the search for agreement in negotiations', *Journal of Applied Social Psychology*, 1: 205–39.

Pruitt, D. G. and D. Johnson. (1970) 'Mediation as an aid to face saving in negotiation', *Journal of Personality and Social Phsychology*, 14: 239–46.

Pruitt, D. G. and J. Z. Rubin. (1986) *Social Conflict: Escalation Stalemate, and Settlement*. New York: Random House.

Putnam, L. L. and M. S. Poole. (1987) 'Conflict and negotiation', in *Handbook of Organizational Communication Yearbook*, F. M. Jablin, L. L. Putnam, K. H. Roberts, and L. W. Porter (eds). Newbury Park, CA: Sage.

Putnam, L. L. and S. R. Wilson. (1982) 'Communication strategies in organizational conflicts: Reliability and validity of a measurement scale', in *Communication Yearbook*, M. Burgood (ed.). Beverly Hills, CA: Sage.

Ross, W. H., D. E. Conlon and A. Lind. (1990) 'The mediator as a leader: effects of behavioural style and deadline certainty on negotiation', *Group and Organizational Studies*.

Rouhana, N. N. and H. C. Kelman. (1994) 'Promoting joint thinking in international conflicts: an Israeli–Palestinian continuing workshops', *Journal of Social Issues*, 50: 157–78.

Saunders, H. H. (1991) 'Officials and citizens in international relationships: The Dartmouth Conference', in *The Psychodynamics of International Relationships*, vol. 2, V. D. Volkan, J. V. Montville and D. A. Julius (eds). Lexington, MA: Lexington Books.

Sheppard, B. H. (1984) 'Third party conflict intervention: a procedural framework', *Research in Organizational Behavior*, 6: 141–90.

Silbey, S. and S. Merry. (1986) 'Mediator settlement strategies', *Law and Policy*, 8: 7–32.

Stern, P. C. and D. Druckman. (1995) 'Has the "earthquake" of (1989) toppled international relations theory?', *Peace Psychology Review*, 1: 109–22.

Stevens, C. M. (1963) *Strategy and Collective Bargaining Negotiations*. New York: McGraw-Hill.

Thibaut, J. (1968) 'The development of contractual norms in bargaining: reliction and refinement', *Journal of Conflict Resolution*, 12: 102–12.

Thomas, K. W. (1992) 'Conflict and negotiation processes in organizations', in *Handbook of Industrial and Organizational Psychology*, M. D. Dunnette and L. M. Hough (eds). Palo Alto, CA: Consulting Psychologists Press.

Touval, S. and I. W. Zartman. (eds) (1985) *The Man in the Middle: International Mediation in Theory and Practice*. Boulder, CO: Westview.

van de Vliert, E. (1985) 'Conflict and conflict management', in *A New Handbook of Work and Organizational Psychology*, H. Thierry, P. J. D. Drenth and C. J. de Wolff (eds). Hove, Sussex: Lawrence Erlbaum.

Vasquez, J. (1983) 'The tangibility of issues and global conflict: a test of Rosenau's issue area typology', *Journal of Peace Research*, 20: 179–92.

Wall, J. A. (1981) 'Mediation: an analysis, review and proposed research', *Journal of Conflict Resolution*, 25: 157–80.

Wall, J. A. and M. Blum. (1991) 'Community mediation in the People's Republic of China', *Journal of Conflict Resolution*, 35: 3–20.

Wall, J. A. and R. R. Callister. (1995) 'Conflict and its management', *Journal of Management*, 21: 515–58.

Wall, J. A. and D. Rude. (1985) 'Judicial mediation: Techniques, strategies, and situational effect', *Journal of Social Issues*, 41: 47–64.

Wall, J. A. and J. Stark. (1996) 'Techniques and sequences in mediation strategies: a proposed model for research', *Negotiation Journal*, 12: 231–9.

Walton, R. E. (1987) *Managing Conflict*. Reading, MA: Addison-Wesley.

Walton, R. E. and R. B. McKersie. (1965) *A Behavioral Theory of Labor Negotiations: An Analysis of a Social Interaction System*. New York: McGraw-Hill.

Zechmeister, K. and D. Druckmam. (1973) 'Determinants of resolving a conflict of interest: a simulation of political decision making', *Journal of Conflict Resolution*, 17: 63–88.

Part III
Extending the Range of Mediation

9
Interactive Problem-solving: Informal Mediation by the Scholar-Practitioner

Herbert C. Kelman

Introduction

For some years, my colleagues and I have been actively engaged in the development and application of an approach to the resolution of international conflicts for which we use the term 'interactive problem-solving'. The fullest – indeed, the paradigmatic – application of the approach is represented by problem-solving workshops (Kelman, 1972, 1979, 1992, 1996b; Kelman and Cohen, 1986), although it involves a variety of other activities as well. In fact, I have increasingly come to see interactive problem-solving as an approach to the macro-processes of international conflict resolution, in which problem-solving workshops and similar micro-level activities are integrally related to official diplomacy (Kelman, 1996a).

The approach derives most directly from the work of John Burton (1969, 1979, 1984). While my work follows the general principles laid out by Burton, it has evolved in its own directions, in keeping with my own disciplinary background, my particular style, and the cases on which I have focused my attention. My work has concentrated since 1974 on the Arab–Israeli conflict, and particularly on the Israeli–Palestinian component of that conflict. I have also done some work, however, on the Cyprus conflict and have maintained an active interest in several other intense, protracted identity conflicts at the international or intercommunal level, such as the conflicts in Bosnia, Sri Lanka, and Northern Ireland.

Interactive problem-solving

Interactive problem-solving – as manifested particularly in problem-solving workshops – is an academically based, unofficial third-party approach, bringing together representatives of parties in conflict for direct communication.

The third party typically consists of a panel of social scientists who, among them, possess expertise in group process and international conflict, and at least some familiarity with the conflict region. The role of the third party in our model differs from that of the traditional mediator. Unlike many mediators, we do not propose (and certainly, unlike arbitrators, we do not impose) solutions. Rather, we try to facilitate a process whereby solutions will emerge out of the interaction between the parties themselves. The task of the third party is to provide the setting, create the atmosphere, establish the norms, and offer the occasional interventions that make it possible for such a process to evolve.

Although the distinguishing feature of the approach (in contrast, for example, to traditional mediation) is direct communication between the parties, the objective is not to promote communication or dialogue as an end in itself. Problem-solving workshops are designed to promote a special type of communication – to be described below – with a very specific political purpose. Problem-solving workshops are closely linked to the larger political process. Selection of participants and definition of the agenda, for example, are based on careful analysis of the current political situation within and between the conflicting parties. Moreover, the objective of workshops is to generate inputs into the political process, including the decision-making process itself and the political debate within each of the communities. Most broadly stated, workshops try to contribute to creating a political environment conducive to conflict resolution and to transformation of the relationship between the conflicting parties – both in the short term and in the long term.

Practically speaking, this emphasis usually means that problem-solving workshops are closely linked to negotiation in its various phases, although negotiation does not by any means fully encompass the process of changing international relationships (see Saunders, 1988). In our work on the Israeli–Palestinian conflict in earlier years, problem-solving workshops were designed to contribute to the prenegotiation process: to creating a political atmosphere that would encourage the parties to move to the negotiating table. Thus, in planning and following up on workshops, we focused on the barriers that stood in the way of opening negotiations and on ways of overcoming such barriers – for example, through mutual reassurance. With the beginning of official Israeli–Palestinian negotiations in the fall of 1991, our focus of necessity shifted (Rouhana and Kelman, 1994). During the active negotiation phase, workshops can contribute to overcoming obstacles to staying at the table and negotiating effectively, to exploring options for resolving issues that are not yet on the table, to reframing such issues so as to make them more amenable to negotiation, and to beginning the process of peace-building that must accompany and follow the process of peace-making. Workshops can also be of value in the postnegotiation phase, where they can contribute to implementation of the negotiated agreement and to long-term peace-building.

Despite the close link between workshops and negotiations, we have been very clear in emphasizing that workshops are not to be confused with negotiations as such. They are not meant to be negotiations, or simulated negotiations, or rehearsals for negotiations, nor are they meant to serve as substitutes for negotiations. Rather, they are meant to be complementary to negotiations.

Binding agreements can only be achieved through official negotiations. The very binding character of official negotiations, however, makes it very difficult for certain other things to happen in that context – such as the exploration and discovery of the parties' basic concerns, their priorities, their limits. This is where problem-solving workshops – precisely because of their non-binding character – can make a special contribution to the larger process of negotiation and conflict resolution. This special relationship to the negotiation process underlines one of the central differences between interactive problem-solving and traditional mediation: Problem-solving workshops are generally not designed to facilitate or influence the official negotiation process directly, although they do play a significant indirect role. Insofar as we mediate, it is not between the negotiators representing the two parties, but between their political communities. What we try to facilitate is not the process of negotiation itself, but communication that helps the parties overcome the political, emotional, and at times technical barriers that often prevent them from entering into negotiations, from reaching agreement in the course of negotiations, or from changing their relationship after a political agreement has been negotiated.

Central features of problem-solving workshops

Until the fall of 1990, the Israeli–Palestinian workshops we organized were all self-contained, one-time events. Some of the participants were involved in more than one workshop and many were involved in a variety of other efforts at communication across the conflict line. For these and other reasons, there was continuity between these separate events and they seem to have had a cumulative effect in helping to create a political environment conducive to negotiations. However, because of logistical and financial constraints and a lack of political readiness, we made no attempt before 1990 to reconvene the same group of participants over a series of meetings.

In the fall of 1990, Nadim Rouhana and I convened our first continuing workshop with a group of high-level, politically influential Israelis and Patestinians. The full group met five times between November 1990 and August 1993 – a period that included the Persian Gulf crisis and war, the beginning of official negotiations, and the election of a Labor party government in Israel (see Rouhana and Kelman 1994).[1] After the Oslo agreement (September 1993), Rouhana and I initiated a new project, a Joint Working Group on Israeli–Palestinian Relations (see Kelman, 1996b). This group began meeting in 1994 and held a total of 15 plenary meetings and a number of sub-committee meetings between the spring of 1994 and the summer of 1999. In contrast to our earlier workshop efforts, the working group was designed to generate and disseminate concrete products in the form of a series of concept papers on final-status issues in the Israeli–Palestinian negotiations and on the long-term relationship between the two societies.[2] The group published three papers: one on general principles for the final-status negotiations (Joint Working Group, 1999), one on the problem of Palestinian refugees and the right of return (Alpher and Shikaki *et al.*, 1999), and one on the future Israeli–Palestinian relationship (Joint Working Group, 2000). A fourth paper, on Israeli settlements, is close to completion, but there are no immediate plans to publish it.

To provide a more concrete sense of problem-solving workshops and their underlying logic, I shall describe the format of a typical one-time workshop. It should be stressed, however, that most workshops are in fact 'atypical' in one or more respects. Workshops (including continuing workshops) conform to a set of fundamental principles, but they vary in some of their details, depending on the particular occasion, purpose, and set of participants. What I am presenting, then, is a composite picture, which most workshops approximate but do not necessarily correspond to in all details.

Most of our one-time workshops have been held at Harvard University, under the auspices of the Center for International Affairs or in the context of my graduate seminar on international conflict. Workshop sessions usually take place in a seminar room, with participants seated at a round table, although in some cases we have used a living-room setting or a private meeting room at a hotel. The typical workshop is a private, confidential event, without audience or observers. The discussions are not taped, but members of the third party take notes.

Participants in an Israeli–Palestinian workshop usually include three to six members of each party, as well as three to eight third-party members. The numbers have been smaller on some occasions. For example, I have arranged a number of one-on-one meetings, with the participation of one or two third-party members. These meetings have served important purposes and have retained many important features of problem-solving workshops, although one major feature – intra-party interaction – is missing. In quite a few of our workshops, the size of the third party has been larger than eight. As an integral feature of my graduate seminar on international conflict, I organized an annual workshop, in which the seminar participants – usually about twenty in number – served as apprentice members of the third party. Only eight third-party members sat around the table at any one session, however: three 'permanent' members (including myself and two colleagues with workshop experience) and five seminar participants on a rotating basis. When they were not around the table, the seminar participants were able to follow the proceedings (with the full knowledge of the parties, of course) from an adjoining room with a one-way mirror.

They were fully integrated into the third party: They took part in all of the workshop activities (pre-workshop sessions, briefings, breaks, meals, a social gathering) and were always bound by the requirements and discipline of the third-party role. Apart from the large size of the third party, the workshops linked to this graduate seminar were similar to 'regular' workshops in their purpose and format, and were widely seen as not just academic exercises, but serious political encounters.

The Israeli and Palestinian participants in workshops are all politically active and involved members of the mainstream of their respective communities. Many, by virtue of their positions or general standing, can be described as politically influential. Depending on the occasion and the political level of the participants, we may discuss our plans for a workshop with relevant elements of the political leadership on both sides, in order to keep them informed, gain their support, and solicit their advice on participants and agenda. For many potential workshop participants, approval and at times encouragement from the political leadership is a necessary condition for their agreement to take part. Recruitment, however, is generally done on an individual basis and participants are invited to come as individuals rather than as formal representatives. Invitees, of course, may consult with their leadership or with each other before agreeing to come. Whenever possible, we start the recruitment process with one key person on each side; we then consult with that person and with each successive invitee in selecting the rest of the team. At times, the composition of a team may be negotiated within the particular community (or subcommunity) that we approach, but the final invitation is always issued by the third party to each individual participant.

As an essential part of the recruitment process, we almost always discuss the purposes, procedures, and ground rules of the workshop personally with each participant before obtaining her or his final commitment. Whenever possible, this is done during a face-to-face meeting, although at times it is necessary to do it over the telephone. In addition to the individual briefings, we generally organize two pre-workshop sessions, in which the members of each party meet separately with the third party. In these sessions, which generally last four to five hours, we first review the purposes, procedures, and ground rules of the workshop. We then ask the participants to talk about their side's perspective on the conflict, the range of views within their community, the current status of the conflict as they see it and the conditions and possibilities for resolving it, and their conceptions of the needs and positions of the other side. We encourage the participants to discuss these issues among themselves. We make it clear that the role of the third party – even in the pre-workshop session – is to facilitate the exchange, in part through occasional questions and comments, but not to enter into the substantive discussion or to debate and evaluate what is being said.

The pre-workshop sessions fulfill a number of important functions. They provide an opportunity for the participants to become acquainted with the setting, the third party, and those members of their own team whom they had not previously met, without having to confront the other party at the same time; to raise questions about the purposes, procedures, and ground rules of the workshop; to begin to practice the type of discourse that the workshop is trying to encourage; to gain a better understanding of the role of the third party; and to 'do their duty' by telling the third party their side of the story and enumerating their grievances, thus reducing the pressure to adhere to the conflict norms in the course of the workshop itself. The pre-workshop sessions also give the third party an opportunity to observe some of the internal differences within each team, and to compare the ways in which the parties treat the issues when they are alone and when they are together.

The workshops themselves generally last two-and-a-half days, often taking place over an extended weekend. The opening session, typically late Friday afternoon, begins with a round of introductions, in which the participants are encouraged to go beyond their professional credentials and say something about their reasons for coming. We then review, once again, the purposes, procedures, and ground rules of the workshop, stressing the principles of privacy and confidentiality, the nature of the discourse that we are trying to encourage, and the role of the third party. This review, in the presence of all of the participants, serves to emphasize the nature of the contract to which all three parties are committing themselves. After dinner, shared by the entire group, we reconvene for the first substantive session. On the second day, we have two sessions (each lasting one-and-a-half hours) in the morning, with a half-hour coffee break in between. The same pattern is repeated after lunch. That evening, there is a dinner and social gathering for all participants, typically held at the home of the Kelmans. On the third day, there are again two sessions in the morning and two in the afternoon, and the workshop closes late that afternoon. Thus, in addition to the ten sessions around the table, the workshops provide ample opportunities for informal interaction during meals and coffee breaks. Sometimes participants create additional opportunities for themselves.

In opening the first substantive session, the third party – after describing the political context and the focus of the workshop – proposes a loose agenda. The specific agenda must depend, of course, on the stage of the conflict and the character of the group. The agenda followed in most of our workshops prior to 1992 was appropriate for initial workshops (i.e. workshops whose participants were convening for the first time as a group) in a conflict that was still in a pre-negotiation phase. The main task that we have set for our workshop participants in recent years has been to generate – through their interaction – ideas for bringing the parties to the negotiating table, or for negotiating more productively if they are already at the table. To get the interaction started, we ask the participants to describe their view of the conflict and its current status, to define the spectrum of positions *vis-à-vis* the conflict in their own societies, and to place themselves along that spectrum.

We try to move as rapidly as possible from this more conventional, descriptive discussion into the analytic, problem-solving mode of interaction that is at the heart of the agenda. First, we ask the participants on both sides to talk about their central concerns: the fundamental needs that an agreement would have to satisfy and the fundamental fears that it would have to allay in order to be acceptable to their communities. Only after both sets of concerns are on the table and each side's concerns have been understood by the other, are the participants asked to explore the overall shape of a solution that would meet the needs and calm the fears of both sides. Each is expected to think actively about solutions that would be satisfactory to the other, not only to themselves. Next, the participants are asked to discuss the political and psychological constraints that make it difficult to implement such solutions. Finally, the discussion turns to the question of how these constraints can best be overcome and how the two sides can support each other in such an effort. Depending on how much time is left and on the prevailing mood, the participants may try to come up with concrete ideas for unilateral, coordinated, or joint actions – by themselves or their communities – that might help overcome the barriers to negotiating a mutually satisfactory solution.

The agenda described here is not followed rigidly, but rather serves as a broad framework for the interaction. The discussions are relatively unstructured and, insofar as possible, are allowed to maintain their natural flow. We are careful not to intervene excessively or prematurely, and not to cut off potentially fruitful discussions because they appear to be deviating from the agenda. If the discussion goes too far afield, becomes repetitive, or systematically avoids the issues, the third party – usually with the help of at least some of the participants – will try to bring it back to the broad agenda. In general, the third party is prepared to intervene in order to help keep the discussion moving along productive, constructive channels. At times, particularly at the beginning or at the end of sessions, we also make substantive interventions, in order to help interpret, integrate, clarify, or sharpen what is being said or done in the group. On the whole, however, the emphasis in our model is on facilitating the emergence of ideas out of the interaction between the participants themselves. Consistent with that emphasis, we try to stay in the background as much as possible once we have set the stage.

Having drawn a general picture of the format and proceedings of a typical workshop, let me now highlight some of the special features of the approach.

Academic context

In my colleagues' and my third-party efforts, our academic base provides the major venue of our activities and source of our authority and credibility. The academic context has several advantages for our enterprise. It allows the parties to interact with each other in a relatively non-committal way, since the setting is not only unofficial, but also known as one in which people engage in free exchange of views, in playful consideration of new ideas, and in 'purely academic' discussions. Thus, an academic setting is a good place to set into motion a process of successive approximations, in which parties that do not trust each other begin to communicate in a non-committal framework, but gradually move to increasing levels of commitment as their level of working trust increases (Kelman, 1982). Another advantage of the academic context is that it allows us to call upon an alternative set of norms to counteract the norms that typically govern interactions between conflicting parties. Academic norms favor open discussion, attentive listening to opposing views, and an analytical approach, in contrast to the polemical, accusatory, and legalistic approach that conflict norms tend to promote.

Nature of interaction

The setting, norms, ground rules, agenda, procedures, and third-party interventions in problem-solving workshops are all designed to facilitate a kind of interaction that differs from the way parties in conflict usually interact – if they interact at all. Within the workshop setting, participants are encouraged to talk to each other, rather than to their constituencies or to third parties, and to listen to each other – not in order to discover the weaknesses in the other's argument, but in order to penetrate the other's perspective. The principles of privacy and confidentiality – apart from protecting the interests of the participants – are designed to protect this process, by reducing the participants' concern about how each word they say during the workshop will be perceived on the outside. In order to counteract the tendency to speak to the record, we have avoided creating a record, in the form of audio or videotapes or formal minutes. The absence of an audience, and the third party's refusal to take sides, to evaluate what is said, to adjudicate differences, or to become involved in the debate of substantive issues, further encourages the parties to focus on each other, rather than attempt to influence external parties. These features of the workshop are in no way designed to encourage the participants to forget about their constituencies or, for that matter, about relevant third parties; ideas generated in workshops must be acceptable to the two communities, as well as to outside actors, if they are to have the desired impact on the political process. Rather, these features are designed to prevent the intrusion of these actors into the workshop interaction itself, thus inhibiting and distorting the generation of new ideas.

A second central element in the nature of the interaction that workshops try to promote is an analytic focus. Workshop discussions are analytical in the sense that participants try to gain a better understanding of the other's – and indeed of their own – concerns, needs, fears, priorities, and constraints, and of the way in which the divergent perspectives of the parties help to feed and escalate their conflict. It is particularly important for each party to gain an understanding of the other's perspective (without accepting that perspective) and of the domestic dynamics that shape the policy debate in each community. To appreciate the constraints under which the other operates is especially difficult in a conflict relationship, since the parties' thinking tends to be dominated by their own constraints. But an analytic understanding of the constraints – along with the fundamental concerns – that inform the other's perspective is a *sine qua non* for inventing solutions that are feasible and satisfactory for both sides.

Analytical discussions proceed on the basis of a 'no fault' principle. While there is no presumption that both sides are equally at fault, the discussions are not oriented toward assigning blame, but toward exploring the causes of the conflict and the obstacles to its resolution. This analytical approach is designed to lead to a problem-solving mode of interaction, based on the proposition that the conflict represents a joint problem for the two parties that requires joint efforts at solution.

Dual purpose

Workshops have a dual purpose, which can be described as educational and political. They are designed to produce both *changes* in attitudes, perceptions, and ideas for resolving the conflict among the individual participants in the workshop, and *transfer* of these changes to the political arena – i.e. to the political debate and the decision-making process within each community. The political purpose is an integral part of the workshop approach, whatever the level of the participants involved. Workshops provide opportunities for the parties to interact, to become acquainted with each other, and to humanize their mutual images, not as ends in themselves, but as means to producing new learnings that can then be fed into the political process. Some of the specific learnings that participants have acquired in the course of workshops and then communicated to their own political leaderships or publics have included: information about the range of views on the other side, signs of readiness for negotiation, and the availability of potential negotiating partners; insights into the other side's priorities, rock-bottom requirements, and areas of flexibility; and ideas for confidence-building measures, mutually acceptable solutions to issues in conflict, and ways of moving to the negotiating table.

Because of their dual purpose, problem-solving workshops are marked by a dialectical character (Kelman, 1979; Kelman and Cohen, 1986). Some of the conditions favorable to change in the workshop setting may be antagonistic to the transfer of changes to the political arena, and vice versa. There is often a need, therefore, to find the proper balance between contradictory requirements if a workshop is to be effective in fulfilling both its educational and its political purpose. For example, it is important for the participants to develop a considerable degree of working trust in order to engage in joint problem-solving, to devise direct or tacit collaborative efforts for overcoming constraints against negotiation, and to become convinced that there are potential negotiating partners on the other side. This trust, however, must not be allowed to turn into excessive camaraderie transcending the conflict, lest the participants lose their credibility and their potential political influence once they return to their home communities. Workshops can be seen as part of a process of building a coalition across the conflict line, but it must remain an uneasy coalition that does not threaten members' relationship to their own identity groups (Kelman, 1993).

The selection of participants provides another example of a central workshop feature for which the dialectics of the process have important implications. The closer the participants are to the centers of power in their own communities, the greater the likelihood that what they learn in the course of their workshop experience will be fed directly into the decision-making process. By the same token, however, the closer participants are to the centers of power, the more constrained they are likely to feel, and the greater their difficulty in entering into communication that is open, non-committal, exploratory, and analytical. Thus, on the whole, as participants move closer to the level of top decision-makers, they become less likely to show change as a result of their workshop experience, but whatever changes do occur are more likely to be transferred to the policy process. These contradictory effects have to be taken into account in selecting participants for a given occasion, or in defining the goals and agenda for a workshop with a given set of participants. In general, the best way to balance the requirements for change and for transfer is to select participants who are politically influential but not directly involved in the execution of foreign policy. The approach can be adapted for use with decision-makers themselves, as long as the facilitators are aware of the advantages and drawbacks of participants at that level.

The workshops and related encounters that we have organized over the years have included participants at three different levels of relationship to the decision-making process: political actors, such as parliamentarians, negotiators, party activists, or advisers to political leaders; political influentials, such as former officials and diplomats, senior academics (who are leading analysts of the conflict in their own communities and occasional advisers to decision-makers), community leaders, writers, or editors; and pre-influentials, such as younger academics and professionals or advanced graduate students, who are slated to move into influential positions in their respective fields. The lines between these three categories are not very precise; moreover, many participants who may have been 'pre-influentials' at the time of their workshop have since become influential, and some of our 'influentials' have since become political actors. Whatever the level of the participants, a central criterion for selection is that they be politically involved – at least as active participants in the political debate and perhaps in political movements. From our point of view, even this degree of involvement is of direct political relevance since it contributes to the shaping of the political environment for any peace effort. Another criterion for selection is that participants be part of the mainstream of their community and that they enjoy credibility within broad segments of that community. We look for participants who are as close as possible to the center of the political spectrum, while at the same time being interested in negotiations and open to the workshop process. As a result, workshop participants so far have tended to be on the dovish ('moderate' or pro-negotiation) side of the center.

Third-party contributions

Although workshops proceed on the principle that useful ideas for conflict resolution must emerge out of the interaction between the parties themselves, the third party plays an essential role (at certain stages of a conflict) in making that interaction possible and fruitful. The third party provides the context in which representatives of parties engaged in an intense conflict are able to come together. It selects, briefs, and convenes the participants. It serves as a repository of trust for both parties, enabling them to proceed with the assurance that their confidentiality will be respected and their interests protected even though – by definition – they cannot trust each other. It establishes and enforces the norms and ground rules that facilitate analytic discussion and a problem-solving orientation. It proposes a broad agenda that encourages the parties to move from exploration of each other's concerns and constraints to the generation of ideas for win/win solutions and for implementing such solutions. It tries to keep the discussion moving in constructive directions. And, finally, it makes occasional substantive interventions in the form of content observations, which suggest interpretations and implications of what is being said and point to convergences and divergences between the parties, to blind spots, to possible signals, and to issues for clarification; process observations at the intergroup level, which suggest possible ways in which interactions between the parties 'here and now' may reflect the dynamics of the conflict between their communities; and theoretical inputs, which help participants distance themselves from their own conflict, provide them conceptual tools for analysis of their conflict, and offer them relevant illustrations from previous research.

Process observations are among the unique features of problem-solving workshops. They generally focus on incidents in which one party's words or actions clearly have a strong emotional impact on the other – leading to expressions of anger and dismay, of relief and reassurance, of understanding and acceptance, or of reciprocation. The third party can use such incidents, which are part of the participants' shared immediate experience, as a springboard for exploring some of the issues and concerns that define the conflict between their societies. Through such exploration, each side can gain some insight into the preoccupations of the other, and the way these are affected by its own actions. Process observations must be introduced sparingly and make special demands on the third party's skill and sense of timing. It is particularly important that such interventions be pitched at the intergroup, rather than the interpersonal level. Analysis of 'here and now' interactions is not concerned with the personal characteristics of the participants or with their personal relations to each other, but only with what these interactions can tell us about the relationship between their national groups.

Social–psychological assumptions

The practice of interactive problem-solving is informed by a set of assumptions about the nature of international/intercommunal conflict and conflict resolution. These assumptions are meant to be general in nature, although they refer most directly to conflicts between identity groups and may not be equally applicable in other cases. The problem-solving approach is likely to be most relevant in conflicts in which identity issues play a central role and to which these assumptions most clearly refer.

In my particular conception of the problem-solving approach, the guiding assumptions derive from a social–psychological analysis, which provides a bridge between individual behavior and social interaction, on the one hand, and the functioning of social systems (organizations, institutions, societies) and collectivities, on the other (Kelman, 1997b). Social–psychological assumptions enter into the formulation of the structure, the process, and the content of problem-solving workshops.

Workshop structure

Workshop structure refers primarily to the role of workshops in the larger political context and their place within the social system in which the conflict is carried on. In effect, the focus here is on the relationship between the micro-process of the workshop and the macro-process of conflict management or resolution. Several assumptions underlie our view of this relationship and hence the way in which workshops are structured.

Conflict as an intersocietal process

International conflict is not merely an intergovernmental or interstate phenomenon, but also an intersocietal phenomenon. Thus, in addition to the strategic, military, and diplomatic dimensions, it is necessary to give central consideration to the economic, psychological, cultural, and social–structural dimensions in the analysis of the conflict. Interactions along these dimensions, both within and between the conflicting societies, form the essential political environment in which governments function. It is necessary to look at these intrasocietal and intersocietal processes in order to understand the political constraints under which governments operate and the resistance to change that these produce. By the same token, these societal factors, if properly understood and utilized, provide opportunities and levers for change.

This view has a direct implication for the selection of workshop participants. To be politically relevant, workshops do not require the participation of decision-makers or their agents. In fact, as proposed in the earlier discussion of the dual purposes and dialectical character of workshops, the ideal participants may be individuals who are politically influential but not directly involved in the foreign-policy decision-making process. The important consideration is that they be active and credible contributors to the political debate within their own communities and thus can play a role in changing the political environment.

Another implication of the view of international conflict as an intersocietal phenomenon is that third-party efforts should ideally be directed not merely to a settlement of the conflict, but to its resolution. A political agreement may be adequate for terminating relatively specific, containable interstate disputes, but it is an inadequate response to conflicts that engage the collective identities and existential concerns of the societies involved.

Conflict resolution as transformation of the relationship

Following from the stress on the intersocietal nature of conflict is the assumption that conflict resolution represents an effort to transform the relationship between the conflicting parties. This assumption has direct implications for the type of solutions that third-party intervention tries to generate. First, solutions must emerge out of the interaction between the parties themselves: The process of interactive problem-solving itself contributes to transforming the relationship between the parties. Secondly, solutions must address the needs of both parties, thus providing the foundation of a new relationship between them. Finally, the nature of the solutions and the process by which they were achieved must be such that the parties will be committed to them: Only thus can they establish a new relationship on a long-term basis.

Diplomacy as a mix of official and unofficial processes

Another corollary of the stress on the intersocietal nature of conflict is the view of diplomacy as a broad and complex mix of official and unofficial processes. The peaceful termination or management of conflicts requires binding agreements that can only be achieved at the official level. Unofficial interactions, however, can play a constructive complementary role, particularly by contributing to the development of a political environment conducive to negotiations and other diplomatic initiatives (Saunders, 1988). Problem-solving workshops and other informal efforts, as pointed out at the beginning of the chapter, can make such contributions precisely because of their non-binding character. In such settings – in contrast to official fora – it is much easier for the parties to engage in non-committal, exploratory interactions, which allow them, for example, to test each other's limits, to develop empathy, or to engage in creative problem-solving. Accordingly, many of the features of problem-solving workshops are specifically geared to maximizing the non-committal nature of the interaction: the academic context; the assurance of privacy and confidentiality; the absence (at least in our earlier work) of expectations of specific products; and the emphasis on interactions characterized by exploration, sharing of perspectives, playing with ideas, brainstorming, and creative problem-solving – rather than bargaining.

Impact of intragroup conflict on intergroup conflict

A further assumption relates to the interplay between intragroup and intergroup conflict. In many international and intercommunal conflicts, internal divisions within each party shape the course of the conflict between the parties. This phenomenon represents a special instance of the general observation of continuities between domestic and international politics. Understanding of the internal divisions within each party is essential to the selection of workshop participants, since the political significance of workshops depends on the potential impact these participants can have on the internal debate. The internal divisions in each society are also a major focus of concern within workshops, particularly when the discussion turns to the political and psychological constraints against compromise solutions and ways of overcoming these constraints.

More generally, I have already alluded to my conceptualization (Kelman, 1993) of workshops and related activities as part of a process of forming a coalition across the conflict line – a coalition between those elements on each side that are interested in a negotiated solution. It is very important to keep in mind, however, that such a coalition must of necessity remain an uneasy coalition. If it became overly cohesive, it would undermine the whole purpose of the enterprise: to have an impact on the political decisions within the two communities. Workshop participants who become closely identified with their counterparts on the other side may become alienated from their own co-nationals, lose credibility, and hence forfeit their political effectiveness and their ability to promote a new consensus within their own communities. One of the challenges for problem-solving workshops, therefore, is to create an atmosphere in which participants can begin to humanize and trust each other and to develop an effective collaborative relationship, without losing sight of their separate group identities and the conflict between their communities.

The world system as a global society

At the broadest level, my assumptions about international and intercommunal conflict rest on a view of the world system as a global society – a term used here not only normatively, but also descriptively. To be sure, the global society is a weak society, lacking many of the customary features of a society. Still, conceiving of the world as a society corrects for the untenable view of nation states as sole and unitary actors in the global arena. Clearly, nation spates remain the dominant actors within our current global society. The nation state benefits from the principle of sovereignty and from its claim to represent its population's national identity – perhaps the most powerful variant of group identity in the modern world. (In intercommunal conflicts within established nation states, the ethnic community is seen as representing the central element of identity and seeks to restructure, take over, or separate from the existing state in order to give political expression to that identity.) Despite the dominance of the nation state, the world system has many of the characteristics of a society: It is formed by a multiplicity of actors, including – in addition to nation states – individuals in their diverse roles, as well as a variety of subnational and supranational groups; it is marked by an ever-increasing degree of interdependence between its component parts; it is divided along many complex lines, with the nation state representing perhaps the most powerful, but certainly not the only cutting line; and it contains numerous relationships that cut across nation-state lines, including relations based on ethnicity, religion, ideology, occupation, and economic interests. The embeddedness of the nation state in a global society, in which ethnic and other bonds cut across nation-state lines, accounts in large part for the continuity between the domestic and foreign policies of the modern stable.

The view of the world system as a global society provides several angles for understanding the role of interactive problem-solving within a larger context of conflict resolution.

First, the concept of a global society with its emphasis on interdependence suggests the need for alternative conceptions of national and international security, which involve arrangements for common security and mechanisms for the nonviolent conduct, management, and resolution of conflicts. Such arrangements and mechanisms, in turn, call for the development of governmental, intergovernmental, and nongovernmental institutions to embody the emerging new conceptions of security. Interactive problem-solving can be seen as the germ of an independent (nongovernmental) institutional mechanism, which can contribute to security through the nonviolent resolution of conflicts.

Secondly, by focusing on multiple actors and cross-cutting relationships, the concept of a global society encourages us to think of unofficial diplomacy in all of its varieties as an integral part of diplomacy and of a larger process of conflict resolution, and not just as a side-show (as it tends to be viewed in a state-centered model).

Finally, the multiple-actor framework central to the concept of a global society provides a place for the individual as a relevant actor in international relations. Interactive problem-solving uses the individual as the unit of analysis in the effort to understand resistances to change in a conflict relationship despite changes in realties and interests, and in the search for solutions that would satisfy the human needs of the parties. Moreover, interactive problem-solving is a systematic attempt to promote change at the level of individuals (in the form of new insights and ideas) as a vehicle for change at the system level.

Workshop process

Several social–psychological assumptions underlie our view of the kind of interaction process that workshops are designed to promote.

Direct bilateral interaction

One assumption follows directly from the structural analysis that has just been presented – i.e. from the role of workshops in the larger political context. Somewhere within the larger framework of conflict resolution, there must be a place for direct, bilateral interaction between the parties centrally involved in a given conflict – such as the Israelis and the Palestinians, or the Greek and the Turkish Cypriots. Such direct, bilateral interactions are not a substitute for the multilateral efforts that are almost invariably required for the resolution of protracted conflicts. Greece and Turkey cannot be excluded from negotiations of the Cyprus conflict, nor can the Arab states and major world powers be bypassed in efforts to resolve the Israeli–Palestinian dispute. Within this larger framework, however, there must be an opportunity for the parties immediately involved – the parties that ultimately have to live with each other – to penetrate each other's perspective and to engage in joint problem-solving designed to produce ideas for a mutually satisfactory agreement between them.

Opportunities for interaction at the micro-level can also contribute some of the needed interactive elements at the macro-level: a binocular orientation, such that each party can view the situation from the other's perspective as well as from its own; a recognition of the need for reciprocity in the process and outcome of negotiations; and a focus on building a new relationship between the parties.

Emergent character of interaction

A second assumption underlying the workshop process is that products of social interaction have an emergent character. In the course of direct interaction, the parties are able to observe at first hand their differing reactions to the same events and the different perspectives these reflect; the differences between the way they perceive themselves and the way the other perceives them; and the impact that their statements and actions have on each other. Out of these observations, they can jointly shape new insights and ideas that could not have been predicted from what they brought to the interaction. Certain kinds of solutions to the conflict can emerge only from the confrontation of assumptions, concerns, and identities during face-to-face communication.

The emergence of ideas for solutions to the conflict out of the interaction between the parties (in contrast, for example, to ideas proposed by third parties) has several advantages: Such ideas are more likely to be responsive to the fundamental needs and fears of both parties; the parties are more likely to feel committed to the solutions they produce themselves; and the process of producing these ideas in itself contributes to building a new relationship between the parties.

In keeping with our assumption about the emergent character of interaction, we pay attention to the nature of the discourse during workshops (see Pearson, 1990): How does the way parties talk to each other change over the course of the workshop? What are the critical moments in a workshop that have an impact on the continuing interaction? How do new joint ideas come to be formulated in the course of the interaction?

Exploration and problem-solving

Workshops are designed to promote a special kind of interaction or discourse that can contribute to the desired political outcome. As noted in the earlier discussion of the nature of the interaction, the setting, ground rules, and procedures of problem-solving workshops encourage (and permit) interaction marked by the following elements: an emphasis on addressing each either (rather than one's constituencies, or third parties, or the record) and on listening to each other; analytical discussion; adherence to a 'no-fault' principle; and a problem-solving mode of interaction. This kind of interaction allows the parties to explore each other's concerns, penetrate each other's perspectives, and take cognizance of each other's constraints. As a result, they are able to offer each other the needed reassurances to engage in negotiation and to come up with solutions responsive to both sides' needs and fears.

The nature of the interaction fostered in problem-solving workshops has some continuities with a therapeutic model (Kelman, 1991b). The influence of the therapeutic model can be seen particularly in the facilitative role of the third party, the analytical character of the discourse, and the use of 'here and now' experiences as a basis for learning about the dynamics of the conflict (as mentioned in the earlier discussion of process observations). It is also important, however, to keep in mind the limited applicability of a therapeutic model to problem-solving workshops. For example, the focus of workshops is not on individuals and their interpersonal relations, but on what can be learned from their interaction about the dynamics of the conflict between their communities. Furthermore, there is no assumption that nations can be viewed as equivalent to individuals or that conflict resolution is a form of therapy for national groups.

Establishment of alternative norms

The workshop process is predicated on the assumption that the interaction between conflicting parties is governed by a set of 'conflict norms' that contribute significantly to escalation and perpetuation of the conflict (Kelman, 1997b). There is a need, therefore, for interactions based on an alternative set of norms conducive to de-escalation. Workshops are designed to provide an opportunity for this kind of interaction. As noted earlier, the academic context provides an alternative set of norms on which the interaction between the parties can proceed. The ground rules for interaction within the workshop make it both possible and necessary for participants to abide by these alternative norms. The safe environment of the workshop and the principle of privacy and confidentiality provide the participants with the protection they need to be able to deviate from the conflict norms.

Individual change as vehicle for policy change

Finally, workshops operationalize a process that is social–psychological par excellence: a process designed to produce change in individuals, interacting in a small-group context, as a vehicle for change in policies and actions of the political system (Kelman, 1997a). Thus, workshops have a dual purpose – educational and political, or change and transfer – as discussed above in some detail. This dual purpose, at times, creates conflicting requirements that have to be balanced in order to fulfill both sets of purposes. I have already illustrated how such conflicts may affect the selection of workshop participants and the atmosphere of trust that workshops seek to engender. The relationship between change at the individual level and at the system level – which often lends a dialectical character to problem-solving workshops – is at the heart of the workshop process.

Workshop content

A set of social–psychological assumptions also inform the substantive emphases of workshop discussions. These emphases include human needs, perceptual and cognitive constraints on information processing, and influence processes, as these enter into conflict relationships.

Parties' needs and fears

The satisfaction of the needs of both parties – as articulated through their core identity groups – is the ultimate criterion in the search for a mutually satisfactory resolution of their conflict (Burton, 1990; Kelman, 1990). Unfulfilled needs, especially for identity and security, and existential fears about the denial of such needs typically drive the conflict and create barriers to its resolution. By pushing behind the parties' incompatible positions and exploring the identity and security needs that underlie them, it often becomes possible to develop mutually satisfactory solutions, since identity, security, and other psychological needs are not inherently zero-sum. Workshop interactions around needs and fears enable the parties to find a language and to identify gestures and actions that are conducive to mutual reassurance. Mutual reassurance is a central element of conflict resolution, particularly in existential conflicts where the parties see their group identity, their people's security, their very existence as a nation to be at stake.

Escalatory dynamics of conflict interaction

The needs and fears of parties involved in a conflict relationship impose perceptual and cognitive constraints on their processing of new information. One of the major effects of these constraints is that the parties systematically underestimate the occurrence and possibility of change and therefore avoid negotiations, even in the face of changing interests that would make negotiations desirable for both. Images of the enemy are particularly resistant to disconfirming information. The combination of demonic enemy images and virtuous self-images on both sides leads to the formation of mirror images, which contribute to the escalatory dynamic of conflict interaction and to resistance to change in a conflict relationship (Bronfenbrenner, 1961; White, 1965).

By focusing on mutual perceptions, mirror images, and systematic differences in perspective, workshop participants can learn to differentiate the enemy image – a necessary condition for movement toward negotiation (Kelman, 1987). Workshops bring out the symmetries in the parties' images of each other and in their positions and requirements, which arise out of the dynamics of the conflict interaction itself. Such symmetries are often overlooked because of the understandable tendency of protagonists in a conflict relationship to dwell on the asymmetries between them. Without denying these important asymmetries, both empirical and moral, we focus on symmetries because they tend to be a major source of escalation of conflict (as in the operation of conflict spirals) and a major reason for making the conflict intractable. By the same token, they can serve as a major vehicle for de-escalation by helping the parties penetrate each other's perspective and identify mutually reassuring gestures and actions (Kelman, 1978, 1991a).

Mutual influence in conflict relationships

Finally, the content of workshop discussions reflects an assumption about the nature of influence processes in international relations. Workshops are predicated on the view that the range of influence processes employed in conflict relationships must be broadened. It is necessary to move beyond influence strategies based on threats and even to expand and refine strategies based on promises and positive incentives. By searching for solutions that satisfy the needs of both parties, workshops explore the possibility of mutual influence by way of responsiveness to each other's needs. A key element in this process, emphasized throughout this chapter, is mutual reassurance. In existential conflicts, in particular, parties can encourage each other to move to the negotiating table by reducing both sides' fear – not just, as more traditional strategic analysts maintain, by increasing their pain. At the macro-level, the present approach calls for a shift in emphasis in international influence processes from deterrence and compellence to mutual reassurance. The use of this mode of influence has the added advantage of not only affecting specific behaviors by the other party, but contributing to a transformation of the relationship between the parties.

The expanded conception of influence processes that can be brought to bear in a conflict relationship is based on a view of international conflict as a dynamic phenomenon, emphasizing the occurrence and possibility of change. Conflict resolution efforts are geared, therefore, to discovering possibilities for change, identifying conditions for change, and overcoming resistances to change. Such an approach favors 'best-case' analyses and an attitude of 'strategic optimism' (Kelman, 1978, 1979), not because of an unrealistic denial of malignant trends, but as part of a deliberate strategy to promote change by actively searching for and accentuating whatever realistic possibilities for peaceful resolution of the conflict might be on the horizon. Optimism, in this sense, is part of a strategy designed to create self-fulfilling prophecies of a positive nature, balancing the self-fulfilling prophecies of escalation created by the pessimistic expectations and the worst-case scenarios often favored by more traditional analysts. Problem-solving workshops can be particularly useful in exploring ways in which change can be promoted through the parties' own actions and in discovering ways in which each can exert influence on the other (Kelman, 1991a, 1997b).

Conclusion: relevance of interactive problem-solving

The principles of interactive problem-solving have some applicability in a wide range of international conflict situations. Indeed, I would argue that problem-solving workshops and related activities – along with other forms of unofficial diplomacy – should be thought of as integral parts of a larger diplomatic process. This type of intervention can make certain unique contributions to the larger process that are not available through official channels – for example, by providing opportunities for non-committal exploration of possible ways of getting to the table and of shaping mutually acceptable solutions. Moreover, the assumptions and principles of interactive problem-solving can contribute to a reconceptualization of international relationships at the macro-level by encouraging shifts in the nature of the discourse and the means of influence that characterize international relations today (Kelman, 1996a). Nevertheless, it must be said that problem-solving workshops, particularly in the format that has evolved in our style of practice, are more directly relevant in some types of conflict than in others and at certain phases of a given conflict than at others.

Since my primary case has been the Israeli–Palestinian conflict, it is not surprising that my approach is most relevant to situations that share some of the characteristics of that conflict. The approach is most directly relevant to long-standing conflicts, in which the interests of the parties have gradually converged, and large segments of each community perceive this to be the case, but nevertheless they seem to be unable or unwilling to enter into negotiations or to bring the negotiations to a satisfactory conclusion. The psychological obstacles to negotiation in these cases are not readily overcome despite the changes in realities and in perceived interests.

Interactive problem-solving is not feasible if there is no interest among the parties – or significant elements within each party – in changing the *status quo*. It is not necessary if there are no profound barriers to negotiations; in that event, other forms of mediation – designed to enhance negotiating skills or to propose reasonable options – may be equally or more useful. However, when the recognition of common interests is insufficient to overcome the psychological barriers, interactive problem-solving becomes particularly germane. These conditions are likely to prevail in intense, protracted identity conflicts at the international or intercommunal level, particularly conflicts in which the parties see their national existence to be at stake. The Israeli–Palestinian conflict, the Cyprus conflict, and the conflicts in Northern Ireland and Sri Lanka, clearly share these characteristics. There are many other conflicts, however, that can benefit from a process designed to promote mutual reassurance and to help develop a new relationship between conflicting parties that must find a way of living together.

Since the goal of workshops is to help the parties translate their interest in changing the *status quo* into an effective negotiating process, by overcoming the barriers that stand in the way of such a process, it is necessary to select workshop participants from those segments of the two communities that are indeed interested in a negotiated agreement. They may be skeptical about the possibility of achieving such an agreement and suspicious about the intentions of the other side, but they must have some interest in finding a mutually acceptable way of ending the conflict. In addition, workshop participants must be prepared to meet and talk with members of the other community at a level of equality within the workshop setting, whatever asymmetries in power between the parties may prevail in the relationship between the two communities. Thus, 'participants from the stronger party must be *willing* to deal with the other on a basis of equality, which generally means that they have come to accept the illegitimacy of past patterns of discrimination and domination; participants from the weaker must be *able* to deal with the other on a basis of equality, which generally means that they have reached a stage of confrontation in the conflict' (Kelman, 1990: 293–4). In their interactions within the workshop setting, it would be inappropriate for members of the stronger party to take advantage of their superior power, as they might in a negotiating situation. By the same token, it would be inappropriate in this setting for members of the weaker party to take advantage of their superior moral position, as they might in a political rally or an international conference. Workshop interactions are most productive when they are based on the principle of reciprocity.

As emphasized at the beginning of this chapter, workshops are not intended to substitute for official negotiations but they may be closely linked to the negotiating process. Thus, our work on the Israeli–Palestinian conflict during the pre-negotiation and early negotiation phases helped lay the groundwork for the Oslo agreement by contributing to the development of the cadres, the ideas, and the political atmosphere required for movement to the table and productive negotiation (Kelman, 1995, 1997c). At a point when active negotiations are in progress, workshops may provide a noncommittal forum to explore options, reframe issues to make them more amenable to negotiation, identify ways of breaking stalemates in the negotiations, and address setbacks in the process. They may also allow the parties to work out solutions to specific technical, political, or emotional issues that require an analytical, problem-solving approach; such solutions can then be fed into the formal negotiating process. In the post-negotiation phase, workshops can help the parties address issues in the implementation of the agreement and explore a new relationship based on patterns of coexistence and cooperation.

The Israeli–Palestinian workshops that we have conducted over the years have suggested some of the ways in which workshops and related activities can contribute to the peace process, helping the parties to overcome the fears and suspicions that keep them from entering into negotiations or from arriving at an agreement. Workshops can help the participants develop more differentiated images of the enemy and discover potential negotiating partners – to learn that there is someone to talk to on the other side and something to talk about. They can contribute to the formation of cadres of individuals who have acquired experience in communicating with the other side and the conviction that such communication can be fruitful. They enable the parties to penetrate each other's perspective, gaining insight into the other's concerns, priorities, and constraints. They increase awareness of change and thus contribute to creating and maintaining a sense of possibility – a belief among the relevant parties that a peaceful solution is attainable and that negotiations toward such a solution are feasible.

Workshops also contribute to creating a political environment conducive to fruitful negotiations through the development of a de-escalatory language, based on sensitivity to words that frighten and words that reassure the other party. They help in the identification of mutually reassuring actions and symbolic gestures, often in the form of acknowledgments – of the other's humanity, national identity, ties to the land, history of victimization, sense of injustice, genuine fears, and conciliatory moves. They contribute to the development of shared visions of a desirable future, which help reduce the parties' fear of negotiations as a step into an unknown, dangerous realm. They may generate ideas about the shape of a positive-sum solution that meets the basic needs of both parties. They may also generate ideas about how to get from here to there – about a framework and set of principles for moving negotiations forward. Ultimately, problem-solving workshops contribute to a process of transformation of the relationship between enemies.

The continuing workshop that Nadim Rouhana and I convened between 1990 and 1993 (Rouhana and Kelman, 1994) enhanced the potential relevance of interactive problem-solving to the larger political process. A continuing workshop represents a sustained effort to address concrete issues, enabling us to push the process of conflict analysis and interactive problem solving farther and to apply it more systematically than can be done with self-contained, one-time workshops. The longer time period and the continuing nature of the enterprise make it possible to go beyond the sharing of perspectives to the joint production of creative ideas. Moreover, the periodic reconvening of a continuing workshop allows for an iterative and cumulative process, based on feedback and correction. The participants have an opportunity to take the ideas developed in the course of a workshop back to their own communities, to gather reactions, and to return to the next meeting with proposals for strengthening, expanding, or modifying the original ideas. It is also possible for participants, within or across parties, to meet or otherwise communicate with each other between workshop sessions in order to work out some of the ideas more fully and bring the results of their efforts back to the next session. Finally, a continuing workshop provides better opportunities to address the question of how to disseminate ideas and proposals developed at the workshop most effectively and appropriately.

The Joint Working Group on Israeli–Palestinian Relations that Nadim Rouhana and I launched in 1994 addressed the issue of dissemination more directly. This project was initiated with the express purpose of producing and disseminating joint concept papers on the final-status issues in the Israeli–Palestinian negotiations and on the future relationship between the two societies and the two polities that will emerge from the negotiations. The participants were politically influential members of their respective communities, some of whom have held official positions in the past and/or may hold such positions in the future. The working group followed the general principles and ground rules that have governed our previous problem-solving workshops. The principles of confidentiality and non-attribution prevailed, as in other workshops, until the group decided that it was ready to make a particular product public. However, the anticipation that there would ultimately be published papers focused the discussion more tightly and reduced the non-committal character of the interaction. It is a price worth paying if it yields products that reflect the joint thinking of influential, mainstream representatives of the two communities and that can be disseminated under their names to decision-makers and the wider public on both sides.

The continuing workshop and the joint working group represent important new steps in the development of interactive problem-solving. The entire field, for which Ronald Fisher (1993, 1997) and others use the term 'interactive conflict resolution', is still at an early stage of development. A relatively small number of scholar-practitioners around the world are engaged in this kind of work and the experience they have accumulated is still quite limited. However, the field is maturing. The number of centers devoted to this work is increasing. A new generation is emerging. My students, among others, are actively engaged in research and practice in the field and are taking increasing responsibility for organizing their own projects. By establishing their personal identities as scholar-practitioners in the field, they are giving the field itself an identity of its own. Both the older and the younger generations are establishing networks, whose members engage in collaborative work and are beginning to think systematically about the further development and institutionalization of problem-solving approaches to the resolution of international conflicts (see Fisher, 1993, 1997). Among the issues that need to be addressed and that are, indeed, receiving increasing attention are: the evaluation of this form of practice, the training of new scholar-practitioners, the requirements and pitfalls of professionalization, the formulation of principles and standards of ethical practice, and the development of institutional mechanisms that would strengthen the contribution of interactive problem-solving to the resolution of intractable conflicts.

Notes

1. The continuing workshop was supported by grants from the Nathan Cummings Foundation, the John D. and Catherine T. MacArthur Foundation, the U.S. Institute of Peace, and Rockefeller Family and Associates. We are greatly indebted to these organizations for making this work possible and to the Harvard Center

for International Affairs for providing the institutional base for it. Nadim Rouhana and I were joined on the panel of third-party facilitators by Harold Saunders of the Kettering Foundation and C.R. Mitchell of George Mason University. We are very grateful to them, as well as to the members of the third-party staff, which included Cynthia Chataway, Rose Kelman, Susan Korper, Kate Rouhana, and William Weisberg.

2. The Joint Working Group is a project of PICAR, the Program on International Conflict Analysis and Resolution (Herbert C. Kelman, Director; Donna Hicks Deputy Director), which was established at the Harvard Center for International Affairs (now the Weatherhead Center) in 1993, with a grant from the William and Flora Hewlett Foundation. The Hewlett Foundation's support of PICAR's infrastructure is deeply appreciated, as is the support of the Working Group itself by grants from the Nathan Cummings Foundation, the Carnegie Corporation, the Ford Foundation, the Charles R. Bronfman Foundation, and the US Information Agency, as well as the Hewlett Foundation, the Renner Institut in Vienna, and the Weatherhead Center. The third-party team, chaired by Nadim Rouhana and myself, included Donna Hicks, Kate Rouhana, Rose Kelman, and (in 1994–95) Eileen Babbitt. Their dedication and skill have been indispensable to the project.

References

Alpher, J. and Shikaki, K., with participation of the additional members of the Joint Working Group on Israeli–Palestinian Relations (1999) 'The Palestinian Refugee Problem and the Right of Return', *Middle East Policy*, 6(3), 167–89. (Originally published as *Weatherhead Center for International Affairs Working Paper No. 98-7.* Cambridge, MA: Harvard University, 1998).

Bronfenbrenner, U. (1961) 'The Mirror Image in Soviet–American Relations: a Social Psychologist's Report', *Journal of Social Issues*, 17(3), 45–56.

Burton, J. W. (1969) *Conflict and Communication: The Use of Controlled Communication in International Relations.* London: Macmillan – now Palgrave Macmillan.

Burton, J. W. (1979) *Deviance, Terrorism and War: The Process of Solving Unsolved Social and Political Problems.* New York: St. Martin's Press – now Palgrave Macmillan.

Burton, J. W. (1984) *Global Conflict: The Domestic Sources of International Crisis.* Brighton, Sussex: Wheatsheaf.

Burton, J. W. (ed.) (1990) *Conflict: Human Needs Theory.* New York: St. Martin's Press – now Palgrave Macmillan.

Fisher, R. J. (1993) 'Developing the Field of Interactive Conflict Resolution: Issues in Training, Funding, and Institutionalization', *Political Psychology*, 14, 123–38.

Fisher, R. J. (1997) *Interactive Conflict Resolution.* Syracuse: Syracuse University Press.

Joint Working Group on Israeli–Palestinian Relations (1999) 'General Principles for the Final Israeli–Palestinian Agreement', *The Middle East Journal*, 53(1), 170–5. (Originally published as *PICAR Working Paper.* Cambridge, MA: Program on International Conflict Analysis and Resolution, Weatherhead Center for International Affairs, Harvard University, 1998).

Joint Working Group on Israeli–Palestinian Relations (2000) 'The Future Israeli–Palestinian Relationship', *Middle East Policy*, 7(2), 80–112. (Originally published as *Weatherhead Center for International Affairs Working Paper No. 99-12.* Cambridge, MA: Harvard University, 1999).

Kelman, H. C. (1972) 'The Problem-Solving Workshop in Conflict Resolution', in R. L. Merritt (ed.), *Communication in International Politics.* Urbana, Ill.: University of Illinois Press, pp. 168–204.

Kelman, H. C. (1978) 'Israelis and Palestinians: Psychological Prerequisites for Mutual Acceptance', *International Security*, 3, 162–86.

Kelman, H. C. (1979) 'An Interactional Approach to Conflict Resolution and its Application to Israeli–Palestinian Relations', *International Interactions*, 6, 99–122.

Kelman, H. C. (1982) 'Creating the Conditions for Israeli–Palestinian Negotiations', *Journal of Conflict Resolution*, 26, 39–75.

Kelman, H. C. (1987) 'The Political Psychology of the Israeli–Palestinian Conflict: How Can We Overcome the Barriers to a Negotiated Solution?', *Political Psychology*, 8, 347–63.

Kelman, H. C. (1990) 'Applying a Human Needs Perspective to the Practice of Conflict Resolution: The Israeli–Palestinian Case', in J. W. Burton (ed.), *Conflict: Human Needs Theory*. New York: St. Martin's Press – now Palgrave Macmillan, pp. 283–97.

Kelman, H. C. (1991a) 'A Behavioral Science Perspective on the Study of War and Peace', in R. Jessor (ed.), *Perspectives on Behavioral Science: The Colorado Lectures*. Boulder, CO: Westview, pp. 245–75.

Kelman, H. C. (1991b) 'Interactive Problem Solving: the Uses and Limits of a Therapeutic Model for the Resolution of International Conflicts', in V. D. Volkan, J. V. Montville and D. A. Julius (eds), *The Psychodynamics of International Relationships, Volume II: Unofficial Diplomacy at Work*. Lexington, MA: Lexington Books, pp. 145–60.

Kelman, H. C. (1992) 'Informal Mediation by the Scholar/Practitioner', in J. Bercovitch and J. Z. Rubin (eds), *Mediation in International Relations: Multiple Approaches to Conflict Management*. New York: St. Martin's Press – now Palgrave Macmillan, pp. 64–96.

Kelman, H. C. (1993) 'Coalitions Across Conflict Lines: the Interplay of Conflicts Within and Between the Israeli and Palestinian Communities', in S. Worchel and J. Simpson (eds), *Conflicts between People and Groups*. Chicago: Nelson-Hall, pp. 236–58.

Kelman, H. C. (1995) 'Contributions of an Unofficial Conflict Resolution Effort to the Israeli–Palestinian Breakthrough', *Negotiation Journal*, 11, 19–27.

Kelman, H.C. (1996a) 'Negotiation as Interactive Problem Solving', *International Negotiation*, 1, 99–123.

Kelman, H. C. (1996b) 'The Interactive Problem-Solving Approach', in C. A. Crocker and F. O. Hampson with P. Aall (eds), *Managing Global Chaos: Sources of and Responses to International Conflict*. Washington, DC: US Institute of Peace, pp. 501–19.

Kelman, H. C. (1997a) 'Group Processes in the Resolution of International Conflict: Experiences from the Israeli–Palestinian Case', *American Psychologist*, 52, 212–20.

Kelman, H. C. (1997b) 'Social–Psychological Dimensions of International Conflict', in I. W. Zartman and J. L. Rasmussen (eds), *Peacemaking in International Conflict: Methods and Techniques*. Washington, DC: US Institute of Peace, pp. 191–237.

Kelman, H. C. (1997c) 'Some Determinants of the Oslo Breakthrough', *International Negotiation*, 2, 183–94.

Kelman, H. C. and Cohen, S. P. (1986) 'Resolution of International Conflict: an Interactional Approach', in S. Worchel and W. G. Austin (eds), *Psychology of Intergroup Relations*, 2nd edn. Chicago: Nelson-Hall, pp. 323–42.

Pearson, T. (1990) *The Role of 'Symbolic Gestures' in Intergroup Conflict Resolution: Addressing Group Identity*. Unpublished PhD Dissertation, Harvard University.

Rouhana, N. N. and Kelman, H. C. (1994) 'Promoting Joint Thinking in International Conflicts: an Israeli–Palestinian Continuing Workshop', *Journal of Social Issues*, 50(1), 157–78.

Saunders, H. H. (1988) 'The Arab–Israeli Conflict in a Global Perspective', in J. D. Steinbruner (ed.), *Restructuring American Foreign Policy*. Washington, DC: Brookings Institution, pp. 221–51.

White, R. K. (1965) 'Images in the Context of International Conflict: Soviet Perceptions of the U.S. and the U.S.S.R.', in H. C. Kelman (ed.), *International Behavior: A Social–Psychological Analysis*. New York: Holt, Rinehart & Winston, pp. 238–76.

10
Mediating Intermediaries: Expanding Roles of Transnational Organizations

Larry A. Dunn and Louis Kriesberg

Introduction

The systematic analysis of the mediating contributions of international transnational organizations is only beginning to match their recent expansion. In this chapter we contribute to that widening body of research, mapping out the various kinds of special contributions transnational organizations (TOs) make to effective mediation of international and other large-scale conflicts involving one or more state actors. Transnational organizations, here, refers to NGOs operating internationally. NGOs may be multinational in their membership and leadership, as international NGOs (INGOs) are generally considered to be, or they may be based in one country and conduct their activities in other countries as well. We first examine some of the intermediary activities of transnational organizations drawing from several case studies and historic examples, and then highlight their special advantages and limitations in performing mediation activities. We conclude the chapter with a discussion of theoretical considerations and practical applications for this type of engagement.

The role of mediators has usefully received a great deal of attention in the field of conflict resolution. Actions by mediators and other intermediaries often contribute significantly to the transformation of conflicts. The wide variety and complexity of activities conducted by mediators and the diversity of social roles performed by them supports a broad definition and understanding of mediation (Touval, 1982; Touval and Zartman, 1985; Bercovitch, 1992; Kelman, 1992). For our purposes, mediation is defined as a form of conflict intervention which is provided to promote the settlement or constructive transformation of a conflict between two or more parties. Admittedly, some of those activities and roles which seem acceptable to us are not regarded by some analysts and practitioners as embodying 'true' or 'good' mediation.

Trends and developments in transnational organizations

Expansion in engagement

Activities normally associated with TOs relevant for peacemaking include humanitarian assistance (e.g. in the provision of emergency aid to refugees and short-term famine relief), intervention assistance (in the form of human rights observation, documentation and advocacy), and the advancement of long-term economic development projects. Alongside these three traditional mandates of European and North American based TOs, Anderson identifies a fourth relevant to this chapter: 'the pursuit of peace, including the promotion of the philosophy and techniques of negotiation, conflict resolution, and nonviolence' (Anderson, 1996a: 344). Peacemaking, then, has emerged as the *raison d'être* of several transnational organizations.

It is not our purpose to provide a comprehensive account of the history of transnational organizations here. We note only those trends and developments that relate to mediation activity. One phenomenon corresponding to such activity is the remarkable expansion of TOs and their recently expanded engagement in conflict settings. Apropos of our concern here are the ways in which problems and conflicts resulting from migration, trade, and increased demands on limited resources have stimulated the formation and exponential growth of transnational actors across the globe. The increase in sheer numbers of actors is matched by an expansion of engagement in situations of crises and conflict. However, this heightened engagement in conflicts should not be surprising, since the conventional kinds of activities conducted early on by TOs such as the International Red Cross (IRC), CARE, the American Friends Service Committee (AFSC), and the Mennonite Central Committee (MCC), were directed in response to needs arising from past or present wars. The widespread global presence of relief and development organizations meant that representatives occasionally found themselves in the midst of emerging violence as they pursued other mandates (Anderson, 1996b).

Varieties of organizational engagement with mediation

For transnational actors attempting to fulfill other objectives, engagement in various kinds of mediating activities is a by-product of their other types of assistance. Established relationships with governments and future antagonists or proximity to conflicts has led to intervention opportunities. Access to and conversations with existing factions as a result of previous and ongoing assistance may allow TOs to be involved in work preparing for and supportive of mediation activity being conducted by other actors. The provision of 'good offices' and the facilitation of communication are two such types of aid. More direct and primary engagement in mediation activity is also on the rise. Of course, these varieties are not offered as rigid types and may exist in combinations or overlap other forms of engagement as well, including *ad hoc* individual mediation and that conducted by 'quasi-mediators' (Kriesberg, 1996b).

The proliferation of new TOs and the expansion of organizational objectives to include conflict resolution reflects an increased understanding of the complexity and multiple causes of global issues and needs. This most recent trend may also reflect a general increase in and awareness of alternative dispute resolution (ADR) activity, at least among TOs based in the United States. Furthermore, the expansion of US-based TOs to include mediation efforts may mirror the preeminence of American mediation in international politics during and after the Cold War (Zartman and Touval, 1996: 447). This type of activity does not necessarily contradict the traditional goals of TOs, as many are dedicated to furthering international understanding, peace, and human rights, while others increasingly recognize the interrelatedness of diverse mandates and activities. It has, however, rendered traditional activities more complex and difficult, and has led agencies to closely examine assumptions about political affiliations and the reality of policies of strict neutrality long honored by many organizations (Betts, 1996).

Stages of mediating activities

We have noted how the role of mediators is prominent in the field of conflict resolution, and that the number of individuals and agencies conducting mediation activities in international and other large-scale conflicts has expanded greatly in the last two decades to include a wide variety of transnational organizations. This points to the many opportunities that parties who are not primary adversaries have to affect the course of a struggle. Both aside from and as part of the mediating role, they may give support and assistance to one side, set limits on the way the conflict is waged, provide models of alternative approaches, pressure or cajole the adversaries to negotiate a settlement, and even facilitate them doing so. In this section we focus on the range of mediating activities provided by transnational actors at four major stages of the settlement phase of large scale conflicts: preparation, initiation, negotiation, and implementation. Of course, the sequence does not occur linearly nor should the stages be considered clearly marked.

Mediating activities are quite diverse and they tend to vary with the mediator, the type of conflict, and the stage of the conflict's de-escalation or avoidance of escalation (Kriesberg, 1982). Each kind of mediating activity can occur at any stage of a conflict, but the specific content, form, and significance of the activities vary at different stages and from one type of intermediary to the next. At least in theory, transnational organizations might be expected to intervene effectively at any point along the life cycle of an international conflict Rubin (1992: 264). Some mediating activities may be performed by TOs particularly well, and others by official organizations. In any case, no intermediary can perform all of the possible services, since many are incompatible with each other. Later, we will discuss the importance of coordinating the great range of activities that may be conducted by different actors.

While it is also useful to discuss the activities that can contribute to constructive conflict transformation and settlement independently of who performs them, our task is to consider some of the services transnational intermediaries may provide. As will be evident in this section, there may be a great deal of overlap of the kind of mediation activities performed by TOs with other actors. However, in the next section we will identify the ways in which TOs are better positioned to conduct certain activities more or less effectively, noting special opportunities and constraints at each of the stages.

Preparation and mediation

Because some TOs maintain an ongoing presence in settings where conflicts may erupt, they are in a position to identify the potential outbreak of a violent struggle and assess opportune moments for initiating mediating actions. Long before any individual or agency is identified as a mediator or any other kind of intermediary, TOs on the ground may conduct fact-finding services and report about emerging conflicts to the adversary sides, their own constituents or the wider public, thus mobilizing support for other intermediaries to intervene. In his discussion of the role of religious actors in the transition from Rhodesia to Zimbabwe, Kraybill notes that the primary role of the Catholic Church in Rhodesia 'was that of "truth-telling" – conveying the reality of what was happening in Rhodesia to the nation and the world' (Kraybill, 1994: 213). This did not lead to direct mediation involvement by the Catholic Church, but their far-reaching ecclesial network helped to mobilize global support of their advocacy for negotiations.

In another instance, we can see how a similar initial role led to more direct intervention involvement. As the program head of International Dialogues in West Africa, Quaker conciliator John Volkmar early on monitored rising Nigerian tensions from his office in Togo. Yarrow (1978) and Sampson (1994) document the involvement that Volkmar and two other Quaker colleagues, Adam Curle and Walter Martin, would eventually have as transnational conciliators. In their capacity as a TO carrying out relief and development projects in conjunction with regional agencies, the Quakers had developed key relationships that had made mediation involvement possible. Lederach (1995a) notes the importance for conducting peacebuilding activities to establish such relationships among indigenous grassroots leaders as well as with persons who function in positions of middle-range leadership in sectors such as education, business, agriculture, or health. These middle range leaders are 'positioned such that they are likely to know and be known by the top-level leadership, yet they are significantly connected to the broader context and the constituency that the leaders claim to represent' (Lederach, 1995a: 20).

As illustrated by Quakers in the Nigerian civil war context, being engaged in conflict settings allows TOs to conduct a variety of mediating activities. Involvement in non-mediating activities such as relief efforts may place organizational agents in contact with existing or future protagonists and in a position to build bridges based on established trust. Some TOs more strictly limit their intermediary involvement, choosing not to parlay established trust into an opportunity to facilitate negotiation. During the 1997 Peruvian hostage crisis, the International Red Cross officials had limited their involvement to talks addressing humanitarian concerns (Knox, 1997). In spite of the contextual importance of identifying the IRC and other interveners as 'guarantors' or 'interlocutors', the significance of their possible activity as mediators remains. Acceptance of this role for the IRC followed initial permission to enter the heavily guarded compound strictly to check on the condition of the hostages. Even in the case of TOs whose stated purpose is conflict resolution, involvement in an environment where conflict exists may still not be directly related to larger civil or international struggles. However, training (or, capacity building) in conflict resolution or organizational skills can become useful for local actors whose overlapping involvements and roles provide opportunities for involvement as intermediaries at other levels of the social structure. For example, during several years of conciliation work in Central America, the Mennonite Central Committee conducted workshops on peacemaking and reconciliation among Moravian church leaders in Nicaragua. With some technical assistance, these leaders subsequently organized a new conciliation commission concerned with the US-backed *contra* war, leading to negotiations between the Miskito Indians and the Sandinistas (Nichols, 1994; Wehr and Lederach, 1996).

In preparing hostile sides for de-escalating movement, TOs can provide new ways of thinking about and framing a conflict and the roles of adversaries. Fisher (1997) examines these and other types of contributions by scholar-practitioners involved in more than 75 interactive conflict resolution (ICR) workshops over three decades. Before adversaries are actually brought together, trusted intermediaries may be relied on for transmitting information from one side to another with relatively little distortion. Such exchanges may probe either side's readiness to de-escalate, make salient the risks of continuing or escalating the struggle, or suggest terms of a possible agreement. The mediator may present concessions informally and off-the-record in a way that either side feels it could not for fear of appearing weak or losing face. In this way Quaker missions of conciliation between Nigerian leader Yakubu Gowon and Biafran leader Emeka Ojukwu helped to reduce suspicions, misperceptions, and fears. Their involvement helped to remove obstacles for negotiation while they continued advocating for a settlement of the destructive conflict. Where antagonists are willing to meet, though not yet negotiate, transnational actors may convene meetings or larger conferences which help representatives of both sides to get to know each other. This type of activity begins to overlap with that in the next stage of mediation intervention: initiation.

Initiation and mediation

Facilitating communication outside of the context of joint meetings may lead to involvement in arranging which parties will come together at a future time, often a considerable concern to adversaries. If unable to gain recognition from or access to more powerful states, minor actors to a conflict may accept the lesser legitimation that comes from dealing with a non-governmental agency. Whether for mediation or other purposes, such involvement may lead to the kind of familiarity that helps an intermediary to develop a common agenda for consideration in future negotiations. Often the trust which accrues will lead both sides to be willing to accept the offer of 'good offices' by a transnational actor; such was the case with Roman Catholic Cardinal Antonio Samore in the conflict between Argentina and Chile prior to official papal mediation (Princen, 1992a: 144). While seemingly a small detail, the provision of an acceptable space for discussions perceived by both sides as safe, confidential, and neutral is often critical for encouraging the pursuit of dialogue.

Being able to recognize and identify who should meet as principal negotiators does not automatically translate into access, nor does it bring them to the negotiation table. As Princen (1992a,b) notes, unlike states, most TOs do not have the resources to punish international actors or threaten to do so. Neither can they promise economic rewards or other material incentives as a means for encouraging belligerents to cease hostilities and enter into negotiations. Accounts of TOs operating as mediators emphasize the significance of personal ties and interaction through organizational networks. When Curle and Volkmar found themselves unable to gain an audience with General Gowon, it was a government minister who had a firsthand acquaintance with Quakers while living in the United States who arranged a critical meeting with the Nigerian leader (Sampson, 1994: 112). This enabled the Quakers to perform another critical mediation function: facilitating a confidential exchange outside the spotlight of officially arranged formal meetings. When the Consultative Committee of six African heads-of-state formed by the OAU to address the Nigerian struggle sided with the government, one of its members, Niger president Hamani Diori, recognized that the Quakers' low-profile might enable them to convene a secret meeting of lower level officials from both sides to search for some possible areas of agreement (Sampson, 1994: 93).

Negotiation and mediation

'The most difficult moment in a dialogue aimed at ending a conflict can be the apparently simple act of convening talks', reflects Cameron Hume in his account of the Mozambique peace negotiations (Hume, 1994: 25). The difficulty arises from the many strategic choices that must be made regarding parties, agenda, issues, format and context, and their degree of appropriateness given the prevailing conditions of the conflict. Generally, the formula for negotiations, presented by the intermediary, is likely to have more appeal and legitimacy than if proposed by any one of the partisans alone. In the likely context of heightened suspicion, the intermediary has to be trusted and know enough about the concerns and interests of each side to be able to propose a formula that has acceptable elements for every side. This is where TOs, particularly those with a long-term presence in settings where conflicts erupt, are able to be especially effective in bringing adversaries together to discuss a common agenda and negotiate about the agreed-upon issues. Indigenous TO representatives may be uniquely in such a position, though they must overcome whatever real or perceived alliances are associated with them as nationals. In Mozambique, the team of 'observers' who eventually took on the collective role of mediator included members of Sant' Egidio, a Vatican-affiliated religious community. Their involvement as mediators became possible because the years of engagement in Mozambique had helped Sant' Egidio members to develop ties of trust and credibility to both the government and insurgent groups. Their close relations with the Holy See and Pope John Paul II allowed them to transcend the alliances which divided the country.

Assuming the formal mediator role facilitates the provision of a primary mediating activity at this stage: making negotiating exchanges more acceptable to the adversaries. This entails giving salience, credibility and legitimacy to offers for settlement and, where necessary, generating new options in the face of rejection. Negotiations do not always indicate cooperativeness or the cessation of hostilities in conducting the conflict elsewhere, but while underway, they can avert the slide toward further destructiveness, as did the Vatican in the Beagle Channel Dispute (Princen, 1992a).

Even as negotiations progress, each side may find it difficult to appear to accept the ideas of the enemy though an offer may be acceptable on its own merit. If the idea is proposed by an intermediary, it can be more seriously considered or even accepted without appearing to be a sign of weakness, compromise, or yielding to an opponent's demands. For example, this type of activity was conducted as part of the Quaker mediation efforts in Nigeria. Not only did Curle and Volkmar make substantive suggestions of their own in order to break an apparent impasse, at one point they presented their own views on an issue of high concern, hoping to avert a major outbreak of rebel violence. Shortly thereafter, the Quaker mediators conveyed Biafran concessions which could not be offered openly in formal peace talks for fear of appearing weak (Princen, 1992a; Sampson, 1994). And while non-governmental mediators may not be able to threaten repercussions or promise material benefits, they may warn of potential repercussions or consequences of the ongoing policies.

Implementation and mediation

Agreements often represent an extended process of transformation among disputing parties. Outside the negotiating forum, final agreements can be perceived as inexplicable dramatic turnarounds in the light of earlier or ongoing rhetoric and posturing by adversaries. Therefore, negotiating parties may seek the help of the mediator to win support for the settlement by their respective constituencies. Mediators can help to stage traditional and symbolic rituals that endeavor to represent the transformed nature of the conflict and parties, making the agreement more visible and obligatory. When non-governmental mediators have established contacts on both sides beyond the negotiating actors, and have transnational constituencies of their own who seek to promote support for an agreement, the likelihood of ratification and compliance improves significantly.

Increasingly, although perhaps not always wisely, agreements lead to immediate elections which need monitoring by third parties. Other settlement terms, such as demobilization or redeployment of occupying forces, may require observers as well to help monitor the provisions of such an agreement, all a part of the mediation effort. The need for relieving the pressures of war-torn societies through efforts of aid, conciliation, healing, and sustainable development projects is also being recognized more and more. Holding the strong belief that individual change is the key to larger social change, persons associated with Moral Re-Armament drew on the network of friendships they had developed in the tension-filled Rhodesia of 1980 to bring together Prime Minister Ian Smith and nationalist opposition leader Robert Mugabe on the eve of the announcement of election results. Extensive negotiations had been completed in September of 1979, clearly spelling out the terms of agreement on a transitional government and settlement on a new constitution. But fear of renewed fighting, regardless of results, continued to grip the country. The public announcement of the election results followed the meeting of Smith and Mugabe, and each announced their support of the outcome to their own constituents; Mugabe making his reconciliation speech and Smith his astonishing exhortation encouraging fellow whites to stay (Kraybill, 1994: 224). This activity was no mere monitoring; significant mediation activity was required to bring the two men together and to encourage a shared understanding for how best to respond to the election outcome each had become privy to prior to its public disclosure.

To their traditional responses of relief, reconstruction and conciliation, the Mennonite Central Committee has sought to address the ongoing emotional trauma created by the brutalities of violent conflicts. In Russia and the Caucasus, Central America, and Central and Southern Africa, MCC has sought to help bring healing to those who suffered post-traumatic stress disorder (PTSD) as a result of the torture, rape and other brutalities which are too often a part of war and other forms of violent conflict. In Liberia, for example, an MCC sponsored trauma and conflict resolution team worked with the Christian Health Association of Liberia (CHAL) following that country's civil crisis. Along with existing involvement in education, health work and logistical and relief services, the team expanded Mennonite participation in Liberia, conducting workshops in trauma healing, bias awareness, prejudice reduction, mediation and reconciliation.

Special contributions and constraints of transnational organizations

We turn now to a closer examination of the special contributions which transnational organizations can make to mediation. We discuss how many of the activities noted in the previous section are more effectively carried out by TOs because of their unique relationship to conflict parties and conflict settings. Specific limitations are presented as well. It is useful in our analysis to discuss the activities which occur by the stages of mediating activities, first noting special contributions and then constraints within each phase.

Preparation aid by transnational organizations

Contributions

Lederach (1997) notes the significance for peacebuilding in divided societies of being able to take a long-term view of the situation and the progression of conflict. Even in the most enduring and intractable of conflicts, mediation efforts are frequently short-term crisis interventions (relative to the duration of the conflict) conducted intermittently in the course of the conflict's longer progression or across a relatively brief period of its lifespan. Transnational organizations, in particular humanitarian and service agencies, often establish the kind of long-term presence in conflict settings that allows their agents and representatives to become familiar with the complexities of a conflict situation. Often these complexities require knowledge of the cultural components of the setting beyond the understandings of customs and the etiquette of negotiating behavior, which might be made available to an outside intervener. This is especially difficult for non-local TOs whose *raison d'être*, is crisis intervention, whether mediation or otherwise.

A transnational organization providing multiple long-term services in a region can help to maintain the possibility of mediation involvement even if such intervention is initially rejected. In the case of Quaker conciliation efforts in Nigeria, Nigerian officials – recently independent and sensitive to outside meddling – were cautious about having the Quakers serve as channels of communication before the outbreak of civil war. Accepting this concern, Quaker mediators extended an offer to make other kinds of relief available which provided for ongoing involvement and access in later stages. The more recent crisis between the Tupac Amaru and the Peruvian government provides an example of activity of another kind preparing the way for later mediation involvement. Following the guerrillas' raid on the Japanese Ambassador's residence at a reception to honor Emperor Akihito's birthday, Roman Catholic Archbishop Juan Lus Cipriani is believed to have carried messages between the government and the rebels' leader, Nestor Cerpa Cartolini, even though no talks were yet officially taking place. This preliminary activity was carried out as Archbishop Cipriani, a personal friend of Peruvian President Alberto Fujimori, visited the Ambassador's residence almost daily to say mass (Knox, 1997).

The significance of long-term involvement goes well beyond providing understanding for the purpose of designing effective outside intervention. Long-term agencies are particularly likely to know how to activate the involvement of appropriate local conflict resolution mechanisms. Outside methods of mediation, like outside solutions, often discourage local actors from identifying and building on their own cultural knowledge to establish a lasting infrastructure for developing sustainable, peaceful relationships. In many cases, outside intervention models fail to bring about effective, long-lasting solutions, and can be, at their worst, counterproductive. For example, when relief efforts were hampered by Somali clan infighting over the provision of humanitarian assistance (frequently stolen by warring factions), long-term service agencies sought out community elders and other leaders for solutions to the problem. Not only were struggles that can make later negotiations more difficult avoided, but channels were identified to facilitate later direct peacemaking efforts, particularly among Somali women who had access to warring factions because of cross-clan marriages. The crisis-oriented efforts of outside interveners in Somalia, limited to inviting internationally recognized 'warlords' to the 'universal' forum of international diplomacy, assumed the existence of a classically governed power-wielding state that no longer existed. Intervention processes at this level did not recognize the need for, nor could it have created, such a solution. In fact, the collapse of the Somali state brought a return to traditional forms of association, and it was in this social web of relationships that peacemaking efforts were pursued by TOs.

Intervention and advocacy TOs, especially those with a long-term presence, can provide valuable training and other forms of intervention that effectively prepares individuals and groups for the stages ahead. Short-term interveners, particularly those from North America, are strongly driven to provide results that are recognized as viable contributions and solutions back home and serve to justify budgeted allocations for ongoing involvement in conflict resolution work. The tentative activities of the preparation stage, often simmering for a long time without seeming to have a positive effect, can more easily be waited out and followed up by locally resident intermediaries carrying on with other work.

Constraints

The increase of international agencies offering assistance to people in conflict settings contributes to the complexity and introduces the possibility of additional problems. Anderson (1996a) examines how humanitarian assistance may prolong the conflicts which produce the need they intend to alleviate. Transnational agencies conducting mediation should be aware that the introduction of external resources, including intermediary personnel, into conflict environments can create additional tensions, imply a passive acceptance of the war, bestow legitimacy on warring factions, undermine culturally held peacetime values, and reinforce animosity (Anderson, 1996a: 16–19). While the legitimacy which TOs may provide a lesser adversary can also lead to recognition which spurs constructive movement, TOs lack the kind of resources necessary for providing balance to an otherwise asymmetrical (negotiating) relationship. Such consequences and constraints may not only diminish the likelihood of being invited or accepted to conduct some of the activities discussed above, but may also result in a lack of important constituent support for ongoing involvement which makes mediation possible.

Initiation aid by TOs

Contributions

Some transnational organizations may have special advantages in gaining early mediating access in conflict situations, especially when one of the adversaries is non-governmental in nature. As noted previously in the case of Mozambique, the two sides could not agree to invite the government of the United States, Zimbabwe, Kenya or any other country to mediate. The adversaries had not set out to identify a non-governmental agency to mediate, but those whom they trusted to convene talks about talks eventually became an acceptable mediating group. Drabek's observation that 'NGOs are perceived to be able to do something that national governments cannot or will not do' (Drabek, 1987: xiii) rightly applies to mediation as well as to other activities. For example, official state policies of not talking to 'thugs', 'terrorists', or other non-state actors engaged in conflict preclude performing any role that legitimates hostile non-governmental antagonists in the public sphere. The refusal by World Vision, a relief and development agency founded in 1950 and more recently exploring involvement in conflict resolution work, to be used in any way for US political purposes has allowed them to gain access to Ethiopia, Vietnam and Cambodia, when ruled by governments linked to the Soviet Union or the People's Republic of China (Bolling and Smith, 1982: 176–8). Such access may provide the opportunity to initiate mediation activity in the event of intra- or international hostilities involving these and other countries where World Vision is involved in other projects.

Where access is concerned, the TO-adversary relationship involves something of a paradox. We have already noted the lesser ability of TOs to apply pressure to move toward negotiations. However, as Princen suggests, the bases of a transnational actor's influence are more subtle in their ability to 'help create the conditions for effective negotiating between conflicting parties' (Princen, 1992b, p. 150). For adversaries who may be more readily persuaded to negotiate by the stick or carrot of a powerful state, the increased risk of a difficult withdrawal may reinforce initial reluctance. The more limited ability of TOs to pressure through reward and punishment mechanisms is matched or exceeded by their ability to bring adversaries together by providing a low-pressure context which affords greater deniability and the option of an easier exit. During the Nigerian civil war, formal British participation as either arbitrators or mediators was unacceptable to Biafran leaders "suspicious of British motives based on their interpretation of colonial history and the British role in establishing northern dominance in the Nigerian federation" (Sampson, 1994: 98). Since the OAU's Consultative Committee had already ruled itself out as a potential mediating body by calling on Biafra to renounce secession, Quaker conciliation involvement in support of official mediating efforts was accepted by both sides, although in the end none of the peacemaking attempts was successful in ending the war.

Constraints

Several qualities of TOs tend to limit their mediating contributions at the initiation stage, including problems of access to warring parties and their conflicts. Without other means of leverage or legitimacy to pressure adversaries to accept preliminary intervention, the absence of existing involvement in conflict settings reduces the likelihood of gaining access to conduct capacity-building activities or to facilitate communication directly in relation to an outbreak of hostilities. Without existing contacts, non-governmental mediators often lack the leverage necessary to insert themselves into a conflict in order to initiate the kind of communication that characterizes activities at this stage. Adversaries risk less criticism by rejecting overtures by TOs than by shunning the intervention efforts of powerful states or of international governmental organizations who are in a position to apply and encourage international pressure. And while major powers may be restricted in their access by real or perceived interests in the issues in dispute, on occasion TOs have encountered similar suspicion, criticism and hostility because of their association with state powers, whether financed directly by government funds or not (Bolling, 1982: 4). In the case of US-based TOs, the perception of US interest is not absent, since many TOs receive significant support from or represent interests of the US government. The inability of TOs to transcend such associations as genuinely autonomous actors may limit their ability to successfully initiate mediation activities.

For many non-governmental aid organizations, their primary mission may seem to preclude mediation activities. Humanitarian agencies providing relief to Rwandan refugees in Zaire pulled back from all operations following an escalation of the conflict. Since mediation involvement in response to such conflicts may place more traditional activities at risk, TOs may be reluctant to intervene as mediators, even at opportune times and when no one else may be in a position to do so. A lack of constituency support for any involvement that might possibly interfere with a TO's primary purpose may jeopardize its ability to be involved in any way.

Negotiation aid by TOs

Contributions

As was clearly the case in Nigeria, TOs are more likely to carry out facilitative mediation rather than directed mediation since these are generally the expectations of antagonists. This also may be in part due to the lack of leverage available to TOs, limiting the directiveness used in bringing about a settlement. While Quaker conciliators were involved in discussions concerning the political, economic, and military issues in the conflict, their work more centrally involved behind-the-scenes intermediary activity of 'persuasion, clarification, message carrying, listening, defusing, honest brokering, encouraging and liaison' with other intermediaries (Yarrow, 1978: 256). A similar role was played by Moravian Church leaders as part of the Conciliation Commission mediating between the Sandinista government and the Atlantic-coast resistance represented by the political umbrella group YATAMA. Nichols explains that the role of the Commission 'was to conduct the process and maintain the integrity of the talks, not to deal with the substance' (1994: 76–7). Activities included logistical planning of the sessions, message carrying, and preparation of documents and records. This facilitative function was an extension of living side-by-side with YATAMA leaders, and included eating and relaxing together with both parties (Wehr and Lederach, 1996: 66).

In the Nicaraguan case, the intermediaries responsible for organizing and sponsoring negotiations (in this case the Moravian Church) are identified by Wehr and Lederach as *insider-partials*, 'whose reservoir of trust and mutually recognized stature among conflictants, and cross-cutting affiliations with both sides, are so substantial as to permit a mediating function'

(Wehr and Lederach, 1996: 65). In contrast to the *outsider–neutral* mediator whose legitimacy and authority are created primarily through the role of the mediator as a professional, the acceptability of the Moravian Church officials was based on their culturally valued ability to identify with a group or tradition, for being 'close to, known by, with and for each side' (Wehr and Lederach, 1996: 59). However, while Wehr and Lederach acknowledge that personal trust is always a concern in selecting any mediator, they perhaps too strongly contrast this sense of trust, or *confianza*, with neutrality. As they recognize, antagonists in *all* settings value trust in relation to third party involvement; we stress that trust is *attributed to different sources* in various settings. Along a second dimension, the objectives of the Conciliation Commission's process clearly reflected culturally valued elements of the regionally established Contadora Agreement which called for the Commission's formation. Glossed over outside of the region even by those most concerned with the terms of settlement, the Commission's goals were based on 'spiritual understandings long embedded in the cultural backgrounds of the Sandinista and YATAMA delegations alike' (Nichols, 1994: 74). The likelihood that such objectives might be overlooked by a mediator was averted by the involvement of locally-based, culturally-sensitive intermediaries.

Constraints

Outside of the officially recognized diplomatic field, most TOs lack externally based credentials for playing an extended mediation role in large-scale conflicts. Unable to interject themselves into conflict situations in ways that a governmental mediator or representative of the United Nations or other regional agency might, TOs are likely to remain largely peripheral unless mediation is recognized as their primary organizational function. The Vatican-affiliated observer team was not recognized as likely mediators of the Mozambique conflict, even after conducting substantial mediation activity, until all other qualified potential nation-state intermediaries were ruled out for other reasons as unacceptable to the parties.

Zartman and Touval observe that agencies such as the International Committee of the ICRC can bestow normative approval on and an improved image to a warring group. That ability may be able to provide a powerful incentive for antagonistic parties 'to accept its presence and services and to accede to its proposals' (Zartman and Touval, 1996: 451). However, as they rightly point out, since warring parties are primarily concerned with whether the framework of an agency's involvement as a mediator will further their own party's interests, the effectiveness of a mediator is likely to be based on the ability to fulfill both tangible and intangible needs. Unlike state actors, TOs seldom have the kind of resources which large-scale international conflicts require to achieve and to sustain a settlement. Prior to settlement, negotiations can be costly enterprises. In spite of the substantial amount of money spent by some of the larger humanitarian agencies, most TOs do not have adequate financial resources for sponsoring the kind of extended negotiations often required by complex, multi-party conflicts. While this may be especially true of those TOs whose sole concern is conflict resolution, agencies conducting mediation alongside other activities have perhaps as much difficulty justifying expenditures that have a less observable and immediate impact.

Implementation aid by TOs

Contributions

TOs are especially able to provide particular kinds of assistance for the ratification and implementation of negotiated agreements. Hume (1994: 137) recounts how the legitimation provided by the solemn yet celebratory tone given to the signing ceremony by Archbishop Goncalves helped to overcome a flawed agreement by engendering support for implementation on the ground in Mozambique. In yet another role, many intermediaries who had conducted conflict resolution training in South Africa later served as election observers there. The specialized roles afforded to TOs, combined with a long-term perspective, allows them to go beyond the details of an agreement, fostering cooperation and, in some cases, reconciliation, by facilitating the (re)establishment of relationships necessary for lasting peace, particularly at the lower and middle levels of society. Well aware of the shortcomings following the first world war, several transnational actors actively promoted Franco-German reconciliation after World War Two (Steele, 1994). The newly established World Council of Churches created an independent advisory commission to promote European cooperation. Its support for the Schuman Plan, which established a supranational agency integrating European coal and steel industries which led to both the Common Market and today's European Community, helped to promote European unity. Other efforts to foster reconciliation were carried out by the International Fellowship of Reconciliation (IFOR), Moral Re-Armament (MRA), and Pax Christi.

The involvement of local actors in TO mediation activities, as with Archbishop Goncalves in Mozambique, who was recognized both as a Mozambican and a man of God, allows mediators to develop and apply expert knowledge of local culture. In Somalia, the Mennonite Central Committee published the proceedings and agreements of MCC-sponsored elders' peace conferences to distribute among the broader Somali population. Extraordinary as a form of disclosure in its leveling effect among disparate clans, the culturally sensitive and locally based nature of these publications was reflected in their use of both English and Somali. In other activities, the strength of the Somali oral tradition was reinforced by TO intermediaries through the provision for nonwritten mechanisms (poetry, speeches) and media which remain a powerful means for moving people toward either war or reconciliation (Lederach, 1995: 97).

Constraints

Many of the constraints noted for previous stages apply to the activities required for the ratification and implementation of agreements. On-the-ground involvement which does not engage middle and upper level actors in a context where a state governs may limit a TO's ability to monitor or enforce compliance at the top levels. Although TOs may be able to win support for an agreement by the negotiating parties' constituencies, they may lack either negative or positive leverage to encourage the adoption and implementation by governments of popularly supported settlement provisions. Aside from compliance that may emerge from the kind of obligation that is based on an established relationship between TO mediators and adversaries, TOs may be limited to less direct influence through their own constituents' lobbying of state governments to apply such pressure. Given the multi-national make-up of some TO constituencies, this can be a significant resource. However, before it can be employed as such, the TOs' constituencies must be supportive of the kind of costly, uncertain, and uncontrollable processes that are a part of conflicts.

Coordination by TOs

Transforming large-scale social conflicts is an extended process, proceeding along different paths, and conducted at many levels by a variety of governmental and non-governmental actors (Kriesberg, 2002). The possible contributions of TOs to the resolution of such conflicts can best be understood in that context. Once a conflict has emerged, four major steps can be discerned by which the opposing parties move to negotiate a settlement of the conflict and perhaps resolve it. The steps are: preparing to undertake negotiations, initiating negotiations, negotiating an agreement, and implementing the agreement. As indicated earlier, TOs can make relatively effective contributions at each stage, but they are also limited in some regards at each stage as are all such actors. This provides the setting for effective coordination between TOs or non-official (track 2) and official (diplomatic) mediating activities.

The coordination among mediating intermediaries may occur sequentially as well as simultaneously (Kriesberg, 1996a). Since different kinds of mediating activities are particularly important at various stages, sequential coordination is a likely occurrence. For example, exploratory probing may be provided in the preparation stage by individuals associated with a TO and when formal negotiations seem possible to initiate, official mediators may step in to continue the work begun in the earlier exploratory phase. Because of the complexity of large-scale conflicts, coordination among diverse intermediaries and between them and mediating agencies, can be crucial since the work of any one intermediary is likely to impact on the work of others (Stremlau, 1987; Kriesberg, 1996a). The more closely related the work, the more vital the task of effectively coordinating such initiatives for reducing or eliminating interference and enhancing the overall effectiveness of intervention. Because intermediaries will be limited in their capabilities or constrained in certain ways by other factors, mediating agencies with experience in a broad range of services may be in a better position to assist with coordinating the activities of a range of actors. Kriesberg (1996a) has proposed elsewhere that no one intermediary can reasonably attempt to perform all the useful activities that can promote constructive peacemaking. However, with expansion into the kinds of mediating involvement documented here, TOs may increase their capacity to take the lead in providing such coordinating services in future conflicts.

Conclusion

It is widely accepted that mediation in international settings is a multivalent activity shaped by both the context of the conflict environment and the characteristics of the intervening agent or agency. A more recent addition to this equation is the consideration that official intermediary activities may emerge in association with an INGO or TO whose *raison d'être* may or may not explicitly include the activities normally recognized as those of a mediator. This chapter has examined the characteristics and activities of transnational organizations conducting mediation in large-scale conflicts, noting special contributions and constraints in relation to traditional and emerging roles and types of interventions.

In the context of international conflict, TOs have not been recognized as conducting typical mediation activities. In carrying out a wide range of other activities, TOs have a long history of intervention as intermediaries of another kind in alleviating the effects of war. Out of this long-standing humanitarian involvement, some TOs have taken on a new role as mediating intermediaries.

Peacemaking in large-scale conflicts requires changes, at one stage or another, at different levels and in different directions. TOs do function at all levels, but tend to have relatively more linkages at the grass-roots, middle-rank, and sub-elite levels compared to governmental actors. Again this is the setting for effective coordination, particularly simultaneously. Thus, while official mediators are working with the leading officials of the antagonistic sides, various TOs may be working at the grass-roots or middle-rank level. As we have seen, work at these levels may increase the awareness of the relevance of cultural factors and their salience for the conflict, and places TOs in a position to assess how cultural aspects of conflict and conflict resolution practices are impacted by the conflict at hand. The importance of such knowledge for determining appropriate interventions was noted in several of the cases discussed above. Though perhaps not proposed with culture in mind, Bercovitch's (1992: 18) observation supports such a conclusion: 'For international mediation to be effective, it must *reflect* as well as *affect* the wider conflict system.'

Recognition of the various kinds of activities needed to resolve a large-scale conflict and to attain an equitable and enduring outcome provides the basis for the engagement of many actors to build an enduring peaceful accommodation between former enemies. Whether the scope of activities analysed here rightly comprise mediation or some other subset of peacemaking, peacekeeping, or peacebuilding approaches intended to promote conflict resolution may be debated. The discussion, however, supports the assertion that the lines between the many possible roles, activities and actors contributing to peacemaking may not be as clear in practice as they are in theory (Kelman, 1992). Recognition of the special capabilities and limitations of various kinds of providers, combined with a careful assessment of the most appropriate response or combination of responses, can facilitate effective cooperation in forming a comprehensive approach to bringing about constructive conflict outcomes (Kriesberg, 2002). We are just beginning to see how the characteristics and activities of transnational organizations can contribute to such transformative processes and outcomes.

References

Anderson, M. B. (1996a) *Do No Harm: Supporting Local Capacities for Peace through Aid.* Cambridge, MA: Collaborative for Development Action.

Anderson, M. B. (1996b) 'Humanitarian NGOs in Conflict Intervention', *Managing Global Chaos: Sources of and Responses to International Conflict*, edited by C. Crocker, F. Hampson with P. Aall. Washington, DC: United States Institute of Peace Press, pp. 343–54.

Bercovitch, J. (1992) 'The Structure and Diversity of Mediation in International Relations', *Mediation in International Relations*, edited by J. Bercovitch and J. Z. Rubin. New York: St. Martin's Press – now Palgrave Macmillan, pp. 1–29.

Betts, R. K. (1996) 'The Delusion of Impartial Intervention', *Managing Global Chaos: Sources of and Responses to International Conflict*, edited by C. Crocker, F. Hampson with P. Aall. Washington, DC: United States Institute of Peace Press, pp. 333–41.

Boiling, L. R. with C. Smith. (1982) *Private Foreign Aid: U.S. Philanthropy for Relief and Development*. Boulder, CO: Westview Press.

Drabek, A. G. (1987) 'Development Alternatives: the Challenge for NGOs – An Overview of the Issues', *World Development*, Vol. 15, supplement, Oxford: Pergamon Press, pp. ix–xv.

Drabek, A. G. (ed.) (1987) *World Development*, Vol. 15, supplement. Oxford: Pergamon Press.

Fisher, R. J. (1997) *Interactive Conflict Resolution*. Syracuse, NY: Syracuse University Press.

Hume, C. (1994) *Ending Mozambique's War: The Role of Mediation and Good Offices*. Washington, DC: United States Institute of Peace.

Kelman, H. C. (1992) 'Informal Mediation by the Scholar/Practitioner', *Mediation in International Relations*, edited by J. Bercovitch and J. Z. Rubin. New York: St. Martin's Press – now Palgrave Macmillan, pp. 64–96.

Knox, P. (1997) 'Canadian's Role in Peruvian Crisis Grows'. *The Globe and Mail.*

Kraybill, R. (1994) 'Transition From Rhodesia to Zimbabwe: the Role of Religious Actors', *Religion, the Missing Dimension of Statecraft*, edited by D. Johnston and C. Sampson. New York: Oxford University Press, pp. 208–57.

Kriesberg, L. (1982) *Social Conflicts*, 2nd edn. Englewood Cliffs, NJ: Prentice-Hall.

Kriesberg, L. (1996a) 'Coordinating Intermediary Peace Efforts', *Negotiation Journal*, Vol. 12, No. 4: 341–52.

Kriesberg, L. (1996b) 'Varieties of Mediating Activities and Mediators in International Relations', *Resolving International Conflicts*, edited by J. Bercovitch. Boulder, CO: Lynne Rienner.

Kriesberg, L. (2002) *Constructive Conflicts: From Escalation to Resolutions* 2nd edn. Lanham, MD: Rowman & Littlefield.

Lederach, J. P. (1995) *Preparing for Peace*. Syracuse, New York: Syracuse University Press.

Lederach, J. P. (1997) *Building Peace: Sustainable Reconciliation in Divided Societies*. Tokyo: The United Nations University Press, Washington, DC: United States Institute of Peace.

Nichols, B. (1994) 'Religious Conciliation Between the Sandinistas and the East Coast Indians of Nicaragua', *Religion, the Missing Dimension of Statecraft*, edited by D. Johnston and C. Sampson. New York: Oxford University Press, pp. 64–87.

Princen, T. (1992a) *Intermediaries in International Conflict*. Princeton, NJ: Princeton University Press.

Princen, T. (1992b) 'Mediation by a Transnational Organization: the Case of the Vatican', *Mediation in International Relations*, edited by J. Bercovitch and J. Z. Rubin. New York: St. Martin's Press – now Palgrave Macmillan, pp. 149–75.

Rubin, J. Z. (1992) 'Conclusion: International Mediation in Context', *Mediation in International Relations*, edited by J. Bercovitch and J. Z. Rubin. New York: St. Martin's Press – now Palgrave Macmillan, pp. 249–72.

Sampson, C. (1994) 'To Make Real the Bond Between Us All: Quaker Conciliation During the Nigerian Civil War', *Religion, the Missing Dimension of Statecraft*, edited by D. Johnston and C. Sampson. New York: Oxford University Press, pp. 88–118.

Steele, D. (1994) 'Appendix: the Role of Other Religious Networks in Franco-German Reconciliation', *Religion, the Missing Dimension of Statecraft*, edited by D. Johnston and C. Sampson. New York: Oxford University Press, pp. 58–63.

Stremlau, C. (1987) 'NGO Coordinating Bodies in Africa, Asia, and Latin America', *World Development*, Vol. 15, supplement, edited by A. Gordon Drabek. Oxford: Pergamon Press, pp. 213–25.

Touval, S. (1982) *The Peace Brokers: Mediators in the Arab–Israeli Conflict, 1948–1979*. Princeton: Princeton University Press.

Touval, S. and I. W. Zartman (1985) 'Introduction: Mediation in Theory', *International Mediation in Theory and Practice*, edited by S. Touval and I. W. Zartman. Boulder, CO: Westview Press, pp. 7–17.

Wehr, P. and J. P. Lederach (1996) 'Mediating Conflict in Central America', *Resolving International Conflicts: The Theory and Practice of Mediation*, edited by Jacob Bercovitch. Boulder, CO: Lynne Rienner, pp. 55–74.

Yarrow, C. H. M. (1978) *Quaker Experiences in International Conciliation*. New Haven, Conn.: Yale University Press.

Zartman, I. W. and S. Touval (1996) 'International Mediation in the Post-Cold War Era', *Managing Global Chaos: Sources of and Responses to International Conflict*, edited by C. Crocker, F. Hampson with P. Aall. Washington, DC: United States Institute of Peace Press, pp. 445–61.

11
Mediation in International Business

Jeswald W. Salacuse

Introduction

The playing field for business has become the globe. National boundaries are no longer business boundaries. Spectacular technological advances, especially in computers and communications, and profound political changes, like the end of the Cold War and the creation of new international trade and investment regimes, have encouraged the globalization of business. Companies, large and small, in all countries are shifting from a national to a worldwide field of vision and of action.

The expansion of international business has been accompanied by vastly increased organizational and transactional complexity. No longer is international business merely a series of discrete foreign trade transactions, for example the sale of cloth by a textile broker in New Delhi to a clothing manufacturer in New York, or the export of groundnuts from a cooperative in the Sudan to a food processor in England. Today, international business transactions extend over long periods of time, often many years; create complex legal, financial, and technical relationships; and involve numerous participants from many different countries, including multinational corporations, global financial institutions, sovereign governments, state enterprises, and international organizations. Transnational business transactions include international manufacturing joint ventures, multi-party strategic alliances, huge infrastructure construction projects, high technology licensing agreements, international franchising arrangements, production-sharing petroleum agreements, and 50-year mineral development projects, to mention just a few. Parties from countries throughout the world are negotiating and carrying out these complex transactions in an environment of diverse cultures, political instability, conflicting ideologies, differing bureaucratic and organizational traditions, inconsistent laws, and constantly changing monetary and economic variables (Salacuse, 1991). As a result, the potential for conflict in the world of global business is expanding along with the growth in the magnitude, diversity, and complexity of its transactions.

The international deal: a continuing negotiation

All international transactions are the product of a negotiation – the result of *deal-making* – among the parties. Although lawyers like to think that negotiations end when the participants agree on all the details and sign the contract, this view hardly ever reflects reality. In truth, an international deal is a *continuing negotiation* between the parties to the transaction as they seek to adjust their relationship to the rapidly changing international environment of civil strife, political upheavals, military interventions, monetary fluctuations, and technological change in which they must work.

No negotiation, particularly in a long-term transaction, can predict all eventualities that the parties may encounter, nor can any negotiation achieve perfect understanding between the parties, especially when they come from differing cultures. If they do encounter changes in circumstances, misunderstandings, or problems not contemplated by their contract, the parties need to resort to negotiation to handle their difficulties. In short, negotiation is a fundamental tool for *managing* their deal. And when the parties to a deal become embroiled in genuine conflict – for example, the failure by one side to perform in accordance with other side's expectations – negotiation may be the only realistic tool to resolve the controversy – particularly if the parties want to preserve their business relationship. Thus, negotiation, at least initially, is a means to mend a broken deal. (Salacuse, 1988)

In the life of any international deal, one may therefore identify three distinct stages when conflict may arise and the parties rely on negotiation and conflict resolution to achieve their goals: *deal-making, deal-managing,* and *deal-mending*. Within the context of each of these three kinds of negotiation, one should ask to what extent third parties, whether called mediators or something else, may assist the parties to make, manage, and mend productive international business relationships. This chapter seeks to explore that question.

Deal-making mediation

The usual model of an international business negotiation is that of representatives of two companies from different countries sitting across a table in face-to-face discussions to shape the terms of a commercial contract. While many transactions take place in that manner, many others require the services of one or more third parties to facilitate the deal-making process. These individuals are not usually referred to as 'mediators'. They instead carry a variety of other labels: consultant, adviser, agent, broker, investment banker, among others. These deal-making mediators usually have some sort of a contractual arrangement with one of the parties, and in rare cases both; however, they are not formally employees of either party in the strict sense. Although it could be argued that consultants and advisors should not be considered mediators since they are not independent of the parties, a close examination of their roles in the negotiation of an international business deal reveals that they exercise mediator's functions, as defined in this book, in that they assist the parties to change, affect or influence their behavior so as to manage conflicts or potential conflicts arising in the course of a negotiation. Even if a deal-making mediator has a contract with and is paid only by one side, his or her ability to play an effective mediating role is crucially dependent on the willingness of the other side to accept that person as a participant in the deal-making process. Indeed, in most cases, one of the principal assets of deal-making mediators is the fact that they are known and accepted by the other side in the deal.

Deal-making mediation in Hollywood

The acquisition in 1991 by Matsushita Electric Industrial Company of Japan, one of the world's largest electronics manufacturers, of MCA, one of the United States' biggest entertainment companies, for over $6 billion illustrates the use of mediators in the deal-making process (see Bruci, 1991). Matsushita had determined that its future growth was dependent upon obtaining a source of films, television programs, and music – what it termed 'software' – to complement its consumer electronic 'hardware' products. Matsushita knew that it could find such a source of software within the US entertainment industry, but it also recognized that it was virtually ignorant of that industry and its practices. 'For Matsushita executives, embarking on their Hollywood expedition may have felt almost interplanetary. They were setting out for a place that was … foreign to their temperament, culture, and business experience …' (Bruci, 1991: 39–40). They therefore engaged Michael Ovitz, the founder and head of Creative Artists Agency, one of the most powerful talent agencies in Hollywood, to guide them on their journey.

After forming a team to assist in the task, Ovitz, a man who was fascinated with Asian cultures and who had been a consultant to Sony when it had purchased Columbia Pictures, first extensively briefed the Japanese over several months, sometimes in secret meetings in Hawaii, on the nature of the US entertainment industry, and he then proceeded to propose three possible candidates for acquisition, one of which was MCA. Ultimately, Matsushita chose MCA, but it was Ovitz, not Matsushita executives, who initiated conversations with the MCA leadership, men whom Ovitz knew well. Indeed, Ovitz assumed the task of actually conducting the negotiations for Matsushita. At one point in the discussions, he moved constantly between the Japanese team of executives in one suite of offices in New York City and the MCA team in another building, a process which one observer described as 'shuttle diplomacy', a clear reference to the mediating efforts of Henry Kissinger in the disengagement talks between the

Israelis and the Arabs following the 1973 October War. Although Matsushita may have considered Ovitz to be their agent in the talks, Ovitz seems to have considered himself to be both a representative of Matsushita and a mediator between the two sides.

Because of the vast cultural and temperamental differences between the Japanese and American companies, Ovitz's strategy was to limit the actual interactions of the two parties to a bare minimum. During the first six weeks of negotiations, the Japanese and Americans met only once in a face-to-face meeting. All other interactions took place through Ovitz. He felt that to bring the parties together too soon would create obstacles that would inevitably derail the deal. He was not only concerned by the vast differences in culture between the two companies but also by the greatly differing personalities in their top managements. The Japanese executives, reserved and somewhat serf-effacing, placed a high value on the appearance if not the reality of modesty, while MCA's president was an extremely assertive and volatile personality. Like any mediator, Ovitz's own interests may also have influenced his choice of strategy. His status in the entertainment industry would only be heightened by making a giant new entrant into Hollywood dependent on him and by the public image that he had been the key to arranging one of the biggest deals in the industry's history. It should also be noted that Ovitz's primary interest was in making the deal happen, and only secondarily in creating a foundation that would result in a profitable long-term acquisition for Matsushita.

Although Ovitz launched the deal-making process and moved it a significant distance, he was not able to bring it to completion alone. Eventually the talks stalled over the issue of price, and meetings between the two sides ceased. At this point, a second deal-making mediator entered the scene to make a crucial contribution. At the start of the negotiation, Matsushita and Sony together had engaged Robert Strauss, a politically powerful Washington lawyer who had been at various times US Ambassador to the Soviet Union and US Trade Representative, as 'counsellor to the transaction'. Strauss, a member of the MCA board of directors and a close friend of its chairman, was also friendly with the Matsushita leadership and did legal and lobbying work in Washington for the Japanese company. In effect, his strong personal and business relationships with the two sides led them to appoint him to represent them both. Although his letter of appointment merely stated that Strauss was to 'co-ordinate certain government relations matters', and even excluded his participation in the negotiations themselves, it appears that both MCA and Matsushita felt that he might be useful in other, unspecified ways.

When the talks stalled on the question of price, Strauss' close relationship to the two sides allowed him to act as a trusted conduit of communication who facilitated a meeting between the top MCA and Matsushita executives that ultimately resulted in an agreement on what Matsushita would have to pay to acquire the American company. In arranging that meeting over some fifteen hours, he apparently gained an understanding of the pricing parameters acceptable to each side and then communicated them to the other party. The Japanese, at that point, apparently had greater trust in Strauss, particularly because of his former role as high US government official, concerning the delicate issue of price than they did in Ovitz, who they sensed had a dominant interest in simply getting the deal done, regardless of the price the Japanese would have to pay for it (Bruci, 1991: 66). In the end, as a result of that meeting, the two sides reached an agreement by which Matsushita acquired MCA.

The Matsushita-MCA case shows clearly how two mediators facilitated the deal-making process, a deal that the parties probably would not have achieved by themselves. The factors that allowed Ovitz and Strauss to play successful roles were their knowledge of the two parties and their industries, their personal relationships with the leadership of the two sides, their respective reputations, the trust that they engendered, and their skills and experience as negotiators. On the other hand, although Matsushita did succeed in purchasing MCA, the acquisition proved to be troubling and ultimately a disastrous financial loss for the Japanese company. One may ask whether Ovitz' strategy of keeping the two sides apart during negotiations so that they did not come to know one another contributed to this unfortunate result. It prevented the two sides from truly understanding the vast gulf which separated them and therefore from realizing the enormity – and perhaps impossibility – of the task of merging two such different organizations into a single coordinated and profitable enterprise.

Other deal-making mediators

An opposite mediating approach from that employed by Ovitz is the use of consultants to begin building a relationship between the parties *before* they have signed a contract and indeed before they have actually begun negotiations. When some companies contemplate long-term relationships, such as a strategic alliance, which will require a high degree of cooperation, they may hire a consultant to develop and guide a program of relationship building, which might include joint workshops, get-acquainted sessions, and retreats, all of which take place before the parties actually sit down to negotiate the terms of their contract. The consultant will facilitate and perhaps chair these meetings, conduct discussions of the negotiating process, make the parties recognize potential pitfalls, and discuss with them ways to avoid possible problems. Once negotiations start, the consultant may continue to observe the process and be ready to intervene when the deal-making process encounters difficulties (Buhring-Uhle, 1996: 318–19).

Not all mediators in an international business negotiation have the reputation and prestige of a Robert Strauss or a Michael Ovitz or receive specific authorization to engage in relationship building. Sometimes persons involved in the negotiation because of their technical expertise or special-ized knowledge, may assume a mediating function and thus help the parties reach agreement. For example, while language interpreters ordinarily have a limited role, they may facilitate understanding by explaining cultural prac-tices that seem to complicate discussions or by finding linguistic formulas that lead to agreement, formulas that the parties would not be able to arrive at on their own. Similarly local lawyers or accountants engaged by a foreign party to advise on law or accounting practices in connection with international negotiation may assume a mediating role in the deal-making process by serving as a conduit between the parties, by suggesting approaches that meet the other side's cultural practices, by explaining why one party is behaving in a particular way, and by proposing solutions that are likely to gain agreement from the other side.

Deal-managing mediation

Once the deal has been signed, consultants, lawyers, and advisers may con-tinue their association with one or both parties and informally assist as mediators in managing conflict that may arise in the execution of the transaction. In some cases, the parties to a complex or long-term transac-tion, seeking to minimize the risk of conflict, may include specific provi-sions in their contract stipulating a process to manage conflict and prevent it from causing a total break down of the deal. For example, the contract may provide that in the event of a conflict cannot be settled at the opera-tional level, senior management of the two sides will engage in negotiations to resolve it. Generally, top management, not directly embroiled in the conflict and with a broad view of the transaction and its relationship to the company's over all strategy, may be in a better position to resolve a dispute than persons at the operating level, who have come to feel that they have a personal stake in 'winning' the dispute. Once top management of the two sides have reached an understanding, they may have to serve as mediators with their subordinates to get them to change behavior and attitudes with respect to interactions at the operational leve (Buhring-Uhle, 1996: 317).

Deal-managing mediation in the construction industry

The international construction industry has developed an important form of deal-managing mediation that employs a designated third person, such as a consulting engineer, to resolve disputes that may arise in the course of a major construction project, such as a dam or a power plant. International construction projects typically include many parties, involve highly techni-cal complexities, and take a long time to complete. The possibilities for conflict among the participants are virtually endless, yet it is essential for all concerned that disputes among the parties not impede the progress of the project. The construction contract will therefore usually designate a consulting engineer, review board, permanent referee, or dispute advisor, with varying powers, to handle disputes as they arise in a way that will allow the construction work to continue. Sometimes, as in the case of a consulting engineer, the third person will have the power to make a decision, which may later be challenged in arbitration or the courts; sometimes as in the case of dispute advisor the third person plays the role of a mediator, by engaging in fact finding or facilitating communication among the disputants.

One particular type of mediator worthy of note is the Dispute Review Board, which was used in the construction of both the Channel Tunnel between England and France and the new Hong Kong Airport and is now required by the World Bank in any Bank-financed construction project having a cost of more than $50 million (Bunni, 1997: 14). Under this procedure, a Board, consisting of three members, is created at the start of the project. One member of the board is appointed by the project owner and a second by the lead contractor. The third member is then selected either by the other two members or by mutual agreement between the owner and the contractor. The Board functions according to rules set down in the construction contract. Generally, it is empowered to examine all disputes and to make recommendations to the parties concerning settlement. If the parties to a dispute do not object to a recommendation, it becomes binding. If, however, they are dissatisfied, they may proceed to arbitration, litigation or other form of mandatory dispute settlement (Bunni, 1997).

Deal-managing mediators in the international construction industry approach their task with advantages that mediators in other domains usually lack. First, the parties designate them at the time they sign their contract and before any specific conflict arises. Thus, the mediators have a clearly defined role, and their acceptance by the parties is assured. They approach their task with a high degree of legitimacy. Secondly they are intimately familiar with the transaction from its very start and are in continuing contact with the parties through meetings and visits to the construction site. Thirdly, they have recognized technical expertise which is applicable to most disputes that may arise in the course of the project.

The use of such dispute review boards or dispute advisors in construction contracts has proved to be a cost-effective means of settling disputes while permitting a continuation of construction project in an expeditious manner. This mechanism would seem to have application in other areas of international business. For example, in a complex multi-party strategic alliance, the participants might designate a person or organization to serve as a permanent mediator to assist the parties to manage conflicts that may arise in the course of their business relationship. Thus far, however, this device does not appear to have reached much beyond the construction industry.

Deal-mending mediation

The parties to an international business relationship may encounter a wide variety of conflicts that seem irreconcilable. A host government may expropriate a foreign investor's factory. A poor developing country may stop paying its loan to a foreign bank. Partners in an international joint venture may disagree violently over the use of accumulated profits and therefore plunge their enterprise into a state of paralysis. Here then would seem ideal situations in which mediation by a third party could help in settling conflict. In fact, mediation is relatively uncommon once severe international business conflicts break out. To understand why, one must first understand the basic structure of international business dispute settlement.

International commercial arbitration

Nearly all international business contracts today provide that any disputes that may arise in the future between the parties are to be resolved by international commercial arbitration. The parties choose this option for a variety of reasons: to avoid the vagaries of national courts, to secure a neutral and expert forum for their disputes, to conduct dispute resolution in private, and to have legal assurance that arbitral awards will be enforceable. International arbitration is of two types: *ad hoc*, which is basically administered by the parties according to an agreed upon set of rules, or institutional, which is administered by an established institution such as the International Chamber of Commerce, the London Court of Arbitration, the American Arbitration Association, the Stockholm Chamber of Commerce, or the International Centre for Settlement of Investment Disputes, an affiliate of the World Bank.

The parties by agreement are free to shape the arbitral process as they wish. Normally, most opt for a three-person arbitral panel consisting of an arbitrator appointed by each of the disputants, and the third, the panel's chairman, selected by the two arbitrators. By virtue of the Convention on the Recognition and Enforcement of Arbitral Awards, now signed by over a hundred countries, both arbitration agreements and arbitral awards are enforceable throughout the world (see Streng and Salacuse, 1986, chapters 30 and 31).

At the outset, it should be emphasized that arbitration is not mediation. International commercial arbitration is a legalistic, adversarial process whose purpose is to decide on the respective rights and obligations of the parties to the dispute, not to help them change their attitudes and behavior to resolve their conflict. Essentially it is private litigation. The failure of arbitrators to decide a dispute according to the applicable law is ground for invalidating such award by the courts.

Thus in the background of virtually all international business disputes is the prospect of binding arbitration if the parties, alone or with the help of a third person, are unable to resolve the conflict themselves. This factor influences the ways in which the parties deal with their dispute and it also affects the strategy of any mediator who may be invited to help the disputants settle their conflict. In this regard, international business disputes are unlike virtually all international political disputes between states where no such adjudicative process is waiting in the wings to impose a binding decision. As result, when parties to an international business transaction find themselves embroiled in a dispute which they judge to be irreconcilable, they will invariably commence arbitration to settle the matter.

Arbitrating a dispute is not, however, a painless, inexpensive, quick solution. Like litigation in the courts, it is costly, may take years to conclude, and invariably results in a final rupture of the parties' business relationship. Even when an arbitral tribunal makes an award in favor of one of the parties, the losing side may then proceed to challenge it in the courts, thus delaying or even preventing a final resolution of the dispute. For example, one arbitration between Egypt and foreign investors took five years in its first phase and resulted in legal and administrative costs of nearly $1.5 million (International Chamber of Commerce Court of Arbitration, 1983). But thereafter, the arbitral award was appealed in the courts and the case was rearbitrated in another forum. The parties finally settled the matter through negotiation 14 years after the dispute began.

The prospect of such a costly, lengthy and potentially destructive process does encourage the two sides to negotiate a settlement of their dispute. For example, approximately two-thirds of all arbitration cases filed with the International Chamber of Commerce Court of Arbitration are settled by negotiation before an arbitral award is made (Schwartz, 1995: 99). Third persons, whether called mediators or otherwise, could in theory help parties embroiled an international business dispute settle their conflicts without the intervention of an arbitrator's decision.

Initially, one may ask whether the arbitrators themselves can and should seek to facilitate a negotiated settlement of the dispute. On this question, practice seems to vary considerably among countries. Generally, Americans and some Europeans consider it improper for an arbitrator to facilitate a settlement of the dispute. In their view, an arbitrator should do no more that to suggest the possibility of settlement but should not actively engage in mediating efforts. In other cultures, for example, China and Germany, arbitrators often take a more active role by proposing at the parties' request possible formula for settlement, by participating in settlement negotiations, and even meeting separately with the parties with their consent. In Asian cultures, which have a particular aversion to confrontation, arbitrators are even more energetic than their European and American counterparts in seeking to facilitate agreement among the disputants rather than merely imposing a decision (Buhring-Uhle, 1996: 127–217).

Generally speaking, an arbitrator's efforts, however minimal to facilitate settlement, tend to have the effect of persuading the parties that if they allow the dispute to be arbitrated they will not achieve all that they hope. Such efforts by arbitrators have a predictive effect. When arbitrators strongly encourage settlement, they are actually saying to the claimant company that it probably will not receive all that it claims, and they are also telling the respondent that if the case goes to an award it will have to pay something. The strategy of arbitrators who seek to play a mediating role is to give the parties a realistic evaluation of what they will receive or be required to pay in any final arbitration award.

Mediation in international business disputes

Traditionally, companies engaged in an international business dispute have not actively sought the help of mediators. They have first tried to resolve the matter themselves through negotiation, but when they judged that to have failed, they have immediately proceeded to arbitration. Various factors explain their failure to try mediation: their lack of knowledge about mediation and the availability of mediation services, the fact that companies tend to give control of their disputes to lawyers whose professional inclination is to litigate, and the belief that mediation is merely a stalling tactic that only delays the inevitability of an arbitration proceeding.

With increasing recognition of the disadvantages of arbitration, some companies are beginning to turn to more explicit forms of mediation to resolve business disputes. Increasingly, when a dispute can be quantified, for example the extent of damage to an asset by a partner's action or the amount of a royalty fee owed to a licensor, the parties will engage an independent third party such an international accounting or consulting firm to examine the matter and give an opinion. The opinion is not binding on the parties but it has the effect of allowing them to make a more realistic prediction of what may happen in an arbitration proceeding.

Conciliation

One type of deal-mending mediation used occasionally in international business is *conciliation*. Many arbitration institutions, such as the International Chamber of Commerce (ICC) and the International Centre for Settlement of Investment Disputes, offer a service known as conciliation, which is normally governed by a set of rules (e.g. ICC Rules of Optional Conciliation, 1995). In addition, the United Nations Commission on International Trade Law has prepared a set of conciliation rules which parties may use without reference to an institution.

Generally, in institutional conciliation, a party to a dispute may address a request for conciliation to the institution. If the institution concerned secures the agreement of the other disputant, it will appoint a conciliator. While the conciliator has broad discretion to conduct the process, in practice he or she will invite both sides to state their views of the dispute and will then make a report proposing an appropriate settlement. The parties may reject the report and proceed to arbitration, or they may accept it. In many cases, they will use it as a basis for a negotiated settlement. Conciliation is thus a kind of non-binding arbitration. Its function is predictive. It tends to be rights-based in its approach, affording the parties a third person's evaluation of their respective rights and obligations. Conciliators do not usually adopt a problem-solving or relationship-building approach to resolving the dispute between the parties. The process is confidential and completely voluntary. Either party may withdraw from conciliation at any time.

Deal-mending mediation in Trinidad

Since conciliation is confidential, public information on the process itself is scant. One of the few published accounts concerns the first conciliation conducted under the auspices of the International Centre for Settlement of Investment Disputes (ICSID) (Nurick and Schnably, 1986). ICSID, an affiliate of the World Bank created by treaty in 1964, provides arbitration and conciliation services to facilitate the settlement of investment disputes between host countries and foreign investors. One such dispute, between Tesoro Petroleum Corporation and the government of Trinidad and Tobago, arose out of a joint venture which the two sides established in 1968, each with a 50 per cent interest, to develop and manage oil fields in Trinidad. By their joint venture contact and subsequent agreements, the two partners developed a complex arrangement on the extent to which profits would be paid as dividends or reinvested to develop additional oil properties. Their joint venture agreement also provided that in the event of a dispute the parties would first attempt conciliation under ICSID auspices, but if the dispute was not settled within six months from the date of the conciliation report, either party could then commence ICSID arbitration.

By 1983, following the rise of oil prices and continued turbulence in world petroleum industry, Tesoro and the Government of Trinidad and Tobago were embroiled in a conflict over whether and to what extent to use accumulated profits for payment of dividends to themselves or for reinvestment to develop new oil properties. Finally, Tesoro decided to sell its shares and pursuant to their agreement offered them first to the Trinidad and Tobago government. The two parties then began to negotiate a possible sale, but appeared to make little progress. In August 1983, Tesoro filed a request for conciliation with the ICSID Secretary-General, claiming that it was entitled to 50 per cent of the profits as dividends and that the government had breached the joint venture agreement on dividend payments.

The ICSID rules, recognizing the importance of a conciliator in whom the parties have confidence, gives the parties wide scope in the conciliator's appointment. The rules allow them to choose anyone, provided he or she is 'of high moral character and recognized competence in the fields of law, commerce, industry, or finance, who may be relied upon to exercise independent judgment'. Tesoro and the Trinidad and Tobago government agreed to a single conciliator (instead of a commission of three or more conciliators as the Rules allow) and through direct negotiations chose Lord Wilberforce, a distinguished retired English judge, in December 1983 to serve as their conciliator.

Lord Wilberforce held a first meeting of the parties in March 1984 in London, where they agreed upon basic procedural matters, including a schedule for the filing of memorials and other documents by the parties in support of their positions. The parties proceeded to file their memorials and then met once again with Lord Wilberforce in July 1984 in Washington, DC. In this meeting, at the conciliator's suggestion, they agreed that no oral hearing or argument by the parties would be necessary, that the parties could submit to Lord Wilberforce their views in confidence on what might constitute and acceptable settlement, and that thereafter Lord Wilberforce would give them his recommendation.

In February 1985, Lord Wilberforce delivered a lengthy written report to the parties, in which he stated that his task as a conciliator had three dimensions: (1) to examine the contentions raised by the parties; (2) to clarify the issues in dispute; and (3) to evaluate the respective merits of the parties positions and the likelihood of their prevailing in arbitration. Thus, he saw his task as giving the parties a prediction of their fate in arbitration, with the hope that such prediction would assist them in negotiating a settlement. He concluded his report with a suggested settlement, which included a percentage of the amount sought by Tesoro, based on his estimate of the parties' chances of success in arbitration on the issues in dispute.

Following receipt of the report, Tesoro and the Trinidad and Tobago government began negotiations, and by October 1985 they had reached a settlement by which the joint venture company would pay dividends to the two partners in cash and petroleum products totaling $143 million. The conciliation thus helped the parties reach an amicable settlement of their dispute with minimum cost, delay, and acrimony. The whole conciliation process from start to finish took less than two years to complete, and administrative costs and conciliator fees amounted to less than $11,000. Equally important, conciliation preserved the business relationship between the parties. After the conciliation, the Trinidad and Tobago Government purchased a small portion of Tesoro's shares so as to gain a majority interest, but Tesoro continued as a partner in the venture. Had the matter proceeded to arbitration, without conciliation, the case would have lasted several years, cost many hundreds of thousands of dollars and perhaps more, and would have resulted in a complete rupture of business relationships between Tesoro and the Government.

Thus far few disputants in international business avail themselves of conciliation. For example, out of a total of ten cases on the docket of ICSID in 1996, only one was for conciliation (ICSID, 1996). Similarly, from 1988 to 1993, a period in which over 2000 arbitration cases were filed at the International Chamber of Commerce, the ICC received only 54 requests for conciliation. Of that number, the other party in the dispute agreed to conciliation in only 16 cases; however, the ICC appointed only ten conciliators, since the parties settled the dispute or withdrew the request in six cases. Of the ten conciliations, nine had been completed by 1994, five resulting in complete settlement (Schwartz, 1995: 98, 107–17).

Conclusion

The use of mediators in international business is fragmented and uneven. If one defines a mediator broadly as a third person who helps the parties negotiate an agreement, then their use in deal-making is fairly extensive. Their use in deal-managing seems to be growing, particularly in the international construction industry, but in deal-mending, where the parties to a transaction are embroiled in a genuine conflict, the use of mediators is relatively rare. In all three types of negotiations, mediators participate only because the parties have specifically sought them out and invited them into the process. It is extremely rare for persons to volunteer their services as mediators in an international business transactions. In all cases, mediators in international business are private individuals, rather than organizations, institutions, or governmental officials. Institutions such as the International Chamber of Commerce or the International Centre for Settlement of Investment Disputes only facilitate the search for an appropriate mediator or conciliator. They do not themselves participate in mediation. Once on the job, the mediator works independently of these organizations, is not their representative, and does not operate under their direction.

Like any mediation, effective international business mediation requires three things: disputant motivation, mediator opportunity, and mediator resources, including skills. No mediation can take place unless the parties to the business conflict want or at least acquiesce in the presence of a mediator. Variations in the degree of disputant motivation in deal-making, deal-managing, and deal-mending may explain the difference in the frequency of use of mediators in these three types of negotiation. Motivated to achieve a deal because of expectations of profit, parties have a strong incentive to use third persons to achieve their deal-making goals and may view the alternatives as the loss of the deal with no compensation. Similarly, agreement to use mediators in deal-managing may be a condition for achieving agreement or for securing financing from institutions such as the World Bank; consequently, disputant motivation may also be high in these cases. However, in the case of a broken deal, at least one of the parties will lack motivation so long as it believes that it can obtain compensation or secure enforcement of its version of the deal in the courts or in international commercial arbitration. In short, that party does not see the failure to mend a deal through mediation as an absolute loss. So long as it considers litigation or arbitration as an acceptable alternative to a mediated agreement, it will have little motivation to accept the presence of a mediator. Unfortunately, most of the time, one of the parties to a business dispute does in fact believe that it will gain more in litigation or arbitration than it could through the services of a mediator.

Mediators have an opportunity to mediate international business disputes only if both parties invite them into the process. Parties to international business transactions can enhance mediator opportunity by agreeing at the time they make their contract to use third persons, such as Dispute Review Boards, to help them with future disputes; however, outside of the international construction industry, such provisions are relatively rare. To a certain extent, the low degree of disputant motivation to use mediators in international business disputes is also caused by the general lack of knowledge by businesses and their lawyers of the potential value of mediation and their belief that mediation will be used by one of the parties merely to stall and delay the inevitability of a law suit or arbitration case.

To be effective, mediators in international business, like mediators in other domains, must possess certain resources, including skills. The essence of their resources resides in their ability to influence the parties to arrive at an agreement. Mediators in international business transactions derive their power to influence the parties from various factors. Unlike some mediators in the political arena, business negotiators generally have no coercive power. The basis of their power first and foremost resides in their expertise. The power of Ovitz, Wilberforce, and consulting engineers in major construction projects to influence the parties clearly resided in their knowledge about the respective industries and issues they were dealing with. In the kind of rights-based mediation engaged in by Wilberforce, where the source of his influence was to give the parties a clear prediction of how they might fare in arbitration, expertise in the law and the functioning of the arbitral process was an important source of mediator power.

Mediators may also have power because of their relationships with the disputants. This referent power is particularly present in deal-making mediation in international business. Thus, the relationships of Ovitz and Strauss with both sides in the MCA–Matsushita negotiation gave weight to their advice and recommendations to both sides. And finally, international business negotiators may also rely on legitimacy in influencing the parties to a dispute. Wilberforce had legitimacy because the parties specifically selected him to make a recommendation, a Dispute Review Board for a major construction project has legitimacy because the parties created it at the time they signed the construction contract to resolve future disputes, and Strauss had great legitimacy because MCA and Matshushita had designated him in a formal document as 'counselor to the transaction'.

Mediation and the future of global business

The magnitude, complexity, and duration of international business transactions creates a substantial and continuing risk of conflict. International commercial arbitration, the primary dispute settlement mechanism designed for international business, has proven itself to be expensive, destructive, time consuming, and in some cases lacking in finality. Mediation of varying types offers international business executives a possible attractive alternative, an alternative that they should explore at the time they negotiate their transactions. They might include in their contracts from the outset mechanisms such as dispute advisors to help in the problem of deal management, and they might also commit themselves to try mediation or conciliation before they take the usually irrevocable step of submitting their disputes to arbitration.

References

Bruci, C. (1991) 'The World of Business – leap of faith', *The New York*, 9 September, pp. 38–74.

Bunni, Nael G. (1997) 'Major Project Dispute Review Boards', *In-House Counsel International*, June–July, pp. 13–15.

Buhring-Uhle, C. (1996) *Arbitration and Mediation in International Business*. The Hague: Kluwer Law International.

ICC (1995) 'International Chamber of Commerce Rules of Optional Conciliation', reprinted in *ICSID Review*, 10, pp. 158–61.

ICSID (1996) *1996 Annual Report*. Washington, DC: ICSID.

International Chamber of Commerce Court of Arbitration. (1983) 'Award in the Arbitration of S.P.P. (Middle East) Limited, Southern Pacific Properties Limited, and the Arab Republic of Egypt, the Egyptian General Company for Tourism and Hotels [March 11, 1983], *International Legal Materials*, 22, p. 752.

Nurick, L. and Schnably, S. J. (1986) 'The First ICSID Conciliation: Tesoro Petroleum Corporation v. Trinidad and Tobago', *ICSID REVIEW*, 1, pp. 340–53.

Salacuse, J. W. (1991) *Making Global Deals – Negotiating in the International Marketplace*. Boston: Houghton Mifflin.

Salacuse, J. W. (1988) 'Renegotiations in International Business', *Negotiation Journal*, 4, pp. 347–54.

Schwartz, E. (1995) 'International Conciliation and the ICC', *ICSID Review*, 10, p. 98.

Streng, W. P. and Salacuse, J. W. (1986) *International Business Planning: Law and Taxation*. New York: Matthew Bender.

12
Two's Company But Is Three a Crowd? Some Hypotheses about Multiparty Mediation

Chester A. Crocker, Fen Osler Hampson and Pamela R. Aall[1]

Introduction

The increasing complexity of international third-party mediation efforts – whether consisting of many different types of mediating bodies or an intergovernmental mediation effort undertaken under the auspices of an international organization or an informal coalition, and whether occurring simultaneously or sequentially – means that these operations are difficult to orchestrate in many of today's conflicts. The vicious nature of these conflicts, however, and the high costs for the international community of failing to prevent or end these conflicts highlight the need for a better understanding of the consequences of multiparty mediation, and of the requirements for leadership and cooperation in these third-party interventions (Kriesberg, 1996b).

A number of important developments in international politics have changed both the content and nature of international mediation. Some of these developments can be traced to the end of the Cold War and bipolarity, but others are reflective of a more general trend of civil society engagement in international conflict management and resolution processes. First, the end of the Cold War has to some extent freed international organizations from their bipolar constraints and allowed them to take on new roles in mediation and conflict management (Skjelsbaek, 1991; Durch, 1993, 1996; Blechman, 1996). Regional organizations, and coalitions of small and medium-sized powers, have also become more active as mediators, facilitators, and conflict managers (Wedgwood, 1996). Even in those situations in which great powers have intervened as a result of domestic political pressure or threatened national interests, there is seemingly a greater willingness to share the costs of intervention – military and political – with other states and international actors (Etzioni, 1995).

Secondly, the widespread presence of religious, humanitarian and development NGOs in countries and regions of conflict has created a third tier of actors beyond states and international organizations which not only seek to alleviate the plight of refugees and other victims of violent conflict but also see themselves as having the capacity, expertise, and knowledge to initiate a process of dialogue between warring parties and factions (Assefa, 1987; Mitchell, 1994; Zartman, 1995; Weiss, 1996). In some instances, governments are willing to support these groups because they offer an entry point into the conflict.

Thirdly, the renewed interest in mediation as an instrument of conflict management is prompted by the recognition that civil or inter communal conflict is not easily dealt with by other modes of conflict management, such as international legal tribunals, arbitration, or even the use of force which is costly and has obvious limitations as an instrument of third party intervention (Bercovitch and Houston, 1996; Brown, 1996; Bilder, 1997). Mediation represents a relatively low cost alternative between the choices of doing nothing and large-scale military intervention (Bercovitch, 1984, 1986).

Finally, it is arguably the case that international norms are changing. There does appear to be a growing sentiment that something must be done to prevent further eruptions of wide scale intercommunal violence that threaten regional stability. Some of these sentiments are fueled by the media and the publicity given to the victims of genocide and civil war on television (Strobel, 1997). But there is also a growing sense of moral responsibility premised on the recognition that the international community has an interest in advancing human rights, democracy, and the rule of law because these are universal values that will contribute to the development of a more peaceful and stable international order (Hadden, 1987; Damrosch, 1993; Cortright, 1997).

That mediations are being undertaken by a diversity of institutions, including individual states, coalitions of the willing, international organizations, and NGOs, raises interesting questions about how and why these multiparty interventions come about; whether and how they are coordinated; who provides leadership; what determines the level of commitment in terms of human and financial resources; and who is responsible for keeping an already mediated settlement on track and preventing the collapse of the agreement lest it become orphaned. As more countries and institutional actors become involved in mediation, particularly in trying to mediate an end to violent conflict in an intercommunal setting, a judicious assessment is required not only of their comparative institutional strengths and weaknesses, but also of how to encourage complementary efforts and how to coordinate the process when one actor/institution is handing off the responsibilities for mediation to others. In addition, we also need to know more about the main obstacles to achieving coordination and coherence among different mediators in such settings and how to over-come the problems faced by multiple mediators working without a common script in trying to mediate a negotiated resolution to conflict.

Definition of multiparty mediation

Multiparty mediation refers to attempts by many third parties to assist peace negotiations in any given conflict. These attempts may occur sequentially – one institution at a time – over the life of the conflict, or may occur simultaneously, involving many different mediators with various institutional bases on the ground at the same time, as happened in 1997 in Zaire. Diplomatic interventions by IGOs or coalitions are in themselves multiparty mediations. In these circumstances, the mediation is on the behalf of a number of sovereign states, each of which has its own objectives, interests, priorities, and domestic constraints. These factors complicate the essential tasks of imposing coherence on the mediation effort: establishing an agreed mandate, defining and delegating responsibilities, and ensuring a coordinated response and support among the interests involved in the mediation effort.

The situation is further complicated by the fact that multiparty mediations may also refer to a number of attempts at mediation by different actors over the life cycle of the conflict. In the early stages of a conflict, for example, non-official groups may be the only third parties active in the attempt to bring groups together or alert the international community to the need for preventive diplomacy or some kind of action. If the conflict has escalated to full-scale violence, however, mediation may be undertaken by an international organization or by a representative of a national government that has the necessary influence and ability to move the parties to the conflict toward a negotiated solution. After a conflict is over or a negotiated settlement has been reached, many outside organizations may be involved in post-conflict reconstruction.

Multiparty mediation may be undertaken by international or regional organizations, national governments, and non-governmental organizations. It may also be undertaken by a collective body such as a coalition of states which represent more than one set of national interests (Umbricht, 1989; Archer, 1994). The mediations undertaken by this range of institutions may occur simultaneously or sequentially, and may involve a variety of mediators who intervene in the conflict at different points in time. Our definition of multiparty mediation therefore includes an important temporal component and is intended to suggest that more than one mediator may be involved in a conflict at any given point in time or over the total life cycle of the conflict itself. The concept of multiparty mediation refers to simultaneous interventions by more than one mediator in a conflict, interventions by composite actors such as regional organizations or contact groups, as well as sequential mediated interventions which again involve more than one party.

The term 'multiparty' therefore has a triple meaning and we recognize at the outset that the range of issues associated with multiparty interventions in a sequential setting may well differ from those where a variety of mediators intervene in the same conflict at the same point in time. That being so, we also recognize that some conflicts may include mediated interventions that comprise both components, i.e. simultaneous and sequential interventions that occur during more than one phase of the conflict.

Part of the problem of examining multiparty mediation is the increasing variety of activities that can legitimately claim a place under the umbrella term 'mediation', and consequently, the numbers of organizations that can legitimately qualify as mediators. The activities include formal assistance to the negotiation process as well as the use of humanitarian, economic, social, and political tools outside the negotiation arena to influence the parties to a conflict and to increase their propensity to seek or keep a peace agreement. The organizations range from superpowers to volunteer church-based NGOs.

The purpose here is not to put forward a 'new theory of mediation', but to situate the multiparty mediation phenomenon – a classic case of impro-vised and transitional policy practice – in the academic literature. The problems posed by multiparty mediation are, at one level, essentially prob-lems of managing complexity, coordinating the use of comparative advan-tages, maximizing leverage, avoiding crossed wires and conflicting agendas, and maintaining focus and coherence. Stated another way, they are prob-lems of leadership, whether of the intellectual, entrepreneurial or structural variety, to use the terminology of Oran Young (Young, 1991).

The problems posed by multiparty mediation can also help us explore under a new light the categories and paradigms prevailing in this field. Rather than reinvent the wheels of mediation theory, we explore the possi-bility that multiparty mediation may add further weight to the need for a synthesis between structural and process paradigms. We look at multiparty mediation from the standpoint of timing and conflict cycles, and seek to explore how the comparative contributions of different actors may unfold. But these ideas represent simply a suggestive and exploratory probe of an emerging phenomenon, one that is briefly illustrated in the ensuing case study of Bosnia. This chapter concludes with a discussion of the particular practical and operational challenges posed by multiparty mediation and the implications for policy.

Two paradigms of mediation

Analysing mediation raises some basic questions about what third parties can do in a conflict, under what circumstances, and to what effect. Over-simplified, the debate over these issues can be classified into two major paradigms: the structuralist paradigm (Hopmann, 1995) and the social–psychological. These two paradigms involve alternative assessments about appropriate bargaining strategies and entry points, as well as about comparative advantage, coordination, and leadership of different kinds of mediators. Each paradigm also points to a different set of conclusions about the possibilities for effective mediation when there is more than one mediator and the kinds of bargaining strategies that are likely to be most effective in a multiparty setting.

These paradigms are presented, however, with a lively awareness that in the real world, negotiators generally find themselves with a foot in each approach, and that choices are rarely as stark as suggested by each school's proponents. Furthermore, viewing the conflict in terms of a life cycle marked by different phases or stages opens up a wider range of possibilities for mediated interventions by a more inclusive set of actors and institutions than is contemplated by either school.

Structuralist paradigm

The structural paradigm of mediation is based on a belief that through the use of persuasion, incentives, and disincentives, parties to a conflict can be led to and through a negotiated settlement. This paradigm views the causes of conflict as objective – as opposed to subjective – issues which can yield to negotiation. It is premised on the familiar notions of 'ripeness' and 'hurting stalemate' as advanced in the work of I. William Zartman, Richard Haass, and others. As defined by Haass, ripeness is associated with 'the prerequisites for diplomatic progress, that is … particular circumstances … conducive for negotiated solution or even progress. Such prerequisites may include characteristics of the parties to a dispute as well as considerations about the relationship between or among parties' (Haass, 1988: 232). Of the various factors that may make resolution more attractive, thereby enhancing the prospects for successful third party intervention, Zartman suggests that the prime 'condition' is if neither side in a conflict feels it can win a conflict and the parties perceive the costs and prospects of continuing war to be more burdensome than the costs and prospects of settlement (Zartman, 1985). The prospects for a negotiated settlement to a dispute are thus greater when war weariness has set in among the parties and a conflict has reached a plateau or 'hurting stalemate' in which unilateral solutions are no longer believed to be credible or achievable.

Timing, of course, is all important if mediated interventions are to be successful and potential mediators are well advised, according to the theory of ripeness, to wait until the parties are sufficiently 'exhausted' on the battlefield to push for a negotiated political settlement (Rubin, 1981). It may well be that in some circumstances the issue of who does the mediating is less important than the matter of timing and ripeness to the conflict itself.

In stressing the importance of timing, ripeness theory has its greatest utility in setting up benchmarks and signposts that help mediators calibrate their strategies to help ripen the conflict. Parties have to be coaxed or cajoled to the bargaining table through a combination of carrots and sticks, and skilled mediators use a variety of ripening agents: coaching, discrediting, legitimizing, making themselves indispensable, leaning and shifting weight, exploiting changes in military balance, exploiting changes in party leadership, as well as promises of resources or threats of withdrawal (Crocker, 1992: 469–72).

Mediation therefore involves more than just assisting highly motivated parties in reaching a negotiated solution to their disputes. It also requires the use of various side payments and/or penalties and sanctions to get the parties to the dispute to change their cost/benefit calculations about the utility of a negotiated settlement (Touval, 1996a,b). Thus, what is required in some situations is what Saadia Touval calls 'mediators with muscle' (Touval, 1982). According to this formulation, impartiality and objectivity are less important to achieving influence than 'power potential considerations' (Touval and Zartman, 1985: 256). The ability to exercise leverage may also be positively influenced by close ties between a mediator and one or more parties to the dispute thus allowing the mediator to elicit cooperative behavior and concessions (Princen, 1991). The less 'muscle' a mediator has, and the more removed or distant it is from the conflict, the weaker will be its mediation efforts (Zartman and Touval, 1985; Zartman, 1989). The question of how much leverage mediators must exercise to bring about a negotiated settlement before mediation strays into the realms of coercive diplomacy and, in effect, ceases to be mediation is a matter of some contention (Azar and Burton, 1986; Burton, 1987).

Structuralists are generally silent on the question whether one mediator is better than many. However, great powers are considered to be at an advantage when it comes to mediation because leverage depends upon persuasion, extraction, termination, manipulation, and the ability to offer and withhold resources. Acting in concert, a coalition of great power mediators should in principle be able to exert greater leverage than a single state, but this assumes that the members of the coalition share similar goals and are willing to work together and not at cross purposes. International organizations can potentially play an effective mediation role provided they enjoy the backing of key members and are not overwhelmed by other tasks. However, some argue that their ability to do so has been hampered by divisions among their most powerful members and ongoing problems of inadequate credibility and resources (Touval, 1994).

Social–psychological approaches

The second paradigm of third-party intervention in conflict focuses on the processes of communication and exchange as a way to change perceptions and attitudes. This approach to mediation centers on providing a forum in which parties can explore options and develop solutions, often outside of the highly charged arena of a formal negotiating structure. To this school, the establishment of a dialogue, of a pattern of exchanges and contacts between and among official parties or other influential representatives, helps set the stage for a lasting peace built on an agreement developed by the parties in a collaborative process. A key to this process is often the involvement in the dialogue not just of the principal political authorities but of a wider group of civil and opinion leaders whose support is essential for the long-term sustainability of the peace process.

One of the driving assumptions behind the social–psychological approach is that although parties identify specific issues as the causes of conflict, conflict also reflects subjective, phenomenological, and social fractures and, consequently, analysing 'interests' can be less important than identifying the underlying needs that govern each party's perception of the conflict (Doob, 1993; Lederach, 1995). Because much of human conflict is anchored in conflicting perceptions and in misperception, the contribution of third parties lies in changing the perceptions, attitudes, values, and behaviors of the parties to a conflict (Kriesberg, 1992, 1997). This process begins with interventions that allow conflict parties to glean a better understanding of the different dimensions of the conflict and works to develop means to allow them to recognize mutual gains and craft joint strategies towards a solution. Attitudinal change can be fostered through a variety of instruments. including, for example, consultative meetings, problem-solving workshops, training in conflict resolution at the communal level, and/or third party assistance in developing and designing other kinds of dispute resolution systems which are compatible with local culture and norms and are directed at elites as different levels within society (Bloomfield, 1997).

The problem-solving workshop is directed at communication and creating more open channels of communication which allow the participants to see their respective intentions more clearly and to be more fully aware of their own reactions to the conflict (Kelman, 1996). Workshops are aimed at cultivating respect and objectivity so that the parties develop a mutual commitment to cooperative exchanges in their relationship. Based on findings which show that individuals are more disposed to cooperative behavior in small, informal, intergroup activities, the problem-solving workshop establishes relations among significant players who may be in a position to influence the parties to the conflict and, in so doing, to contribute to the de-escalation of conflict. The approach seems to work best if individuals are middle-range elites such as academics, advisers, ex-officials, or retired politicians who continue to have access to those in power. By helping to establish communications between parties at the sub-elite level, these workshops help to undermine 'we–they' images of conflict, establish linkages among influentials, begin a discussion of framework solutions, identify steps that will break the impasse, and in general create an understanding of these steps and processes that the participants can feed back into the Track I effort where actual decisions get made.

A somewhat different kind of pre-mediation activity is third party assisted dialog, undertaken by both official and non-governmental structures. This activity is directed at ethnic, racial, or religious groups who are in a hostile or adversarial relationship (Wehr and Lederach, 1991). Like 'circum-negotiation' this dialog occurs at a quasi-official level around or prior to the formal peace process (Saunders, 1996). Dialog is directed at both officials and civic leaders, including heads of local nongovernmental organizations, community developers, health officials, refugee camp leaders, ethnic/religious leaders, intellectuals, and academics. This dialog process can be assisted by specialized training programs that are directed at exploring ways of establishing and building relationships, furthering proficiency in facilitation, mediation, and brokering, data collection, fact-finding, and other kinds of cooperative decision-making. As Kriesberg notes, much of this activity is directed at developing 'constituency support for peace efforts' (Kriesberg, 1996b: 228).

The practice of dialog and communication is not confined to the non-governmental sector, but in fact underlies the approach of a number of regional organizations' attempts at mediation. Lacking in some instances the resources of individual states or the UN and in other instances reluctant to use the resources they have, regional organizations have used consultation, problem-solving, dialog, and a kind of moral example to shift perceptions and change attitudes among conflict parties. A prime example of the use of this approach is found in the conflict prevention work of the Organization for Security and Cooperation in Europe's (OSCE's) High Commission on National Minorities (Chigas with McClintock and Kamp, 1996).

Social–psychological approaches to mediation are directed at finding ways of establishing communication channels between different groups in society, initiating discussions of framework solutions to problems of mutual concern, identifying steps for breaking impasses, developing new norms, and creating an understanding of the kinds of decision-making processes that can lead parties out of conflict. In these kinds of activities, third parties are supposed to play a neutral and essentially facilitating role, enabling and encouraging a mutual learning process rather than guiding or still less influencing and directing the parties to mutually acceptable approaches to problem-solving. Their involvement is based on their expert and/or reputational authority or on their ability to represent a normative or real community to which the combatants aspire.

Towards a synthesis of perspectives

The value of establishing paradigms is that they allow us to isolate and analyse the different assumptions and beliefs and consequent conclusions and patterns of behavior the each school embraces. For instance, each of the above paradigms offers different insights into appropriate mediation intervention strategies. The structuralist school places considerable importance on the dynamics of conflict and the interests of the parties, arguing that mediated interventions that are not timed to coincide with hurting stalemates run a real risk of failure. Even so, there is a general consensus that ripeness is more of a cultivated and not just an inherited condition. In fact, there are a myriad of techniques and measures which mediators can deploy to foster the ripening process in order to move the parties from a hurting stalemate to a political settlement. In addition to timing, it is crucial is to have a strategy of peacemaking and mediation, to know how to move the parties, to have a sense of how they can be engaged in a process and how unripe conditions can be modified into riper ones, i.e. to understand the dynamics of the conflict cycle and the point at which the mediator decides to enter it.

Social–psychological approaches stress the importance of changing attitudes and the creation of new norms in moving parties towards reconciliation. Early intervention, according to this formulation, is preferable because once relations have deteriorated because of violence, and attitudes are embedded in 'we–they' images of the enemy, it becomes much more difficult for mediators to move the parties towards sober reflection about their real world choices and change perceptions (Wehr and Lederach, 1996). These interventions, however, may take place at any point in the conflict cycle, because part of their function is to reach beyond elites to the level of civil society by creating mobilized domestic constituencies who are supportive of the peace process and are in a position to influence the policies and positions of those who hold power.

The trouble with establishing paradigms, on the other hand, is that these categories rarely translate well into reality. Another shortcoming of this use of paradigms is that it can imply – wrongly – that one approach will be more successful than the others in dealing with all of the issues and events of the conflict cycle. The fact that more than one set of factors are at play in any given conflict argues against an intervention strategy that is directed at a single cause or at alleviating only one set of social or political pressures. As Charles King observes, there is a wide range of obstacles to settlement of civil wars (King, 1997). He concludes that there is no single formula for all conflict, and external powers are likely to be more effective at reducing some obstacles (influencing key leaders, leveling organizational and status imbalances, and overcoming security dilemmas) than others. Similarly, Keashly and Fisher point out that protracted or intercommunal conflicts contain a large number of constituencies with different demands, interests, and belief systems. 'With such a large number of elements, it seems unreasonable to expect that a single intervention strategy could deal with all of them. It seems more useful to envision interventions as a coordinated series of concurrent and consecutive strategies directed towards the long-term goal of resolving the conflict' (Keashley and Fisher, 1990).

Such a sequencing strategy, which lends support to the proposition that more than one mediator may be required to help manage an ongoing conflict, is premised on the notion that most conflicts-even protracted ones – have life cycle of their own, characterized by various phases or stages (Bercovitch and Langley, 1993; Mitchell, 1994; Lund, 1996). These include a period of rising tensions between or among parties, followed by confrontation, the outbreak of violence, and the escalation of military hostilities. In the postagreement or postsettlement phase, a conflict may go through several stages de-escalatory phases as well, such as a ceasefire, followed by a formal settlement, rapprochement, and eventual reconciliation. And in unfortunate cases, as the situation in Angola in the late 1980s and early 1990s reminds us, some conflicts reverse themselves, doubling back into violence even in the implementation stage (Hampson, 1996).

During these various phases or stages of conflict, the intensity of the security dilemma among rival communal groupings is likely to vary. Parties will tend to feel more secure in their relations with other groupings when the level of violence is low, formal ties exist between different groups, and institutionalized channels of communication, though perhaps frayed, are still available. At this stage of the conflict style, there may well be more chances for mediation because attitudes and perceptions have not hardened and parties are still willing to talk to each other (Jones, 1995; Lund, 1996; Adelman and Suhrke, 1996; Carnegie Commission on Preventing Deadly Conflict, 1998). As Princen notes, negotiation at this stage is a relatively low risk strategy for the disputants 'because it is not equated as conceding' (Princen, 1992: 54). The downside is that negotiated solutions will seem less attractive because the parties, having not yet experienced the full cost and limits of what can typically be achieved on the battlefield, may consider violence in support of unilateral goals to be a viable alternative to compromise and politically based solutions and this will tend to limit the mediator's leverage over the parties.

As violence increases, different groups start to arm themselves, and factions become increasingly aware of the real power asymmetries that exist between themselves and other groups, the security dilemma will become more acute and the desire for peaceful and cooperatively based strategies of conflict will weaken (Lake and Rothchild, 1996). This will tend to reduce the likely effectiveness of most potential mediators unless their mediation is linked to instruments of outright strategic leverage and coercive diplomacy, as was the case in orchestrating both the Madrid peace talks and the

Namibia–Angola settlement (Crocker, 1992; Corbin, 1994; Hampson, 1996). Once violence has reached a threshold where no further escalation is possible without major costs, the disputants may be willing to consider other alternatives than the use of force. At this point, the alternatives to mediation have worsened. Although mediators may experience difficulty gaining entry to the conflict because of the sustained pattern of violence, once they do gain entry they will tend to have greater leverage – sometimes termed 'procedural control' – over the negotiating process (Princen, 1992: 54).

However, for conflicts that fall within the middle range of the escalation curve, i.e. violence is ongoing and episodic but not sufficient to make the idea of a political solution an attractive alternative to the status quo, mediators will have to work harder to convince parties to accept mediation and to develop the credibility and leverage to engage the parties in a meaningful exploration of options. Such conflicts are sometimes referred to as 'protracted social conflicts' because they are marked by self-sustaining patterns of hostility and violence with no apparent end in sight (Azar, 1990; Albin, 1997). Lacking any apparent deadline, impending disaster, or sense of time shifting to the other side's advantage, these conflict can be sustained for years. For third parties intent on offering their mediation services and other 'good offices' it may be difficult to identify a formula or pattern in which issues can be resolved in order to lend momentum to the peace-making process. And in situations that get frozen by previous interventions – Cyprus is an obvious case in point – there must be an intervening shock to the system to drive the parties out of the comfort zone or it may be necessary to wait for a change in leadership or for broader attitudinal change.

In sum, the notion of a conflict cycle suggests that while the level of violence is low (a condition that may occur at the beginning and at the end of a conflict cycle) there are greater opportunities for a variety of mediators to engage both the parties and the larger society in a wide range of activities, investing on a long-term basis in the peace. These conditions, however, present fewer opportunities for a real movement towards settlement on disputed issues. As one approaches higher levels of violence, the opportunities for mediators to engage the parties may diminish but the likelihood of mediation success, i.e. helping the parties to negotiate an agreement increases (see Table 12.1). The escalatory and de-escalatory dynamics of the conflict cycle therefore suggest that there is an inverse relationship between opportunities to engage the players in a political dialogue and direct assistance to a peace negotiation process.

In examining Table 12.1, it is important to remember that mediators gain or fail to gain entry into a conflict for a variety of reasons besides the level of violence and the hardening of attitudes. Outside actors, particularly great powers, also may not want to intervene because the costs and risks of intervention outweigh any perceived potential political benefits for

Table 12.1 Entry points in the conflict cycle

Level of violence	No. of potential entry points	Barriers to entry	Opportunity to exercise procedural control
Low	Large	Low–moderate	Low
	(Attitudes and perceptions have not hardened or opened have opened up again)	(Parties may not want to risk escalating the stakes by inviting high level mediators)	(Parties are not yet prepared to eschew violence if demands cannot be met through negotiation)
Medium	Moderate and Declining	Moderate–high	Low
	(Attitudes and perceptions are hardening)	(Increasing risks of negotiation coupled with status and legitimacy concerns)	(Parties still believe that they have the option of escalating conflict and/or accepting resulting costs/losses)
High	Few	High	Moderate–high
	(Hardened 'we–they' images of the enemy)	(Parties are locked into a continuing struggle)	(Alternatives to mediation have worsened as conflict reaches a plateau or 'hurting stalemate')

them (Mitchell and Webb, 1988). The parties themselves may wish to exclude international organizations and great powers from mediation at low levels of conflict because they fear that interventions by these actors will further complicate the issues and raise the stakes in ways that polarize attitudes (Chigas with McClintock and Kamp, 1996) or are considered to be unwarranted intrusions in the internal affairs of a state (Chayes and Chayes, 1995). This is not to say that great-power intervention is undesirable or should be avoided at lower rungs on the escalatory ladder – sometimes, a dramatic intervention or shock is just what is needed to bring the parties to their senses and avert violent conflict and effectively to engage the parties in a process which limits their options – but there may well be resistance to early mediated interventions by the parties themselves.

Comparative advantage of different kinds of mediators

What are the implications of the above hypothesis of the inverse relationship between mediator opportunity and mediator effectiveness? Do some mediators have a greater comparative advantage over others in gaining entry, initiating dialogue, and/or bringing the parties to settlement at different points along the escalation curve? And if so, what does this mean for the multiparty mediation in which many actors may be trying to influence the course of peacemaking?

Jeffrey Rubin has suggested that there are several different kinds of resources and influence that mediators can bring to the negotiating table and that these are related to six different bases of power:

1. reward power, when the mediator has something to offer to the parties such as side payments in exchange for changes in behavior;
2. coercive power that relies on threats and sanctions to carry them out, again with the intention of changing the behavior of the parties;
3. expert power based on the mediator's greater knowledge and experience with certain issues;
4. legitimate power which is based on certain rights and legally sanctioned authority under international law;
5. referent power that is based on the relationship between the mediator and the recipient and a relationship that is valued; and
6. informational power which works on the content of the information conveyed as in the case of a go-between or message carrier (Rubin, 1992).

As Rubin and others have argued, whereas private individuals and non-governmental mediators are low in reward/coercive power capabilities, they may be strong in expert and referential power capabilities (Rothchild and Hartzell, 1991). The scholar/practitioner also tends to enjoy high levels of reputational authority which itself creates its own form of legitimacy. Regional and international organizations tend to enjoy legitimate power because they speak with the authority of their members (Thornton, 1992) but they also tend to be weak on the reward/coercive power dimensions (Edmead, 1971; Skjelsbaek, 1991; Amoo and Zartman, 1992; Skjelsbaek and Fermann, 1996; Wedgwood, 1996). The most powerful states in the international system generally tend to have strong reward and coercive power capabilities, although their hegemonic status may, in some instances, weaken their legitimacy and informational power capabilities because they are not trusted by one or more of the parties.

How an organization is structured and to whom or what it is ultimately accountable also have consequences for the efficacy of the mediation effort. Johannes Botes and Chris Mitchell perceive a 'paradox' in which a mediator's flexibility and freedom from constraints imposed by its internal structure and constituency demands shape both the methods and the potential effectiveness of a mediation: the absence of constraint widens the choice of possible conflicts to be tackled, entry points, tactics and approaches. Yet, at the same time, this absence of constraint is associated with an absence of capacity and, hence, flexibility, to bring influence to bear on the conflicting parties (Botes and Mitchell, 1995).

These remarks highlight the varying bargaining capabilities and resources as well as perceived legitimacy of different mediators. These differences, however, enable the disparate organizations to perform widely varying roles depending upon where the conflict stands on escalation curve or conflict life-cycle. As argued by the social-psychological school of mediation, when violence is low, parties may handle disputes on their own or to consider interventions by a wide range of mediators, including various nonstate actors. However, the extent to which parties to the conflict are willing to resort to violence if negotiations fail, limits mediator leverage, and these third parties will face an uphill struggle keeping the negotiations on course. Mediation efforts at this level should therefore be directed at 'lengthening the shadow of the future' (Axelrod, 1984) by dramatizing the long-term costs of violence to the parties if negotiations fail. Ideally, they should also be directed at changing the attitudes of the parties by creating domestic constituencies that are supportive of negotiation and political as opposed to military options. This analysis points to a multiple track mediation strategy that is directed at both elites and various factions and groups within civil society, i.e. a series of simultaneous mediated interventions by governmental and non-governmental mediators that are targeted at different groups in the conflict (Rupesinghe and Kuroda, 1992; Marks and Fraenkel, 1997).

The middle range of the conflict curve is typically resistant to entry because the conflicting parties' attitudes and perceptions have hardened towards each other with the escalation of violence. Opportunities to exercise effective leverage by would-be mediators are limited because the conflict has not yet reached a level where the parties are prepared seriously to explore negotiation as a viable option to a continued unilateral pursuit of military options. Where sovereignty and recognition issues lie at the heart of conflict, one of the main challenges is to establish direct communication between the parties in order to initiate a process of prenegotiation. Various non-governmental actors and scholar/practitioners may enjoy a comparative advantage in this sort of task because they can help to establish informal channels of communication without compromising the interests of the parties or formally committing them to a politically risky course of action.

That being said, once entry is gained and communication between the parties involving some kind of mutual recognition is established, mediators who exercise reward and coercive power will likely have to be brought into the formal negotiating process – what is sometimes called 'mediation with muscle'. This is because offers of side-payments, or coercive threats such as sanctions and the use of force by an external third party, and the full panoply of leverage-based diplomatic mediation techniques may be required to change the cost/benefit calculus of warring parties away from violence to a consideration of various political alternatives (Stein, 1985; Rabie, 1995). Absent these externally induced incentives, parties will have little incentive to come to the table and may, in fact, be willing to escalate the conflict in the hope of achieving their objectives. It is at this stage of conflict where entry points are few and leverage is limited that a combined strategy that draws on the different resources and influence of different kinds of mediators may be most essential.

In situations of medium to high levels of protracted conflict and violence where parties are deadlocked and yet worried enough to consider direct communication without preconditions, second-track initiatives by small powers or non-governmental organizations can assist with prenegotiation processes and negotiation as in the case of Norway's role in the Oslo peace talks between Israelis and Palestinians (Corbin, 1994). But such interventions, if they are to be translated into concrete agreements require concerted engagement and follow-up by states or groups of states.

The use of sanctions and side payments may also be required to bring the parties to the table. Creative uses of shifting military balances on the ground can become a key ingredient in the arsenal of this kind of mediation. As in the case of NATO air strikes in Bosnia, discussed below, the use of force against recalcitrant elements who refuse to come to the table may be critical to prenegotiation strategies (Holbrooke, 1998).

At the upper end of the escalation curve, a different kind of mediator with muscle may be called for as the mediator is required to develop and deploy those pressures and inducements which keep the mediation moving forward deter parties from exiting or blowing up the process. Also, mediators will often be expected to come up with innovative and credible ideas for confidence-building measures, cease-fire monitoring, verification proposals to assure that commitments are being carried out, and other forms of political guarantee that help address the most difficult security dilemmas faced by the parties.

The conflict has now reached a point where further escalation is not possible, or, at least not possible without greatly raising costs, and the warring parties' alternatives to a mediated solution have appreciably, perhaps dramatically, worsened. Success depends upon mediators who can exercise effective procedural control and carry out the following tasks: meeting with stakeholders to assess their interests, helping to choose spokespersons or teach leaders, identifying missing groups or strategies for representing diffuse interests, drafting protocols and setting agendas, suggesting options, identifying and testing possible tradeoffs, writing and ratifying agreements, and monitoring and facilitating the implementation of those agreements (Carnevale, 1986; Bercovitch, 1997).

It would be wrong to suggest that these kinds of skills are tied to the capabilities and resources of a single kind of actor in international politics. Great powers, middle and small-sized powers, and international and regional organizations have all at one time or another played this kind of role although demonstrable qualities of leadership are essential (Hermann, 1996). Given the complexity of the assignment, organizational capacity, staying power, and flexibility are also key to the multitasking needs of this kind of mediation.

Based on the above analysis, Table 12.2 links mediators to activities which they may undertake effectively at different levels of violence.

This classification of mediators, entry points, and their respective comparative advantage should not, however, be taken too literally. The fact that more than one set of factors are at play in any given conflict argues against a mediation intervention strategy that is directed at a single cause or at alleviating only one set of social or political pressures. The list of causes in any conflict is long, and different third-party intervenors may enjoy different kinds of comparative advantage depending upon the actual situation at hand and the specific issues that lies at the heart of a particular dispute. Furthermore, some situations may be more ripe for certain kinds of intervention than others, depending upon who does the intervening.

Table 12.2 Type of third-party assistance and the conflict cycle

Level of violence	Type of third-party assistance	Mediator	Multiparty initiative
Low	Second track coupled with 1st track diplomacy	NGOs, International and Regional Organizations	Simultaneous
Medium	Second track to gain entry and assist with prenegotiation/ negotiation followed by 'mediation with muscle'	Scholar-practitioner, NGOs for pre- and post-negotiation; great powers or coalitions for formal negotiation	Sequenced
High	Second track to gain entry followed by procedural mediation	Scholar-practitioner, NGOs for pre- and post-negotiation; great powers, international and regional organizations for formal negotiation	Sequenced

The kinds of confidence-building measures set in motion by mediators will also vary from one setting to another depending upon the intensity of the conflict and the pressures that are brought to bear upon the disputants themselves.

As noted above, it is important to recognize that effective third-party mediation also depends upon the mediator's capabilities and leverage, as well as the linkage between the third party and the conflict and the extent to which the mediators see themselves as stakeholders. Those third parties that are not stakeholders in the conflict or do not have a relationship with the parties may have greater difficulty engaging them than those who do. It may well take several false starts to figure out what works, what does not, and who has the most to offer as a third party mediator. Most conflicts, in fact, cry out for more than one set of hands at the tiller. The fact that more than one mediator may be involved in a conflict as it moves through the various stages of the conflict 'life cycle' suggests that maintaining coherence, coordinating and sequencing initiatives, and having staying power are essential in any sort of multiparty mediated intervention.

The war in the Balkans: an illustration

The wars in the Balkans since 1991 illustrate some of the points which this paper has made: the difficulty of mediation when so many voices are speaking at the same time; the difficulty of keeping a multiparty mediation on track; the comparative advantage of different third-party institutions at different times during the conflict; and the particular qualities a powerful state brings to the mediation process when disputants are at their most intractable. It should not be taken, however, as the best or only illustration of the validity of the foregoing statements. Mediation is a multifarious activity which calls on all of the powers that Rubin lists. The Bosnian case shows that both reward and coercive power, provided finally by the United States in late 1995, were needed to help stop the fighting. The case of Sant' Egidio in Mozambique shows how a non-official organization can borrow the necessary skill and leverage, as well as exercise its own referent power, in order to become an effective mediator. The case of Norway in the Oslo process is an example of a small, relatively powerless – in every sense that Rubin employs – state turning these characteristics to good advantage in facilitating an agreement when other channels were blocked.

The case of the conflict in the former Yugoslavia, especially the Serbian–Croatian war in 1991–92 and the Bosnian war in 1992–95, provides a good example of multiparty mediation in several senses of the definition. First, there were a number of third parties which offered their services or more or less compelled the parties to accept them as intermediaries: the UN, the EC/EU, the United States, and in a private capacity, former president Jimmy Carter. These concerted interventions were by-and-large sequential: first the

EC (now EU), then the UN, then a joint UN/EU effort, the brief Carter-negotiated ceasefire in late 1994–early 1995, and then the US. A number of the interventions also represented mediations by institutions – the UN and the EU – that are composed of governments with high degrees of sovereignty in the foreign policy arena. Consequently, despite the EU's attempt to create a common foreign policy among its member nations, both institutions are subject to strong, often contradictory expressions of national interest among their memberships. As discussed earlier in the chapter, these interventions by IGOs are included in our definition of multiparty mediation because the mediator, whether UN Special Representative Yasushi Akashi or the Vance–Owen team, is subject to the multiple pressures of the organization's membership. And finally, some of the mediation efforts were simultaneous. Jimmy Carter's effort to arrange a ceasefire occurred while Owen and Stoltenberg were still active and the US government, in the person of Robert Frasure, was negotiating with Milosevic to end the sanctions in return for recognition of Bosnia (Holbrooke, 1998: 63).

The conflict in the former Yugoslavia was in part a by-product of the end of the Cold War. The regime of Josip Broz Tito, who ruled over a unified Yugoslavia for 35 years, had repressed ethnic identification as part of campaign to build a nation-state out of the disparate communities of Serbia, Macedonia, Montenegro, Bosnia, Slovenia, and Croatia. Even the traditional enmity between Serbians and Croatians, intensified by the activities of the Croatian Ustashe and the Serbian Chetniks during World War II, seemed to fade into competition for political and economic power between the two largest Yugoslav states. Intermarriages among the ethnic groups became common and when Bosnian Muslims mobilized in the 1960s and 1970s, it was as a political force in order to strengthen their position against the larger states of Serbia and Croatia rather than a religious grouping (Malcolm, 1996: 202). Yugoslavia seemed to support several anomalies: an open Communist system and a unified ethnically diverse state. Unnoticed by the outer world, this model developed cracks along ethnic and political faultlines before Tito died in 1980 but really started to crumble after his death and accelerated with the fall of the Berlin Wall and the political transitions that overtook Eastern and Central Europe as a consequence. In the midst of this political transition in Yugoslavia, politicians such as Slobodan Milosevic and Franco Tudjman began to use ethnic nationalism as a political platform to increase their own power base.

The Yugoslavian wars began in 1991 with the conflict first between Slovenia and Belgrade, and then between Croatia and Belgrade. The trigger for the latter's turn to mass violence was Croatia's declaration of independence. This declaration coincided with Slovenia's declaration of independence, provoked in both cases by a Serbian refusal to recognize a Croatian as head of the rotating federal presidency. Belgrade failed to subdue the Slovenians militarily and so turned to Croatia. Compared to the later

Bosnian conflict, this was a short war. The Croatians, poorly armed and vulnerable to the UN arms embargo on Yugoslavia, and the well-equipped and trained Serbian federal army, fought for four months. During this time, the Croatians found ways around the arms embargo and were recognized internationally as a sovereign state. These changes strengthened the Croatian position against the Serbs and may have contributed to Serbs' understanding that this early conflict was headed for an impasse, a hurting stalemate which increased the parties' willingness to negotiate rather than continue military action.

The international response to this war and the later Bosnian War, which were simultaneously intra-state and inter-state, was equally a product of the post-Cold War period. After its attempts to stop the dissolution of Yugoslavia had failed, the United States claimed that European institutions should take responsibility for this European conflict. The European Community (later the European Union) agreed and stepped up to the challenge, first enlisting Henry Wijnaendts as the Community's envoy to Yugoslavia and later appointing Lord Peter Carrington, former British Foreign Minister, to intervene on its behalf. The European Community then teamed up with the United Nations to negotiate a peace in the former Yugoslavia in 1991. Former US Secretary of State Cyrus Vance, acting for the United Nations, was successful in negotiating a cease-fire in Croatia but the final end to the war came about because of changes on the battlefield and in international recognition for Croatia's independence. Lord Carrington on behalf of the European Community had a more difficult time in getting the Yugoslav republics to negotiate a joint future (Zimmerman, 1996: 161), an effort undercut by the German recognition of Croatian independence. From these first third party attempts at intervention, the deleterious effects of multiple voices making conflicting statements was apparent in this complex conflict.

The problems caused by competition among the peacemakers were even more apparent in the diplomatic interventions in the war in Bosnia. In the spring and summer of 1992, the war in Bosnia began, sparked in part by the profoundly different political futures the three ethnic groups envisioned for Bosnia. While the Croats and the Serbs wanted to carve Bosnia up along ethnic lines, the Muslims wanted to keep the nascent country together. Again the UN and the EU were teamed as the agents of third party intervention. A stronger duo is hard to imagine. Cyrus Vance again represented Secretary General Boutros Boutros Ghali, bringing with him years of experience and a gloss of US involvement in addition to the moral authority of the United Nations. Former British Foreign Secretary David Owen was appointed as envoy on behalf of the European Union, representing the collective power of Yugoslavia's close neighbours and largest trading partners.

The joint mediating team painstakingly put together a proposal for the resolution of the conflict, a plan which involved recognizing

Bosnia–Herzegovina as a decentralized state composed of ten provinces and the eventual demilitarization of the whole country. The proposal was accepted as a basis for negotiation by all three parties, although both Muslim and Serb authorities had strong reservations about it. Its reception in the United States, however, was mixed. *Time* magazine claimed that the plan clearly favored the Serbs and a critical opinion piece by Anthony Lewis in the *New York Times*, entitled 'Beware of Munich', drew parallels between the Vance–Owen peace plan and Chamberlain's negotiations with Hitler in 1938. While members of the departing Bush Administration were cautiously supportive, the new Secretary of State, Warren Christopher, expressed doubts on the day following Bill Clinton's inauguration that the plan would work (Owen, 1995: 94–101). His ambivalence developed into skepticism by mid-February and set the pattern for US reluctance to engage with the European/UN mediation effort, a pattern which continued until the United States put its weight behind the creation of the Federation of Bosnia–Hercegovina in March 1994. This agreement ended the war between the Croats and Muslims in Bosnia, and was the result of an intensive effort by Charles Redman, appointed by Christopher as the Bosnian negotiator during this period. The agreement was important, although as Daniel Serwer (the US special coordinator for the Federation) notes, the State Department remained ambivalent about devoting the attention and resources needed to make the agreement a success (Serwer, 1999).

A private effort occurred in December 1994 when former president Jimmy Carter traveled to Pale and Sarajevo and managed to secure an agreement among the parties for a four-month ceasefire. How private this effort was is not clear. Certainly, in carrying out his initiative, Carter acted independently of the American diplomatic corps. On the other hand, he may have had White House backing – or at least tacit support – for his work (Owen, 1995: 310). On the official side, the US was becoming more involved in the peacemaking effort, principally through a quiet – and ultimately unsuccessful – series of negotiations between US Special Envoy Robert Frasure and Milosevic (Holbrooke, 1998: 63).

As public criticism about US unwillingness to play a role in ending the war in the former Yugoslavia increased, pressure mounted for the Clinton administration to do something. Rumors of a massacre at Srebrenica and the horrifying late August 1995 mortar attack on a Sarajevo market seemed to galvanize the administration (Holbrooke, 1998: 74, 93). NATO bombing of Serb positions around Sarajevo and then more generally around western and northern Bosnia started on August 30. At the same time, a Bosnian Croatian military advance, supported by the Muslim authorities and by the Croatian army, streamed into the Krajina region, pushing back Serb forces on the ground at the same time as the international community was pounding them from the sky. Changes in the military equation on the ground, and in the third parties' willingness to use force quickly altered the reckoning for the Serbs. Ripening in this case occurred when the Serbs overplayed their hand and a previous military imbalance (favoring the Serbs) was transformed by the Croat–Muslim advance and the use of NATO air power. This created for the first time a mutually hurting stalemate which mediators could manipulate to bring the Bosnian Serbs and their patron, Slobodan Milosovic, to the table.

The Dayton Accords which followed this changed understanding of the costs and benefits of continued fighting was an agreement imposed by the United States on three reluctant ethnic groups. The full engagement of the United States gave the US mediator, Richard Holbrooke, a tremendous amount of leverage – both positive and negative – with which to impress upon the parties the absolute necessity of coming to settlement. The mediation took every ounce of leverage that the superpower could bring to bear (Holbrooke, 1998), including the personal attention of the president and the offer of 60,000 peacekeeping troops available for the implementation phase. The re-emergence of the US however, changed this mediation from a diffuse multiparty peacemaking effort to a much more focused, single-party one. The Europeans were frozen out of the key decision-making processes and the UN was thrust to the background, replaced in the implementation by the almost non-existent Organization for Security and Cooperation in Europe and the newly established Office of the High Representative.

Looking at the Bosnian case, what does it tell us about the complexities of multiparty mediation? The first and most costly lesson in terms of human lives is that the propensity of individuals and institutions to try to run the show themselves – as the Europeans did in the early years of the Yugoslav wars – works only if they have the necessary willingness, resources and persuasiveness to back it up. The UN/EU mediation had resources in the member states that compose the institutions but found it difficult to marshal them. Individual states, protecting and pursuing their own interests, effectively diluted the mediation effort, and the mechanism to compel them to act concordantly was lacking. Further, the failure to engage – or to convince – the United States lost valuable leverage for the UN/EU effort and meant that member states added to their balance ledgers the possibility of antagonizing the US: a minor cost to some but more significant to Germany and Britain.

On the American side, it proved possible to muster both willingness and resources to gain entry and to impose a settlement – in one sense a measure of a high degree of effectiveness. The American reluctance, however, to support the Vance–Owen plan undercut these early mediators and led to a long period of mutual recriminations, the Europeans blaming the US for its unwillingness to commit troops on the ground and its propensity to criticize the European/UN plan without offering an alternative. The Americans blamed the Europeans for a failure of nerve and an incompetency that allowed the Serbs to commit atrocities under the noses of the peacekeepers.

Bosnia also presents some interesting reflections on when institutions – no matter which they are – can intervene effectively. During the long war, while the Serbs were winning on the battlefield, they were uninterested in considering the possibility of negotiating. This posture changed only when the combined force of the Croatian offensive and NATO bombing attacks changed the situation on the ground. Does this mean that the Bosnian War was ripe for resolution in the fall of 1995? In a sense, yes. The Serbs, the most aggressive party to the conflict at this late stage in the war, had to refigure in these new circumstances the costs and benefits of continuing to lose soldiers, territory, prestige, and the patronage of Slobodan Milosovic. On the other hand, however, it seems that the Croatians had more fight in them and were prepared to pursue a military victory. In addition, the Muslims became more eager to exploit the change in the military balance rather than to negotiate a deal. This is hardly the definition of a mutually hurting stalemate.

The role of the third party intervenors in managing this situation, in changing the Serbs' perceptions and in restraining the Croatians was critical to developing a state of ripeness. The combination of the use of force and the figurative (and one wonders if it was at times literal) strong-arming of Milosovic to bring his clients to the negotiating table provide an extreme example of the use of leverage to change the parties' appreciation of costs. Only a very powerful state, capable of pulling along a military alliance such as NATO and of providing incentives and disincentives could have played this role in 1995. It does not mean that, given another constellation of circumstances – including a unity of purpose and coordination among the third-party actors – that the EU/UN effort was incapable of bringing peace at an earlier stage. These efforts, however, were stymied as third parties looked for scapegoats among allied partners and undercut their own – and all other – efforts. And this raises a final point that this case illustrates: in order for multiparty mediation to succeed, political will and unity of purpose among the intervenors to end the conflict and to forge the necessary coordination are essential elements, all too often missing from joint international engagements.

Challenges of multiparty mediation

When more than one mediator is involved in a conflict, there is clearly a need to not only time and sequence interventions so that the right mix of skills and resources is being brought to bear on the parties to the conflict, but also to ensure that interventions by different parties are pursued consistently and coherently over time in order to move the parties to an agreement. Where direct leverage is limited it may have to be borrowed from others (Crocker, 1996: 188). Episodic interventions in conflicts which have not ripened to the point where parties are willing to consider mediated alternatives to a continuing campaign of violence will offer outsider little chance to gain leverage. Sometimes it may take external military intervention or major shifts in the military situation on the ground to create fresh openings for mediation, as was the case in Bosnia. Needless to say, in a complex or multiple mediation setting, this requires the careful orchestration of carrots and sticks to create leverage between the mediating party and those who have the ability to exercise force or offer side-payments.

Different mediators should also be aware that the parties will be more disposed to play mediators off each other in particular sets of circumstances, e.g. if the conflict has not ripened and the potential for escalation is rife or, on the other hand, when they face the toughest choices and the discussion is edging closer to bottom line positions. Even at the point of ripeness when escalation is no longer considered a viable option by the parties to the conflict, opportunities to intervene and exercise effective procedural control will be missed if different mediators are sending mixed signals and there is no clear delegation of authority. Such mismanagement only invites 'forum shopping' and other unhelpful behavior.

Ideally, the party or parties that mediated the settlement should stay engaged in the peace process in the post-settlement or implementation phase (Hampson, 1996: 227). But this may not be possible because of restrictive third party mandates, changing personnel, or because other actors and institutions have the responsibility for implementation. In this case, coordination and properly timed hand-offs are essential. Negotiation and implementation phases of the peace process are overlapping, intertwined, and mutually interdependent. Failure to recognize the interdependence of mediation roles and functions during the de-escalation phase may lead to an unraveling of the peace process as rival factions or 'spoilers' attempt to undermine the settlement in question (Stedman, 1997).

There is almost an inverse relationship between the number of participants and issues in a multiparty mediation and the likelihood of developing and sustaining a coordinated intervention strategy. The larger the number of participants – as in a mediation undertaken by a coalition of states – the greater the likelihood of conflicting interests and positions, and the more complex the interconnections among the parties concerned. Increasing numbers and difficulties in negotiation are related to heterogeneity of interests and perceptions. However, the fact that mediation is backed by a coalition need not pose insurmountable barriers if preferences are homogenous or convergent and/or the coalition is willing to delegate authority and responsibility to the mediator while allowing the mediator to bargain for the group as a whole.

Coalitions will generally choose representatives to bargain or mediate for the group if sufficient trust has developed among the members of the coalition. Clear lines of delegation and authority are obviously critical to simplifying the negotiation process so that the mediator is not just a spokesperson or mouthpiece for the group. Patterns of representation and authority obviously vary from one institutional setting to another. In a more formal institutional setting, the norms and rules governing lines of authority are generally demarcated in advance. In a more informal setting, the absence of clear lines of authority can create problems if the members of the coalition are unhappy with the mediator's actions or the direction in which negotiations are moving. Effective mediation obviously depends upon a number of conditions being fulfilled, including close links between the group and the party doing the mediating, but also delegated authority so that the mediator has some leeway to make independent decisions during the actual course of negotiations that will be binding on the group as a whole (Botes and Mitchell, 1995).

Depending on the kind of mediation that is being undertaken, different organizational capacities, structures, and lines of authority may be required to ensure that mediation is effective and not undermined by the institutional weaknesses and deficiencies of the mediating individual or organization. If parties feel that the mediator is an independent actor who has little capacity to make good on promises or threats this will tend to undermine the mediator's leverage. Furthermore, if other mediators are present who are communicating different signals, or are in a position to offer a more attractive package of offers/inducements, this will also undermine the mediator's position.

Experience in such varied places as the former Yugoslavia, Somalia, Cyprus, Mozambique, Central America, and Central Africa points to the growing need for comprehensive thinking and coherence of unity of action. While it may be gratifying to professionals and specialists in various types of third party intervention to imagine that each can operate unburdened by the other's baggage and free from heavy-handed coordination mechanisms, the reality is that chaotic interventions will produce at best random results. Practitioners of all sorts can agree, presumably, on some form of the Hippocratic oath to 'do no harm' and rise to the challenges of incremental learning in complex diplomatic-political interventions just as they are starting to do in the field of military intervention in complex emergencies (Anderson, 1996). There is, in other words, some obligation to avoid simply exporting confusion, organizational and fund-raising agendas, as a result of an eagerness to help and to be seen helping to peoples in conflict who already have enough problems. Successful peacekeepers and peace enforcers will keep in view the necessity for a center of gravity and a critical mass of efforts focused on clearly defined goals. Obviously, such operational coordination does not just happen; nor can it be imposed by one set or type of practitioners on another. A start can be made, however, by recalling that more will be accomplished when there is a laser-like focus on solving the problem at hand as distinct from getting the credit for being involved.

Note

1. This chapter is based on the introduction to their volume *Herding Cats: The Management of Complex International Mediation* (Washington, DC: United States Institute of Peace Press, 1999). The authors would like to thank Greg Maruszecka for research assistance.

Bibliography

Adelman, H. and A. Suhrke. (1996) 'Early Warning and response: Why the International Community Failed to Prevent the Genocide', *Journal of Disaster Studies and Management*, 20: 295–304.

Albin, C. (1997) 'Negotiating Intractable Conflicts: On the Future of Jerusalem', *Cooperation and Conflict*, 32: 29–77.

Allouche, B. (1994) 'La mediation des petits Etats: retrospective et perspective', *Etudes Internationales*, 25: 213–36.

Amoo, S. G. and I. W. Zartman. (1992) 'Mediation by Regional Organizations: the Organization of African Unity (OAU) in Chad', in J. Bercovitch and J. Rubin (eds), *Mediation in International Relations: Multiple Approaches to Conflict Management*. New York: St. Martin's Press – now Palgrave Macmillan.

Anderson, M. (1996) 'Humanitarian NGOs in Conflict Intervention', in C. A. Crocker and F. O. Hampson with P. Aall (eds), *Managing Global Chaos: Sources of and Responses to International Conflict*. Washington, DC: United States Institute of Peace Press, pp. 343–54.

Archer, C. (1994) 'Conflict Prevention in Europe: the Case of the Nordic States and Macedonia', *Cooperation and Conflict*, 29: 367–86.

Assefa, H. (1987) *Mediation of Civil Wars: Approaches and Strategies; the Sudan conflict*. Boulder, CO: Westview Press.

Axelrod, R. (1984) *The Evolution of Cooperation*. New York: Basic Books.

Azar, E. E. (1990) *The Management of Protracted Social Conflict: Theory and Cases*. Dartmouth: Aldershot.

Azar, E. E. and J. W. Burton. (eds) 1986 *International Conflict Resolution: Theory and Practice*. Sussex: Wheatsheaf Books.

Bailey, S. D. (1990) *Four Arab–Israeli Wars and the Peace Process*. London: Macmillan – now Palgrave Macmillan.

Bendahmane, D. and J. MacDonald. (eds) (1986) *Perspectives of Negotiation*. Washington, DC: Foreign Service Institute.

Bercovitch, J. (1984) *Social Conflicts and Third Parties: Strategies of Conflict Resolution*. Boulder, CO: Westview Press.

Bercovitch, J. (1986) 'International Mediation: a Study of the Incidence, Strategies and Conditions of Successful Outcomes', *Cooperation and Conflict*, 21: 155–68.

Bercovitch, J. (ed.) (1997) *Resolving International Conflicts: The Theory and Practice of Mediation*. Boulder, CO: Lynne Rienner.

Bercovitch, J. and J. Langley. (1993) 'The Nature of the Dispute and the Effectiveness of International Mediation', *Journal of Conflict Resolution*, 37: 670–91.

Bercovitch, J., J. T. Anagnoson and D. L. Willie. (1991) 'Some Contextual Issues and Empirical Trends in the Study of Successful Mediation in International Relations', *Journal of Peace Research*, 28: 7–17.

Bercovitch, J. and A. Houston. (1996) 'The Study of International Mediation: Theoretical Issues and Empirical Evidence', in J. Bercovitch (ed.), *Resolving*

International Conflicts: The Theory and Practice of Mediation. Boulder, CO: Lynne Rienner Publishers, pp. 11–35.

Bilder, R. B. (1997) 'Adjudication: International Tribunals and Courts', in J. Bercovitch, (ed.), *Resolving International Conflicts: The Theory and Practice of Mediation*. Boulder, CO: Lynne Rienner, pp. 155–90.

Blechman, B. M. (1996) 'Emerging from the Intervention Dilemma', in C. A. Crocker and F. O. Hampson with P. Aall (eds), *Managing Global Chaos: Sources of and Responses to International Conflict*. Washington, DC: United States Institute of Peace Press, pp. 287–96.

Bloomfield, L. P. (1997) 'Why Wars End: a Research Note', *Millenium: Journal of International Studies*, 26: 709–26.

Botes, J. and C. Mitchell. (1995) 'Constraints on Third Party Flexibility', *The Annals of the American Academy of Political and Social Science*, 542 (November): 168–84.

Brookmire, D. and F. Sistrunk. (1980) 'The Effects of Perceived Ability and Impartiality of Mediator and Time Pressure on Negotiation', *Journal of Conflict Resolution*, 24: 311–27.

Brown, M. (1996) *International Dimensions of Internal Conflict*. Cambridge, Mass.: MIT Press.

Brown, S. J. and K. M. Schraub. (eds) (1992) *Resolving Third World conflict: Challenges for a New Era*. Washington, DC: US Institute of Peace.

Burton, J. W. (1987) *Resolving Deep-Rooted Conflict: a Handbook*. Lanham, MD.: University Press of America.

Carnegie Commission on Preventing Deadly Conflict. (1998) *Preventing Deadly Conflict: Final Report*. New York: Carnegie Corporation of New York.

Carnevale, P. J. D. (1986) 'Strategic Choice in Mediation', *Negotiation Journal*, 2: 41–56.

Chan, S. and Vivienne Jabri. (1993) *Mediation in Southern Africa*. London: Macmillan – now Palgrave Macmillan.

Chayes, A. and A. Handler Chayes. (1995) *The New Sovereignty: Compliance with International Regulatory Agreements*. Cambridge, Mass.: Harvard University Press.

Chayes, A., A. Handler Chayes and G. Raach. (1997) 'Beyond Reform: Restructuring For More Effective Conflict Intervention', *Global Governance*, 3: 117–46.

Chigas, D. with E. McClintock and C. Kamp. (1996) 'Preventice Diplomacy and the Organization for Security and Cooperation in Europe: Creating Incentives for Dialogue and cooperation', in A. Chayes and A. Handler Chayes (eds), *Preventing Conflict in the Post-Communist World*. Washington, DC: The Brookings Institution, pp. 25–98.

Corbin, J. (1994) *The Norway Channel: The Secret Talks that Led to the Middle East Peace Accord*. New York: Atlantic Monthly Press.

Cortright, D. (1997) *The Price of Peace: Incentives and International Conflict Prevention*. Lanham, MD: Rowman and Littlefield.

Crocker, C. A. (1992) *High Noon in Southern Africa: Making Peace in a Rough Neighborhood*. New York: W.W. Norton.

Crocker, C. A. (1996) 'The Varieties of Intervention: Conditions for Success', in C. A. Crocker and F. O. Hampson with P. Aall (eds), *Managing Global Chaos: Sources of and Responses to International Conflict*. Washington, DC: United States Institute of Peace Press, pp. 183–96.

Crocker, C. A., F. O. Hampson, and P. R. Aall. (eds) (1999) *Herding Cats: The Management of Complex Mediation*. Washington, DC: United States Institute of Peace Press.

Doob, L. W. (1993) *Intervention: Guides and Perils*. New Haven, Com.: Yale University Press.

Durch, W. J. (1996) *UN Peacekeeping, American Policy, and the Uncivil Wars of the 1990s*. New York: St. Martin's Press – now Palgrave Macmillan.

Durch, W. J. (ed.) (1993) *The Evolution of UN Peacekeeping: Case Studies and Comparative Analysis*. St. Martin's Press – now Palgrave Macmillan.

Edmead, F. (1971) *Analysis and Prediction in International Mediation*. UNITAR Study.

Etzioni, A. (1995) 'Mediation as a World Role for the United States', *Washington Quarterly*, 18: 75–87.

Fisler Damrosch, L. (1993) *Enforcing Restraint: Collective Intervention in Internal Conflicts*. New York: Council on Foreign Relations.

Forsythe, D. P. (1985) 'Humanitarian Mediation by the International Committee of the Red Cross', in S. Touval and I. W. Zartman (eds), *International Mediation in Theory and Practice*. Boulder, CO: Westview Press, pp. 223–50.

George, A. L. (1993) *Bridging the Gap: Theory and Practice in Foreign Policy*. Washington, DC: United States Institute of Peace Press.

Haass, R. N. (1988) *Conflicts Unending: The United States and Regional Disputes*. New Haven, Conn.: Yale University Press.

Hadden, T. (1987) 'The Role of International Agencies in Conflict Resolution: Some Lessons from the Irish Experience', *Bulletin of Peace Proposals*, 18: 567–72.

Hampson, F. O. (1996) *Nurturing Peace: Why Peace Settlements Succeed or Fail*. Washington, DC: United States Institute of Peace.

Hermann, M. G. (1995) 'Leaders, Leadership, and Flexibility: Influences on Heads of Government as Negotiators and Mediators'. *The Annals of the American Academy of Political and Social Science*, 542 (November): 148–67.

Hopmann, P. T. (1995) 'Two Paradigms of Negotiation: Bargaining and Problem Solving', *The Annals of the American Academy of Political and Social Science*, 542: 24–47.

Holbrooke, R. C. (1998) *To End and War*. New York: Random House.

Inbar, E. (1991) 'Great Power Mediation: the USA and the May 1983 Israeli–Lebanese Agreement', *Journal of Peace Research*, 28: 71–84.

Jones, B. D. (1995) 'Intervention Without Borders: Humanitarian Intervention in Rwanda, 1990–94', *Millennium: Journal of International Studies*, 24: 225–49.

Keashley, L. and R. J. Fisher. (1990) 'Towards a Contingency Approach to Third-Party Intervention in Regional Conflict: A Cyprus Illustration', *International Journal*, 45: 425–53.

Kelman, H. C. (1996) 'The Interactive Problem-Solving Approach', in C. A. Crocker and F. O. Hampson with P. Aall (eds), *Managing Global Chaos: Sources of and Responses to International Conflict*. Washington, DC: United States Institute of Peace Press, pp. 501–20.

Kelman, H. C. (1997) 'Social–Psychological Dimensions of International Conflict', in I. W. Zartman and J. Lewis Rasmussen (eds), *Peacemaking in International Conflict: Methods and Techniques*. Washington, DC: United States Institute of Peace Press, pp. 191–238.

King, C. (1997) 'Ending Civil Wars', *Adelphi Paper* #308. London: International Institute of Strategic Studies.

Kleibor, M. (1994) 'Ripeness of Conflict: a Fruitful Notion?', *Journal of Peace Research*, 31: 109–16.

Kleibor, M. and P. Hart. (1995) 'Time to Talk? Multiple Perspectives on Timing of International Mediation', *Cooperation and Conflict*, 30: 307–48.

Kriesberg, L. (1992) *International Conflict Resolution: The U.S.–USSR and Middle East Cases.* New Haven, Conn.: Yale University Press.

Kriesberg, L. (1996a) 'Coordinating Intermediary Peace Efforts', *Negotiation Journal,* 12: 341–52.

Kriesberg, L. (1996b) 'Varieties of Mediating Activities and Mediators in International Relations', in J. Bercovitch (ed.), *Resolving International Conflicts: The Theory and Practice of Mediation.* Boulder, CO: Lynne Rienner, pp. 219–34.

Kriesberg, L. (1997) 'Preventing and Resolving Destructive Communal Conflicts', in D. Carment and P. James (eds), *The International Politics of Ethnic Conflict: Theory and Evidence.* University of Pittsburgh Press, pp. 232–51.

Kriesberg, L. and S. J. Thorson. (ed.) (1991). *Timing the De-escalation of International Conflicts.* Syracuse: Syracuse University Press.

Lake, D. A. and D. Rothchild. (1996) 'Containing Fear: the Origins and Management of Ethnic Conflict', *International Security,* 21: 41–75.

Lederach, J. P. (1995) *Building Peace: Sustainable Reconciliation in Divided Societies.* Washington, DC: United States Institute of Peace Press.

Lund, M. S. (1996) 'Early Warning and Preventive Diplomacy', in C. A. Crocker and F. O. Hampson with P. Aall (eds), *Managing Global Chaos: Sources of and Responses to International Conflict.* Washington, DC: United States Institute of Peace Press, pp. 379–402.

Malcolm, N. (1996) *Bosnia: A Short History.* New York: New York University Press.

Marks, J. and E. Fraenkel. (1997) 'Working to Prevent Conflict in the New Nation of Macedonia', *Negotiation Journal,* 13: 243–52.

Mitchell, C. (1994) 'The Process and Stages of Mediation', in D. R. Smock (ed.), *Making War and Waging Peace: Foreign Intervention in Africa.* Washington, DC: United States Institute of Peace Press, pp. 139–59.

Mitchell, R. and K. Webb. (1988) (eds) New Approaches to International Mediation (New York: Greenwood Press).

Owen, D. (1995) *A Balkan Odyssey.* New York: Harcourt, Brace and Company.

Princen, T. (1991) 'Camp D.: Problem Solving or Power Politics as Usual?', *Journal of Peace Research,* 28: 57–69.

Princen, T. (1992a) 'Mediation by a Transnational Organization: the Case of the Vatican', in J. Bercovitch and J. Rubin (eds), *Mediation in International Relations: Multiple Approaches to Conflict Management.* New York: St. Martin's Press – now Palgrave Macmillan.

Princen, T. (1992b) *Intermediaries in International Conflict.* Princeton: Princeton University Press.

Rabie, M. (1995) *U.S.–PLO Dialogue: Secret Diplomacy and Conflict Resolution.* University Press of Florida.

Rothchild, D. and C. Hartzell. (1991) 'Great and Medium Power Mediations: Angola', *The Annals of the American Academy of Political and Social Science,* 518: 39–57.

Rubin, J. Z. (1992) 'Conclusion: International Mediation in Context', in J. Bercovitch and J. Z. Rubin (eds), *Mediation in International Relations.* New York: St. Martin's Press – now Palgrave Macmillan, pp. 249–72.

Rubin, J. Z. (ed.) (1981) *Dynamics of Third Party Intervention: Kissinger in the Middle East.* New York: Praeger.

Rupesinghe, K. and M. Kuroda. (eds) (1992) *Early Warning and Conflict Resolution.* New York: St. Martin's Press – now Palgrave Macmillan.

Saunders, H. H. (1996) *Prenegotiation and Circum-negotiation: Arenas of the Peace Process,* in C. A. Crocker and F. O. Hampson with P. Aall (eds), *Managing Global*

Chaos: Sources of and Responses to International Conflict. Washington, DC: United States Institute of Peace Press, pp. 419–32.

Serwer, D. (1999) 'A Bosnian Federation Memoir', in C. A. Crocker, F. O. Hampson and P. R. Aall (eds), *Herding Cats: The Management of Complex Mediation*. Washington, DC: The United States Institute of Peace Press, pp. 547–58.

Sick, G. (1985) 'The Partial Negotiator: Algeria and the U.S. Hostages in Iran', in S. Touval and I. W. Zartman (eds), *International Mediation in Theory and Practice*. Boulder, CO: Westview Press, pp. 21–66.

Skjelsbaek, K. (1991) 'The UN Secretary-General and the Mediation of International Disputes', *Journal of Peace Research*, 28: 99–115.

Skjelsbaek, Kjell and Gunnar Fermann. (1996) 'The UN Secretary-General and the Mediation of International Disputes', in J. Bercovitch (ed.), *Resolving International Conflict: The Theory and Practice of Negotiation*. Boulder, CO: Lynne Rienner, pp. 75–104.

Smock, D. R. and C. A. Crocker. (eds) (1995) *African Conflict Resolution: The U.S. Role in Peacemaking*. Washington, DC: United States Institute of Peace.

Stedman, S. J. (1997) 'Spoiler Problems in the Peace Process', *International Security*, 22: 5–53.

Stein, J. G. (1985) 'Structures, Strategies, and Tactics of Mediation: Kissinger and Carter in the Middle East', *Negotiation Journal*, 1: 331–47.

Stein, J. G. (1989) 'Getting to the Table: Triggers, Stages, Functions, and Consequences of Prenegotiation', *International Journal*, 42: 475–502.

Strobel, Warren P. (1997) *Late Breaking News*. Washington, DC: United States Institute of Peace Press.

Thornton, T. P. (1992) 'Regional Organizations in Conflict Management', *The Annals of the American Academy of Political and Social Science*, 521: 132–42.

Thornton, T. P. (1985) 'The Indo-Pakistani Conflict: Soviet Mediation in Tashkent, (1966)', in S. Touval and I. W. Zartman (eds), *International Mediation in Theory and Practice*. Boulder, CO: Westview Press, pp. 141–71.

Thornton, T. P. (1991) 'Regional Organizations in Conflict Management', *The Annals of the American Academy of Political and Social Science*, 518: 132–42.

Touval, S. (1982) *The Peace Brokers: Mediators in the Arab–Israeli Conflict 1948–1979*. Princeton: Princeton University Press.

Touval, S. (1994) 'Why the UN Fails', *Foreign Affairs*, 73: 44–57.

Touval, S. (1996a) 'Coercive Mediation on the Road to Dayton', *International Negotiation*, 1: 547–70.

Touval, S. (1996b) 'Lessons of Preventive Diplomacy in Yugoslavia', in C. A. Crocker and F. O. Hampson with P. Aall (eds), *Managing Global Chaos: Sources of and Responses to International Conflict*. Washington, DC: United States Institute of Peace Press, pp. 403–18.

Touval, S. and I. W. Zartman (eds) (1985) *International Mediation in Theory and Practice*. Boulder, CO: Westview Press.

Umbricht, Victor H. (1989) *Multilateral Mediation: Practical Experiences and Lessons*. The Hague: Martinus Nijhoff Publishers.

Vayrynen, Raimo. (1985) 'The United Nations and the Resolution of International Conflicts', *Cooperation and Conflict*, 20: 141–71.

Wedgwood, Ruth. (1996) 'Regional and Subregional Organizations in International Conflict Management', in C. A. Crocker and F. O. Hampson with P. Aall (eds), *Managing Global Chaos: Sources of and Responses to International Conflict*. Washington, DC: United States Institute of Peace Press, pp. 275–86.

Wehr, P. and J. P. Lederach. (1991) 'Mediating Conflict in Central America', *Journal of Peace Research*, 28: 85–98.

Wehr, P. and J. P. Lederach. (1996) 'Mediating in Central America', in J. Bercovitch (ed.), *Resolving International Conflicts: The Theory and Practice of Mediation*. Boulder, CO: Lynne Rienner, pp. 55–74.

Weiss, T. G. (1996) *The United Nations and Civil Wars*. Boulder, CO: Lynne Reinner.

Yarrow, C. H. Mike. (1978) *Quaker Experiences in International Conciliation*. New Haven, Conn. Yale University Press.

Young, O. R. (1967) *The Intermediaries: Third Parties in International Crises*. Princeton: Princeton University Press.

Young, O. R. (1991) 'Political Leadership and Regime Formation: on the Development of Institutions in International Society', *International Organization*, 45: 281–308.

Zartman, I. W. (1989) *Ripe For Resolution: Conflict and Intervention in Africa*. New York: Oxford University Press.

Zartman, I. W. (ed.) (1995) *Elusive Peace: Negotiating an End to Civil Wars*. Washington, DC: The Brookings Institution.

Zartman, I. W. and S. Touval. (1985) 'International Mediation: Conflict Resolution and Power Politics', *Journal of Social Issues*, 41: 27–45.

Zimmerman, Warren. (1996) *Origins of a Catastrophe*. New York: Times Books.

13
Conclusion: Some Thoughts on the Process and Potential of Mediation

Jacob Bercovitch

Introduction

As the chapters above make clear, mediation is practiced daily, its role, relevance and scope have increased, new actors in international relations engage in mediation, and new forms of mediation have made this method of conflict management an integral instrument of diplomacy. In this concluding chapter I propose to pull together some of the strands presented above, and attempt a few broad reflections on the process of mediation, the importance of mediator power or resources, on determinants of success, and on extending the role and relevance of mediation.

Mediation is a form of cooperative and horizontal decision-making. It contrasts with such conflict arrangement methods as coercion or arbitration which are examples of non-cooperative, vertical modes of decision-making. In the 21st century hierarchical modes of making decisions are breaking down everywhere. Trying to *compel* others to resolve a conflict seems all but impossible today. We rely more and more on cooperative approaches to conflict, on voluntarism, on non-coercive modes, and other aspects which are typical of mediation. This is not to suggest that mediators are motivated by altruism only, nor that mediation is a panacea, or the answer to all our social problems; it is simply that mediation offers the prospect or potential of containing, settling or resolving a conflict in the factory, at home, in the community, and, above all, in the international environment.

Initiating mediation

Much of the emphasis in studies on mediation is on who does the mediation, and on what they bring with them to the process. The process, however, cannot begin unless certain prerequisites are met. Rubin (1992) suggests that three things are required: parties' motivation, an opportunity to get involved, and mediation skills.

For mediation to take place, parties in conflict, be they individuals, organizations or states, must have some resources that the other wants or needs, they must be mutually interdependent, and realize that any alternative to a mediated settlement could actually be much worse. These sets of perceptual conditions, which we rather broadly designate as 'the ripe moment', or 'readiness', offer a perfect opportunity for a mediator to enter a conflict and reconcile different interests by focusing on *relationship*, not *power*, or *rights*.

The focus on relationships and collaborative decision-making makes the lure of a joint gain via mediation a very attractive option which in turn increases the parties' desire to engage in it. Mediators do not need to determine who is right or who is wrong, nor do they need to use power, instead they try and *help* parties get to the core of their conflict and resolve it. As such mediation is a wonderful social invention that may prove easier for both parties to accept. A mediator strives for outcomes that *satisfy* both parties, without in any way challenging the legitimacy of either.

Opportunities to get involved in mediation are plentiful. There is so much conflict around us that in a way everyone of us is a potential mediator seeking an appropriate opportunity to become involved. In the international arena, where much of the most destructive conflict takes place, there are individuals, states – small and large, regional and international organizations, as well as a myriad of transnational organizations, all of whom have a mandate, or search for the chance, to mediate. The truth is that there are simply unprecedented opportunities to intervene in conflict – individually or collectively. What is lacking is the willpower to do so.

Motivation, opportunity and a strong willpower to intervene need to be supplemented by appropriate skills. The list of necessary and desirable attributes for interventions is no short list. Among many other attributes it includes knowledge, experience, process and content skills, courage and adaptability (Doob, 1993). The possession of such attributes helps to make a mediator acceptable, and establish a sense of trust during an intervention.

The salience of different traits and attributes will vary from conflict to conflict, but in general third parties with strong process skills (e.g. ability to do something about the way the parties interact) may have greater relevance in interpersonal conflict, or in the early phases of a conflict, whereas those with stronger content skills (e.g. ability to shape an outcome) may be more effective in organizational and international conflicts. Either way, conflict principals and a third party can participate in intervention when motivation is high, opportunities for intervention are present, and a useful mediator with appropriate skills is available.

Once mediators intervene in a conflict, they utilize various resources, strategies and tactics with the hope of helping the parties address the issues and/or resolve them. The full range of mediator strategies and tactics has been described by Bush and Folger as *settlement-oriented* or *transformative*

(Bush and Folger, 1994), and by Riskin as *evaluative* or *facilitative* (Riskin, 1996). These ways of categorizing mediation may explain some wide variation of behavior, but we can only understand such variations if we appreciate that any mediation effort must use some resources, some influence or some leverage to achieve change. The resource and influence base to which mediators have access, determines their goals, orientation and behavior in mediation.

Resources and influence in mediation

Rubin (1992) identified six bases of resources for influencing the behavior of another party. These are: reward, coercion, expertise, legitimacy, reference and information. Reward is used by parties who can offer tangible or intangible benefits in exchange for compliance. Coercion is here used to describe mostly threats (e.g. withdrawal of economic or diplomatic aid) to induce compliance. Expertise refers to the ability of parties with greater knowledge and expertise to change the behavior of others. Legitimacy refers to the parties' perception that a person or an organization has the *right* to intervene in a conflict, and do something about it. Referent resources describe an interdependent, and valued relationship between one of the parties and a mediator, a relationship which may be used to influence the course or outcome of a conflict. And informational resources describe a third party's ability to change or affect a conflict by relying on information which it possesses and to which the disputants might like to have access.

This typology is useful in reviewing the behavior and performance of all kinds of mediators. Individual mediation, of the sort described by Aggestam in Chapter 4, have little or no access to such resources as reward or coercion, but, relying instead on their referent and informational resources, they can be highly effective especially when confronted by antagonists with serious communicational problems. Egeland, Larsen and Holst were able to open up new avenues for dialog by facilitating the parties' negotiation and providing a supportive cognitive framework. This kind of mediation is very useful in opening lines of communication that have broken down.

Extending traditional avenues of mediation into new realms, scholars such as Burton, Doob and Kelman, and others who follow in their footsteps, act (despite the differences between them) more like teachers addressing such basic issues as poor communicational skills and antagonistic relationship between the parties. There is no question whatsoever of utilizing reward, coercive or referent bases of influence; what these people bring with them to a conflict are information resources and expertise. Kelman's chapter reminds us how frustrated needs (for identity, autonomy, etc.) and poor communications create conflict everywhere. Undertaking interventions in this context means using one's knowledge, information and expertise to analyse problems, disseminate information, explore ideas and, above all, encourage disputants to understand their situation and come up with their own suggestions.

The chapters by Zartman and Fretter point out unmistakably the increasing role of regional and international organizations in the area of conflict management and mediation. Although newspaper and popular accounts may give the impression that only states or their representatives engage in mediation, the reality is that more than 50 per cent of all mediation cases in the 1945–95 period were undertaken by regional organizations or the UN (see Bercovitch and Diehl, 1997). Regional organizations and the UN have credible claims as mediators because of their moral authority, the fact that they embody some generally agreed upon norms, and, above all, their legitimacy. Such organizations have neither power, nor 'teeth', they give concrete expression to the legitimate voices of a regional or the global community, and use this legitimacy to intervene effectively.

Peacekeepers offer an interesting variation on the theme of legitimacy. Peacekeepers are called upon by a regional organization, or more often than not, the UN, to interpose themselves between hostile parties and stop a conflict from escalating further. Sometimes peacekeepers go further, and, as Wall, Druckman and Diehl remind us, engage in mediation. Experiments with peacekeepers as mediators are not all that numerous in international relations. It seems that peacekeepers may, if sanctioned by the organization that had despatched them, use coercive means to enforce peace, use violence to pre-empt further violence. Thus we have peacekeepers enjoying the legitimacy they derive from their organizations, but also having at their disposal power and coercive means to be used if necessary. The unusual combination of legitimacy and coercion creates a rather confusing dual track which may impede peacekeepers' efforts to mediate effectively.

Kleiboer (Chapter 7), while critical of many aspects of leverage and resources, reminds us that great powers, with their obvious capabilities, resources and network of significant links, are the only actors that can use coercive means and rewards as part of an influence strategy in mediation. There is no suggestion here or in that chapter that coercion or reward always elicit a desired response, merely that these are available to states, and states only. There are many conflicts in which great powers will not think about intervening, and many others in which coercion and reward may be inappropriate means of influence. Equally, there could be some situations where such resources might be quite useful. Successful intervention is one that reflects a specific conflict, and responds appropriately to its context. We must not lose sight of this reciprocal relationship.

Mediation success

Possessing resources, capabilities and means of influence, or leverage, enables a mediator to enter a conflict, it does not guarantee success. To be successful requires a confluence of coincidences involving an awareness of the context of a conflict, the nature of the parties involved, appropriate timing, relevant capabilities and the right strategies, and, some would claim, a considerable measure of luck. Successful mediation is the result of many interacting factors. A mediator may have control over some of these factors, many others are beyond the purview of a mediator. As we travel along the 'Holy Grail' of mediation, many of our efforts are directed toward searching for accurate descriptions of when or why mediation succeeds. Ultimately, it seems, that is the big question at the heart of much mediation research.

Much has been written – both theoretically and empirically – about conditions leading to successful or effective mediation (for a useful review of the literature, see Henderson, 1996 and Kleiboer, 1996). Whatever we mean by successful or effective mediation (Sheppard's list revealed 21 different criteria for assessing intervention outcomes, see Sheppard, 1984), it is clear that conditions such as conflict dimensions, types of issues, commitment to mediation, relative power of disputants, mediator resources and the stage of a conflict vary from case to case, and they can thus all be postulated as important determinants affecting the consequences of mediation. Carnevale (Chapter 2) and Pruitt (Chapter 3) examine these last two factors respectively.

Resources really matter. You cannot separate resources from mediation. Resources determine the nature of intervention, and influence its likely outcome. Different resources will, of course, be useful in different contexts, but in general we can say that increasing strategic or tactical resources of a mediator, and using these in the right context, increases the chances of mediation success. Mediation resources are of course multi-faceted and quite elusive, even so it seems wholly reasonable to suggest that any factor or condition which enhances mediation (as possession of relevant resources must do), will have a restraining effect on a conflict. Mediation is a three-way interaction in which resources – be they intellectual, perceptual or tangible – are paraded, used, and exchanged.

While mediators may have little control over the resources they possess, they have considerable control over the issue of entry and exit. Engaging in mediation, or the timing of mediation, appears to affect its effectiveness. Pruitt makes it clear that the notion of timing must not be defined in terms of some temporal perspective, but rather in terms of the parties' psychological readiness. When the parties are 'ready', they are strongly motivated to accept mediation. Identifying when the parties are psychologically ready is obviously quite difficult; there are no empirical guideposts for assessing readiness. Although generalizations are hardly possible with respect to 'best timing'; one of the early and difficult decisions a mediator must make is whether and when to intervene, or whether to postpone, delay or give up the effort.

The two broad factors examined here (resources, and 'timing'), both increase the power of mediation and its likely effectiveness.

Extending the range of mediation

How can we explain, better still organize, the explosion of mediation across all domains? How can we describe the nature of mediation in various arenas (e.g. environmental, business, organizational, etc.), and the emergence of so many new actors as mediators? The chapters in Part III of the book discuss mediation progress into new territories, and the emergence of new actors such as individuals, transnational organizations and multiple parties as mediators. It seems that wherever there is conflict, there are practitioners, with knowledge, experience and resources who could assist the parties with their conflict.

In the current international arena states have lost their monopoly over the use of violence and mediation. There are many conflicts, over relationship, identity and fears, for instance, which will simply not respond to mediation by states. Representatives of transnational organizations, or individuals with diagnostic or analytical skills, who score high on legitimacy, expertise and referent resources, may achieve greater success as third parties than the more traditional mediators who score higher on reward and coercive resources. Mediation, in sum, may be applicable to any conflict, but the difficult task is to know what kind of mediation matches a particular conflict. It embraces potential actors who could pursue mediation as an official process of diplomacy, actors who pursue it as quasi-officials, actors who pursue it informally, and private citizens working in a wide array of organizations.

Whether we are talking about informal mediation by individuals, the quasi-formal mediation by consultants, lawyers and others in commercial disputes, mediation by representatives of transnational organizations, or the new form of multi-party mediation, we are in a way talking about broadening the role, relevance and applicability of mediation. Successful mediation today is not just about addressing one issue in conflict, but about changing a conflict relationship. To change a relationship, indeed to address the full array of a conflictual relationship, requires new actors, new approaches and different instruments of intervention.

A useful way of capturing the complexity and variety of mediation in its new, expanded mode, is suggested by Ury (1999). Bill Ury argues that we are in the midst of a paradigm shift; from power and hierarchy as modes of decision-making to cooperation, negotiation and mediation. This paradigm shift creates unprecedented opportunities for a great variety of persons and institutions to act as mediators. As mediators these persons and institutions can operate in any arena, use any resource they possess that may be useful in changing a relationship, and engage in intervention that may range in form all the way from preventive diplomacy to coercive diplomacy.

Thus we have mediators whose activities are organized around the need to *prevent* a conflict. Such mediators could well be prestigious individuals, business people or representatives of transnational organizations. Such actors mediate mostly through informal and unofficial channels, where they teach people skills, joint problem-solving, and create a safe environment in which parties in conflict can think about their situation, and ensure it does not escalate into violence. Preventive mediation represents an expansion on the role of mediation. It may not be as visible as other forms of mediation, but it is no less significant.

Moving along the spectrum of an expanded mediation range, we have individuals, groups and institutions trying to *contain* a conflict. Here we see peacekeepers interposing themselves between disputants, or representatives of regional, transnational or international organizations offering support and reassurance by being there as witnesses, or working hard to contain a conflict (as many mediators have in Northern Ireland, or the Middle East, for instance).

Then we have a large group of potential mediators who try to *resolve* a conflict. Here we see mediators, relying on their legitimacy, expertise or referent resources, try and reconcile conflicting interests, facilitate communication, engage the parties in a sensible dialog, equalize power, and generally promote new norms that can help to resolve a conflict.

Finally, certain actors with the ability to utilize reward or coercive resources, may act as potential mediators who try to *manage* a conflict. As conflict managers, mediators nudge the parties toward certain settlements, promote their own ideas and proposals regarding the outcome, and generally address divergent interests and issues at stake, rather than needs and relationships. As conflict managers mediators seek to regulate the parties' interaction, or change their perception of the conflict through a judicious mix of carrots and sticks.

The range of mediation has been so radically expanded over the last two or three decades as to become at times quite indistinguishable from leadership, diplomacy or foreign policy. The number of actors who can undertake mediation now runs the whole gamut from individuals to supranational organizations. Given so wide a range, it is perhaps understandable if we occasionally encounter some confusion of concepts or policies. It is only when practitioners and scholars get together – as we have here – that confusion can be reduced and better guidelines for promoting tripartite conflict management can be promoted.

Final thoughts

We are now in the second year of the International Decade of Peace and Nonviolence. One way to stimulate broader support for these objectives is to understand the role, relevance, diversity and performance of some instruments of conflict resolution. Mediation is undoubtedly one of the most significant of these instruments. Using mediation is no easy matter; it is often difficult and messy, and usually requires some good fortune, but even when it fails to achieve its stated goals, mediation teaches us how to cooperate in the midst of conflict. Today, when there is so much conflict at home, at work, in the community and internationally, there can be few more challenging tasks than the removal of barriers to cooperative conflict management. More than twenty years ago Jeff Rubin began the task of removing some of the intellectual barriers that surround mediation. Here we have tried to dismantle a few more.

References

Bercovitch, J. and Diehl, P. (1997) 'Conflict Management of Enduring Rivals: The Frequency, Timing and Short Term Impact of Mediation', *International Interactions*, 22: 299–320.

Bush, R. and J. P. Folger (1994) *The Promise of Mediation*. San Francisco: Jossey Bass.

Doob, L. (1993) *Intervention: Guides & Perils*. New Haven, Conn.: Yale University Press.

Henderson, D. A. (1996) 'Mediation Success: An Empirical Analysis', *Ohio State Journal of Dispute Resolutions*, 11: 105–48.

Kleiboer, M. (1996) 'Understanding Success and Failure of International Mediation', *Journal of Conflict Resolution*, 41: 360–89.

Riskin, L. (1996) 'Understanding Mediators' Orientations, Strategies and Techniques', *Harvard Negotiation Law Review*, 1: 7–52.

Rubin, J. Z. (1992) 'Conclusion: International Mediation in Context', in J. Bercovitch and J. Z. Rubin (ed.), *Mediation in International Relations*. London: Macmillan – now Palgrave Macmillan and New York: St. Martin's Press – now Palgrave Macmillan.

Sheppard, B. (1984) 'Third Party Conflict Intervention: A Procedural Framework', *Research in Organizational Behavior*, 6: 141–90.

Ury, W. (1999) *Getting to Peace: Transforming Conflict at Home, at Work, and in the World*. New York: Viking.

Name Index

Subject Index